The Politics of Hallowed Ground

Wounded Knee and the Struggle for Indian Sovereignty

Mario Gonzalez
and Elizabeth Cook-Lynn

University of Illinois Press

Urbana and Chicago

© 1999 by the Board of Trustees of the University of Illinois
Manufactured in the United States of America
1 2 3 4 5 C P 5 4 3 2 1

This book is printed on acid-free paper.

Library of Congress Cataloging-in-Publication Data
Gonzalez, Mario, 1944–
The politics of hallowed ground : Wounded Knee and
the struggle for Indian sovereignty / Mario Gonzalez
and Elizabeth Cook-Lynn.
p.   cm.
Includes bibliographical references (p.) and index.
ISBN 0-252-02354-4 (cloth : acid-free paper). —
ISBN 0-252-06669-3 (pbk. : acid-free paper)
1. Teton Indians—Government relations. 2. Wounded Knee
Massacre, S.D., 1890. 3. National monuments—South Dakota.
4. Teton Indians—Legal status, laws, etc. I. Cook-Lynn,
Elizabeth. II. Title.
E99.T34G65   1998
973.8'6—dc21   97-4777
CIP

"Brown Hat's Vision" is reprinted by permission from
Cultural Survival Quarterly (Winter, 1996).

Photo courtesy of *Indian Country Today*

Dedicated to Sam Eaglestaff

A "FLAG CAPTURE" SONG OF THE SIOUX NATION

milahanska mayucanze ca
    tawapaha na wipeki ko
wayankan iwacuwe

the enemy has made me angry
and I have taken his flag and
his weapons captive

Contents

Preface

Mario Gonzalez

This book is what we in the legal profession would call *sui generis,* that is, it is the only one of its own kind. Elizabeth Cook-Lynn has taken selected diary entries between the years 1989 and 1992 from my daily diary, added commentary called "Chronicles," and created a new format to tell the story of the 1890 Wounded Knee Massacre as interpreted by the Sioux Indians. The format allows the story of the massacre to be told against the backdrop of federal laws and historical events that give the reader a better understanding of Sioux culture, history, and government.

Stories about military confrontations between the Sioux bands and the United States in the nineteenth century are stories about the Sioux peoples' struggle for survival against a colonial power that invaded their homelands and embarked on a policy of genocide to eliminate them from the face of the earth. It is important to understand, however, that the United States has sought to destroy Native American culture and nationalism, not only on the battlefields in past centuries but also through its political and legal institutions from the time of the Declaration of Independence in 1776 up to the present, under an international legal principle called the "Doctrine of Discovery."

The colonization of Native American tribes actually began in the sixteenth century when the European explorers landed on the shores of the Americas, planted their flags on the beach, and proclaimed the land to be the property of the king or queen they represented. Although such scenes make good movies, they also had a legal significance under the Doctrine of Discovery, which was described in 1823 by Chief Justice John Marshall:

On discovery of this immense continent, the great nations of Europe were eager to appropriate to themselves so much of it as they could respectively acquire. Its vast extent offered an ample field to the ambition and enterprise of all; and the character and religion of its inhabitants afforded an apology for considering them as a people over whom the superior genius of Europe might claim an ascendancy. The potentates of the old world found no difficulty in convincing themselves that they made ample compensation to the inhabitants of the new, by bestowing on them civilization and Christianity, in exchange for unlimited independence. But, as they were all in pursuit of nearly the same object, it was necessary, in order to avoid conflicting settlements, and consequent war with each other, to establish a principle, which all should acknowledge as the law by which the right of acquisition, which they themselves asserted, should be regulated as between themselves. *This principle gave title to the government by whose subjects, or by whose authority, it was made, against all other European governments, which title might be consummated by possession.*

The exclusion of all other Europeans, necessarily gave to the nation making the discovery the sole right of acquiring the soil from the natives, and establishing settlements upon it. It was a right with which no Europeans could interfere. It was a right which all asserted for themselves, and to the assertion of which, by others, all assented.

In the establishment of these relations, the rights of the original inhabitants were, in no instance, entirely disregarded; but were necessarily, to a considerable extent impaired. They were admitted to be the rightful occupants of the soil, with a legal as well as just claim to retain possession of it, and to use it according to their own discretion; but their rights to complete sovereignty, as independent nations, were necessarily diminished and their power to dispose of the soil at their own will, to whomsoever they pleased, was denied by the original fundamental principle, that discovery gave exclusive title to those who made it.

While the different nations of Europe respected the right of the natives, as occupants, they asserted the ultimate dominion to be in themselves; and claimed and exercised, as a consequence of this ultimate dominion, a power to grant the soil, while yet in possession of the natives. These grants have been understood by all, to convey a title to the grantees, subject only to the Indian right of occupancy.

The history of America, from its discovery to the present day, proves, we think, the universal recognition of these principles. . . .

The United States, then have unequivocally acceded to that great and broad rule by which its civilized inhabitants now hold this country. They hold, and assert in themselves, the title by which it was acquired. They maintain, as all others have maintained, that discovery gave an exclusive right to extinguish the Indian title of occupancy, either by purchase or by conquest; and gave also a right to such a degree of sovereignty as the circumstances of the people would allow them to exercise. [Emphasis added.][1]

The doctrine of discovery, then, has been used by European governments and the U.S. government as the basis to claim fee title (European title) to Indian lands, to extinguish the underlying aboriginal title to the same lands,[2] and to limit the sovereignty of Indian tribes over their remaining territories.

As the United States extended its dominion over the North American continent, Indian tribes found themselves in a very unusual relationship with the United States, a relationship that the Supreme Court, in 1831, said was marked by "peculiar and cardinal distinctions which exist nowhere else,"[3] that is, Indian tribes were sovereign nations within a sovereign nation; sovereign nations that are located within the geographic sphere of what is said to be the boundaries of the United States of America.

Over the years, Congress has diminished tribal sovereignty, through legislation such as the Major Crimes Act of 1885, in which tribal sovereignty was diminished by transferring jurisdiction over major crimes on Indian reservations from the tribes to the federal courts,[4] and Public Law 280 in 1953, in which tribal sovereignty was further diminished by transferring criminal and civil jurisdiction over cases involving Indians from the tribes to several state governments.[5]

The federal courts, however, have also played a major role in diminishing tribal sovereignty by developing rules of law in court decisions, called "federal common law"; this is possible because court decisions have the force of law in common law countries and the United States is a common law country. For example, in 1832, the Supreme Court ruled in *Worcester v. Georgia* that Indian sovereignty was a complete bar to state encroachment and jurisdiction on Indian reservations; that Indian tribes are distinct political entities with the right of self-government, have exclusive authority within their territories, and are not subject to the laws of the state within whose geographical boundaries they are located.[6] But as more non-Indians settled on Indian reservations in the twentieth century, the Supreme Court developed new rules of law that modified its decision in the *Worcester v. Georgia* case. These rules of law were articulated in the 1959 case *Williams v. Lee:* "Essentially absent governing Act of Congress, the question has always been whether the state action infringed on the right of reservation Indians to make their own laws and be ruled by them."[7] Under *Williams v. Lee,* state governments can now encroach on Indian reservations if their actions are not preempted by federal legislation (governing acts of Congress) or do not infringe on tribal self-government.[8] Today, Indian tribes resist, day by day, the encroachments on their sovereignty by both the United States government and state government in the halls of Congress and in the federal courts.

Indian sovereignty was described in a 1934 Interior Department Solicitor's Opinion as follows: "Perhaps the most basic principle of all Indian law, supported by a host of decisions . . . , is the principle that *those powers which are lawfully vested in an Indian tribe are not, in general, delegated powers granted by express acts of Congress, but rather inherent powers of a limited sovereignty which has never been extinguished* [emphasis added]."[9] The sovereignty of the Sioux tribes, therefore, predates the sovereignty of the United States, and remains intact until extinguished by congressional act. However, Congress's power to extinguish Indian sovereignty (or confiscate Indian property in violation of treaties) is said to be "plenary."[10]

Another justification for congressional extinguishment of Indian title that must be mentioned is the common law principle of "trust responsibility." According to the *Johnson v. McIntosh* case, the primary basis for the United States' general trust responsibility over Indians is *conquest*: "The title by conquest is acquired and maintained by force. The conquerer prescribes the limits. Humanity, however, acting on public opinion, has established, as a general rule, that the conquered shall not be wantonly oppressed, and that their condition shall remain as eligible as is compatible with the objects of the conquest. . . . *[A] wise policy requires, that the right of the conquered to property should remain unimpaired.*"

The relationship between the conqueror (the United States) and conquered (the Indian nations and tribes), was defined in the *Cherokee Nation v. Georgia* case. Indian tribes are, according to the Supreme Court, "domestic, dependant nations . . . in a state of pupilage" whose relationship with the United States "resembles that of a ward to his guardian."

Trust responsibility based on conquest is hard to define when Indian tribes desire to enforce it against the United States. It is looked upon as a moral obligation assumed by the United States. It is easy to define, however, when the United States wants to expropriate Indian lands for non-Indian settlers, such as the surplus land acts passed at the beginning of the twentieth century.[11]

Much of federal Indian policy and law in the United States is derived from the Doctrine of Discovery. Hence, this doctrine was used to justify the theft of the Black Hills in 1877 and of 48 million acres of Sioux territory under the 1946 Indian Claims Commission Act in the 1980s.[12] Ultimately, it was also the Doctrine of Discovery that was used by the United States to justify the murder of over 350 to 375 unarmed Sioux men, women, and children at Wounded Knee.

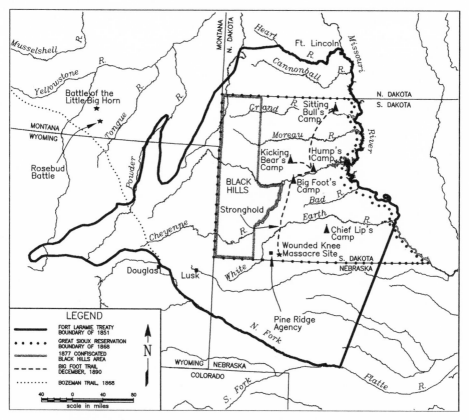

Map 1. Territory of Docket 74 Sioux west of the Missouri River, September 17, 1851, to March 2, 1889. Not shown: the expanded 1868 treaty hunting rights area westward to the summits of the Bighorn Mountains and southward to the Republican River. Map by Matt Watson, Watson Engineering, Inc.

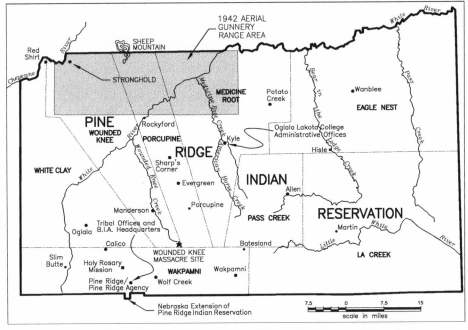

Map 2. Pine Ridge Indian Reservation, 1988–92. Map by Matt Watson, Watson Engineering, Inc.

The Politics
of Hallowed Ground

Introduction

Elizabeth Cook-Lynn

This is an account of a contemporary political effort by the Minneconjou and Oglala people of the Sioux Nation to establish as a national American monument the site of the Wounded Knee Massacre, where in 1890 over three hundred of their relatives were murdered, in a place they called their homelands. This effort, taking place at the close of the twentieth century, is in recognition of the fact that there is no national monument anywhere in the United States that honors the history of an indigenous nation's *defense of itself.* There is no place for Lakota tribal heroism to be recognized in the United States. *The failure to take note of this indigenous inalienable right is at the heart of America's racism.*

This book is neither historiography, biography, nor autobiography, nor is it ethnographic biography. It is what might be called a "mixed genre," informal anecdotal writing of social and political history. Anecdotes, unlike history, are not large things and so if this art, with a will of its own, is thought by those who read it to be more promissory than structured, that is its nature.

When I first looked at the diaries kept by Oglala attorney Mario Gonzalez, I immediately started referring to them as "the Mario diaries," and when I wondered out loud in his presence whether or not we could use them to tell a story about our people's nationalism, he agreed. The Mario diaries, which have been emended by the author in order to ensure accuracy, cover the brief period from April, 1989, through April, 1992. Though originally intended for no eyes but the author's, the diaries have become interesting to others because they are at least in part a tribal accounting of the conflicting demands in a political relationship between a First Nation and its colonial dispossessor. As you will come to realize, it is not a pretty sight.

Though the diaries begin in 1989, this story has many beginnings. One of the important beginnings occurred when, in 1985, an Oglala Wi(n)yan, Claudia Iron Hawk Sully of the Pine Ridge Wounded Knee Survivors' Association, requested Gonzalez's attendance at a meeting she called to ask whether or not the people wanted to start work on a national memorial to the victims by December 29, 1990, the anniversary date of the Wounded Knee Massacre. This was agreed upon as the sole objective but very soon, in discussions with the National Park Service on the required collaboration, other matters came up. The Minneconjou Wicasa, Sam Eaglestaff, brought his people's wishes to the discussion table and this act signified another beginning.

The daily diaries written by Mario Gonzalez, which form the book's essential narrative voice, discuss matters which are of interest to a tribal lawyer who has made a career of trying cases for and of the people, writing legislation for tribal defense and improvement, and taking up the challenge of moving forward into what will surely become a decolonization period. Many inquiries emerge. What are those interests? Who is in charge? Who leads? Who follows? How is leadership determined in contemporary tribal life? What has been the role of those outside of the tribal circle? What have been the effects of historical colonialism on the ability of tribal leaders to do what is necessary for the people in a modern world? Who are the antagonists? And why? The Mario diaries and the accompanying chronicles will begin to answer some of these inquiries.

This book, with its pattern of intermittent chronicles, features the second narrative voice of historical tribal revisionism and is meant to praise the courage and tenacity of a people who know that the past is always possessed of its own truth. In the attempt at honest and regular self-examination which occurs on these pages, then, the cultural and historical balance of being a Lakota/Dakota in the modern United States stems, as it always has, from collaboration.

First, two terms need definition, *diaries* and *chronicles*.

Diaries are the daily records of a writer's own experiences, observations, and attitudes. They are sometimes kept secretly, expressing secret feelings: emotion- and personality-laden writings. Sometimes they are kept so that the author can record specific events which have to do with work. Professionals of every sort, teachers, lawyers, shopkeepers, have kept diaries throughout the ages. In the case here, the diaries of Mario Gonzalez, an Indian lawyer, are wonderfully noncommittal and filled with the important events of his daily life, just as one would expect a lawyer's quick daily diaries to be, just as one would expect of a man who deals in truth and reality.

Chronicles, on the other hand, are a certain kind of historical writing. They most often revise already existing records, old news, but, significantly, they can also be firsthand accounts of the author's own times. They include all sorts of miscellaneous items, and while sometimes they seem ambiguous and detached, at other times they are very partisan. They almost always have to do with nationalistic themes. The chronicles here are intermittent commentaries and I make no excuses for their anecdotal nature. I am, after all, a poet and fictionist. I believe what a very famous poet and philosopher, Maya Angelou, whose work I much admire has so eloquently said: "History, despite its wrenching pain, / cannot be unlived, but *if faced / with courage,* need not be lived again."[1] Her view and mine agree with Plato's assertion that the world will not be rid of evil until philosophers acquire political power or until those with political power become philosophers. More germane to the arguments of this book, perhaps, are the thoughts of Rigoberta Menchú on the importance of treaties and accords to indigenous peoples.[2]

The structure of the book, dependent as it is on the dual voices of the diary and chronicle, is an organizational pattern devised to reflect more appropriately the nature of tribal discourse. Here we make accessible the many tribal voices of narration, not just the formal assessment by the professional scholar. The structure is an attempt by the authors to present history in a more conversational and anecdotal way, more in tune with oral discourse.

The tellers of this story have a long and intertwined history. In the late 1980s, Mario Gonzalez (Nantan Hinapan)[3] was doing pro bono work on the Black Hills Claim for an organization of Lakota elderlies called the Grey Eagle Society. The society had chapters on several reservations and was developing federal legislation to resolve the Black Hills Claim. A principal leader of the Cheyenne River Reservation chapter was Sam Eaglestaff, a Minneconjou Lakota, a respected elder and astute politician.

During the course of their work on the Black Hills Claim, Mario and Sam became close friends. In 1989, Sam learned that Mario was also representing the Pine Ridge Wounded Knee Survivors' Association. Mario had become involved with the Wounded Knee Massacre work in 1985 when Claudia Iron Hawk Sully reactivated the Survivors' Association and asked him to represent them in obtaining an official apology from the United States government and establishing a national monument at the massacre site by December 29, 1990, the centenary of the massacre. Sam, whose uncle was killed in the massacre, decided to reactivate the Cheyenne River Survivors' Association and work with the Oglalas to accomplish its goals.

Sam had recognized Mario as a leading modern Lakota defender of the people when, not long out of law school, he litigated for the Sioux Nation a successful challenge to the United States government's effort to legitimize its theft and plunder of the Black Hills in 1877 by offering the Sioux tribes $17.1 million to forget about the crime. It was at that time, on July 18, 1980, when everything seemed hopeless, that Gonzalez filed suit on behalf of the Oglala Sioux Tribe against the United States, challenging the United States' "ownership" of the Black Hills and demanding $11 billion in damages for the denial of the Sioux tribes' exclusive use and occupation of the Black Hills for 103 years as guaranteed by the 1868 Fort Laramie treaty.[4] A man who came of age during the era of the civil rights movements of the 1960s and 1970s, Gonzalez knew what was at stake. He and his tribal compatriots were adamant in their refusal to accept the racist arena through which Indian land claims are contested, often referring to the Indian Claims Commission as a "complete sham." To refuse the millions of dollars in what the tribe called a giant "pay-off" was shocking to those who had never before understood the Lakota commitment to their homelands.

In 1988 Mario resigned as Oglala Sioux tribal attorney, after serving as general counsel to the tribe for ten years, and went into private practice at Black Hawk, South Dakota. He nevertheless continued to do pro bono work for the Grey Eagles in developing legislation to resolve the Black Hills Claim.[5] He informed the society that he would not accept compensation for any work he did on the Black Hills Claims because of his dedication to the Oglala Sioux Tribe and Sioux Nation. He said, "the fight for the Black Hills is a fight for the survival of the Sioux people, it is the same fight that our grandfathers fought in the 1800s. Our leaders didn't get compensated for their efforts to defend our homeland then, so I can't accept compensation to carry on the same fight today."

Although many saw the Supreme Court's 1980 award of $105 million to the Sioux Nation for the Black Hills, placer (surface) gold removed from the Black Hills prior to 1877, and three rights-of-way across the remainder of the Great Sioux Reservation as a great victory, Gonzalez saw it as a devious attempt to extinguish title to the sacred Black Hills and to terminate treaty benefits for a few token dollars, and he influenced the Sioux tribes to reject it on that basis. He argued that the Black Hills are the religious property of the Sioux Nation and cannot be sold for any amount of money; that the compensation offered was also totally inadequate and designed to simply extinguish title and terminate treaty benefits guaranteed under articles 5 and 8 of the 1877 Black Hills Act.[6] Although many antagonists existed then and still do, the tribal councils have agreed with Gonzalez's views on the 1980

Supreme Court award and have consistently rejected the award in favor of land restoration, even though the award has now grown (with interest) to over $540 million.

On June 30, 1980, when the U.S. Supreme Court affirmed the Indian Claims Commission's award and the fight to retain the Black Hills seemed hopeless, everyone looked to Gonzalez to lead the way in developing the legal theories to contest the United States' claim of ownership of the Black Hills, to write the briefs and form the dialogue for the people. Gonzalez was tired of reading in the history books that the Sioux were hopelessly inept, that they did nothing but complain bitterly, that Sitting Bull (when he resisted the theft of lands and the proposed Allotment Act) was an "extremist," and that sovereignty was "unknown," for he knew all of it to be a false history. Instead, he set about doing what needed to be done.

While much of the United States wrung its collective hands over the historical issue that it had robbed the Sioux of "a way of life," a "bleeding heart" theory held in contempt by many Indians, while other Americans fought back in defense of their wrongful claim of historical innocence, Gonzalez acted on the Lakota/Dakota/Nakota theory that the theft of the Black Hills was a crime, that someone must be indicted, and that stolen land must be returned.

Acting in professional isolation, against the best advice and to the chagrin of the white attorneys who had husbanded this matter through the federal courts for sixty years, for months Gonzalez worked sixteen-hour days with Oglala Sioux leadership to prevent the General Accounting Office from paying the Black Hills judgment award to the Oglala Sioux Tribe (through its federal trustee and GAO's collaborator the secretary of the interior), and thereby extinguishing its title to the Hills.

The team of Washington-based attorneys Arthur Lazarus, Jr., Marvin Sonosky, and William Howard Payne who won the $105 million Supreme Court award eventually became Gonzalez's strongest critics. Their arguments, advanced in the book *Black Hills, White Justice* by Edward Lazarus, the son of Arthur Lazarus, Jr.,[7] can best be summarized as follows: The Sioux had no representation in the 1950s when attorney Ralph Case nearly lost the Black Hills case in the Indian Claims Commission, and were begging for representation. Lazarus, Sonosky, and Payne stepped forward, saved the case, and won the largest land claims award in the history of the nation. The Sioux people should be grateful. But, instead, along comes Mario Gonzalez and gives them bad advice and convinces them to believe in unrealistic expectations of land restoration and compensation. They should come back to reality, ignore Gonzalez, and accept the money and better their lives with it.

But Gonzalez isn't the only lawyer who has criticized the work of the Laz-arus/Sonosky/Payne team and the ultimate dealings of a colonial power struc-ture. Another Lakota attorney and scholar, Vine Deloria, Jr., has made the following observation, which Gonzalez believes is applicable to the work done by Lazarus, Sonosky, and Payne:

> Tribal claims attorneys must be approved by the Department of Interior and they are awarded 10 (ten) % of the amount recovered. With some nice provisions in the Internal Revenue Code they can keep a good part of this amount. Since the attorneys must be approved by the U.S. before they can sue the U.S. on behalf of their Indian clients, they are a remarkably congenial group. One need only check the number of stipulations in the course of an Indian case to see that such attor-neys are most cooperative with the U.S. so that in many instances one could hardly say that an adversarial system of litigation exists.[8]

Gonzalez's and Deloria's views are corroborated by Indian Law Resource Center attorneys Steven Tullberg and Robert Coulter in *Rethinking Indian Law,* where they point out that the attorney representing the Sioux Nation, Arthur Lazarus, Jr., in the 1980 Supreme Court case "conceded that the United States government, and not his Sioux clients, was the actual owner of all Sioux lands."[9]

In the face of great odds, then, in a move which some believe to be cru-cial, Gonzalez gave hope to the people in their struggle to save the sacred Black Hills and to secure the inalienable right of the Lakota/Dakota people to ex-ist on the planet Earth as a separate and distinct culture and society. Many believe that without his work and guidance on the longest-fought battle for native land restoration in the history of the United States, the Indians would have been relegated, as they had been so many times before, to oblivion. But he, unlike the white Washington attorneys, knew that the land return move-ment of the latter decades of this century was not just a momentary resis-tance. He knew it was historical, a century-long desire of the people. And he was right. The Sioux Nation turned its back on the court's huge monetary award and, as this book is prepared, continues to do so in spite of great pres-sure from many quarters to accept it. This is a significant tribal nation stance and an extraordinarily courageous thing to do because it has occurred within what is considered the physical boundaries of one of the most materialistic nations on the planet. Many factions in the mainstream still do not compre-hend what this tribal reaction means.

The Sioux Oyate believe they now walk with a renewed pride in themselves instead of walking around with their heads hanging in defeat and shame, which would have been their fate if they had accepted the monetary award for the Black Hills.

What this all means, perhaps, is that a people's national history cannot simply be stamped out or ignored or relegated to obscurity. A nation does not cease to exist simply because another nation wishes it so. It means, also, that no event in a tribal history stands in isolation from any other. Had the antagonists known about the meaning of the theft of the Black Hills and its connection to the killings at Wounded Knee, or had they cared, they might have seen their efforts to cram money down the throats of the Sioux Oyate as futile.

Everyone knows that any story of any consequence is a continuing one. Thus, on that spring day, Sam Eaglestaff, already frail but clear-headed, by enlisting the aid of an accomplished and dedicated attorney, took up the task again in the tradition of his ancestors. As the Wounded Knee Memorial fight began, Mario held Sam Eaglestaff in high regard; he knew him as a man with a good heart, a fierce loyalty to the Lakota people and his family; a man with uncommon wisdom and useful skills in diplomacy.

Eaglestaff knew of the work already in progress on the Pine Ridge Reservation regarding the establishment of a national monument at the Wounded Knee Massacre site. Until the time of his death, he took the leadership role in pushing for atonement for the Wounded Knee Massacre, for the passage of Senate Concurrent Resolution No. 153[10] in which Congress would apologize for the crime. He organized a coordinated effort to get a bill to establish a national park (now a national tribal park) and monument at the site. The struggle goes on as this book goes to press and will continue until the people receive justice, a fair and honorable recognition of their rights.

It is to such men as Eaglestaff that this book is dedicated, although several people can be said to have been crucial to the movement toward developing a major Indian site for the Wounded Knee Memorial in the last decade of the twentieth century. It should be noted, however, that few people have chosen to seek support for the project on such a long-term basis as has Mario Gonzalez.

When Sam Eaglestaff asked Mario Gonzalez to represent the Cheyenne River Sioux Wounded Knee Survivors' Association in developing a historical monument at the site, he realized something very unique about the attorney. Mario was willing to represent clients who had no money to pay for attorney's fees and court expenses. He had already been representing the Grey Eagle Society in drafting legislation for the Black Hills Claim on a pro bono basis. Even as Claudia Iron Hawk Sully of the Pine Ridge Wounded Knee

Survivors' Association promised to raise money to pay for representing their tribal association, Gonzalez had already worked with her and invested three years of work without compensation and advanced all the costs associated with the effort. To this day he has not received a penny from either Survivors' Association.

This was the kind of dedication to Native American issues that Sam said he saw in Mario. He also saw that Mario possessed Lakota values and virtues such as generosity, wisdom, bravery, fortitude, and humility, an inheritance from his full-blooded grandmother and half-breed mother. He saw that Mario had a strong sense of his Lakota identity.

Mario is a descendant of Chief Lip's Band who settled on Pass Creek on the northeastern part of the Pine Ridge Indian Reservation after the Battle of the Little Big Horn, when the buffalo disappeared from the prairies, themselves the victims of the whiteman's power and greed. Lakota elder Paul High Horse described the history of Mario's *tiospaye* (camp), the Breast/Lip/Quiver tiospaye, as follows:

> In the old days, the Indian nations [were a] very big generation on this mother country of earth. The Indian tribes kept moving around different direction[s]. At that time they had no wagon or team to drive so they had to walk and use dogs and horses to move.
>
> Finally, one Indian band moved along [the] Missouri River to [the] mouth of Platte [R]iver and from there, some travel[ed] south, hunting as they went. This band finally came to a high hill to rest and looked around and they saw a big draw running from the Missouri River on the West. They saw two little things in the bush so they got up and walked to the bush and found one little boy and girl. The little boy and girl were big enough to talk but they had a different language, so they didn't realize. The boy and girl were adopted into the tribe.
>
> When this boy [grew] up he marrie[d] twice, first to a Hunkpapa woman and then to a Blackfeet woman. The first wife bears a boy which is called Breast. The second bears a son which is called Short Bull. From these two boys grew Wanblee camp.
>
> . . . Breast camp was founded in 1880, on the east side of Pass Creek. At that time, Lip's father [Breast] was getting old so Lip was put in his father's place.
>
> Breast found a place for this generation where there was plenty of wood, water, grass, and a good place to raise livestock. Breast sought to secure it for the generations to come in the near future. Lip was made head man. From there his name was well known and [his band] was called Lip Camp or Band.
>
> At that time, Lip Camp was enrolled on Rosebud Reservation getting their rations, distribution material, and beef from Rosebud. . . . Pute [Lip] visited

Washington, D.C., to request a school . . . so that the children in his band [could] go to school. In 1885, Lip's people hauled lumber from Cody, Nebraska, by oxen and the school was established. The school was opened on September 16, 1885, with Mr. Frank E. Louise as the first teacher.

In 1886, Lip contacted William H. Hare, D.D., at Rosebud Agency and requested a church for his young people. Bishop Hare reacted favorably to Pute and gave him a church at Bad River. The Pute brothers [took an] oxen team and wagon and they went and tore the church down and hauled it home. The church was connected to the school. The first minister was John Long Commander, an Indian.

At the time, Rosebud line was from Bear Creek to the Nebraska state line and north to the White River. . . . Lip-Pute was appointed head chief of the band of Indians composed of relations and Indians who wished to join the Lip band, among whom are the names of many familiar to the people living in Wanblee today, Breast's sons and daughters. Breast's first wife was Earth Nation Lope Walks Woman (Maka Oyate Anaonk Mani Win). Breast had children: Deaf Woman, Lip-Pute, Crier. Breast's second wife was Jealous at (Nakiwgzi Pi). From his second wife Breast had children: Mrs. Quiver (Rattling Hawk),[11] Lucy Breast, Red Breath Woman, Alfred Whirlwind Breast, John Breast, William Breast. Two babies died before Silas Breast was born. Relatives were Twin, Short Bull, Four Knives, White Cow River, Swift Thunder, Iron Thunder, Little Commander, John Long Commander, Two Elk, Sitting Up, and Crazy Horse. Breast had a third wife, but her name has been lost in history. She had two daughters, Her Good Land and Cloud Shawl Woman.[12]

In 1990, in an official ceremony held at an Oglala Sioux Tribal Council meeting, Grey Eagle president Royal Bull Bear placed two eagle feathers (representing the Pine Ridge and Cheyenne River Grey Eagle Society chapters) in Mario's hair and declared that "from here on, you are the official *Eyapaha* of the Black Hills bill." Thus, under traditional Lakota custom, Mario is obligated to work on the Black Hills Claim until it is finally resolved. Taking his responsibility seriously, he has said: "I have no choice but to continue working on the Black Hills Claim. In a traditional religious ceremony, I was named *Eyapaha* [spokesman] and given that responsibility. I'm prepared to fulfill that role. Hopefully, within my lifetime, my pipe, which was wrapped when the Black Hills litigation was initiated in 1980, will be unwrapped."[13]

All of these things played into the collaboration of Sam Eaglestaff and Mario Gonzalez as they worked together for the people. It would turn out to be an important journey for both men.

Diaries and Chronicles, 1989-93

Introduction to Diaries and Chronicles

Stories told by the modern Sioux Oyate (Lakota/Nakota/Dakota) are stories of a struggle which has its origins in genocide and colonization. This means that the United States has sought to destroy Indian nationalism and sovereignty *by law*. The preface has examined legal concepts such as the doctrine of discovery. Here it is necessary to say that throughout the making and testing of the United States' own nationalistic resolve vis-à-vis the development of its legal attitude toward Indians, the U.S. Supreme Court has upheld the right of the United States to "convert the discovery of an inhabited country into conquest."[1] This has been done through an underpinning doctrine called Manifest Destiny. As a result of that thinking, the United States assumed virtual absolute power (called plenary power) over the First Nations. These legal concepts rose out of what a nineteenth-century court decision called "peculiar and cardinal distinctions which exist nowhere else," that is, the location of the Indian Nations within the geographic sphere of what is said to be the boundaries of the United States.[2]

The Sioux people, recognizing themselves within that history as citizens of a tribal nation and believing that they enjoy dual citizenship, namely, tribal and federal, see themselves as representing an interesting but unthreatening phenomenon in the United States. Though they do not have the protections of the Constitution as nations of people[3] and have only partial protection as individual citizens, nonetheless they represent a historical reality: they are not vanishing (as had been hoped by early historians and politicians), nor do they today submit to a federal policy which insists that they be completely absorbed by assimilation.

They see themselves as a nation that has never lost a military conflict with the United States, as the victors of the Powder River War of 1866–68, which resulted in a treaty of peace in 1868. They see themselves as an unconquered people who have honored their commitment to reside on their reservation as provided in the treaty.

The challenge for the United States, then, is to move away from its over two hundred years of dirty history of genocide and acquisition, recognize clear crimes of land thefts (those land acquisitions unsustainable through treaty negotiations), and begin to view First Nation nationalism as a concept of cohabitation for the twenty-first century. With appropriate return of stolen lands, protection from further theft of lands and resources, and development of political processes in defense of their unique presences in the United States, Indian Nations will no longer be excluded from dialogues of democratic idealism.

In memory, all of the people whose lives ended before present lives began help in telling the nation's history which "cannot be unlived" and inform the events and attitudes spoken of here in *The Politics of Hallowed Ground*. They are the cause of work done by Celane Not Help Him, Marie Not Help Him, Sam Eaglestaff, Mario Gonzalez, Claudia Iron Hawk Sully, Marcella LeBeau, Florence Arpan, Mike Her Many Horses, Alex White Plume, Milo Yellow Hair, Suzan Shown Harjo, John Yellow Bird Steele, Harold Salway, Birgil Kills Straight, Belva Hollow Horn, Royal Bull Bear, Oliver Red Cloud, William Horn Cloud, Melvin Garreau, Elaine Quick Bear Quiver, and dozens more in the defense of the homelands.

For the most part, the United States believes it can ignore the political and legislative agenda of its native citizens. It's not like going to war, they believe, nor is it like reorganizing the savings and loan banking system. Defrauding Indians doesn't really hurt the national economy nor does it even damage the national psyche all that much. Yet, the denial of its own history as it concerns its earliest beginnings, the failure to analyze the links between politics and morality inherent in all relations between the indigenes and the colonist cannot sustain a nation's future in a world which has become more critical of the deliberate colonizer.

The parts of *The Politics of Hallowed Ground*, 1 (The Dilemma), 2 (The Antagonists), 3 (Wicowoyake ["true stories"]), and 4 (Restoration), are not intended as a complete analysis. They are meant to illustrate, only, that a moment in history is the preface for all that follows.

Thus, the reader of *The Politics of Hallowed Ground* is asked to read the story of Alice Ghost Horse as a preface to the modern Diaries and Chronicles.

It is a story that many Lakotas have known from the oral traditions, from the passing down of stories through the generations. Sam Eaglestaff came into the current activities of working for legislation for a monument to the Lakota dead by presenting to Mario Gonzalez a translated manuscript which he attributed to the English/Lakota language skills of a Minneconjou man named Sidney Keith, who told the history of how the story was related to a relative and kept by that relative until he decided to share it with the people.

Alice Ghost Horse/Kills the Enemy/War Bonnet was born in 1878 and died in 1950. She was Hohwoju Lakota of the Spotted Elk or Big Foot band located at the mouth of the Cherry Creek in those days. She told this story to her son, John War Bonnet, who wrote it down in Lakota. From there, Goldie Iron Hawk kept the letters and documents until 1979, when she gave them to Keith for safe keeping and translation. The story, one which Eaglestaff said every American should know, is reprinted here:

> "They Killed My Father and Brother . . . *for no reason at all.*"
> By Alice Ghost Horse
>
> We were camped at the mouth of Cherry Creek, last part of December, 1890. I was 13 years old at the time. There was my father (Ghost Horse) and my mother (Alice Her Shawl) and two younger brothers. The *wicasa itacan* (male leader) was Spotted Elk (Big Foot), up the creek was Hump and his followers our people were scattered all up and down the Cheyenne River towards Bridger, South Dakota, a place called now *takini* (barely surviving), they all lived the farthest away but they were all *hohwoju's* just as we are all *minneco[n]ju.*
>
> Rest of the Lakotas were already assimilated with the whites out towards east end and were already under military rule, they were being trained to be farmers and were given land to plant things.
>
> At this time, my people were ghost dancing above Plum Creek, straight east of Cherry Creek across the river. We went up there when they have the dances but children were not allowed in so my brothers and I play near the wagons. The dances usually last four days and quite a few camp up there during that time, we usually go back to Cherry Creek when they get through.
>
> The agent at Fort Bennet (Cheyenne agency) was a military officer and he would send Lakota scouts to the camp to ask questions about the ghost dance.
>
> The ghost dance was like a sun dance, which was held once a year about August. In the ghost dance they form a circle, holding hands and they dance stationary not like the Sun Dance. But they sing and dance. Usually starts at almost sundown and last for couple hours. They do this till someone falls or several fall. They wait till they tell what they saw or hear during their trance, the purpose of the dance was to see their dead relatives and converse with them and they continue.
>
> One day some people came from Standing Rock and told Big Foot that Sitting Bull was shot and killed by Indian Police, provoked by agent.
>
> Big Foot decided they should flee to Pine Ridge. They thought that Sitting Bull

was killed because of the Ghost Dance. On short notice, it was decided to move out the very next day so they all staked out their horses close by and all went to bed.

Next day, we packed up in a hurry that morning and we were ready to move out. I was on my horse and my two brothers rode in the wagon. My mother rode in the back with the youngest brother and the other one rode up front with my father. We had an extra horse tied to the team, this one can be rode or used as one of the team.

We crossed Cherry Creek at the mouth where it empties into the river. We were to follow the wagon trails that went west all along the river, on the north side. The old wagon trails lead to *takini*.

We ran all the way, bottom of the river and stopped half way to water the horses and cook something to eat. My mother had some pemmican which we all shared before we continue on towards *takini*.

Late afternoon we pulled into *takini* amid clusters of lean-tos and tents. Most of the people were getting ready for winter by looking at the wood piles. Some had stocks of wood piled high. After we put up our tents my mother started her cooking. She had good soup and kabubu bread and hot government coffee. After a hearty meal my mother and father went to a meeting at Big Foot's tent so my brothers and I went down to the river and played for a while and then came to bed.

Early next morning I heard my father hitching up the horses so I got up and saddled up my own horse and was ready to go. I planned to ride all the way to Pine Ridge.

First wagon to leave was Big Foot's wagon, followed by all his relatives. All the horse backs and some were walking for a time up the hill. We fell in, about the middle of the wagon train and were headed up a long hill east side of the river.

I looked back and I could see more wagons joining in and coming and many children were on horse back, too. It was a sight to see. It was also exciting because we were running from the military.

We ran like this all morning without stopping, some times some riders would fall back to check on us at the request of Big Foot. By noon, we stopped to rest but we were not allowed to start a fire so we ate what little mother had for us. In a short while, we were again on our way with Big Foot and his wagons still leading the way. We were trotting all the way, southerly direction, keeping to the low area, valleys and creek beds.

My younger brother sat in the back with my mother who kept an eye on me. The other brother rode up front as before, the extra horse still tied to the side of the team.

By mid-afternoon the going was tough but we went below Porcupine Butte still keeping in the draws and gullies, sometime there was no trail so the going was really rough in the wagons.

Sometime later the head wagons stopped on top of a hill and they were all looking down at something, my father went to see, and my mother came over and started to tighten my cinch and said, there were some cavalry camped below on Wounded Knee creek. She told me we might have to make a run for it and she asked me to stay close to the wagon.

My father returned and said Big Foot was very sick and laying in the back of the buggy all bundled up. My father said they picked some men to go down and talk to the officers.

I saw four riders riding down towards the center of the camp where they have big guns on wheels. One of the riders had a white flag, a white material tied to a stick, riding in front of the other three riders. Soon as they cross the creek all the soldiers laid down and aim their rifles at them but they kept on going and arrived at the big gun on wheels where there were some soldiers and officers standing. They dismounted and had a short talk.

A lone rider galloped up the hill to Big Foot's wagon and they told him that the officers wanted to talk to him but his relatives said "no," that he was very sick so the rider went back to tell them.

Sometime later, a buggy was sent up with a doctor to examine the old man. The doctor said he had pneumonia. He gave him some medicine and they loaded him in the special wagon and they took him down.

They talked a long time and finally a lone rider came back and told them to camp along the creek on the west side of the creek.

Everyone pitched their tents as ordered and pretty soon an army wagon was coming along the camp, issued bacon, flour, coffee beans, army beans and hard tack.

By sundown we were completely surrounded by foot soldiers, all with rifles. My mother and I went down to the creek to pick up some wood and to go to the bathroom but two soldiers followed us so we hurried back with some sticks.

Everyone went to bed as they were all tired from the hectic trip. Some of the young men stayed up all night to watch the soldiers. Some of the soldiers were drunk, saying bad things about the Lakota women. Early next morning, a bugle woke us up. I went outside and noticed all the soldiers were gone but there was lot of activity at the military camp.

We ate in a hurry because most of the Lakotas were loading their wagons and my father had the horses and he was saddling my horse.

At this time a crier was making his way around the Lakota camp, telling the men folks to go to the center for more talks so they dropped everything and left but the women continued to pack their belongings in the wagon. I was on my horse just standing there. In a little while there seem to be an argument at the confrontation which developed into a shouting match. Pretty soon some cavalry men rode in from the center at a fast gallop and they started to search the wagons for axes, knife, guns, bow and arrows and awls. They were really rude about it. They scattered the belongings all over the ground.

The soldiers picked up everything they could find and tied them up in a blanket and took them. They also searched the Lakotas in the center. They emptied the contents on the ground in the center in front of the officers and continued to argue with the Lakotas but the Lakotas did not give in.

During the heated discussion a medicine man by the name of Yellow Bird appeared from nowhere and stood facing the east right by the fire pit which was now covered up with fresh dirt. He was praying and crying. He was saying to the eagles that he wanted to die instead of his people. He must sense that something was going to happen. He picked up some dirt from the fireplace and threw it in the air and said this is the way he wanted to go back . . . to dust.

At this time there were cavalry men all on bay horses all lined up on top of the hill on the north side. One officer rode down towards the center at a full gallop. He made a fast halt and shouted something to his commanding officers and retreated back up on the hill and they all drew their rifles and long knife (swords) and you can hear them load it with bullets.

In the meantime some more cavalry men lined up on the south side. A big gun was also aimed down towards the center and towards where we were. . . . I heard the first shot coming from the center followed by rifles going off all over, occasionally a big boom came from the big guns on wheels. The Lakotas were all disarmed so all they could do was scatter in all directions. The two cavalry groups came charging down, shooting at everyone who is running and is a Lakota.

My father made it back to our wagon and my horse was trying to bolt so he told me to jump so I got off and the horse ran for all its worth toward the creek. We fled to the ravine, where there was lots of plum bushes and dove into the thicket. The gunfire was pretty heavy and people were hollering for their children. With children crying everywhere, my dad said he was going to go out and help the others. My mother objected but he left anyway. Pretty soon, my father came crawling back in and he was wounded below his left knee and he was bleeding. He took my youngest brother who was six years old and he said he was taking him further down the river.

Soon he came crawling back in and said "Hunhun he, micinsi kte pelo." He had tears in his eyes so we cried a little bit. Because there was no time to think, my father said we should crawl further down but my mother said its better we die here together and she told me to stand up so I did but my father pulled me down.

With a little effort we were able to crawl to a bigger hiding place, bullets were whistling all around us but my father went out again to help and he never came back for a long time.

Some people crawled in. They were all wounded. I recognized Philip Black Moon and his mother. They were okay. More women and children came crawling in. The young ones were whimpering. Groups at intervals came in. Four of the wounded died right there but there was nothing anybody can do.

A man named Breast Plate (Wawoslal Wanapin) came in and told us that my father was killed instantly. We all cried but for a short while lest we would be heard.

Charge in Kill and Nistuste (Back Hips) came in later but they left again.

They were brave, it seemed like eternity but actually it didn't last that long. It was getting late, towards sundown more people straggled in. It got dark, and the shooting stopped all of a sudden and we heard a wagon moving around, probably to pick up the dead, killed in the crossfire. None of the Lakotas had guns so they had been engaged in hand to hand combat. At a given signal we all got up, those who could, and walked or limped to the north, tip-toeing our way through creek beds and ravines. Occasionally, we stumbled over dark objects which turn out to be dead animals or sometimes dead Lakotas. We heard a child crying for water some place in the dark, cold night. Many more wounded were crying for help.

We walked in the creek bed a ways north. It must have been Wounded Knee Creek, where we separated into four groups, each to take different routes, to better chance of escaping. By morning our group reached a hill, from there we can see long ways. We stopped there, being careful to find whatever cover there was, by trees. We had traveled mostly a northwesterly direction all night, for the sun-up showed the plains and more level landscape to the east, the higher buttes and pine-covered hills to the west. The sky showed polka-dotted white puffs with blue background, changing patterns by the wind strong enough to make eyes water. We had two boys to go stay up on the hill to watch for soldiers in all directions. "A rider is following our tracks," the boys hollered down, and like cottontails we dove deeper into the ravine among the brushes and trees. But it turn out some moments later it was a Lakota wearing a woman's scarf. It was Nistuste (Back Hips) whom we met earlier. After we shook hands with him we all cried. He told us that after the shooting he escaped to Pine Ridge found all the Oglalas had run away toward the hills. He had stayed up in the hills while scouting the Pine Ridge encampment. He then walked back to Wounded Knee where he found his horse, luckily catching it. He then started tracking our several trails northward hoping to meet up with somebody. He insisted that our group go with him back towards Pine Ridge.

Before our group could decide which way to go, some more riders appeared so [we] took off for the creek to hide. But this one man stayed behind and they rode in yelling, "We are Lakotas. Do not run." They dismounted at the sight of the four Lakota people, all got up there and shook hands with them, one woman and three men, we all cried. We hadn't eaten anything since we left Wounded Knee a day and a half earlier, they had some pemmican which they shared with us. One of the man said there were cattle foraging over the hill that he was going after one. The other two men who had rode in with him went with him. Soon they brought in a quarter of beef, one lady did the cooking from a pail and dishes she had gotten from a deserted log house not far from there. We really ate for once, thanks to the men and nice lady. Nistuste (Back Hips). Then the three men rode back towards Wounded Knee but the woman stayed with us. That left us with 13 people, mostly women and children. I was with my mother and brother; a lady who had her braids cut off—she was slightly wounded, a lady that always carried a little one on her back; and, there was Alex High Hawk, Blue Hair, and five members of the Many Arrows family. We were all there that night.

Next morning we got ready to leave and found Dog Chasing with two women had come in some time during the night. The men who rode out must have sent them in, with them upping our numbers to 16. We left bright and early, the men walking ahead a little ways. Very good fortune it was, for I was again riding a horse with my little brother and my mother on foot was leading the horse.

Along the way I must have dozed off and on, half asleep and half awake. I didn't know anything for a while. When I became clear headed again, we were heading down a hill. Down at the bottom of the valley stood a long house with even a wooden floor and a fire place which they fired up and we rested and got warmed up. Some daylight left, we started off again covering some miles before dark. It started to cloud up, clouds rolling in from the west and the north, cloud waves seeming to roll over the high hills and valleys like water, from misty fine drops somewhere closer to a drizzle.

It started then, the wind came. Some minutes later it turned into a blizzard but one of the men had steered us toward a cabin which he had spotted from a butte some miles back. This blessed haven we reached along a creek, so we stayed warm sitting out the storm. We had plenty of meat from the last butchering to keep us fed. Later in the night their voices woke me up, loud voices, high pitched women arguments to scatter or stay together, the calmer voices of the male sometimes whispering as we listened. I sat up in a hurry when a new meaning came to my senses. I got scared for the first time. My heart was beating faster, my breathing becoming shorter and harder. Quickly moving closer to my mother and squirming closer to my mother's body was to me natural as a cottontail jumping from danger into its lair. The noise the women thought they heard was maybe a rumbling of horse running or of buffalo, animals stampeding, maybe even cavalrymen.

But it turned out that they may have heard something then imagined their fears into loud noises. For sometime we just sat there staring at the darkness only the occasional, flickering firelight and dying embers to see by. During the night riders went some place and later they came back and said in a low voice, "It is time to go." No one complained, all acted on instinct to survive. It was still cloudy and dark when we left the cabin. The men loaned us their horses, so some of us rode double, sometimes the snow would blow but we kept on moving into a deep draw, where the wind wasn't blowing so much, so, we kept to the low lands.

Finally, we stumbled into a camp of Oglalas who ran away from Pine Ridge during the shooting. They were camped in a nice place among the pine trees. At the end of the camp we came across Short Bull's tent. All of the people came to welcome us and the rest of the group were all taken into different tents and were all fed good. We stayed at this camp for three months and the sun kept coming out higher and higher. Soon the snow was melting and all knew it was spring.

One day a rider came into the camp and said there was going to be a meeting [treaty] at Pine Ridge. Next day, early as usual, we headed for Pine Ridge again. It must be quite a ways because we camped in a deep gully. When we started out again the next day, it was a long caravan of bugg[ie]s, travois, horseback and on foot. The chiefs were walking in front, followed by young warriors on horseback.

Over the last hill we could see many tents and cavalry all over the place, dust was flying, horses were tied to hitching posts face to face.

We made camp near the post. Can Hahaka (Plenty Limbs) and Iron Thunder came to the camp and said they came after all the *hohwojus,* Cheyenne River people who were wounded or deceased, that they belonged to our band.

In Pine Ridge my mother reluctantly signed our names as survivors, along with the rest of the family.

They pitched up 3 big tipis in the center where they told us to go. I remember there was Black Moon and his mother and brothers, Iron Horn and Wood Pile was there. There were many *hohwojus* that showed up at the tipi. Even some we thought had been killed. Ashes was a young girl then and she was there too. I noticed other people were Blue Hair, Axe, Brown Eagle, and Can Hahaka (Plenty Limbs).

We left for *hohwoju* country towards Cherry Creek. We were traveling in five wagons, one wagon was loaded with oats and hay, another one of rations, one wagon full of soldiers were leading the way as escorts, out of Pine Ridge in a different direction so we won't have to go through Wounded Knee.

Despite all these nice things being done for us, I can't forget what happened at Wounded Knee. Some nights I cried thinking about it. Many months afterwards. I have never touched a white man during my lifetime. I just couldn't trust any whitemen and never will because they killed my father and brother for no reason at all.[4]

PART 1

The Dilemma of Ethical Systems and Legal Ideas

(May 5, 1989–October 30, 1990)

What I do as a lawyer is base my legal paradigms on the Indian perspective of Treaties: that the Treaties are the supreme law of the land. Unfortunately, others see these Treaties as less than Sacred.

What I mean to say about the 1868 Treaty of Fort Laramie is that it was a Treaty of Peace, not a treaty for the cession of Lakota territory.

What I say about the Wounded Knee Massacre of 1890 is that it was a crime against humanity for which the United States must be indicted.

Mario Gonzalez, Oglala, attorney-at-law
Interview, *National Law Journal*, August 3, 1988

DIARY: MAY 5, 1989

When I called Democratic senator Tom Daschle's office in Washington, D.C., his assistant Sara Yager said she was too busy to talk and would get back to me this afternoon or Monday. I then got Libby Conrad at Congressman Tim Johnson's office (D-SD) on the phone and informed her about our organization and our legislative proposal to establish a national monument at the Wounded Knee Massacre site.

She indicated that the congressman was not very excited about sponsoring our proposed bill (which he had heard about) for two reasons: first, because of the federal deficits, and, second, because it would set a national precedent for other Indian organizations to demand compensation for massacres. I explained the importance and uniqueness of the Lakota historical event and told her that all South Dakotans who understand their own history should support the proposed bill. I emphasized that the Survivors' Associations' claims for atonement are not just moral claims; they were also legal claims because there was an express statutory prohibition against the slaughter committed by the United States government on the unarmed men, women, and children of Chief Big Foot's band of Minneconjou on that infamous day in December, 1890. In the 1877 Black Hills Act, article 8, it states that "each individual will be protected in his person, property and life."[1] This was an express promise made by the U.S. government to the Lakota people. These victims, that is, the Big Foot people buried in the mass grave, were murdered by the military forces of the U.S. government while they were under a white flag of truce within the exterior boundaries of the Pine Ridge Indian Reservation. There was no state of war at this time between the Minneconjous and the United States. I re-

minded her that the U.S. agreed in article 1 of the 1868 treaty that: "From this day forward all war between the parties to this Agreement shall forever cease. The government of the United States desires peace, and its honor is hereby pledged to keep it."²

Her next objection, which indicated that a lot of discussion about our legislative proposal had occurred in Representative Johnson's office prior to my phone call, was that this was a "stale" claim. I explained that it should not be characterized as "stale," since the Survivors' Association has been continuously pressing its claim for atonement for the past one hundred years; that there is historical documentation of that continuity.

I also discussed the Lakota people's interest in helping the United States to move out of its colonial history and asserting their own history, and that no one should be afraid of that. The truth is, I told her, there are no national monuments to Native American patriots who defended themselves and their homelands, and there was no reason for that except the oppressive political system which has denied that idea since its inception in 1776. You go out to the Little Bighorn battlefield in Montana, I told her, and the only grave markers that have been placed there are those of the soldiers of Lt. Col. George Armstrong Custer's Seventh Cavalry. Yet, we Native American patriots also have relatives who died there in defense of our people, culture, and homeland. We talked for several minutes and she eventually agreed to set up a meeting between the Survivors' Association and the congressman for the purpose of explaining our bill and seeing if he would sponsor and introduce it into the U.S. Congress. She said she would try to coordinate the meeting with Sara Yager so we could meet with Senator Daschle on the same day.

It is a first step.

CHRONICLE

This section of the diaries reveals the political no-man's land in which contemporary Indians live their lives. The strategy employed by the Minneconjou and Oglala Wounded Knee Survivors' Association was to write legislation which would do the following things: (1) for the loss of life and injuries, *compensate* the descendants of the victims of the 1890 Wounded Knee Massacre; (2) for the "reconciliation" between Whites and Indians in the country that had been called for in 1987 by South Dakota governor George Mickelson, *render an official* governmental *apology* to the Sioux People for the 1890 Wounded Knee Massacre; (3) for the future relationship between sovereigns, *establish* the Wounded Knee national monument and memorial park, and (4) *authorize and appropriate* funds for the project.

These requests were made partially on the basis of the 1868 treaty and the 1877 act. (For more information on the 1868 treaty and the 1877 act, see appendix A.)

It is the thesis of the Sioux that such actions on the part of tribal people(s) stem from a reassertion of Lakota history for the purpose of protecting and defending postcolonial rights and resources. Before that defense can occur, however, the truth of the United States' colonial relationship with the Sioux must be faced by both Indians and Whites. Many people concede that Indians have suffered unjustly at the hands of their colonizers. Few except the Indians themselves (and, sometimes, not even they) are willing to do the work to critique and change the internal affairs, structures, and methods of congressional Indian policy.

DIARY: JUNE 10, 1989

When I talked to William Horn Cloud today he told me a story about his father who died in 1920. He said that his father, just a little while before his death, had sold all of his good things to pay for a trip to Washington, D.C., on behalf of the Pine Ridge Survivors' Association. William talked about compensation in the form of scholarships for descendants of massacre victims, a national day of mourning, an eternal flame at the mass grave, and a museum near the mass grave.

Horn Cloud also said that long ago, the descendants of Chief Big Foot's band had a Decoration Day in June for relatives buried in the mass grave.

It is interesting that in the 1920s, the Lakota tribes also initiated litigation on the first Black Hills case. The massacre and the theft of 7.3 million acres of Black Hills land have always been interconnected in important ways in Lakota thought and history; ways that non-Indian historians have rarely understood. The Ghost Dance religion and resulting Wounded Knee Massacre in 1890 were caused by (among other things) the theft of the Black Hills in 1877[3] and of nine million additional acres in 1889,[4] not other reasons given by apologists in history. Lakota people were looking for salvation in a messiah that would rid them of the non-Indian intruders and the terrible conditions they were living under in the late 1880s; the famine, sickness, and death. They wanted their stolen lands and way of life restored. This is often overlooked in mainstream historical and political discussions.[5]

In 1863, Congress withdrew its consent to be sued in the Court of Claims for violation of Indian treaties,[6] which meant that after that date,

Indian tribes had no judicial remedy in the United States for violation of their treaty rights. This is the period that historian/activist Helen Hunt Jackson called a "century of dishonor." After that date it became necessary for Indian tribes to petition Congress for special jurisdictional acts waiving the United States sovereign immunity in the Court of Claims. This was the reason the Sioux tribes found it necessary to lobby Congress for a special jurisdictional act in 1920 to have their treaty claims heard in the Court of Claims.[7]

The Sioux treaty claims were filed in the Court of Claims in 1923 as Docket C-531 and dismissed on jurisdictional grounds in 1942.[8] Over twenty claims were filed in Docket C-531; the Black Hills Claim was designated as Docket C-531 (7). But it was theft of Indian land in which the Sioux tribes were mainly interested in 1920, not money. Unfortunately, nations who steal the lands of other nations rarely want to talk about their crimes, and the U.S. legal system wasn't designed to protect Indian interests; it was designed to protect non-Indian interests. What the Sioux tribes didn't understand when they filed Docket C-531 was that the United States intended to extinguish title to their treaty lands by payment of monetary compensation. Many Indian tribes are going to wake up in the twenty-first century and realize that even though they were forcibly removed from these treaty lands in the nineteenth century, they continued to hold legal title to these lands into the twentieth century. They will realize that title to these lands was extinguished by payment of monetary compensation through the Indian Claims Commission subsequent to 1946![9]

The steadfast refusal of the United States to provide a judicial forum with jurisdiction to return tribal lands is based on the common law principle of "sovereign immunity," that a party cannot sue the sovereign in any court without its consent. Colonizing nations such as the United States have successfully invoked the principle in federal courts as a means of preventing tribes from recovering their homelands. When tribes are allowed to sue the United States, sovereign immunity is waived only to the extent that tribes are allowed to sue for the recovery of monetary damages for the theft of their lands. To this day, tribes remained barred from using the federal courts to recover their treaty lands.

Chronicle

In spite of the fact that general public or scholarly talk about "colonization" as it applies to American Indians has been absent from much of the historical discourse because of the national obsession with "assimilation" in the first part of this century, and "multiculturalism" or "diversity" in the latter decades, anticolonial forces have always been at work on the native homelands of the United States and in Sioux Country in particular.

The history of the Oglalas, especially, during the forty-year period of Red Cloud's rise to power (1850–90), the years when the theft of the Black Hills and the massacre at Wounded Knee occurred, years and events which set the stage for almost all subsequent political action, can be seen as crucial to understanding the present dilemma of colonialism. Often, non-Indian political mythmakers, with their unifying themes attendant on "manifest destiny" and inevitable "Americanization," refuse to have an open mind concerning the Lakota position on history, often describing Indian discourse as delusional or pitiful. For the Lakotas, however, the history they know and tell can almost be described as liberation theology and it accounts for daily behavior even today. Refusal to give up language and religion in spite of massive attempts at American institutionalized oppression are not rarities in any Lakota community.

The current "self-determination without termination" era (proclaimed such by President Richard M. Nixon in a policy statement to Congress on July 8, 1970), then, for the Sioux is not a new idea and it would be wrong and misleading to dismiss this longing for sovereignty as a modern manifestation of revisionism. It is not a case of new information which is brought to bear on the condition of American Indian tribes like the Lakotas so much as it is a case of a minority voice finally being heard in a majority setting. On the other hand, the United States' dealings with the First Nations of America, which have always sought to weaken ideas of tribal nationalism, cannot be discounted because they have succeeded to a disheartening degree.

A colonial government whose main governing principle is theft is what Lakotas say has confronted them from the beginning of their relationship with the United States and, they say, it continues in this stance toward them. This principle of legalized theft has caused thousands to die horribly (including the hundreds at Wounded Knee) and has had wretched consequences of poverty and demoralization. The principle of theft confronted the tribes during the treaty period and in the decades immediately following in the era of the big federal water projects and dam construction, and has been seen only reluctantly, at the close of the twentieth century, as having consequences of distrust and failure in Indian/White relations in the United States. Not by everyone, to be sure, but by many historians and scholars and humanitarians.

Once one understands the objectives, one begins to understand the methods. The objective from the beginning was the breaking up of the tribal system and the theft of the Black Hills and thousands of acres of homelands for the enrichment of whites. The methods were astonishingly effective then and they continue to be. For example, finally, in 1905, Red Cloud accepted an allotment of 320 acres though he had opposed it throughout his long life.[10] This historical fact can be seen as a testament to the efficacy of the methods. Today, Indians accept one colonial solution after another though they oppose them. Examination of the past and present dealings of Indian Nations with the federal government illuminates those methods.

The federal government's approach began early but, in the nineteenth century, was perfected. The successful defense of the people's lands by the Oglalas, Hunkpapas, Minneconjous, Sicangu, Yanktons, Santees, Northern Cheyennes, and Arapahoes in 1866–68 was called "Red Cloud's War" by white politicians and the complicit popular press and scholars have ever since accepted that term. It was, of course, nothing of the kind. It was the united Sioux national forces and their Cheyenne and Arapahoe allies who fought and won that struggle, a native military with many commanders. Yet, Red Cloud was touted by whites as "the most powerful Indian on the Plains." The method by which native government(s) and indigenous leadership mechanisms that had developed over a period of thousands of years were corrupted, misunderstood, and dismissed began with that kind of media/political storytelling. By making Red Cloud "the most powerful Indian on the Plains," the whites began the imposition of new methods of governing and the erosion of the sovereign rights of a people to claim their own identity and definition. Legislative, judicial, and executive colonialism took root. It was decades before Oglalas began to accept the fact that the chaotic and disturbing history of Red Cloud was a history of their own times, but, of course, eventually they did.

To read the reports and to listen to the people's remembrances of that era is to see a steady erosion of their sovereign rights not only to choose their own leadership but also to make the rules by which the people would live. In the beginning, it was said, Red Cloud was a member of the band of the Oglala chief Smoke, but his father was Sicangu (Brule) Lakota, a fact of birth which in those days and in times since exempted him from certain stages of political and religious hierarchical influence among the Oglala bands.

Unlike many Oglala/Lakota leaders of the period he did not belong to the very old families revered for centuries because of patrilineal descent necessary to the people's sensibility for acceptability to other cultural groups that made up the national consciousness (the Hunkpapas, the Minneconjous, even the Santees, and others). Careful marriage patterns embedded in the tiospaye mechanisms for survival were adhered to in Red Cloud's early life and the violations of those rules were a serious matter to people who lived in the tribal way. Not so for the whites, the outsiders. During this time of incessant warfare, however, warriors attracted the attention of those outsiders and it was said by the people that this warrior's fame among the whites would distort the leadership mechanisms of the people.

In addition, an early incident would forever besmirch Red Cloud's character as far as his people were concerned. In 1841, the Oglala bands of Chief Bull Bear and Chief Smoke went to Fort Laramie to trade. Chief Bull Bear was shot in an altercation and it was said that the young Red Cloud fired the shot. This dubious information about Red Cloud's youthful past was given by Philip F. Wells, an interpreter who was himself called a liar by many Indians of the period. Nonetheless, the odiousness of such an act made the story one which was told over and over again and believed by many.

According to Mario's account, this is a true story that affects the Oglala even today. Bull Bear was a tyrant, coming to Smoke's camp and belittling him, taking any woman he wanted without offering horses, etc. Eventually Smoke's people confronted Bull Bear. The next morning, the altercation occurred. Bull Bear was shot and wounded. According to Royal Bull Bear, Red Cloud ran up and finished the chief off with a shot in the head.

The two bands split, with the Smoke people moving to the Powder River country and the Bear people staying along the North Platte. Red Cloud was a nephew of Smoke. This is why the Smoke people were involved in the Powder River War of 1866–68.

Mario says he has heard Royal Bull Bear talk about Red Cloud shooting his great-grandfather in the head several times over the past ten years.

The flaws of Red Cloud were never overlooked by the people who understood their nationalistic/sovereign legacy; though they recognized him as an accomplished warrior, they passed him over at least twice during the years of his war exploits and political fame for the position of "shirt wearer," a position of the highest and most influential status. The first time was in 1866, during the so-called Red Cloud War, when those chosen were Sword, American Horse, Young Man Afraid of His Horse, and Crazy Horse; the second time was at a later Bear Butte Council, when Black Twin was appointed instead. What this meant in tribal terms is that, according to the people themselves, there were other Indians on the Plains with power, and Red Cloud's acceptance of that supreme title was, at the very least, ambiguous.

Eventually, in spite of what Red Cloud considered snubs by his people, he became a decision maker for agency politics. He was a signer of the Peace Treaty of Fort Laramie in 1868, which designed a permanent homeland consisting of 26 million acres called "the Great Sioux Reservation" and included the stipulation that any further cessions of the reservation required the signatures of three-fourths of the eligible male populations of each Sioux band. By participating in the negotiation of those terms he has become, in the eyes of some, a figure of grand historical proportions because this treaty has stood up against the attacks of anti-Indian interests far better than most of the treaties of the land.[11]

In 1872, when Sitting Bull, Gall, Crazy Horse, Black Twin, Little Wound, and hundreds of other tribal leaders would not go to the designated reservations nor enter into negotiations which they considered stacked against them, Red Cloud was available to white politicians for the framing of the dialogues concerning the eventual defense and ultimate theft of the Black Hills.

In 1873, when he had finally settled along the White River and his influence among the people had diminished considerably, there was every indication that though he had accepted the reservation as a homeland, he had not given up his commitment to sovereignty. For example, when a new agent, Dr. J. J. Saville, arrived at Pine Ridge, he relayed Red Cloud's position to his superiors as follows: "He says that the Oglalas will regulate affairs here and that everything will be done as they wish."[12]

The reasons Red Cloud gave were significant, ethical, and collective: the Oglalas had already forfeited much, they had sacrificed, and they expected their sovereign rights to be upheld as provided for in the treaty they had signed. Looking at it from today's perspective, it doesn't seem too much to ask. But what we know from history is that America's brand of colonialism, in which Red Cloud was a predestined collaborator, transformed the Indian world forever and initiated the ideological struggles which have plagued the United States ever since, making it virtually impossible for appropriate institution building to occur on the homelands in the name of sovereignty.

In more recent discussions of the ethical ideas here, lawyers like Gonzalez quote article 8 of the 1877 act and *Ex Parte Crow Dog* (1883),[13] which say that the Lakota/Dakota people have control of their own legal systems and are entitled to an orderly government. In the famous *Ex Parte Crow Dog* case, the Supreme Court held that federal courts were courts of limited jurisdiction, though one would never know it to look at the history of cases diminishing tribal sovereignty and Sioux territory. Since *Crow Dog* there has been an erosion of Lakota sovereignty by both the federal courts and Congress and, indeed, by historians and social scientists who have written with little or no documentation that the notion of sovereign nationhood was unknown to the Sioux and to indigenous peoples in general. Social infrastructures such as reservation courts with recognition and support by federal agencies were nonexistent until the 1880s and this neglect allowed other entities to almost overwhelm tribal powers.[14]

DIARY: SEPTEMBER 10, 1989

> *When I spoke to attorney Pete Taylor of the Senate Select Committee on Indian Affairs today, he gave me a detailed account of the attempt (nearly thirteen years ago) by Senator James Abourezk to pass legislation to compensate descendants of massacre victims. This effort was spearheaded by former Oglala Sioux president Johnson Holy Rock. He said the author Dee Brown, who wrote* Bury My Heart at Wounded Knee, *and Alvin Josephy, another well-known scholar in history, and several members of the Survivors' Associations attended the hearing. But except for Abourezk, there was no politician in Washington who aggressively pushed for passage of the proposed legislation.*
>
> *I suspect he wanted me to understand how difficult it will be to get Congress to pass our proposed legislation. The Lakota people, however, now have the expertise and commitment to get the job done and we are determined to do it.[15]*

DIARY: SEPTEMBER 21, 1989

> *Ivan Star Comes Out, a reporter for the* Lakota Times, *called and asked for my opinion about William Horn Cloud's desire to create a new "umbrella" organization for the Pine Ridge and Cheyenne River Wounded Knee Survivors' Associations members to work under. I told him that the whole thing was "a bunch of baloney, instigated by people who do not have the best of intentions." When I talked to Sam Eaglestaff about the umbrella organization at the Rapid City Regional Hospital (he has heart problems) he told me not to worry about it, that "it is an internal Oglala problem" and "they [the Oglalas] will have to resolve it themselves."*

CHRONICLE

About a week after this interview, an article appeared in the *Lakota Times* headlined "New Wounded Knee Survivors' 'Umbrella' Group Causes Furor." This group was apparently formed at a meeting honoring William and Nancy Horn Cloud at their home at Pine Ridge on September 8 and 9. The newspaper named the new board members as William Horn Cloud (president), Edgar High Whiteman, Angelita Blackstone, and Victoria Friday Scares. Cheyenne River descendants serving on the board were also named: Eaglestaff was still the president, and other new members were Isaac Long, Burdell Blue Arm, and Melvin Garreau. Factions opposed to the new Oglala organization saw it as a snub to the work that had been done by Celane Not Help Him (the granddaughter of Dewey Beard) and believed that William Horn Cloud's initiative was simply a way to give his brother-in-law Oliver Red Cloud more influence than he would otherwise have had in the matter. This was not a surprise to those who throughout the years have been critical of Oliver's notion that as a great-grandson of the warrior chief Red Cloud, he himself is "chief of all the Oglalas," as he often proclaims, as though chieftainship were only a hereditary matter. Oliver has served as chairman of the Black Hills Sioux Nation Council since the death of Edwin Red Door of Fort Peck, Montana, in 1982. There has been a continuous struggle within that organization to get Oliver to call a meeting so that new officers can be elected. He refuses. His inaction serves to maintain his control and allows him to go about saying he is head traditional chief of all the eight reservation councils involved in the Black Hills Claim.

In reality, Gonzalez knew that the umbrella organization could not easily be dismissed as "a bunch of baloney." More than most, he understood the relationships and issues involved here. He knew that they reflected behaviors of a long history of traditionalism corrupted by the last hundred years of interference with those traditions. Nonetheless, the need for careful problem solving was apparent and it would be the work of the committees and associations to head off the unnecessary delay which would surely follow.

The Sioux Nation is a confederation made up of several cultural groups, each of which possesses the sovereign power to enter into treaties with the United States, in brief: the Oglala and Minneconjou already mentioned, and the distant Santee, the Yankton, Yanktonai, Hunkpapa, Sicangu, Sihasapa—all of whom are related in a complex system of nationalistic organization which implies particular cultural loyalties and responsibilities. These cultural groups display old-time behaviors which persist in contemporary Sioux life and are often thought of by outsiders as "tribal antagonisms and factionalisms" which are trivial. Almost any outsider who has worked in tribal enclaves becomes frustrated and angry in the face of tribal behaviors and, certainly, American scholars and historians bent upon seeing the world in global and assimilative terms have had a difficult time giving credibility to these time-consuming episodes.

Intertribal ethnicity of this sort is not a new idea to tribal societies nor is it seen by the people themselves as a hindrance to the good life. Such political order has never led to pandemic violence amongst the people, nor to a civil war as far as we know, and there has never been a case in history of one Nakota/Lakota/Dakota cultural group mounting warfare against another because of these kinds of interests. Though there are many political matters which need to be resolved, most of the people do not believe that ridding themselves of their intertribal ethnic identities will help them toward the solutions of these matters. Thus, when Gonzalez talks to the Minneconjou Sam Eaglestaff about his concerns, he is given the tribal solution: that is an internal Oglala matter which *they* must resolve.

This kind of problem solving is almost unknown in the United States, the fixer of all international conflicts for the last fifty years. Europe, too, has had a very different experience with tribalism and ethnicity and international conflict. In the case of the native peoples of the United States, however, some have suggested that, left to their own devices with appropriate relationships to outside interests, they might thrive more vigorously than if the U.S. government continues to intervene.

DIARY: OCTOBER 7, 1989

> Charles Blindman came into my office today. We spent the afternoon discussing issues confronting the WKSA, including the "umbrella" organization William Horn Cloud and his family want to create to assume control of the Survivors' Associations' lobbying effort. He said, based on discussions he had with Edgar High Whiteman and others, the purpose of the organization should be limited to organizing the centennial "celebration"; it should not deal with lobbying our proposed legislation through Congress.
>
> He said Millie Horn Cloud was upset about my statement in the Lakota Times, that the move to create an "umbrella" organization is all a bunch of "baloney." I told him that Millie should attend WKSA meetings

*and support our existing lobbying effort if she and her family want to help;
that I will still have to do all the work and cover all the expenses regardless
of who's in charge and I would rather work with people I like and respect
like Claudia Iron Hawk Sully, Celane Not Help Him, Marie Not Help
Him, Belva Hollow Horn and the members of the Cheyenne River WKSA.
I told him that the Horn Cloud family, largely under the influence of Oliver Red Cloud because of their in-law status, is being disrespectful and their
desire to create an "umbrella" organization is merely a power play to take
control of both Survivors' Associations, and do something stupid like replace the people who are doing all the work as officers and terminate the
contract with their attorney.*

*I told him how Oliver and his son Lyman Red Cloud showed their true
colors while we were working on the Black Hills Claim a few months ago.
Lyman misused Phil Stevens's credit card at a meeting in Rapid City,
which caused divisions among the traditional people from the different
reservations that were totally unnecessary. I made it clear to him that I
work only for the Survivors' Associations, as I committed myself to do in
1985, and I am willing to do everything necessary to make our proposed
legislation a reality.*

*An October 15 meeting of the umbrella organization has been sched-
uled. Charles wanted know if I would be willing to attend the meeting.
I told him I could not attend because of a conflict in my schedule.*

CHRONICLE

The reference to Phil Stevens in the October 7 diary entry refers to a rather
fascinating chapter in the search for a solution to the Black Hills theft.
This claim, that the sacred lands in western South Dakota were taken from
the Sioux Nation illegally by the United States Congress, started in 1920,
went through the courts, was said by the Supreme Court to be a legitimate
claim on the basis of the 1868 Treaty of Fort Laramie and was called by the
Court in 1980 "the most ripe and rank case of dishonorable dealing" in
the nation's history.

Unfortunately, because of the protocol (thought by Indians to be simple racist strategy) by which Indian Nations are allowed to take land
claims to U.S. courts, only money damages could be rendered. The Sioux
Nation has, since then, sought land reform through congressional legislation and refused to accept the money which was to be funneled through
the Bureau of Indian Affairs. Lakota thinking is that if Congress can steal
land, it can also return land.

Mario Gonzalez has been a major player in this tribal effort, filed a federal court action in July of 1980 for injunctive relief to stop the payment, defined issues, and framed the debate through proposed legislation called the Bradley Bill (S. 1453), which was introduced by Senator Bill Bradley from New Jersey in 1985. He also drafted the Martinez Bill (H.R. 5680, an emended version of the Bradley Bill), introduced by Congressman Mathew Martinez of California in 1990. This matter is far from finished, according to the Sioux. The Black Hills Claim is the longest-lasting Indian land claim in the history of the United States and is, according to the Sioux, unresolved.

Phil Stevens, a millionaire California businessman who was previously unknown to the Sioux, showed up in 1987 during the formation of the Bradley Bill at the invitation of Paul Iron Cloud, aligned himself with certain factions of the Oglalas, claimed to be a Standing Bear descendant (an unproven claim contested by the Standing Bear descendants themselves), and, for several years in the 1980s, purported to be "Great Chief of All the Sioux." He even went with them to Washington, D.C., during certain negotiating periods on Black Hills Claim matters, though it is said the Pine Ridge Grey Eagles did not support making him a chief.[16] It is quite possible that Stevens stepped into a leadership vacuum, during a chaotic period for the Sioux political factions, and took more control of the dialogue than would have been acceptable to them otherwise.

Lakota Times editor Tim Giago, a member of the Pine Ridge Sioux Tribe, accused Stevens of divisive tactics for the purpose of control and personal power.[17] Bumper stickers on reservation cars read "Stevens is not my chief!" and, in general, there was much media coverage of the entire fiasco. Stevens has, since then, made a reputation for himself in California by dressing in full regalia and visiting school children, still billing himself as "Sioux Nation Chief." His "antics," say many, are an "embarrassment to the real Lakota people,"[18] and there is much discussion concerning his motives. More significantly, his "antics" have made the legitimate political work of the people look ridiculous. Today some tribal members on the reservation question the loyalty of Stevens—that is, does Stevens serve the interest of the tribe or the government?—but he continues to appear on the reservation scene occasionally, distributing donated goods and talking about poverty issues.

Stevens's unproved claim to be a Lakota is not a new phenomenon, in spite of the fact that Indian Nations have always claimed the sovereign right to say who their citizens are for exactly the same reasons other nations and governments do.

Such racial masquerades as Stevens participated in probably need more study in order to define motives and consequences, but there have been several famous cases documented. For example, Donald B. Smith's *From the Land of the Shadows* presents the story of Archie Belaney, an Englishman who created the fantasy of being an Indian named Grey Owl and was only unmasked at his death in 1938. He wrote many books and became a well-known conservationist in Canada, using his so-called Indian identity to get an audience for his ideas. This celebrated case of fraud was finally and belatedly investigated by the Department of Indian Affairs. Stevens's motivations are still to be determined; but while such masquerades are puzzling, there is evidence that suggests the presence of infiltrators and frauds for what turns out to be anti-Indian political motives at every level of Indian life. In addition, there exists in the "new age" movement of the last two decades the idea that being Indian is a right that anyone can claim. Such people seem to make little distinction between the right that everyone has to seek a spiritual path to God and the right to claim "Indianness." It is simply another example of the denial of the right of sovereign nations to be in charge of their citizenship rules and regulations.

In a recent informal discussion Mario Gonzalez says he does not put the blame for the failure of the Bradley Bill legislation at the doorstep of Phil Stevens, though many others in the tribe do so. Gonzalez says that Stevens had good intentions of helping the Sioux people and his involvement has had a positive effect on the people because he forced the groups to focus on the compensation issue.[19] "I feel he made a mistake, however, in asking the traditional people to confer a traditional Indian title upon him so he could use that title when he helped lobby a Black Hills bill in Congress. The real problem is a lack of leadership within the tribal councils."

Many of the Sioux are not as generous as Mario is in this debate.

Diary: November 2, 1989

I spoke with Joe Horn Cloud (brother of William) this morning. During the course of our conversation he told a story that I've heard many times. In December, 1890, Chief Red Cloud sent a runner to Cherry Creek to invite Chief Big Foot to come to Pine Ridge. Then, when Chief Big Foot and his people were surrounded by the Seventh Cavalry, Red Cloud failed to come to their rescue. The insinuation is that Red Cloud was used to lure Chief Big Foot to Pine Ridge on a pretext so the Seventh Cavalry could have an excuse to get revenge for Custer's death at the Battle of the Little Bighorn. It is true that the defeat of the Seventh Cavalry was very much on the minds of every U.S. military person on the Plains at that time, and Col. George Forsyth and his drunken soldiers talked about revenge throughout the night of December 28, 1890. Even past the turn of the century, Joe indicated, Indians off the reservation were considered "hostile by white settlers and could be shot on sight."[20]

DIARY: JANUARY 20, 1990

A WKSA meeting at Oscar Hollow Horn's residence was held today for the purpose of discussing and explaining the sixth draft of our proposed legislation, which was redrafted to address the concerns of the South Dakota congressional delegation.

Some Survivors' Association members expressed their concern that the National Park Service, whose mentality has pretty much been the creation of national parks on Indian lands, will be involved. The National Park Service is often in conflict with Indian tribes concerning its mission, especially when national parks contain Native American religious sites and shrines. The National Park Service's participation in lobbying our proposed legislation through Congress is nevertheless essential if we are going to succeed in our legislative effort since Congress will not pass our proposed legislation without an NPS Study of Alternatives.

CHRONICLE

The National Park Service came into being in 1916, some years after the Teddy Roosevelt era when "carrying a big stick" and stealing Panama and "opening up" treaty-protected lands by executive order went unchallenged. Roosevelt had a direct role in the creation of the Forest Service in 1905. He also "restored" a 50-square-mile area of the Pine Ridge Reservation located in the state of Nebraska to the public domain so non-Indians could come in and homestead it in that year. (See appendix A.) There's not a Lakota who can forget that 180,000 acres of the Rosebud Reservation treaty-protected lands were "opened up" in 1904 by Teddy Roosevelt (with just a signature and presidential seal) and that's why, they say, he is carved by the whites on the Mount Rushmore National Monument in the heart of the Black Hills. Nonetheless, Mario tells those at the meeting this day that they must find a way to work with the park service if they are to accomplish their goals. These federal agencies, one in Agriculture and the other in the Interior, are thought to be quite different; yet, their bureaucracies often seem to be equally unresponsive to issues of native land and resource use.[21]

DIARY: FEBRUARY 24, 1990

A couple of days ago, I sent copies of the sixth draft of our proposed legislation to Senator Tom Daschle, Congressman Tim Johnson, Professor Merylee Shelton of San Jose College, a good friend of Sam Eaglestaff, and Steve Young of the Sioux Falls Argus Leader, *as they requested.*

In my conference with Sam Eaglestaff today, we discussed the problems of getting the South Dakota congressional delegation to sponsor our proposed legislation in Congress. Sam expressed his amazement at how difficult it is to get the congressional delegation to even look at it. He said: "It is not that they're bad. It's just that they don't have any need to do what's right as far as Lakotas are concerned, since they are elected to defend their own people's behavior in history. I can understand that, because they are not Indians. Still we must continue to break down their unwillingness to do what's right and support our bill."

I am very concerned about Sam's health. I mentioned this to Dorothy (my wife).

CHRONICLE

Steve Young, a reporter for the largest newspaper in the state of South Dakota, was preparing to do a March, June, and August newspaper series on Wounded Knee history as the *Sioux Falls Argus Leader* centennial story and contacted many Indians throughout the state for information and opinion. After the series was published, many thoughtful Indian readers felt that the same history was told, the same language, the same bias, and they were disappointed in the piece considering the fact that they felt they had exerted considerable effort to write and tell a correct history. The need for a new and reasonable history, they said, was one of the main reasons for the contemporary work to be done with the Congress on the Wounded Knee monument.

Young posed many of the same questions and answered them in much the same way: Who started the *Battle?* The *Mystery* Remains. Contemporary Oglalas and Minneconjous, particularly, but the Sioux in general, dispute that it was a *Battle* since the dead were essentially unarmed and the peace treaty had already been signed.

Young's question, "What Went Wrong at Wounded Knee?" distorted the Lakota perception and seemed to imply that there was some unaccountable error in the planning of a military engagement when, on the contrary, the Indian story has suggested all along that the *political* motivations are probably more revealing than the military motivations for this cataclysmic event and need to be examined fully. Today, there are many Indians who believe this event to have occurred during a period of "ethnic cleansing" though the term was not publicly used until recently and has never been applied officially to any event in U.S. or colonial history. That's because the United States has written its own story and Indians have not, and the point was not made in the current newspaper analysis.

Young quoted University of South Dakota history professor and author Herbert Hoover, who said: "I don't believe for a minute that it was a Massacre. I think, more appropriately, it had to be an 'affair,' an emotional outburst that got carried away." Neither has Hoover given much credence to the 1937 story told by South Dakota politician Ralph Case, who noted this about his conversation with the son of Maj. Samuel Whiteside, who was stationed at Wounded Knee: "I will say for the record that his son, Lt. Cl. Warren Whiteside, told me that the Seventh Cavalry went to Pine Ridge with the full intent of getting even for the loss of Custer at the Little Big Horn 14 years before." The Sioux would like this motive of revenge to take a clearer place in the historical discussion of this event.[22]

Some scholars, now called "revisionists," who are now writing of this period in history, Patricia Limerick of the University of Colorado, for example, suggest that the history written by white historians according to "winners" and "losers" still pervades much of the public discourse found both in the popular press and in scholarly works.

Hoover, who does not claim to be a revisionist, is generally considered by his colleagues in history to be a respected scholar of South Dakota history. In his "Historical Adaptation to Natural Features" essay for the 1989 "Centennial West's Celebrations of the Northern Tier States' Heritage" booklet, he says about the famous Black Hills case: "As quickly as tribal groups *relinquished* their claims, farmers and livestock growers occupied the land and miners and foresters moved into the Black Hills" (p. 45, emphasis added).

This statement was written and published only a few years after the Supreme Court called the land case "the most ripe and rank case of dishonorable dealings." Hoover could hardly have been unaware of the discussion in the lower courts, yet his essay says little or nothing about the

century-long litigation, the resistance by tribal politicians, or the lower
court decisions on the matter. Oral historians from the tribes believe that
to suggest there was a wholesale "relinquishment" of lands by Sioux Indians is racist history. 'To relinquish' means 'to forego, renounce, abandon,
cede'. None of these terms is an accurate description of Lakota thought on
the subject. They believe they did not give these lands up, either voluntarily or involuntarily. They believe lands were stolen. A study of how language is used in the political dispossession of the Lakotas is long overdue.

   In another paragraph of this essay Hoover says, "Early in the 1870's a
body of mining prospectors *muscled its way* into the Black Hills. Prospectors violated the 1868 Fort Laramie Treaty but federal officials declined to
enforce its terms. Sitting Bull's followers fought back successfully until the
demise of George Custer and his Seventh Cavalry of 1876. *Through the 1877
agreement, however, western Sioux Tribes gave up the Black Hills,* then their
arms and ponies, and then their freedom in exchange for confinement
around six new agencies" (p. 45, emphasis added). Such inaccuracies must
be challenged. Indeed, the so-called 1877 agreement has been interpreted
in quite a different light by Gonzalez, who calls it an "unconstitutional
act." It began as a proposed agreement in which the Sioux would relinquish 7.3 million acres of their 1868 treaty reservation (the Black Hills),
but when the Manypenny Commission could not obtain the requisite
three-quarters adult male signatures to constitute a cession under article
12 of the 1868 treaty, Congress simply enacted the "agreement" into law in
1877; it therefore became an act of Congress. Gonzalez says that the Fifth
Amendment to the Constitution specifically states that private property
shall not be taken unless it is for a public purpose, and then with due process of law and just compensation, that, in fact, the "taking" of the Black
Hills was for the "profit" of miners and homesteaders, not public use at
all. And that, therefore, "compensation" is the immoral, illegal, and uneth-
ical solution to outright "theft." This theory has not been summarily dismissed, as was predicted by white lawyers and historians, but continues to
be the basis for further tribal action. A major reason for this state of affairs
in telling the story, that is, in writing the history, is that it is in general, in
South Dakota at least, written by non-Indian scholars who seem to have a
vested interest in the continued dispossession of Sioux Indians.

   From the point of view of any scholar or reader of history, it is hardly
sensible to believe that the Sioux Oyate would give up their freedom and
their sacred lands in the hills "for confinement." Plain logic and a history
of twenty-five years (1851–76) of largely successful military resistance says

that reasonable people simply would not do this. Mario Gonzalez's argument concerning the 1877 act, available to historians throughout the state, is noticeably absent from this and many other historical discussions, which means that biases in historical accountings are commonplace in this region.

The following is an excerpt from the oral argument presented by Gonzalez to the U.S. Court of Appeals for the 8th Circuit, located at St. Louis, Mo., in the 1981 case *Oglala Sioux Tribe v. United States*.[23] It remains an argument which the Sioux have faith in as it concerns their legal history and sets forth the legal theory utilized by the Lakota in their own defense. The Wounded Knee Survivors' Associations, in particular, are convinced that unless the people of the United States can be persuaded that a legal wrong has been done and then justified through a falsified history, there will continue to be opposition to the official nation-to-nation apology that has been called for and that reconciliation between the races will not occur.

Mario Gonzalez speaking on behalf of the Oglala Sioux Tribe in the Black Hills Claim:

MR. GONZALEZ: Pursuant to Rule 34-C we have reserved one-half of our time today for rebuttal argument.

THE COURT: You want to reserve half of your time?

MR. GONZALEZ: Yes, 15 minutes.

THE COURT: That's an awful lot to reserve but you are free to do so.

MR. GONZALEZ: And my co-counsel, Mr. [Russel] Barsh, will give rebuttal argument.

THE COURT: (inaudible) Your opening argument does not respond (inaudible) to go into those issues. So keep that in mind, too.

MR. GONZALEZ: Yes, I understand that.

This case involves vested property rights, protected by the Fifth Amendment to the Constitution. That property is described more fully in Paragraph 16 of the amended complaint.

These property rights are vested under the 1868 Fort Laramie Treaty and under the Act of March 3rd, 1871.[24]

The United States confiscated this property by direct Act in 1877. This was done in clear violation of the Fifth Amendment, in that: that land was taken for purposes, other than public purposes; no due process of law was ever accorded the condemnee; and no just compensation, to this date, has ever been afforded to the Oglala Sioux Tribe.

The 1877 act is unconstitutional. We still own the confiscated area because the 1877 act is void *ab initio*. Also, the confiscated area was taken in violation of the First Amendment. This land is sacred to the Oglala Sioux Tribe. The United States took the only place in this world where we could practice our religion by taking away our church, if you will, by taking away the cemeteries where our grandfathers lie buried today.

These matters have all been alleged in the amended complaint and for the purposes of this appeal must be taken as admitted and true.

The United States doesn't actually oppose these factual allegations. They simply argue that [an article 3 Court]: Quote, "with general equity jurisdiction," namely the United States District Court for the District of South Dakota, "has no jurisdiction to hear this case and declare the 1877 Act unconstitutional." Although we cite jurisdictional statutes which we believe confer jurisdiction on the United States District Court, the United States erroneously, we feel, convinced the district court to dismiss the case.

In effect, the United States has successfully convinced the district court to overrule *Marbury v. Madison.*[25] We are here today to request that this court restore *Marbury* as rule of law for the district of South Dakota.

In Britain parliamentary supremacy is a rule of law. In the United States the Constitution is supposed to be the supreme law of the land. However, the United States today urges this court, as it did the district court, to hold that the Constitution is no longer supreme, that congressional power is now above the Constitution and is supreme. The United States desires to have this court hold that legislative supremacy is now the law in the United States, that Congress, in effect, is now parliament and no longer Congress.

Thus, dismissal of the amended complaint raises an important constitutional issue, an issue which must be decided in this case. Is—

THE COURT: Isn't there something else here that's involved? It may—it has been determined in a prior case that the Act of 1877 was the taking under the power of eminent domain; and that there is a [forum] for the adjudication of the amount to be paid through the Indians' Claims Commission.

MR. GONZALEZ: The fact which we alleged in our complaint, your honor, and which must be taken as true for the purposes of this appeal is that the Oglala Sioux Tribe was not a party to the 1980 decision.

THE COURT: Whether or not it's a party, however, we have to look at those statutes to determine whether or not we have jurisdiction. And it could have been a party. And, of course, there's some question whether it was or was not; but assuming it was not a party; it could have been a party.

Isn't that the exclusive measure of (inaudible). Congress had the right to limit our jurisdiction. Isn't that the exclusive means by which the tribe can obtain just compensation for the alleged wrongful taking?

MR. GONZALEZ: The tribe, your honor, does not seek monetary damages in this action. [It seeks] only equitable relief. In terms of the exclusivity of the remedy, we feel that the Indian Claims Commission act is an unconstitutional limitation on a remedy which we have a right to; namely, quiet title and equitable relief.

THE COURT: Then, what you're saying we have to—don't we have to declare that act unconstitutional in order to reach the issue that you pose?

MR. GONZALEZ: That may be so, your honor.

THE COURT: I don't think that question of the Constitution—the constitutionality of that act is really (inaudible).

MR. GONZALEZ: We think this case can be decided without reaching that question. But if need be, we would certainly request the court to consider that constitutional question.

THE COURT: Mr. Gonzalez, I'd like to ask you one question in connection with the procedures and claims here. Now, is there a valid Sioux Tribe—the only tribe that's complained, that claims the possession of this particular area, the so-called Black Hills area—or are there other Indian tribes that also claim a right to (inaudible)?

MR. GONZALEZ: The Oglala Sioux Tribe is the only tribe requesting a return of the land. There are other tribes who are involved and have claims [to] the particular area involved here but they may have gone for a money remedy.

THE COURT: Well, then how do you divide up, then, the rights to the possession of the land? You're not entitled—if your claim is correct, you're not entitled to the whole complete possession. There are others who would be entitled to possession of it too?

MR. GONZALEZ: The fact of the matter is, your honor, that in a claim for quiet title, it's not important that we be able to segregate what portions of the area that we are entitled to. I think that's an issue of fact which must be decided on the merits then. Really, it is immaterial on the question of jurisdiction. It goes to fashioning a remedy after the merits are heard. And in this particular proceeding, we are only concerned, as you know, with jurisdictional issues.

I would like to respond to the question of the Indian Claims Commission being an exclusive remedy. We feel that—since we are not going after monetary damages which only can be granted by the Indian Claims Commission and the Court of Claims—both of those tribunals clearly, as admitted in the briefs, as admitted in the testimony below, and in the memorandums filed below, cannot give us the relief we desire. And the only court that can give us the relief we desire is the United States District Court for the District of South Dakota, namely quiet title and equitable relief.

Getting back to the [question] that must be decided today by this court is this, your honor: is *Marbury versus Madison* still the law? Do federal district courts, the only courts with equity jurisdiction, still have an obligation to the American people to review and declare acts of Congress unconstitutional? Issues in this case are actually basic and simple. The principles involved here can be learned in almost any high school civics class. It involves limited and delegated powers, separation of powers, and a system of checks and balances, and the principle of judicial review. The Oglala Sioux Tribe is here today to urge the preservation of these principles and ultimately the survival of the United States Republic. If this court affirms the district court, the doctrine of separation of powers will cease to exist. As in Britain, federal courts will become mere enforcers of the law, rather than a check on the excesses of the other two branches of government.

The United States contends today that Congress is immune from suit. They argue that the jurisdictional statutes we cite in the amended complaint do not waive this immunity and that Congress can, thus, excuse itself from constitutional excesses by simply providing, prohibiting, or failing to authorize jurisdiction. In essence, they contend here today that congressional authority can override the United States Constitution. Our response is that it makes no difference whether the jurisdictional statute, that we cite in the district court, conferred jurisdiction because the United States Constitution is self-executing. It is the supreme law of the land. Any time the Constitution limits congressional authority, United States district courts must assume jurisdiction and declare acts of Congress unconstitutional if they violate the Constitution.

The appellees filed three responsive briefs consisting of well over 100 pages, and only approximately 4 pages address these very important constitutional issues. Instead, the appellees attempt to detour this court's attention away from the constitutional issues, to issues not relevant to jurisdiction, but only relevant to the merits.

We suspect that they will attempt to do the same thing today at oral argument.

This case makes one wonder whether the Oglala Sioux Tribe believes in the United States Constitution more than the United States, for it seems ironic today that we come here asking the court to uphold the Fifth and First Amendments as a supreme law of the land. The United States apparently no longer believes the Constitution to be the supreme law and requests a declaration that congressional authority is supreme, that Congress can excuse itself from violations of the Constitution by refusing to consent to jurisdiction and judicial scrutiny and compel the victims to involuntary monetary compensation.

As Chief Justice Marshall noted in *Marbury versus Madison,* and I quote: "The government of the United States has been emphatically termed a government of laws and not men. It will certainly cease to deserve this high appellation if the laws furnish no remedy for a vested legal right."

And in *Cohens versus Virginia*[26] the Supreme Court said, and I quote: "It is true that this court will not take jurisdiction if it should not. But, it is equally true that it must take jurisdiction if it should."

Since we allege violation of basic fundamental constitutional rights, these statements apply to this case at bar.

Also, as Chief Justice Marshall noted in *Marbury,* all federal judges are sworn to uphold these constitutional rights.

In closing, I want to emphasize that this case involves issues which affect all Americans, not just Indians. If the U.S. is to remain a nation of laws and not of men, the Constitution must apply equally to everyone, including Indians. Our Fifth Amendment property rights must be protected as equally as everyone else's.

Appellees argue, however, that Indians should be excepted out of [the] Constitution for some unknown reason, and we would like to know what that reason is today.

But this court cannot and should not make exceptions in the application of important constitutional principles. This is dangerous precedent. This may embolden Congress to expand exception and to create new exceptions to the point where one exception will lead to another exception, to the detriment of the American people. The district court should be reversed.[27]

DIARY: MARCH 6, 1990

It is now almost a year since the WKSAs contacted the South Dakota congressional delegation for assistance in sponsoring their proposed legislation for a national monument and an apology for the 1890 massacre. I telephoned Karen Page Hunt of Tom Daschle's office in Rapid City and asked when we could expect to hear from Senator Daschle. She said we would be getting a response before the end of the day. Daschle has been opposed to the idea of an apology for the massacre.

Conferred with Sam Eaglestaff by telephone concerning a letter from Tribal Chairman Wayne Ducheneaux, a letter of support from the Cheyenne River Sioux Tribal Council.

I was also informed by Sara Yager of Senator Daschle's office that Dashle wants to make sure he works with the tribal councils in developing the proposed legislation on the Wounded Knee Massacre. She thought there was a letter from Paul Iron Cloud (Oglala political support) in the files but she wasn't sure. This run-around by Senator Daschle is so time consuming.

DIARY: APRIL 11, 1990

It's been a full year now since we began our lobbying effort in Washington, D.C., and two years of drafting and redrafting our proposed legislation.

While Senator Daschle and Congressman Johnson have continued to carry on a dialogue with us, they do not appear to be sympathetic to our cause.

The Wounded Knee Memorial Ride, which was organized in 1986 is being planned again for this coming December. It is a pilgrimage to commemorate the murder of Chief Big Foot's people and will culminate on December 29, 1990, the one-hundredth anniversary of the massacre, with a "Wiping of the Tears" ceremony for the descendants of those killed and wounded there. This ride is a five-year spiritual journey which the whole world will be watching. The press in South Dakota will likely portray it as part of Governor Mickelson's "reconciliation" effort. Nobody will talk about the real causes of the massacre, like the theft of the Black Hills in 1877, or the need for an official apology from the United States for the murder of over 350 unarmed men, women, and innocent children by colonial military forces in 1890. Restoration of the Lakota/Dakota people's land and sovereignty will never come about if there is no meaningful discussion about history, law, and politics.

People are still suggesting changes in our proposed legislation and we have bent over backwards to incorporate their suggestions. I conferred by telephone with Clara Spotted Elk (a consultant to the Oglala Sioux Parks and Recreation Authority) regarding OSPRA's concerns about including a museum in our proposed legislation. She is vice president of Karl A. Funke and Associates, Inc., 729 Second Street, N.E., Washington, D.C. 20002.

I also had a very interesting discussion today with Patti Rudge of Congressman Tim Johnson's office in Rapid City about the recent Sioux Falls Argus Leader articles. I expressed my disappointment about Congressman Johnson's statement that he does not support our proposed legislation *because he is concerned about the federal deficit. According to the article, he voted against the Japanese World War II reparations act[28] because of the federal deficit, and he is against the Wounded Knee legislation for the same reason. She avoided further discussion by saying that I should talk to John Devereaux, Johnson's press secretary in Washington, D.C.*

Instead, I called Mark Rubin of Johnson's office in Washington, D.C., who said Johnson would not make such a remark publicly, insinuating that the remark was a misquote. I replied by saying that Congressman Johnson should consider sponsoring our legislative proposal since he is running for reelection this fall and needs every Indian vote he can get (in this overwhelmingly Republican state). But what concerns me most, I told him, was all the changes that everyone is trying to make the Survivors' As-

*sociations accept. I said: "this is our bill, not Johnson's; there is a history
here and the WKSAs know what they want."*

*I am worried about how much time my representation of the Wounded Knee Survivors' Associations is taking out of my law practice here at
Black Hawk. I have covered all expenses out of my own pocket and I
haven't received a cent for services rendered since I took the case in 1985.
My family has had to make sacrifices for this effort, yet many Indian people fail to realize how my family has been affected. It is extremely hard to
operate a law office with a nonpaying client, but I am determined to help
make our proposed legislation a reality for those who lost their lives or
were wounded, and their descendants. If I withdraw my representation of
the Survivors' Associations, the lobbying effort will probably die, and in a
few years nobody will really care about protecting the massacre site and it
will eventually be destroyed. It seems like the only people who understand
that the site is sacred are those who have relatives buried in the mass
grave. It is just commercial property to everyone else, a potential tourist
attraction.*

DIARY: APRIL 17, 1990

*Conferred with Mike Her Many Horses at his home northwest of Wounded Knee about archival research that needs to be done to support our legislative effort. We agreed that more publicity must get out and that the
Wounded Knee Memorial Ride, to be led again by Arvol Looking Horse,
Alex White Plume, Jim Garrett, and Birgil Kills Straight, will be an important cultural event and we should assist in whatever ways we can. Although some members of the Pine Ridge Survivors' Association feel that
the ride might overshadow their efforts to get a bill introduced, I feel that
everyone should work together. Mike is working on a research project gathering photographs of the massacre, which should help our effort to get people to understand Lakota history.*

DIARY: APRIL 20, 1990

*Mark Rubin informed me that Congressman Johnson has decided to introduce our proposed legislation with two changes: first, we must delete the
compensation language regarding a right to a free public education for
Sioux Indians and second, we must delete the $10,000,000 authorization
language using instead the phrase "there are authorized to be appropriated
such sums as may be necessary to carry out this Act."*

Sara Yager called and informed me that Senator Daschle will decide next week on whether he will sponsor our proposed legislation. We discussed the possibility of a national press conference to announce the introduction of our proposed legislation in Congress. I suggested that the press conference should be held at Wounded Knee, South Dakota, instead of Washington, D.C.

I had lunch today with a Dr. Sally Roesch Wagner, a native South Dakotan now a professor at the University of California, Davis, who is doing research and giving workshops on prejudice against women and Indians, and Vic Runnels, a Lakota artist. Roesch Wagner indicated that she may be able to generate support in the academic community for our proposed legislation. She is going to Pierre to do research at the South Dakota Historical Society and promised to send me copies of documents that may help our lobbying effort.

CHRONICLE

Although Gonzalez is more fundamentally interested here, as his diaries indicate, in detailing the stonewalling by the South Dakota political delegation, and in issues concerning access to higher education and problems with the media, it is an interesting aside that feminist scholars in the eighties and nineties have added their historically silenced voices to the dialogue. These voices have not escaped scrutiny and controversy. For instance, C. H. Sommers calls this the voice of "advocacy research" and, more specifically, suggests that much of the research done by feminist scholars is "filler feminism" which she says "pads history with its own facts designed to drive home lessons feminists wish to impart giving it a 'feel good' spin."[29] Women's studies scholars like Roesch Wagner have embraced this new "feminism" by writing criticism of male-centered histories and by asserting the specific nature of political and historical knowledge possessed by women.

As far as feminist interest in Indian history is concerned, there has been an attempt on the part of some scholars to align the subordination of white women in the West with the subordination of Indians. Many have been interested in becoming social historians committed to social change. What this has meant in terms of much of the actual research has been an attempt to mute the responsibility of pioneer women in the dispossession of Indians. The thinking is that since men were in power in the West during these initial periods, women could not be held responsible for what happened. The extent to which this "new historicism" will be helpful to Indians is still to be determined. There is, also, an interest by women's scholars to show that white women in the East during early historical periods were influential in protecting the rights of Indians. Helen Hunt Jackson is always used as a major figure to bolster this scholarly assertion. Indians would be the last to cast aspersions on feminist-directed research and history for, if white women and Indians share anything, it is the idea that history is constructed on many levels, not just in public written works which have been, quite obviously, the province of white male domination.

DIARY: APRIL 24, 1990

I conversed with the following people today regarding our proposed legislation, viz.: Eddie Little Sky about a Centennial Commission meeting to be held at Wounded Knee Catholic Church; Jon Kilpatrick of Arvada, Colorado, about organizing a national news conference to announce the introduction of our bill in Congress; and Rabbi Glazer, a well-known Jewish lobbyist in Washington, D.C., who has agreed to assist us as executive director for the Central Conference of American Rabbis.

Ann Davis, a freelance writer who works at Sinte Gleska College on the Rosebud Reservation, called. She is writing an article about the Big Foot Memorial Ride and our proposed legislation, and asked me for some information. I gave her background information about the Survivors' Association and our lobbying effort and sent her a copy of the sixth draft of our proposed bill. I told her, also, that we are hoping to hold a national press conference when our proposed legislation is introduced in Congress, but we can't get the South Dakota congressional delegation to make a commitment to sponsor it.

DIARY: APRIL 28, 1990

Newly elected president of the Oglala Sioux Tribe, Harold Salway, is quoted in the Rapid City Journal *as announcing the groundwork for a permanent memorial at Wounded Knee. When I spoke to him on the phone today he said he was misquoted. Although he appears unaware of all the work the Survivors' Associations have done to get a Wounded Knee bill introduced in Congress, he appears to be supportive.*

DIARY: APRIL 29, 1990

In a meeting today with Marie Not Help Him and Sam Eaglestaff, we decided it was time to get serious about what we see as the "foot dragging" of

Senator Daschle and Congressman Johnson, who while suggesting their interest in our project, are refusing to sponsor our proposed legislation in Congress.

Sam thought Suzan Shown Harjo, a former executive director of the National Congress of American Indians and now the director of the Morning Star Foundation in Washington, D.C., should be contacted to see if she could assist us. Sam indicated that he would also talk to Monsignor Lenz who could, in turn, contact Senator Daniel Inouye for cosponsorship. It is becoming obvious that we may have to go around the South Dakota congressional delegation and seek sponsorship from a senator or congressman from another state. Members of the South Dakota congressional delegation are too timid to support controversial Indian issues because they fear anti-Indian interests in the state; Daschle in particular supports noncontroversial legislation like appropriations for health care, education, law and order, etc. The congressional delegation is totally lacking in leadership on important controversial issues like resolving the Black Hills Claim, or supporting our proposed Wounded Knee legislation.

When I telephoned Francis White Bird (South Dakota governor Mickelson's liaison, current occupant of the so-called Indian Desk) at the state capital in Pierre, he informed me that the governor wants to work only with elected officials like tribal president Harold Salway on the proposed Wounded Knee bill, suggesting that he would not work with unofficial people like the officers of the Wounded Knee Survivors' Associations. He said that if Salway would write a letter indicating that he supports our proposed legislation, the governor would probably support it. He also expressed his concern about the Oglala Sioux Parks and Recreation Authority's opposition to our proposed bill. I informed him that is not the case; that I currently represent the Parks and Recreation Authority under an attorney's contract and it simply wants to make sure that the establishment of a museum at or near the massacre site remains under its control. I assured Francis that the Parks and Recreation Authority and the Survivors' Associations are currently working together to get the Survivors' Associations' draft legislation introduced in Congress.

DIARY: MAY 7, 1990

Received a rather surprising return call from Sara Yager today. She said she wasn't able to find out what date our proposed bill would be introduced but Daschle would like to introduce it with just the apology and national monument provisions; he wants to delete the compensation provi-

sion. I was surprised that Daschle had agreed to support the apology! The compensation provision was crafted in a manner that would minimize opposition, since we were told by legislative assistants that descendants of massacre victims are too far removed from the time of the massacre to warrant the payment of compensation for the killing and wounding of their grandfathers and grandmothers. This is all so repetitious. History keeps repeating itself again and again.

Later, I telephoned Robert "Tim" Coulter, executive director of the Indian Law Resource Center in Washington, D.C., to discuss Native American legal issues. During our conversation, I mentioned our proposed Wounded Knee legislation and Daschle's desire to excise the compensation provision from our current draft. He suggested that we include a provision that would provide for compensation in the form of funding to public schools that would require a curriculum on Sioux history and culture. It's very doubtful, however, that the Survivors' Associations would accept a compensation provision that would compensate them for the killing and wounding of their ancestors in this manner.

Tim also mentioned a meeting in Geneva, Switzerland, on the Declaration on Indigenous Rights that the NGOs have been working on for several years, which is to begin about July 23, 1990. He suggested that I attend. I'm considering it. I am one of the founding directors of the Indian Law Resource Center and Tim is one of my closest friends. I strongly supported the center's representation of Native Americans in Latin America and the United States when I served on the board of directors from 1978 to 1988.

CHRONICLE

Ms. Yager may have been uninformed concerning her boss's position, for Senator Tom Daschle, who sits on the powerful Senate Select Committee on Indian Affairs, has refused to support the idea of a U.S. "apology" to the Minneconjou descendants who now reside on the Cheyenne River and Pine Ridge Reservations from the beginning and has held to that refusal throughout the months and years that have followed.

This has been a keen disappointment to the many Indians who worked for Daschle's election in the rigorously Republican state of South Dakota. In addition to his opposition to an apology, he also remains adamantly opposed to the return of stolen lands in the Black Hills and has been unwilling to participate in any discussions concerning land reform. The strategy of silence on the part of local and federal politicians has been powerfully effective.

Though at this point in the monument/apology/compensation struggle, Daschle was seen by Indians as engaging in a simple avoidance strategy, he was destined to become a major obstacle in the defense of Oglala interests concerning the memorial effort in South Dakota, though during
much of the month of April he was out of the country, speaking to the
global and international issues of the dismantling of the Soviet empire.
Some political watchers believe Daschle was at this time looking toward
developing a voice in national affairs and indicate that he was a close and
trusted ally of then majority leader George Mitchell. According to congressional analysts at the American Enterprise Institute: "Daschle has no
enemies, people like him enormously. He generates a lot of respect."[30]
Since the early part of the decade, however, Daschle has become a national
leader in the Senate and often seems preoccupied with non-Indian issues.

Many in Indian country have an ambiguous view of the senator, based
upon his behavior concerning Indian issues. For example, during the first
session of the 105th Congress, Daschle was circulating from his office a
preliminary discussion draft for a bill which would "transfer" certain
lands located in the area of operation of the Pick-Sloan Missouri River Ba-
sin. These lands are called the "taken" area, in which the Corps of Engineers was allowed to flood 550 square miles of treaty-protected lands of
the Missouri River tribes during the 1950s and 1960s for hydropower.
South Dakota governor Bill Janklow and Senator Daschle are now propos-
ing not only another land grab in favor of the state but also a diminishment of tribal jurisdiction over hunting and fishing. The bill was called
the "South Dakota Land Transfer and Wildlife Habitat Mitigation Act of
1997," but the Sioux feel this is just another smokescreen for further land
theft. The Sioux Nation Treaty Council met in Rapid City in February 1997
to oppose the legislation, gearing up for another long and tedious defense
of their lands, resources, and rights. Some may be reminded of the remark
made by the late C. Hobart Keith, a well-respected and long-time tribal
judge on the Pine Ridge Reservation, that the Indian Health Service now
prints in its manual: "The white man cannot pretend to be the doctor
when, in fact, he is the disease."

Even while he has steadfastly refused to discuss land reform issues and
the return of stolen lands, he holds endless hearings in the state of South
Dakota concerning Indian poverty and water rights, issues that do not of-
fend his non-Indian constituents yet gain him support from Indians. He
apparently sees no connection between the obvious poverty on the Indian
homelands on the one hand and a historical murder of hundreds, the sub-

sequent land loss, colonial institutions on the reservations, and jurisdictional and sovereignty conflicts on the other. To many politicians like Daschle, the wonderful sweep of western history carries with it no real crimes on the part of the United States, no dire consequences, no need for returning lands stolen from the poorest people in the nation through congressional and executive action.

Even while Daschle was in the Soviet Union, stories like the following were appearing in local newspapers, including the *Rapid City Journal:* "Moscow (AP)—The Soviet Union apologized Friday for one of the grisliest crimes of the Stalin Era, the murder of thousands of imprisoned Polish officers shot during World War II and buried in the mass graves in Katyn Forest. 'It is good that criminals admit their crimes,' Polish Solidarity leader Lech Walesa said in Gdansk. 'But, other problems remain, including war reparations.'"

Daschle and others apparently made no connection between this news and the American/Lakota historical past.

DIARY: MAY 18, 1990

Sara Yager of Daschle's office returned my call. I said that in good faith we had revised our bill (fully ten months since we met with them initially) and had done all we could to satisfy them, yet Daschle has not made a firm commitment to sponsoring our proposed legislation.

I told her that if he is not going to do it, he should simply inform us of his decision so we can develop an alternative strategy to get our proposed legislation introduced in Congress.

While we still want the South Dakota congressional delegation to introduce our proposed bill, we can get legislators from other states who are not burdened with the negative, racist attitudes of their non-Indian constituencies to sponsor it. I am not unaware of the attitudes of others whom he represents and that it may not be politically expedient from him to do the right thing. Trying to be polite and tactful though I was disappointed in his behavior at the time, I asked her what the proper protocol was for getting additional sponsors. She said she would get back to me on lining up cosponsors.

During this time of increasing activity brought about by the one hundred year observations, Survivors' Association members are complaining about panhandlers bothering tourists who come to view the mass grave. I drafted two resolutions for the Pine Ridge Wounded Knee Survivors' Association to deal with this problem and the problem of individuals selling

*handicraft at or near the mass grave: one to request that the Oglala Sioux
Tribal Council control panhandlers, and another asking the Wounded
Knee District Council to prohibit peddlers from selling within 330 feet of
the mass grave pursuant to authority delegated by the tribal council to
designate places for peddlers to sell their goods. Something must be done to
protect the religious sanctity of the massacre site and mass grave! It is becoming apparent that the massacre site is nothing more than a piece of
commercial property to everyone except the descendants of those killed
and wounded in the massacre. It is a shame that Lakota people—especially those in the Wounded Knee District—do not understand and appreciate
their own history.*

DIARY: JUNE 8, 1990

*I informed survivor association members that there will be a June 21, 1990,
hearing on the establishment of the boundaries for the Wounded Knee National Historic Site. The National Park Service has scheduled a hearing at
the Wounded Knee Catholic Church at 1 P.M. on that day to get "input"
from reservation residents. I informed those who attended today's survivor
association meeting that historic landmarks are under the jurisdiction of
the National Park Service, and placing the massacre site on the National
Register of Historic Places will enhance the possibility of getting our proposed legislation passed by Congress. The massacre site is sacred ground to
the descendants of Chief Big Foot's people and appears to be nothing more
than a tourist attraction to others—including Lakota people who now
think and act like the colonial institutions that control their lives. Maybe
Sitting Bull was right when he said "I am the last Lakota."*

DIARY: JUNE 25, 1990

*Mark Rubin of Congressman Tim Johnson's office notified me that our leg-
islative proposal was submitted to the legislative research council and that
Johnson wants to make some changes (including an appropriation for the
tribal museum). He indicated that Daschle's office was contacted about
the changes. Claudia Iron Hawk Sully, Celane Not Help Him, Marie Not
Help Him, Belva Hollow Horn, Melvin Garreau, Marcella LeBeau, Florence Arpan, and Sam Eaglestaff will be very pleased to hear the news.*

DIARY: JUNE 29, 1990

*Suzan Shown Harjo is on board now. She has a tremendous amount of re-
spect for Sam and agreed to honor his request to assist in lobbying the bill*

through Congress. I'm a little concerned about Suzan's insistence that she not work with Clara Spotted Elk however. Apparently, she feels that Spotted Elk "trashed" her when Wayne Ducheneaux was trying to remove her as executive director of the National Congress of American Indians. She explained that Carl Funke and Clara joined the Ducheneaux faction. We can work around those issues; I have trust in Suzan since I served on the Resolutions Committee of NCAI when she was executive director and developed a lot of respect and admiration for her.

CHRONICLE

Even the most obscure Indian political doings in Washington, D.C. (and, remember, Indians have had a presence there since the earliest times, carrying on treaty negotiations, giving testimony), carry with them long histories. In this instance, Gonzalez, as counsel to the Wounded Knee Survivors' Associations, now has asked Suzan Shown Harjo, an influential Indian politico who lives in D.C., to do some lobbying on the Hill, keeping in mind that she knows firsthand the fascinating milieu in which Lakota politics occurs. Mario served on the NCAI Resolutions Committee for several years, was well acquainted with Harjo's work, and respects her advocacy of Indian rights work.

Harjo had just been in a furious fight (which she lost) with Wayne Ducheneaux (powerful ex-chairman of the Cheyenne River Tribal Council), a man who comes from a dynasty of fifty years of Indian leadership on that reservation. The two fought over the executive directorship of the National Congress of American Indians, a lobbying organization for the Indian Nations since the 1940s, in recent years headed by Harjo, until she was accused of "incompetence" by Ducheneaux.

Their struggle came to a head at the 1988 annual NCAI meeting in Sioux Falls, South Dakota, when Ducheneaux organized a pullout of all the Sioux tribes and their not inconsiderable funding from the conference. Reuben Snake of the Nebraska Winnebago Tribe saved the day and brought funding for the conference through the Winnebagos, perhaps a bit reluctantly, since he had been heard by conference attendees to say, "Hey, I like a good Sioux fight as much as anybody!!" In his more somber mood, he countered, "But, we haven't got the time right now."

Sam Eaglestaff served as tribal councilman at Cheyenne River and occasionally expressed disagreement with Ducheneaux. He naturally supported Harjo in the NCAI dispute. He also got the Cheyenne River Grey Eagle Society (an elders organization) to pass a resolution apologizing to

Suzan and the NCAI for Ducheneaux's behavior in withdrawing Sioux financial support for the 1988 Sioux Falls meeting. Harjo's animosity toward Ducheneaux and her tenuousness in assisting the WKSA with the Democrats on the Hill may have also been complicated by the fact that Senator Tom Daschle's office was said to be giving support to the Ducheneaux regime at that time. Sara Yager, Daschle's assistant, was seen at an Indian art show in Santa Fe, New Mexico, earlier in the year wearing a Ducheneaux campaign T-shirt. Looming as unknown and, perhaps, unreliable figures were (1) Alan Parker, the Standing Rock Sioux/Rocky Boy Chippewa attorney, then counsel for the Senate Select Committee on Indian Affairs, who was sometimes seen by the group as doing the bidding of the committee rather than Indians, and (2) Clara Spotted Elk, a Northern Cheyenne tribal member later elected to her own tribal council at Lame Deer, Montana, but at that time working effectively with Daschle. She was hired by the Oglala Sioux Parks and Recreation Authority as a lobbyist to represent its interests in Washington, D.C.

To what extent these so-called D.C. Indians were "taking sides" or representing particular factions in any dispute or controversy based on their own self-serving needs has always been anyone's guess.

DIARY: JULY 28, 1990

Got a call from Claudia Iron Hawk Sully who asked that I attend a meeting at Linda Hollow Horn's residence north of Wounded Knee (near Tom Casey's trailer), set for August 8 and 9. She said a film crew from London, England, would be there and wanted to do some interviews. She said $100 was donated for food but I should bring something anyway.

I told her that the Survivors' Associations got a $1,000 discretionary grant from the Peace Development Fund in Seattle to pay on the $6,000 Panther Productions fee (a firm out of Atlanta) to do a television production that would be released on national television on December 15 to give our legislative proposal national exposure. She expressed her happiness and said that these kinds of public relations efforts were useful and should bring pressure on the South Dakota congressional delegation to introduce our proposed bill and schedule hearings on it.

DIARY: AUGUST 1, 1990

I participated in a telephonic conference call with Governor George Mickelson and OST president Harold Salway today while I was at Pine Ridge that was very interesting. Mickelson thought we should try to get a presidential

proclamation to establish a Wounded Knee national monument by executive
order by December 29, 1990. He suggested that the Sioux initiate a drive to
get President George Bush to issue the presidential proclamation under the
1906 Antiquities Act.[31] He said that it is very doubtful that anyone would
back a compensation bill but it might be possible to get President Bush to is-
sue the presidential proclamation for the national monument.

The Oglala Sioux Parks and Recreation Authority is conducting a feasi-
bility study that will consist of three phases. It is to be completed by Wyss,
Inc., landscape architects and planners located at 522 7th Street, Suite 214,
Rapid City, South Dakota.

When I spoke to the Pine Ridge WKSA members about the feasibility
study, they indicated that they didn't want to have anything to do with it
because they were not given sufficient input by Wyss, Inc.

I also informed Survivors' Association members that I would contact
Suzanne Firstenberg of Senator Daschle's office and confirm that we will
be available for a meeting in Washington, D.C., on August 28 and 29. Fidel
Moreno, a Yaqui Indian and documentary film maker from Aurora, Illi-
nois, called to express his interest in videotaping the meeting. He got my
name and address from Suzan Shown Harjo, who thought recording the
event would be a good idea.

DIARY: AUGUST 2, 1990

Today I made copies of documents for WKSA members, namely, the enlist-
ment roll of men stationed at McCloud's Ranch during the 1890 massacre,
Doane Robinson's statement, and a Senate Report containing a list of the
persons receiving monetary compensation under the so-called "1891 Sioux
Depredations Act."[32] The 1891 Depredations Act has an interesting history.
After the massacre took place most non-Indian claims and the claims of
"friendly" Indians, whether valid or not, were settled by congressional act.
It is only the claims of the real victims, i.e., Chief Big Foot's band of Min-
neconjou, that remain unresolved to this day since they were classified as
"hostile" Indians in 1890.

Peter Schwartzbauer of Vienna, Austria, in a conference phone call dis-
cussed and explained the massacre commemoration in Hellemmes-Lille,
France, and other European events. Peter is a good friend with whom I first
became acquainted when I traveled to Europe (Switzerland, Germany, Italy,
Austria) in 1981. I attended a United Nations meeting and made an "inter-
vention" (complaint) against the United States government for the illegal

confiscation of the Black Hills in 1877. I also participated in a diplomatic mission and lecture tour with Larry Redshirt and Russel Barsh to generate international support for the Lakota claim to the Black Hills. Peter and Helga Lomosits are the leaders of our Lakota Support Group in Vienna.

CHRONICLE

With the exception of the Austrians, the Lakota support groups spoken of here are a matter of some conjecture. In the 1980s they seemed to be very political in nature and there was some hope that they might influence the international political climate in significant ways. Currently they seem more based in the cultural exchange mode and many Indian people feel that they are being used simply as fund-raising entities with little oversight.

There may not be a Lakota in the country who hasn't gone to Washington, D.C., or had some relatives who made the trip in the past for the political purpose of testifying for the white man's government about his life as an Indian. It is, some say, a part of the national character of the Sioux.

As Gonzalez and members of the Wounded Knee Survivors' Association planned a 1990 journey to the nation's capital to ask that the federal government take seriously their need for a hearing on the Wounded Knee memorial and protection of the massacre site, they had in their thoughts all of the other such trips made by the people. They looked forward to giving testimony to the Senate Select Committee on Indian Affairs, a committee which was formed in the 1980s when the long-established House and Senate Interior Committees were eliminated as subcommittees. Senator James Abourezk from the state of South Dakota had been a powerful advocate for Indian causes on that committee in the seventies, and his work generated much support for Indian causes. Unfortunately, there has been no serious pro-Indian leadership on that committee for more than ten years, since Abourezk left Congress, though its chairman, Daniel K. Inouye, has maintained a sympathetic but largely ineffectual stance.

Those on the committee in 1990 who would okay or deny any Indian requests for a hearing were: John McCain, Arizona; Daniel K. Inouye, Hawaii (chair); Dennis DeConcini, Arizona; Quentin N. Burdick, North Dakota; Thomas A. Daschle, South Dakota; Kent Conrad, North Dakota; H. Reid, Nevada; Frank H. Murkowski, Alaska; Thad Cochran, Mississippi; and Slade Gordon, Washington State.

This committee has become influenced by senators who not only are elected to Congress by anti-Indian white populations in states with large Indian minority populations but who themselves often hold anti-Indian sentiments. The politicians who sit on the Senate Select Committee on Indian Affairs are seen by Indians as a particularly controversial group, sometimes in blatant support of non-Indian factions in states where tribal/state relations have been historically and notoriously contentious. In addition, the Washington-based lobbying group, the National Congress of American Indians, has become a battleground so politicized by power-hungry Indian leaders that it is virtually useless to reservation-based groups.

The truth is, there is nowhere else for Indians to turn for political support but to the Senate Select Committee on Indian Affairs. It is a sad commentary on Indian affairs during this, the last decade of the century, since the committee is now seen by many Indians as having lost much of its integrity.

DIARY: AUGUST 25–SEPTEMBER 1, 1990

Our meeting in Washington, D.C., today was supposed to begin at 9 A.M. but didn't get started until later. Persons from Pine Ridge who attended the meeting organized by Suzanne Firstenberg were Frank (Popo) Means, Alex White Plume, Eddie Little Sky, Paul Little, Celane Not Help Him, Marie Not Help Him, Belva Hollow Horn, Claudia Iron Hawk Sully, and me. Suzan Shown Harjo accompanied us.

One of the most important things to come out of this meeting was a statement by attorney Alan Parker, chief staff person for the committee, who said that Senator Daniel Inouye was willing to hold a Senate oversight hearing on the Wounded Knee Massacre, but Senator Tom Daschle from South Dakota had to make the request.

Parker's statement was orchestrated by Suzan. Parker and Suzan are good friends and adversaries of Wayne Ducheneaux and his supporters. Suzan felt that neither Congressman Johnson nor Senator Daschle had ever intended to introduce our bill, that they were stonewalling us and planned to continue in that mode. Now they would be forced to hold a hearing and a historical record could be made.

DIARY: SEPTEMBER 5, 1990

In a three-way conference telephone call, Suzan Shown Harjo informed me and Tim Edman of the governor's office that a hearing on our legislative proposal before the Senate Select Committee on Indian Affairs is scheduled for Tuesday, September 25, 1990, at 10 A.M., at Room 485, Russell Senate Building. Mr. Erdman indicated that the governor plans to attend the hearing.

CHRONICLE

The hearing would prove to be a study in contrasts and denials. Knute Knudson, deputy assistant secretary of the interior, would talk in euphemistic terms about "a tragic encounter" in which "firing began" and "large numbers of Indians fell," passive language used to suppress the violent, horrific scene. Representative Tim Johnson (D-SD) would talk about "good faith." Daschle would say tentatively: "I would really like us to work something out if we can." Senator McCain, in congratulating his "distinguished colleague" Daschle, would say, to the bewilderment of the Indians present: "There is no one who is more intimately familiar with this issue, and this issue would not be before this committee if it were not for his [Daschle's] efforts." Daschle, who in his early career had had massive Indian political support in South Dakota, had allegedly made Senator Daniel Inouye promise that there would be no hearings on the Black Hills land reform issue in that committee and, to date, there has been no dialogue forthcoming. In addition, he had been instrumental in setting up the Open Hills Association, a South Dakota citizens' committee based in Spearfish, to oppose any legislation which would develop land reform plans in response to the U.S. Supreme Court findings on theft of the sacred ground. Both Daschle and Senator Larry Pressler were calling for statewide plebiscites which, in this case, would amount to asking the criminals to vote on whether or not their crimes were legal. In any statewide vote on this matter the Sioux would lose not only because theirs is a minority vote but because the general white population in the region has a history of understanding Indian status only in terms of dependency, subordination, and exploitation.

It was at this hearing that Senator Daniel Inouye included the proposal that the name of the Montana site of the Sioux Nation/U.S. military encounter of 1876 be changed from the Custer Battlefield to the Little Bighorn Battlefield National Monument. This was welcomed by those present as a way to force a hearing. In his speech, Inouye indicated that it was not only Custer and his men who died fighting for their country, that many Indians died there as well, yet there is no monument to those native patriots and there must be some changes made. He and others expressed the hope that the name would be just the first revision of a one-sided history.

A 1990 HEARING IN WASHINGTON, D.C.

Keyapi

While the soul-trying experience of self-government and political responsibility by a long-colonized people was going on at many levels during this period, testimony in Washington, D.C., was being recorded. First told by the ancient ones in the old gambling language of *wicowoyake* (true stories), translations by modern people filled the Senate room in the nation's capital but no one could say whether or not any of it would matter. On the following pages selected testimonies of September, 1990, are reprinted:

1. In an oratorical gesture which often accompanies important events, Alex White Plume, a Sitanka Wokiksuye Rider, explained before the Senate Select Committee on Indian Affairs the essential ways of seeing or thinking about things that have made Wounded Knee, the place and the story, a thing of grief and beauty and remembrance for the people. His eloquence filled the room:

> My name is Alex White Plume. I am an enrolled member of the Oglala
> Sioux Tribe and reside at Manderson, South Dakota. I presently serve as Fifth
> Member to the Executive Committee of the Oglala Sioux Tribal Council. I am
> also Chairman of the Oglala Sioux Parks and Recreation Authority and member of the Sitanka Wokiksuye, or the Big Foot Memorial Ride.
> Sitanka Wokiksuye was established in 198[6] for two purposes: (1) to build
> character in our membership by making them aware of the hardships our people had to endure in the 1800's and (2) to bring the descendants of the 1890
> Massacre victims out of 100 years of mourning. For the past four years, members of Sitanka Wokiksuye have been retracing Chief Big Foot's flight from
> Cherry Creek to Wounded Knee. They arrive at Wounded Knee on December
> 28th of each year for special prayers. This enables them to experience the hardships our people had to endure a century ago and makes them better appreciate the meaning of life as an Indian person. 1990 will mark the fifth year we
> have retraced Big Foot's trail.
> On December 29, 1990, the riders will honor the descendants of the 1890
> Massacre victims. This will mark the end of 100 years of mourning. The spirits
> of Chief Big Foot and the men, women, and children killed by the Seventh
> Cavalry will be released, in accordance with sacred Lakota ceremonies. The
> "Wiping of the Tears" will take place when the spirits are released.
> Black Elk said that the sacred hoop of the Lakota people was broken by the
> 1890 Massacre. He prophesied that the Seventh Generation of Lakota would

mend the hoop and rebuild the Nation. We are the Seventh Generation and we are making his prophesies come true.

The Lakota people are a proud people who believe in maintaining the traditional ways. We believe in our language and our religion. We believe in our people. We have survived on the North American continent for thousands of years, and we plan to be here forever.

The United States needs to admit that its soldiers were wrong at Wounded Knee when they killed and wounded unarmed men, women and children. The United States needs to make a meaningful apology for the 1890 Massacre and establish a national monument and memorial at the mass grave site. The apology can only be sincere when it is accompanied by something that will bring lasting value to the Indian people. We fully support the efforts of the Wounded Knee Survivors' Association in this regard.

The Oglala Sioux Parks and Recreation Authority also [has] an interest at Wounded Knee. The Oglala Sioux Tribal Council has delegated the authority the responsibility of establishing the museum and cultural center authorized by Congress in the 1968 Badlands National Monument (now Park).[33] The authority has hired an engineering firm to design the structure and now desires that Congress appropriate the necessary funds to complete the structure, which will be located west of the outer boundaries of the Wounded Knee National Landmark.

Pilamaya,

Thank you for your advocacy and good work.

CHRONICLE

At the time of this hearing, the continuing Big Foot Memorial Ride, which may best be described as a ceremonial much like a four-year-winter-horse cycle of prayers and endurance, was set to take place in December, as it had before and as it would again. All manner of journey (both mythic and legendary) is ritualized in Lakota cultural life, and this modern journey was seen as another dramatic illustration of the importance of returning to one's origins and retracing one's history in terms of specific geography.

White Plume was a spokesman for the fact that Americans were not ideal colonizers, if such an ugly phenomenon in the history of nations could be said to exist. He gave a certain amount of education not only to the committee members present but to his own people, who thought of him as being acquainted with two worlds, both Indian and White. This organized ritual was, he told everyone, a significant development in the self-governance of a people long held in captivity.

Many of the participants in the centennial ride believe that the future interpretation of their efforts will be historically significant. They think that for the children of the next generation of the Lakota/Dakota Nation, this Seventh Generation Ceremonial of the Horse will be considered a landmark event because there is no escape from the sacred notions about Death as a companion of the living.

To understand the significance of this cultural event is to understand that to the Lakota, Death must be ritualized and made art of. It is taught that in mythological times the oyate sometimes feared the power of their dead because their essences could be seen lingering near where they died. This was so if and when the death was an unnatural thing, for it is believed that the dead do not want to leave the comforts of the natural world because they come to love the earth. The living, then, the descendants, hearing the cries of the departed, have to pay careful attention to these desires and they have to take it upon themselves to give generously to the dead because Tokahe tells them to do so as a way of appeasement and harmony. In the case of the unnatural death of those loved ones at Wounded Knee, in the case of the incredible massacre of innocents, there is almost no solace except sincere seeking of vision

and truth

and reparation.

2. Further statements from the September, 1990, hearing, those of many persons with notable names among the Sioux such as Blindman, Eaglestaff, Little Sky, Long, High Whiteman, and dozens more, were added to the history collections which would become archival evidence in this matter of reparation. Scholars and politicians wrote papers and submitted them to the Senate committee. Historical documents by the score were researched and copied to become a part of the hearing documented literatures.[34] In a moment of reminiscence and description, opinion and vindication, the people spoke as follows:

MARIE NOT HELP HIM, great granddaughter of survivor Dewey Beard (also known as "Iron Hail"): I remember sitting on his lap and feeling that scar on his thigh and hearing his heartbeat and feeling his breath on the top of my head. He would tell the account of the Massacre and he would cry. That is why I am here today, continuing to pursue what we are after today, and that is an *apology* from the U.S. government for our relatives.

INOUYE: This tragic chapter of American history came at a time of great upheaval and turbulence for the Indians of the Plains. In 1890, ten years passed since the last bison roamed the plains or provided food for the Sioux people. Relentless pressures to force the tribes on to smaller and smaller reservations left the Indians distrustful, feeling betrayed, and with greater dependence on the Federal government for their very survival. Apparently a debate lingers as to whether the events at Wounded Knee should be referred to as a Battle or a Massacre. As late as 1976, the Army responded to a Congressional Hearing on Wounded Knee by objecting to the term "Massacre" in reference to this event, insisting that it was a "Battle." Although the first moments had characteristics of a Battle, I believe everyone will agree that soldiers hunting down unarmed women and children fleeing from gunfire in the December snow is grounds for calling it a Massacre. By way of contrast, it is interesting to note that for many years the U.S. Government considered the Battle of the Little Bighorn, the famous military loss by Col. Custer and the Seventh Cavalry, a Massacre."

GONZALEZ: I am an enrolled member of the Oglala Sioux Tribe and a descendant of Chief Lip's Band. I am appearing here today as the attorney for the Wounded Knee Survivors' Associations and the Oglala Sioux Tribe. I am also related by blood to some of the victims and survivors of the Massacre. Dewey Beard, the last survivor of the Battle of the Little Bighorn and an 1890 Massacre survivor, was a first cousin to my great-great-grandmother, Rattling Hawk. Dewey's real mother, Seen By Her Nation, and my great-great-great-grandmother, Jealous of Her, were sisters.[35]

The Wounded Knee Survivors' Associations have been developing proposed legislation which would have Congress: (1) make a formal apology to the Sioux people for the 1890 Massacre; (2) establish a national monument and memorial at the Massacre site; and (3) compensate the descendants of the Indian victims for the killing or wounding of their relatives in the form of benefits, i.e., educational benefits and multi-purpose buildings, plus direct compensation for property confiscated by the Army.

It is my belief that the Wounded Knee Massacre, and indeed the massacres perpetuated by the 8th Cavalry and Governor Mellette's cowboy militia, are more than just moral claims. They are legal claims which only Congress can resolve.

It is questionable whether the military forces had a right to be *on* the Sioux reservations in 1890. The federal government certainly breached its promise to maintain peace with the Sioux under the 1868 Treaty. It also failed to follow the extradition procedures outlined in the 1868 Treaty when it attempted to arrest Chief Big Foot on the Pine Ridge Reservation.

CLAUDIA IRON HAWK SULLY: History has to be rewritten to show the Indian side. Apologies and Memorials have to be made. It won't just stop here today. Our future generations, as well as mainstream America, must know of the Wounded Knee Massacre from our point of view. However, they will never realize the sadistic treatment given to a peaceful band of Lakota Indians who just wanted to live. It is written in every treaty our people signed in good faith with the U.S. Government, the Fort Laramie Peace Treaty of 1868, "as long as the grass grows, the rivers flow, and the sun rise[s]." Thank you all and God bless you.

MARIE NOT HELP HIM: My grandfather was shot four times: once in the back, in the lap, in the hip and once in the calf. I could put my hand in the scar on his lap and feel the bone. I firmly believe that this Massacre was a revenge for the killing of Custer at the Little Bighorn. And because the soldiers had been drinking they made no effort to discern the children and women from the men. I also believe that the U.S. Cavalry started the Massacre by provoking the Indian men, by searching and holding the guns to the men's foreheads and clicking the empty guns, by interrogating and torturing; by the wanton slaughter of innocent children, helpless babies and unarmed women . . . all while under a white flag of truce.

CHRONICLE

Right after the September 25, 1990, hearing, an important meeting took place between Suzan Shown Harjo, Alan Parker, and Mario Gonzalez. They discussed legislative strategy and agreed that the best way to accomplish the three goals in the existing draft bill (apology, monument, compensation) was to divide it into three separate pieces. They decided that a *concurrent resolution* could be passed through Congress before the one-hundredth anniversary of the massacre and they drafted language to accomplish this. The words "deep regret and sincere apology" were taken out of the draft Wounded Knee bill and inserted into the proposed concurrent resolution.

This new concurrent resolution was later submitted to Congress but when it was passed as Senate Concurrent Resolution 153, on October 15, 1990,[36] the words "sincere apology" were deleted. The Survivors' Associations later found out that Senator Tom Daschle and some of his colleagues had deleted the words, in contradiction to the wishes of the people he was said to be representing. The tribal people were surprised and dismayed to see these essential words deleted from their writing and they expressed their anger amongst themselves. Gonzalez said publicly: "I believe Daschle did this on his own. We believed then and believe now that it would have passed even if he had left it in the resolution." Daschle's behavior was seen as obstructive and cynical.

Association members and their lawyer felt the resolution could have passed Congress as they submitted it had it not been for the opposition of

some of the important white men from states with heavy Indian populations who sat on the Senate Select Committee on Indian Affairs. This is an
Indian perception which would be adamantly denied by those committee
members. Though these matters may seem trivial to those who deal with
the broad issues of world politics, they are essential to understanding the
oppressiveness of white governments on Indian lands.

3. The effort to reassert old authorities and canons of colonialism was
inherent in the speech given by the governor of the state, George Mickelson, the son of a previous governor and heir to the Euroamerican history
of a self-described compassionate primacy on the prairies of South Dakota.

The silence surrounding such expressions is deafening because no one,
least of all Indians, knows how to account for the extraordinary mix of
compassion and imperialism. Non-Indian listeners, if they share his
soothing views, are filled with a feeling of liberation and relief. The Sioux,
internal political dissension aside, see the state becoming stronger, hanging on to the stolen lands and wealth, defending a long, dishonorable relationship with them, promulgating schemes for further theft of lands and
resources.

The failure of such talks is the failure to recognize that the massacre occurred precisely because of odious nineteenth-century empire building,
the point being that it continues to this day.

Thus, Mickelson's speech does not mention the dispossession of the
Sioux people from their lands or the Sioux Nation's autonomy, does not
suggest that their loss might be the result of criminal acts.

There is no reference to the fact that lands stolen from the Sioux were
clearly off-limits as topics in the so-called year of reconciliation declaration,
and in fact still are, and that no mention was made of the fact that the state's
attorney general has been for years in constant litigation in an effort to diminish the sovereignty of the Sioux tribes over their reservations.

If we look at the actual content of such political speeches, it is obvious
that there is not much intellectual complexity nor historical accuracy to
them; yet, there is tremendous power in what political critics might call
the *text of simplification.*

The governor spoke as follows:

> Shortly after taking office in 1987, I established an Indian Commission. The
> hope was to provide a forum for state government and tribal leaders to explore
> solutions to problems that we could deal with *on a state basis* [emphasis

added] . . . problems such as health care and education and economic development. In order to build on that effort, at the suggestion of one of the Indian
leaders of our state, Tim Giago, I also declared the year 1990, as Senator Daschle has indicated, the *Year of Reconciliation* in South Dakota.

Most recently, we have established a formal dispute resolution process and I
have asked that members of the staff of our Congressional delegation be involved in that. The purpose is to sit down and recognize that, while there are
some issues that can be handled only legally or by change in statute, there are
an awful lot of issues that can be handled by agreement.

I have also established a permanent Reconciliation Council to expand on
our state tribal cooperative ventures in South Dakota.

I want to make sure that everyone understands that I have taken this step
not for the sake of any personal credit or personal benefit, but because it was
the right thing to do. For a hundred years . . . all of our hundred years in our
state . . . we have many things in our history of which we are not proud. Certainly, this Nation has many things in its history of which we are not proud.
But, ever since the Battle [*sic*] of Wounded Knee, which was in our first year of
Statehood, one hundred years ago, unfortunately, that, among other incidents
probably set a tone of relationship between the state and tribal governments
that has not been conducive to working out our differences.

So it is my belief that we must continue our efforts to understand each other as individuals with different cultural histories and backgrounds. With that
kind of a better understanding and appreciation I believe we can better work
through our problems.

It is within this context, then, that I am here to support legislation authorizing the establishment of Wounded Knee as a national monument or memorial,
whatever the appropriate term might be. I believe that in order to move forward we must recognize the history of Wounded Knee and provide the resources necessary to adequately protect this important site.

As Senator Daschle indicated, 100 years ago, in December, 1890, soldiers of
the Seventh Cavalry captured a fugitive band of Minneconjou Sioux and held
them prisoner at a place called Wounded Knee Creek. They were 470 men
strong, the troops surrounded 106 Indian warriors and roughly 250 Indian
women and children, aiming Hotchkiss guns at them from emplacements.
They began to search the camp for some weapons. Unfortunately, there was a
shot fired someplace . . . and, as is too often the case in these kinds of tragedies,
nobody knows who started it or why, but the fact is that on the morning of December 29 that shot was fired and it resulted in a Massacre that is infamous in
the history of our Nation.

It also marked another significant event, and that was perhaps the last military encounter between the soldiers of the United States and the Indian war-

riors. From that particular point on, although there was not necessarily armed conflict, as we have read in our history books as being the Indian Wars, the fact is that the conflict continued.

Peter Norbeck was a Senator from South Dakota, and obviously Teddy Roosevelt is well known in history. Both of these gentlemen had some visions for what they thought was appropriate. From their visions was created Custer State Park, Badlands National Park, Mount Rushmore, and the Grand Teton National Park. Teddy Roosevelt certainly as a legendary conservationist with visions of his own, established the U.S. Forest Service, added 125 million acres of land to the forest system, and also established Devils Tower National Monument and so forth.

Like Norbeck and Roosevelt, I think you and I have an opportunity along with other people, to create a vision of our own. Our vision for South Dakota would create a National Park at Wounded Knee. If Wounded Knee were to become a national park, properly interpreted through the visitors centers, it would bring some recognition to a very remote area of South Dakota . . . the Pine Ridge Reservation. We would estimate that 30,000 to 50,000 people would visit there every year. There is a great amount of interest not only in this Nation, but internationally, in the Native American culture. Such visitation could generate jobs. It would also make a significant economic impact and an appropriate recognition of a chapter in our history that we should be involved in and support.

I want to conclude by saying that South Dakota has already devoted a lot of effort and time and expense to turning this project into a reality. State officials have worked closely with tribal leaders and the National Park Service for more than two years. All interested parties . . . the tribal council, both survivor groups, the State and National Park Service . . . agree on three points. It is always nice to be able to testify before a committee when we can come here agreeing on some points:

1. Wounded Knee must be protected and preserved as a very important part of our history.
2. The National Park Service is best equipped to provide the site that we desperately need.
3. Perhaps the most urgent reason for this testimony here today is that 1990 is the ideal year to place the site under National Park Service jurisdiction, whether as a national park or as a national monument. December 29, 1990, is the ideal date for that official ceremony changing the site's designation.

I stand ready to work with the Select Committee on Indian Affairs and the involved tribal representatives to pursue this goal and to improve the site.

I thank you for your time and patience here today.[37]

CHRONICLE

If it was the governor's intention to downplay the differences between the
races, his testimony in Washington, D.C., was a sad disaster. Calling the
Wounded Knee killing a "battle," after all the discussion over the past year
urging people to understand the past, seemed incomprehensible to his Indian listeners, and "placing the site under National Park Service jurisdiction" was the last thing that was on the minds of the Lakotas. His statements caused a stir, but everyone tried to put the best face on it. While
"reconciliation" was a new word in public vocabulary, it was coming under more careful scrutiny by Indians as the days and weeks passed. Tim
Giago, the Oglala Sioux editor and publisher of the powerful *Lakota Times*
(more recently called *Indian Country Today*), who has never been an elected official of the tribe, claimed credit for challenging the state government
to act affirmatively toward its native population. Credit was also claimed
by Harold Iron Shield. Reacting to the challenge, then, from one of only
two Indian-owned private newspapers in the entire country, the governor
officially declared 1990 the "Year of Reconciliation," saying he hoped that
race relations in the state would improve and that during the commemorative year everything would be done by state government to bring peace
and harmony between the races. Whites began to organize meetings with
Indians in an effort to "get to know" each other.

Such philosophical wordplay and evasion, since the passing of the
American Indian Movement era rhetoric of the sixties and seventies, has
become the norm in public discourse in the region. Instead of admitting to
a history of murder, theft, and oppression, the general white population of
the Northern Plains continues to believe that it can escape its history if
only Indians and Whites can "get to know" each other and can "reconcile."
What Indians want whites to know is that it is a fact that ten years after the
Supreme Court decision called the theft of the Black Hills a "most ripe and
rank case of dishonorable dealing," the state and federal governments, private landowners, and corporations still "occupy" the Sioux sacred lands
and that efforts on the part of the tribes to force land reform legislation on
local and national levels of government has met stiff resistance.

The declaration of "reconciliation" followed a decade of largely futile
but intense political activity by the Sioux tribes. Legislation for the return
of lands was rejected by white politicians, and the request to Congress to
honor the Lakota dead was now falling into a discussion of tourism and

"jurisdiction" of the National Park Service. Much of the political work was done by the tribes with the clear knowledge that state interests stood in the way of reform. Issues of jurisdiction concerning tribal resources were in the state courts every day, and the governor refused to allow the Black Hills Claim to be a part of the official discourse. The "Year of Reconciliation," therefore, was met initially with a certain amount of hardened cynicism on the part of many Indians and was in danger of becoming simply absurd. 'To reconcile', thoughtful people said, means 'to get used to', or 'to resign oneself to something', or 'to make the best of'. But, also, they asked, doesn't it mean 'to rectify', 'to correct a situation', or 'to make something right'? If the state wanted to reconcile, the Sioux were saying, they should begin to talk of how we may work together to return specific treaty-protected lands whites stole from Indians, a theft which was the major cause of the Wounded Knee Massacre which everyone was so set upon "commemorating." The specific treaty-protected lands designated in the treaty and later in the Supreme Court decision are still called the "heart" of the Lakota nation. And the people were desperately wanting to talk about land reform, which would allow them to hold land "in common" as they once did.

The debate called for by the Indians did not occur during the commemorative period, either at the local level or at the broader, national level. The state of South Dakota often acts like an innocent third party in the federal/tribal discourse on Wounded Knee when history shows that the South Dakota "home guard" had engaged in its own war against the Indians and its own thefts throughout the years. Renée Flood's *Lost Bird of Wounded Knee* suggests several "militia-type" unprovoked attacks upon Indians and she claims to have uncovered important documentation concerning these outrages. The subject of complicity on the part of the state of South Dakota is still scrupulously avoided by state politicians, whom many of the Sioux believe to be deceitful, even contemptuous of them. In the current era, when certain factions in the country are calling for the reassertion of state power over federal power, and the discourse seems to defend the idea of the "home guard" and little is done to curb the activities of various militia organizations, Indian rights and properties are at grave risk.

An effective defense strategy by those who would like to see Indian treaty rights and historical land ownership absorbed into the ethnic heap that is American multiculturalism has been silence. The prevention of public discussion of particular topics has been made possible through a deliberate political strategy of pretense. Before the sad and untimely death of Governor Mickelson in a plane crash in 1993, he had begun to change his timetable. Instead of "a *year* of reconciliation," it had become "a *century* of reconciliation," during which time everything would be done to bring about "harmony between the races." The WKSAs and their attorney have not abandoned their demands for an apology and for reparations for atrocities.

DIARY: OCTOBER 10, 1990

When I called Suzan Shown Harjo today to get an update on our proposed concurrent resolution, I was disappointed. She said that Senator Tom Daschle will not support the resolution unless the word "apology" is deleted from the draft. She expressed her true feelings about Daschle and said she would consider coming to South Dakota when he runs for reelection just to campaign against him for stonewalling our proposed legislation.

DIARY: OCTOBER 16, 1990

Mike Her Many Horses called this afternoon for a status report on our proposed Wounded Knee legislation. During our conversation, he also chastised me for Phil Stevens's involvement in the Grey Eagle Society's Black Hills bill that was introduced by in Congress by Congressman Matthew Martinez of California on September 19. Martinez was also a cosponsor of the House version of the Bradley Bill (H.R. 1506) in 1987.

I have known Mike Her Many Horses for several years. We traveled to Europe together in the early 1980s to generate international support for the Black Hills Claim. In the mid-1980s, Mike, Jack Runnels, and I traveled to several Great Sioux Nation meetings together. Mike was the person who got Senator Bill Bradley to introduce the first Black Hills bill in Congress in 1985.

DIARY: OCTOBER 22, 1990

The concurrent resolution was introduced in the House of Representatives by Tim Johnson as he had promised. It is House Concurrent Resolution No. 386. [It was introduced in the U.S. Senate as Senate Concurrent Resolution No. 153.]

Suzan Shown Harjo also informed me that we have problems with the Interior Department appropriations bill. Daschle did not include language in the bill to fund the study of alternatives for the massacre site as he said he would. We asked Jerry Rogers of the National Park Service to include the request in his testimony at the September 25, 1990, hearing, since we

are cognizant of the fact that a study of alternatives is needed to justify the
authorization of federal funds to establish a national monument at the
massacre site.

DIARY: OCTOBER 26, 1990

At the WKSA meeting in Eagle Butte, I gave survivor association members
a status report on our efforts to get an apology from the United States. I
told them truthfully what I thought about Daschle's intentional deletion of
the word "apology" from the concurrent resolution and how disappointed
I am with Daschle's betrayal of our efforts to work together to get a mean-
ingful, sincere apology. Because of his lack of courage we ended up with a
hollow, watered-down "apology."

CHRONICLE

WOUNDED KNEE MONUMENT FAILS, read the headline in the October 30,
1990, *Lakota Times.* And the story read as follows:

> Gonzalez, attorney for the Wounded Knee Survivors Associations, erupted
> last Thursday when an appropriations budget for the Department of Interior
> passed through Congress *without* an amendment earmarking $120,000 for a
> feasibility study on the Memorial proposed at Wounded Knee.
> Gonzalez said Senator Tom Daschle, D-SD, had indicated to them he would
> insert the amendment in the appropriations bill. Sara Yager of Daschle's office
> said that, instead, unspecified congressmen would write a letter to Manuel Lu-
> jan, Secretary of Interior, requesting that he scare up money for the study from
> the Interior Budget. Yager said Daschle's signature was a sure thing and the
> same senators would sign it who signed the resolution. The much greater
> transgression in Gonzalez's eyes was Daschle's insistence that the word "apolo-
> gy" be deleted from the concurrent resolution before he would co-sponsor it;
> this sparked the WKSA resolution rejecting the congressional "regret" at an
> apology level. Gonzalez, calling Daschle's actions a betrayal of trust and a
> throw-back to Congress' historical double-dealing toward Indians, heaped
> contempt on the South Dakota delegation, calling Daschle and his fellow Dem-
> ocrat Representative Tim Johnson "right wing Indian haters at heart."
> He told the WKSA members at the meeting in Eagle Butte, October 26 that
> neither Daschle nor Johnson deserve a place in the Democratic tradition of
> John F. Kennedy, Lyndon Baines Johnson or Hubert H. Humphrey.
> "Daschle and Johnson are no more for the rights of Indian people than
> David Duke is for [the rights of] black people in the South. In fact, Daschle is
> the Duke of the North." [Duke is the former Imperial Grand Wizard of the
> Ku Klux Klan who became a Republican and won a seat in the Louisiana

State Senate. He campaigned recently for the U.S. Senate and made a strong showing.]

Tim Johnson was included in Gonzalez's condemnation for "stonewalling."

The inevitable public outburst by an essentially patient and private man might have been predicted, for there is no more troubling dilemma than the United States' policy of discrimination against the indigenous populations as it has tried to absorb, ignore, kill off, or in one way or another be rid of Indian nationhood in its search for democracy on this continent. In light of the ideology of Indian/White relations, it seems to some that until Indian Nations no longer exist, even in their own imaginations, the United States will not be satisfied with its vision of itself. The United States, the great assimilator, continues to be troubled by the powerful force that the indigenous nation-within-a-nation concept predicates.

The shape of that vision in terms of what was happening in the real world was no longer comprehensible to Gonzalez and his clients. The United States and its nineteenth-century creation, the state of South Dakota, they thought, refused to come to grips with the consequences of the invasion and theft of treaty-protected lands, nor can the United States give up the ideal of "Americanization" of people who have their own unique reality. The United States, they thought, cannot face its own history of empire building.

For Gonzalez, the distortions could not any longer be tolerated. His effort to understand the law of a regime which, having for so long denied him and his people their status as human beings, still insisted upon its own innocence and righteousness had simply reached an intolerable point. The colonial history facing the Sioux seemed impenetrable. When Indians talked to each other about matters of this kind they began to know what other philosophers and historians have known: if something happens in history once, it is an anomaly, if it happens again it is coincidence, a third time it becomes mythology. They began to fear that there would be no relief for Indians from the United States' defense of its own self-serving myths which relegated Indians to oblivion.

The *Lakota Times* article went on to describe the situation between the Sioux and their white government more fully:

> In response to Gonzalez's "Duke of the North" remark, Kinsella, from Senator Tom Daschle's office, was quoted as saying: "When people speak out in anger, they are often blinded; comparing Tom Daschle to a racist bigot like David Duke is wrong.

"David Duke's stock in trade for the last 10 years has been burning crosses in the front yards of blacks.

"For the past ten years Tom Daschle has been building hospitals and homes on the nation's reservations."

Gonzalez said it had been an uphill battle getting either of the state's Democratic congressmen to support any legislation relating to Wounded Knee. Senator Daniel Inouye, D-Hawaii, chairman of the Senate Select Committee on Indian Affairs, at length agreed to hold an oversight hearing *if Daschle requested it,* Gonzalez said [emphasis added].

Daschle would do so only if Johnson, Senator Larry Pressler (R-SD), and South Dakota Governor George Mickelson also signed the letter of request to Inouye, Gonzalez said.

Gonzalez said Pressler alone refused to sign the letter. Pressler denies this.

Members of the Wounded Knee Survivors' Association shared Gonzalez's feelings of anger and betrayal.

Sam Eagle Staff [*sic*], chairman of the Cheyenne River chapter of WKSA, said he was most upset with the congressmen, particularly Daschle and Johnson.

"While the Soviets are apologizing for the killing of Polish people, and the Congress recently apologized to Japanese-Americans for their unfair treatment during World War II, Daschle and Johnson can't bring themselves to support a federal apology to the Sioux Indians. That's outrageous, since Indian people voted them both into office."

Claudia Iron Hawk, chairperson of the Pine Ridge WKSA, said she won't vote in national elections again because candidates court the Indian vote but forget about Indian constituents once they get into office.

Florence Arpan, an elderly member of WKSA and newly appointed to Cheyenne River Sioux Tribal advisory council by Gregg Bourland, said accepting monetary reparations without an apology would be like accepting "blood money."

Gonzalez's wrath extended even to the *Rapid City Journal,* which reported on October 27 in an article that made a point of discovering a supposed inaccuracy in the number of massacred Indians accepted in the resolution.

A local historian told the *Journal* the exact number of dead is certainly lower than the 350 to 375 arrived at in the resolution. The author is not quoted as providing a number of his own, and the *Journal* does not provide clues to what it considers significant about the exact number of casualties at Wounded Knee.

Gonzalez took it as a disservice to Indian people, noting that the resolution's numbers are referred to as "Indian counts."

"That could have been a positive story. Instead it plants an idea in white readers' minds that Indian people are incompetent, exaggerate their own history, and can't count.

"I am sick and tired of the media trying to make Indians look like a bunch of buffoons," he added. "I have researched every document I could get my hands on, and I picked 356 as my best estimate. . . . It seems to be what people agree on, but it is uncertain. The actual number is of little consequence anyway, but there has to be this subtle conveyance of racism."

The WKSA resolution, approved by unanimous vote, 38 for and none opposed or not voting, accepts the congressional expression of regret but not as an apology in view of Senator Daschle's actions in omitting the word "apology"; and now calls for an "unequivocal apology" from Congress. It calls for legislation to establish a national monument and memorial, pay "appropriate compensation to Massacre descendants and their respective tribal communities" and fund a museum for the Oglala Sioux Tribe; it requests Mickelson to "continue his efforts to have President George Bush establish a national monument on tribal lands located at the massacre site prior to December 29, 1990, by Executive Order. . . ." Dec. 29 is the 100th commemoration of the massacre at Wounded Knee.

Mickelson was the only South Dakota legislator of national stature Gonzalez and the WKSA spared.

Gonzalez described him to association members as a man of honor genuinely trying to bring about reconciliation with Indians and the other citizens of the state.

The WKSA resolution contends that Daschle's objection to the word "apology" is not in keeping with the Year of Reconciliation proclaimed by the Governor. But, others interpreted the document differently.

The concurrent resolution does not provide reparations to the descendants or declare the remote site a national monument, as the Wounded Knee Survivors' Association had requested.

The resolution says Congress "acknowledges the historical significance of this event as the last armed conflict of the Indian wars." Period. And, "hereby expresses its *deep regret* on behalf of the United States to the descendants of the victims and survivors and their respective tribal communities."

The measure is referred to as "long overdue" and much in keeping with South Dakota's Year of Reconciliation between Indian and Non-Indian communities.

CHRONICLE

In spite of the reaction of Senator Tom Daschle and his aides, who rose to defend the actions of South Dakota's fair-haired son, many activist Indians thought his public behavior reprehensible and they expressed disappointment. In their hearts they knew he had never really wanted to support the legislation but was forced into it by their persistence. They knew that he, like many of his colleagues in government, had never really wanted an "apology." Apologies, they said bitterly, are for the living. Regrets are for the dead. Finally, they knew, if Wounded Knee signifies anything in the modern world, it signifies the failure of the United States to recognize its own criminality.

Hundreds of modern dramas have been written in the last century, staged mostly by Whites, to tell the stories of the Wounded Knee Massacre and the Black Hills, and all of the other stories of the Sioux Nation that have come about since mythological times. They have become the new origin stories of a morality play of considerable significance in the United States, which grew out of an imitation of reality and have been sustained by political racism. What Antonio Gramsci, that Italian intellectual of the early twentieth century, has called "domestic colonialism" seems to be alive and well on the prairies of South Dakota.[38]

In allowing himself the luxury of public statement at this time, Gonzalez was attempting by sheer political will to turn back the falsely told stories. He, like many of his Sioux compatriots, had apparently had his fill of a historical process of dominance and accumulation by white folks in Indian Country. They all held strongly to the stories and the geography of Lakota thought and origin. They knew that Wounded Knee should tell of the largest massacre of innocents in the history of the United States, that it was the direct result of the theft of Lakota property, the Black Hills, in 1877, and of nine million acres in 1889, the loss of things on the land like the buffalo, the loss of a whole way of life. They knew the "trauma" of the Ghost Dance to be symptomatic rather than causal, and they knew that the passive story of "many Indians fell" dehumanized them all.

Activists have always said that the Black Hills case should exemplify the theft of a people's homelands by those who consider their civilization superior, and the gold which is mined from its bowels should represent the substance for which one people will murder another.

Today, it seems to many that the corrupt story of a tourist Mecca prevails in the hills and prairies of the Sioux lands; that the heads of American presidents carved into its mountains, the fifty miles of shops, restaurants, bingo palaces, and cheap Indian-style trinkets tell stories which reflect the heritage of a divided nation.

PART 2

Word Searchers and Big Foot Riders

(November 1, 1990–April 24, 1991)

My greatest fear is that some way or another the government might put a stop to our way of praying and destroy our sacred sites.

Arvol Looking Horse, Minneconjou, Ikta Wicasa,
"a common person, like anybody else, living day by day"
(quoted in Doll, *Vision Quest*).

CHRONICLE

The struggle for indigenous cultural heritage in the United States could not have been provided with a more profound dichotomy than the events witnessed during the winter months of 1990 and 1991 on the white plains of South Dakota and, ultimately, around the world.

The rhetoric of politicians and media, that is, the *word searchers*, controlled by white and powerful America, discussed and evaluated an ideological vision of the United States and its nations-within-a-nation (i.e., Indian Nations) which over a hundred years had failed to make the historical changes upon which contemporaries might agree. What the struggle revealed was that the oppressive bonds between white power and native ethics were, perhaps, bonds of humiliation and hardship which could be broken only by the process of rediscovery and repatriation.

The native voice revealed a difficult history based upon a distinction between the United States and the native so different, so independent of one another as to clarify those differences in a creative way. The intratribal dialogue, revealed not only in the legislative effort to seek justice led by the Wounded Knee Survivors' Associations but in the physical re-creation of the Wounded Knee journey led by Sitanka Wokiksuye (the Big Foot Riders) in order to reclaim the spiritual self, sometimes strangely disagreeable, often revealing a sense of anger and frustration, in the end became a unified discourse on the things that mattered. The challenge for the Dakotapi has always been, of course, to struggle to tell their own story and then go on.

This is what happened for the Lakotas during the crucial months of late 1990 and early 1991. Even while the Big Foot memorial ride, under the brilliant direction of White Plume, Birgil Kills Straight, Looking Horse, Gar-

rett, and dozens more, captured the imagination of the world, South Dakota Indian/White political relations concerning the memorial legislation
became a morass of cant and hypocrisy almost unequaled in modern political discourse. For the white power systems, euphemism took the place
of logic and reasonableness. Prospects for compensation and recognition
of Lakota nationhood seemed bleak at every turn.

Still, Gonzalez continued his struggle toward the legislative goals. The
dialogue began to show more tension. An architectural firm called Wyss
Associates, along with white scholars who have appointed themselves care-
takers of this history, addressed the possibility of a memorial enclave on
Indian lands, and as might have been expected, the storytelling began
drifting toward the deep divisions inherent in racial conflict.[1]

DIARY: NOVEMBER 1, 1990

> When I talked to Christine Jackson of the Rapid City Journal, she asked
> why I called the esteemed senator from South Dakota the "Duke of the
> North," when a few weeks ago I was apparently on good terms with him.
> She asked why I changed my position.
>
> I told her what I really thought; that if it wasn't for Senator Daschle de-
> leting the word "apology" from Senate Concurrent Resolution 153, the
> whole nation would have apologized for the 1890 Massacre!!
>
> I also explained to Christine that the killings at Wounded Knee and the
> theft of the Black Hills are not separate, unrelated stories; that our repeat-
> ed efforts to liberate our homeland is a political matter directly related to
> this country's effort to destroy Lakota identity. No one except Indians can
> define criminal acts such as the Wounded Knee Massacre as they should be
> defined in history. This is a matter I take very seriously, and, I told her, my
> characterization of the senator is not undeserved.
>
> Tim Kostel of South Dakota Public Radio and Margaret Smith, pro-
> ducer at National Public Radio in Washington, D.C., also telephoned for
> my explanations and comments about Daschle.

CHRONICLE

Someone once said, "All politics are local," and then went on to suggest
the courthouses and statehouses of local regions surpass the Congress and
White House in offering the "best government." This is the opinion of all
kinds of citizens these days, from the militias to the man on the street. The
movement toward state power fills people who know anything about Indian history in the West with dread. To the Sioux, the historical legacy of co-

lonial politics and racism resides in both places and neither is "better" than the other. In fact, any states' rights movement has always been detrimental to indigenous peoples. As far as the local situation was concerned, it seemed to Indians that the whole world would apologize to the Lakotas, return lands, and celebrate the human spirit. But not the men who occupied the seats of government representing the United States of America and the state of South Dakota and the counties and cities of the region.

DIARY: NOVEMBER 3, 1990

Daschle's press office is saying that Senate Concurrent Resolution 153 would not have been adopted by Congress without Daschle's support. In reality, the resolution would not have been adopted without the hard work of grassroots Indian people, men and women who struggle day to day to put food on the table for their families. They have no money, no resources, no telephones, and half the time they don't even have cars that run. It is hard for non-Indians to imagine how difficult it is for Indian people to defend the constant assault on their lands, resources, sovereignty, and culture under these conditions.

CHRONICLE

In spite of all their setbacks, Sioux Indians were working hard at this time trying to get things in shape so that they could receive an apology from the United States, a good way to start the new century, which they were counting as 1990, the anniversary date. In light of other outrages around the world, only three to four hundred dead might have seemed like a paltry number of Indians but what people were told they must understand is that *Wounded Knee has come to represent the millions of Indians who died at the hands of the United States and it represents all that is wrong with the United States' past.* It represents the indigenous condition throughout the world.

Some Indian cynics wondered if apologies were only for the living. Like the Japanese after Hiroshima or the Jews after the Holocaust, or the Poles after World War II. Since Indians are supposed to be "vanished," some thought sarcastically, they don't need an apology. After years of propaganda instead of history in the United States, the thinking is, "Well, they aren't nations, anyway. Not really, you know." Just some kind of "pockets of poverty" that need handouts and pity. To refute these misconceptions was the thrust of the entire movement to develop the monument and no one knew better than the survivor/descendant organizers that such a rewriting of history would be its influence. Their resolve was strengthened when they talked together.

DIARY: NOVEMBER 3, 1990 (continued)

Marie Not Help Him informed me that she plans to present the WKSA position on the deletion of the word "apology" from Senate Concurrent Resolution 153 on her weekly KILI Radio Oldie Goldie Country show. She said Milo Yellow Hair plans to host a pre-election program on Monday and she would like to discuss with him the questions on our proposed legislation that he will direct at political candidates.

Sally Roesch Wagner called today. She said that in her research she found that Gutzon Borglum, the Mount Rushmore sculptor, had planned to do a special project in Nebraska before he died, a whole Indian village sculpture, a project in the Pine Ridge area of Nebraska. He was quoted as having expressed his belief that the Black Hills were stolen from the Sioux. She is writing letters to Senator Daschle and Congressman Tim Johnson objecting to the deletion of the word "apology." I thanked her and told her we need all the help we can get.

CHRONICLE

Milo Yellow Hair, mentioned in this diary entry, is a well-known spokesperson for the Oglala traditionalists and treaty organizations. At this time he was an on-the-air reporter for the reservation-based radio station, KILI, which was started in 1983 and is now called "the Voice of the Lakota Nation." Today he is a persistent presence, an elected official of the tribe, a compelling voice for sovereign nationalism, and is much sought after as a public speaker for he is one of the few native spokespersons who is thought to be equally articulate in English and Lakota. He has done much work in the international arena, and recently married a blonde European woman with whom he has a child. Since it is still held by many traditionals that Lakota leaders must not move away from the marriage patterns of the old tiospayes no one knows to what extent this marriage to a white woman will diminish his leadership role among the traditionals. At this time, however, his narration of a 1990 "Frontline" program based on the book *In the Spirit of Crazy Horse* has served to reinforce his role as a major contemporary spokesperson for the tribe.

Milo possesses an old Oglala name. Some say that name came about after the killing of Custer. Others suggest that the name became well known during early reservation days when there were many acts of resistance to colonial practices. One such act occurred during the period of the settling of the Red Cloud Agency back in the late 1800s and a very revealing incident called in history "the flagpole incident" made the name forever a part of tribal resistance and negotiation.

A U.S. flag was put up by the white soldiers in the first few days of the agency's occupancy. The agency erupted in anger, a clear indication that the Oglalas (contrary to a history that is written about their "acceptance" of colonial rule) knew the symbols of colonialism and the meaning of sovereignty and were refusing in this way to give up their rights as a sovereign people. They were not U.S. citizens. They were Lakotas acting in defense of themselves. They would not have the U.S. flag flying over their sovereign lands.

An Indian named Speeder was sent by officials to summon the troops to quell the uprising, but the people killed him before he could do it. The agent and his 140-man occupation force claimed to be astonished at this reaction of the Indians and fully expected that Red Cloud would back them. Red Cloud did nothing. It was thought that a real, forceful rebellion might get out of hand. Others at the agency intervened, most notably Yellow Hair, who restored order through his influence among the people, but the flag did not reappear. The incident, retold in Catherine Margaret Price's dissertation, serves as historical evidence that the Oglalas meant to assert their rights as a sovereign nation and would not have a symbol of nationalism other than their own flying over their homelands. Such acts of resistance were not unheard of but many went unrecorded.

DIARY: NOVEMBER 8, 1990

> When freedom-loving people are rounded up in their own homelands and placed in a small area with a high population density (called reservations), and see their land and natural resources exploited for the benefit of foreigners while they live nearby in a state of abject poverty and dependence on a colonial government, they eventually start acting like caged animals and turn on each other. They become extremely jealous of one another and constantly undermine each other to make sure no one succeeds at anything they want to accomplish. It has happened over the years to reservation Indians. I believe it's a symptom of European colonialism.
>
> In the midst of a flurry of positive activity by people who support our efforts, there are always jealous-hearted people around to criticize and undermine our efforts. Harold Salway, president of the Oglala Sioux Tribe, recently told me that Duane Brewer, a supporter of Wayne Ducheneaux at

that time, made derogatory remarks about Suzan Shown Harjo and how
we Oglalas don't need her "interference." Brewer also told him the reason
the two Survivors' Associations have been unsuccessful with their proposed
legislation is because they have aligned themselves with Suzan; that the
Pine Ridge Survivors' Association was making the Oglalas look bad by
aligning itself with her.

Brewer also said that Sara Yager (of Daschle's office) used to be friendly,
but now she is cold toward Oglala Sioux tribal officials because of my re-
marks about Daschle being the Duke of the North and Suzan's involve-
ment in our lobbying effort.

The reason the Survivors' Associations have been unsuccessful so far is
the same reason they have been unsuccessful in all their previous attempts
to get Congress to atone for the massacre. It's because of underlying racism
at every level of the political process, inherent in South Dakota public
opinion and in the Senate Select Committee on Indian Affairs (which in-
cludes senators from the western states who are busy defending non-Indi-
an interests in their states against Indians).

CHRONICLE

Indian hating is America's oldest racism. There are social forces brought
about by Indian hating and racism which have shaped the Lakota world
over which the Lakota themselves have had little influence, and it may be
that people like Brewer who seem to be at odds with many of the ideals of
the historical past are a significant part of that dangerous change. Tribal
relationships (which many at this time believed Brewer failed to defend)
are the bases of resistance. When petty and ahistorical ideas aren't rejected, it seems difficult for many to keep going. Mario did not feel discouraged by this but told Salway they should reject such silly assessments of
things.

Duane Brewer has been described in Peter Matthiessen's book *In the
Spirit of Crazy Horse* as a "breed," a "goon," and he was accused of con-
cealing evidence of U.S. and tribal governmental crimes on the Pine Ridge
Reservation during the 1973 confrontation between the American Indian
Movement and U.S. marshals sent in by President Nixon.[2] On February 26,
1975, writes Matthiessen, "a goon gang led by Richard 'Manny' Wilson, Jr.,
and Duane Brewer of Dick Wilson's 'Highway Safety Committee' assault-
ed several AIM members in Pine Ridge Village and pursued them in a
running gun fight down the road toward Wounded Knee." Brewer was later indicted for allegedly participating in the vandalization of an airplane

which brought AIM defense lawyers to South Dakota and was thought to be a "gun-runner" between the FBI and the tribal governments bringing illegal weapons onto "trust" lands. Later he admitted as much on a "Frontline" broadcast. Brewer has since that time held several positions on the tribal council and various other tribal positions.

After the "Duke of the North" comment by Gonzalez, Duane Brewer and Mike Her Many Horses (both councilmen of the Pine Ridge Tribal Council at the time) made a special trip to Washington, D.C., at tribal expense to apologize to Daschle on behalf of the Oglala Sioux Tribe for Mario's comments.

DIARY: NOVEMBER 19, 1990

When I was in Washington, D.C., I had an interesting meeting with Sam Eaglestaff and Luke Duncan, chairman of the Ute Tribe, regarding the Treaty organization that was created earlier this year in Salt Lake City and the need to make it a more viable organization in defending Indian treaty rights.

I talked with Marie Not Help Him today. She told me about the Indian and State Relations Conference she attended that was chaired by University of South Dakota law professor Frank Pommershiem, who has written rather extensively on Indian legal issues. She said it was a successful conference, but it was not well covered by the news media.

Marie also informed me that Birgil Kills Straight and others met with Richard Moves Camp about the issue of repatriation of the remains of Lost Bird (an infant survivor of the Wounded Knee Massacre who was later adopted by a U.S. Army officer, and lived and died an early and unfortunate death away from her people through no choice of her own). It was the opinion of Moves Camp that no pipe carrier should be involved in exhuming and reburying Lost Bird's remains at the Wounded Knee mass grave site. Only nonbelievers can do this. Richard is from Eagle Nest District and is the current medicine man for the descendants of many of Chief Lip's people including my family. I therefore give deference to his advice and have not participated in the return of the remains.

CHRONICLE

Like all people confronted with oppressive government and racist colonialism, the Sioux are familiar with hatred. It begins with the hatred felt from others and the hatred felt for others, from outsiders, and, then, it sometimes turns into self-hatred, that is, internalized oppression, which eventually, and mercifully, can become the landscape of resistance. Hatred is a process born of history and it takes decades and decades to become an articulated phenomenon because it is ordinarily an unconscious part of people's daily lives, unthought of and quiescent.

The issue of who to blame for failure in Indian/White relations in the state is taken up frequently and there is a tendency on the part of everyone, even the Indians, to engage in what is now called "blaming the victim," even if they are, themselves, the victims. And it is because of hatred, an irrational emotion much like love, that exploitation and resistance seem to become normal.

Serious scholars of the Sioux/White relationship in South Dakota are beginning to delve into historical attitudes in a public and forthright manner after decades of stubborn silence and it must not be thought an effortless phenomenon. Sally Roesch Wagner who, at the invitation of Gonzalez, testified at the Washington, D.C., hearing on these matters brought some interesting insight into prevailing attitudes, particularly that of the popular press, when she contributed some materials to the hearing committee as follows: "L. Frank Baum, who later wrote *The Wonderful Wizard of Oz,* was editor of the Aberdeen, South Dakota *Saturday Pioneer,* and one year after the Massacre, wrote in an editorial: '*The Pioneer* has before declared that our only safety depends upon the total extermination of the Indian. Having wronged them for centuries, we had better, in order to protect our civilization, follow it up with one more wrong and wipe these untamed and untamable creatures from the face of the earth.'"[3] This, from a man who contributed what is, perhaps, the most influential and popular American story of them all, a fantasy morality tale about Kansas in which there are no Indians. It pretty much sums up the desires of whites in the United States and the history of Indian/White relations in the region. With genocide the historical answer to the question of the unwanted presence of the first occupants of this country, why would anyone think that "reconciliation" would be easy or even possible in our time? Why would anyone think that the Wounded Knee story could be a dialogue between reasonable people even after a hundred years?

Though there is much consternation and denial even among scholars and academics that Baum's sentiment might be the true sentiment of the region, and there is much effort to gloss it over, the complicated matter of who tells the stories of the Indian/White past is still an issue of great urgency. It is at the heart of the argument over "apology" and "compensation." The Baum history would suggest that the story Americans want to tell convincingly to the rest of the world is one in which there are no Indians. Or if they have somehow survived, they are "reconciled" to the fact that their lands have been stolen and their relatives murdered. Nothing, of course, could be further from the truth.

As the crucial years of 1991 and 1992, largely made up of pretenses, go relentlessly forward, the modern stories thematize two diametrically opposed versions of history and story.

American fantasies about a world without Indians are unusually popular. On the other hand, the fantasy world with them, such as *Peter Pan,* seems just as wonderfully seductive. The actualities of pioneer stories have even more claim upon the American imagination. What influence all of this history has had and what it has meant in terms of contemporary Indian politics is that the issue of U.S. imperialism, that is, America's seeking of empire formulated particularly since World War II, has been done in such a way that exempts Indian nationhood (legally reconstructed by the treaties and accounted for since 1934 in the Indian Reorganization Act)[4] from participation. More base than that, it has exempted Indian nationhood from its own existence or reality.

One of the more arresting and vituperative stories about the people of the Sioux Nation entitled *The Black Hills; or, The Last Hunting Ground of the Dakotahs,* was written in 1899 by a white teacher-pioneer. Oddly, it was reissued during the American Indian Movement–led "take-over" at Wounded Knee in 1973 by a South Dakota publishing house and has become a book which continues to be examined and used by many teachers and scholars throughout the region as a reasoned reflection of local thinking and interest during that historical period.[5]

Virginia Driving Hawk Sneve, a Brule Sioux educator, born and raised on the Rosebud Sioux Reservation in South Dakota, wrote in an introduction to the second edition:

> *The Black Hills,* Annie Tallent's malicious, bigoted treatment of the Dakota or Sioux Indians, would best serve mankind if it were burned rather than reprinted in this edition to continue to perpetuate a distorted, untrue portrait of the American Indian. However, Annie Tallent is a revered and sacred figure in South Dakota's history. Schools have been named after this woman, and an annual award to an outstanding female teacher is presented in her name. Destruction of Annie Tallent's book would be considered heresy by the non-Indians in South Dakota.
>
> The Gordon Party started for the Black Hills on October 6, 1874 and traveled surreptitiously westward in defiance of the law. She was proud that the

Gordon Party were trespassers and outlaws. She regarded the furtive maneuvering which the expedition employed to avoid discovery as a "wonderfully
brilliant conception." But she considered the Sioux, who engaged in defensive
warfare as "sneaking savages."

"The Dakotahs, or Nadouwessious . . . ," Annie Tallent wrote on page one
of her book, "were doubtless a valorous people considered from an Indian
standpoint . . . ," but she clearly did not consider them such. She believed that
the Sioux went to war, not in the name of self-defense against extermination,
but because they were natural killers. She asked if treaties should ever have
been entered into for they tended to . . . "arrest the advance of civilization, and
retard the development of the rich resources of our country. . . ."

Mrs. Tallent called medicine men "a class of lazy, but shrewd imposters [sic],
who, claiming supernatural powers, have by their incantations and sorceries, imposed upon the credulity of these benighted people, the most absurd supersti-
tions, among which was the belief that some day a 'Messiah' would appear."

This is a book which, for the better part of a century, has passed for
history in a region which learned and never forgot how to hate Indians.
Sneve, a respected Indian educator in the state, wrote the introduction as
a signal to educators that such distorted histories could no longer be used
in the school systems unchallenged. Though the resistance to revising this
well-loved history is ongoing, fervent, and resilient, there are, however,
signs of change (if only politically correct ones), for in 1992 the white
teacher who was to have received the Annie Tallent award refused to accept it, and a school in Rapid City called Annie Tallent Elementary
changed its name.

DIARY: NOVEMBER 20, 1990

*Jack English of Panther Productions telephoned to express his thought that
the movie* Dances with Wolves *might spark an interest in our effort to get
media coverage for the centennial of the massacre.*

*Sarah Long of the Voice of America also called me for an interview. She
asked for the names of other people involved in our lobbying effort that she
could interview. I told her I would contact several people (who are at the
heart of this effort) and arrange a time and place for her to interview them.*

CHRONICLE

For some reason, the general public seemed to embrace *Dances with
Wolves* as a story (in spite of its inaccurate history) which would make everyone understand better the unhappy relationship between Indians and

Whites. Perhaps even Kevin Costner thought it. Later, however, when he was asked if he was going to make a "sequel," he said he didn't think so because, he said offhandedly, he didn't have a clue to what happened next. For much of the United States that statement is profoundly true. Americans really don't have a clue about Indian history after the Civil War. If they do, they don't want to hear about it.

After the successful film, the Costner brothers began investing some of the millions they made on the Indian story in the old gambling and tourist industries of Deadwood, that frontier town of Dakota Territory, a place where locals restage old shoot-outs in the streets two or three times a day for the tourists and have quick-draw tournaments in the summer. Indians, in costume, sometimes participate in the touristy goings-on in that town but they always seem pitiful and out of place.

In January, 1993, Costner had an apparent change of heart about a continuing story, because in *Entertainment Weekly* magazine he announced plans to "do for Native Americans what *Roots* did for African-Americans." This is an idea which surfaces from time to time in the media. Costner was not specific about what he thought that was, but stated his desire to invest $8 million of his own money in an eight-hour documentary tracing the history of Indians in North America.

Vine Deloria, Jr., Sioux lawyer and scholar, has had this to say in the second edition of *God Is Red* about the matter of imaging history:

> There is the continuing struggle over the Black Hills of South Dakota. Many Americans are now aware of this state, thanks to the success of the movie *Dances with Wolves* that not only depicted the culture of the Sioux Indians but also filled the screen with the magnificent landscape of the Northern Plains. Nineteen ninety-one was a year of great schizophrenia and strange anomalies in South Dakota. Local whites shamelessly capitalized on the success of the movie at the same time they were frothing at the mouth over the continuing efforts of the Sioux people to get the federal lands in the Black Hills returned to them. Governor George Mickelson announced "a Year of Reconciliation" that simply became twelve months of symbolic maneuvering for publicity and renewal of political images. When some of the Sioux elders suggested that the return of Bear Butte near Sturgis [by the State of South Dakota] would be a concrete step toward reconciliation, non-Indians were furious that reconciliation might require them to make good-faith effort to heal the wounds from a century of conflict.

In the past few years when politicians in the state talk publicly, they often say what Governor Bill Janklow was quoted as saying during his recent term,

"The tribes want all of western South Dakota to be given back to them." In spite of the fact that this is not the reality of tribal concerns, Janklow goes on to say that he is against it because he is defending *all* of the citizens of his state. Tribal land loss, however, is rarely considered by the governor of the state in his discussion of justice for *all* citizens. For example, the flooding of 550 square miles of Indian lands for hydro-electric power and the request by tribes for the return of "taken" but unused portions of those lands are rarely given the "fairness" test. It is a politicians' kind of hyperbole, in contradistinction to actual Indian/White experience, that prevents any real problem solving concerning the theft of treaty-protected lands.

In 1995 National Forest Service lands which the Sioux tribes still consider in dispute because they are part of the Black Hills Sioux land claim were exchanged through government intervention (both state and federal) to the Costner brothers to help their one hundred million dollar gambling resort at Deadwood. South Dakota congressman Tim Johnson and senators Larry Pressler and Tom Daschle were quick to support the land exchange in the "interest of public good." It was reported in the local news media that the state of South Dakota made available nearly $14 million in various kinds of "incentives" to assist the Costners with their resort.

In 1997 Senator Daschle, working with the South Dakota governor and legislature, began drafting and sponsoring a bill that would turn over the federally controlled (U.S. Army Corps of Engineers) shoreline of the Missouri River to the state of South Dakota. The bill was euphemistically called the "South Dakota Land Transfer and Wildlife Habitat Mitigation Act of 1997," but it was clearly a land grab of treaty-protected lands and an attack on tribal jurisdiction. In newspaper accounts, tribal leaders, who only learned about this bill when they read about it in the *Federal Register,* voiced their objection, saying that "our federal recognized status is what is supposed to be in place to prevent any encroachment into that territory."[6] A largely uninformed white citizenry, its greed and ignorance fueled by the governor's "community meetings," was saying that the federal government had no place controlling state interests, and called this land grab a "return" of lands to the state when, in fact, the state never owned much of this land. The Daschle bill asks that about 198,000 acres, much of it Indian land, be transferred to the state of South Dakota.

The outrageous exploitation of Indians as tourist and media subjects in the State of South Dakota has been uncommented upon and largely unexamined since Indians, themselves, in many cases, have allowed themselves to be exploited.

DIARY: NOVEMBER 21, 1990

President Salway wants to appoint the Steering Committee suggested by Wyss, Inc., an architectural firm of Rapid City retained by the Oglala Sioux Parks and Recreation Authority to conduct a feasibility study for a visitor center/museum at the massacre site. Members of the committee would include Harold Salway, John Steele as chairman of the Wounded Knee District, Alex White Plume as chairman of the OST Parks and Recreation Authority, Sam Eaglestaff as president of the Cheyenne River WKSA, Claudia Iron Hawk Sully as president of the Pine Ridge WKSA, and Leonard Little Finger (who claims to be a descendant of Chief Big Foot).

Voice of America and the National Public Radio program "All Things Considered" are getting ready for the December 29th Centennial commemorating the Wounded Knee Massacre. The 100th Anniversary ride by the Oglalas and Minneconjous will be, perhaps, one of the most important symbolic events of our time.

DIARY: NOVEMBER 23, 1990

Still doing PR work. I returned a call from the Associated Press in Washington, D.C., and answered numerous questions about the history of the Wounded Knee Massacre. Chuck Haga of the Minneapolis Tribune *also called (for the same information). He got my name from Steve Young of the* Sioux Falls Argus Leader.

A free-lance reporter for the National Catholic Reporter, *Cathy Walsh, also called for information about Wounded Knee. Calvin Jumping Bull, she said, spoke on Wounded Knee at Cincinnati, Ohio, and the place was packed. She said she is also writing an article for the* St. Anthony Messenger, *which has over 400,000 subscribers.*

DIARY: NOVEMBER 30, 1990

National Public Radio called again and wanted more information regarding the September 25th Senate Select Committee hearing. Specifically, NPR wanted to know if any government witnesses testified. I told them that government witnesses did in fact testify, but my list of witnesses would not be complete, since people were invited to submit written testimony and it is probable that they did so. I suggested that they get in touch with Siobhan Wescott of the Senate Select Committee on Indian Affairs, in Washington, D.C., for a complete list of government witnesses and copies of their testimonies.

*Johnson Holy Rock and Patti Marks (a former Abourezk staff person),
and others say that the failure of Senator Abourezk to get a compensation
bill passed in 1976 was caused by the U.S. Army's position (and testimony) that Wounded Knee was not a "massacre"; that it was all justified because the Indians caused it. This is, in my view, not just a matter of se-
mantics; it is a matter of federal strategy to cover up the massacre and
accounts for Daschle's deletion of the word "apology" in Senate Concurrent Resolution 153.*

*Government witnesses are a significant counter to Lakota witnesses in in-
terpreting the 1890 massacre. For example, a former chief historian of the
National Park Service, Robert M. Utley (now living in Moose, Wyoming,
and married to the assistant superintendent of the Grand Teton National
Park) testified in the 1976 Abourezk hearing that there is no evidence the
Black Hills were ever central to Sioux spirituality; that the Sioux didn't even
come into the Black Hills until 1775 when they pushed the Kiowas out.[7]*

*Utley has lost credibility as a historian among the Lakota because of his
efforts to justify the mass murder of Lakota men, women, and children at
Wounded Knee. It is historians like Utley who have prevented the federal
government from acknowledging that it committed an illegal and immoral
act and must now apologize for it. It is also historians like Utley who deni-
grate Lakota claims to the Black Hills by suggesting that they are latecomers,
having arrived in the Black Hills from Minnesota around 1775 (based on a
winter count). The truth of the matter is that the Lakota used and occupied
the Black Hills for a period of time sufficient to establish "aboriginal Indian
title" under U.S. law. Moreover, the Lakota also possess "recognized title" to
the Black Hills under the 1851 and 1868 Fort Laramie treaties.[8]*

CHRONICLE

Utley's latest book, *The Lance and the Shield: The Life and Times of Sitting
Bull,* has been well received by the public and by scholars in general but,
from a Lakota point of view, it is filled with pejorative language and false
supposition. Utley begins by calling Sitting Bull and his warriors "extrem-
ists" (p. 66); the historical truth is that though Sitting Bull had opposition
within tribal enclaves as all politicians do, he represented a very wide segment of Sioux thinking at the time, probably more mainstream than extremist during that period from a tribal perspective; the 1874 Custer expedition is called an "ostensible" search for a site for a fort (p. 116), though
little is said of its illegality; about this matter, he says the Sioux "complained bitterly," and he uses the term "yipping warriors" to describe the

Sioux military (p. 84). He says "unity of action had never been Lakota strength" (p. 85), implying an inferior military force rife with dissension even though the Sioux defeated the U.S. Army in nearly every military engagement of the 1860s and 1870s. Finally, when Sitting Bull was elected "War Chief of the Entire Sioux Nation" in 1869, in a move to head a confederation, Utley sees it only in terms of factionalism:

> The designation of Sitting Bull as Supreme Chief was an astute political move. A faction likely representing no more than minorities of varying size within each tribe lifted him to an office that had never existed and was alien to Sioux thinking about political organization. It could be viewed as a tainted power play, driven by factional and family self-interest and large segments of non-treaty tribes did not accept it. But the deal had been done and as the authors well knew, its success depended on Sitting Bull's ability to convert an office of doubtful legitimacy into one that functioned in practice as its designers intended. (Pp. 87–88)

Utley indexes the Wounded Knee Massacre as "Battle of . . . ," and continues to tout the Ghost Dance phenomenon as the rationale for the atrocity against families at Wounded Knee Creek in 1890.

Utley, a popular writer of historical works, is considered by some an exemplar of American Indian scholarship and historiography, but he is more accurately, perhaps, a historian who is shaping the idea of the United States in such a way as to give it a reassuring identity. American power is continuously reinforced in these kinds of historical interpretations of the Indian experience.

DIARY: DECEMBER 1, 1990

> Eddie Little Sky called, upset because Marie Not Help Him "chewed him out" for suggesting that a Hotchkiss cannon be brought to Wounded Knee on December 29th and fired in honor of those who died there in 1890. Marie did not think it was a good idea; that it would be disrespectful to the Lakota men, women, and children who were killed by Hotchkiss cannons. Although Eddie's intentions are good, I agree with Marie.
>
> Eddie said that Marie was also unhappy about the Oglala Sioux Parks and Recreation Authority hiring Clara Spotted Elk as their lobbyist. I informed him about Clara's politics (i.e., her supposed role in helping Wayne Ducheneaux remove Suzan Shown Harjo as executive director of the National Council of American Indians) and how that might negatively impact our lobbying effort.
>
> I also told him about Clara asking Alex White Plume to step into the hallway to visit just about the time Alex was supposed to testify at the Sep-

tember 25th hearing in Washington, D.C. When Senator Inouye, chairman of the Senate Select Committee on Indian Affairs, called Alex to testify, he wasn't in the room. Claudia Iron Hawk Sully had to testify out of order. Some congressional staff members interpreted this seemingly trivial event as a lack of respect for Inouye, who left the hearing room.

DIARY: DECEMBER 6, 1990

I conferred (by telephone) with Peter Schwartzbauer of Vienna regarding Wounded Knee Centennial events in Europe. He said that an exhibit on the 1890 massacre showed in France, Holland and will show at the Museum of Man in Vienna starting December 12th. It will also be shown in Italy and Hungary. He said that Birgil Kills Straight will be in Vienna for the opening of the exhibit at the Museum of Man. Peter asked me to attend but I don't believe I will have time to go.

Also today, I gave a two hour interview to Patrick Cudmore of Spearfish. He is writing an article for the Rapid City Journal *on the massacre for a special edition to be issued on December 29th.*

DIARY: DECEMBER 7, 1990

Attended a joint meeting of the Cheyenne River/Pine Ridge Survivors' Associations at the Cheyenne River Sioux Tribal Cultural Center in Eagle Butte. Some WKSA members had a hard time getting there. Sam Eaglestaff called to say his car was broke down. When I called Marie Not Help Him about the meeting, she said she and her mother (Celane) wanted to go but didn't have enough gas money. I told her I would provide gas money if she and others could just get there. It was a good meeting; I gave an update on our lobbying effort. We also drafted a letter to Senator Inouye to inform him that the Survivors' Associations will accept Senate Concurrent Resolution 153 as an apology based on his representations (in his letter to Claudia Iron Hawk Sully) that it was the intent of Congress that the resolution be an official apology for the massacre and that he will support our legislative proposal in the next session of Congress if the Survivors' Associations accept it as an apology. The Survivors' Associations' acceptance of the resolution as an apology is conditioned, however, on passage of our proposed legislation by Congress. Passage of our legislative proposal will make the apology meaningful; otherwise, it will remain a watered-down, hollow apology, a mere expression of regret rather than a sincere apology.

I was honored by the WKSA members by being presented a handmade quilt with an eagle on it. Burdell Blue Arm sang the honoring song for me

*and used my Lakota name Nantan Hinapan (Comes Out Charging) in
the song. This was my great-great grandfather Robert Quiver's name. It
was given me by my great uncle Enos Poor Bear, Sr., at a naming ceremony held at Wanblee, South Dakota, in 1979.*

DIARY: DECEMBER 12, 1990

*Sam Eaglestaff stopped by my office this evening to make several telephone
calls. Later I returned a call to Chet Brokaw of the Associated Press in
Pierre and responded to questions he had regarding Senate Concurrent
Resolution 153 and our proposed legislation.*

*Howard Burkus of National Public Radio called from Salt Lake City
and informed me that he received comments from Senator Tom Daschle
regarding the Wounded Knee bill and things he has done for Sioux Indians. Burkus later called from San Francisco to inform me that a member
of Daschle's staff quoted a $10,000,000 figure for a national monument.
This was the amount we initially requested in the authorization section of
our draft bill but changed to the "there are authorized to be appropriated
such sums as may be necessary" language at Congressman Johnson's request. The* Rapid City Journal *also has a story in today's edition about
Daschle and Johnson and their support for Indian projects.*

The Lakota Times *also received a letter from Senator Larry Pressler defending his refusal to accept the word "massacre" to describe the 1890 massacre. They asked if I wished to respond. I declined.*

DIARY: DECEMBER 13, 1990

*I spoke to Suzan Shown Harjo today and informed her of (among other
things) Howard Burkus's statement that Senator Daschle is planning to
pursue our proposed legislation in the next session of Congress.*

DIARY: DECEMBER 15, 1990

*Today is the one hundredth anniversary of the assassination of Sitting Bull.
Before she died in 1971, my grandmother Anna Quiver Wilcox told me that
we are related to Sitting Bull. Sitting Bull is a first cousin to my great-great-
great grandmother Jealous of Her and her sisters Pearl Woman, Returns
Last Woman, and Seen By Her Nation (Dewey Beard's mother).*

DIARY: DECEMBER 16, 1990

*Sam gave me an update on the speeches made at the Cultural Heritage
Center event in Pierre called "Wounded Knee, a Century Past." He said*

Carole Barrett's speech about Agent McLaughlin and Sitting Bull made people angry because it seemed she was trying to whitewash the political assassination of the respected chief. He said Mike Her Many Horse's speech was good and informative but boring. The best speech was given by Arthur Amiotte, the internationally known Lakota artist from Custer, South Dakota. He also said that Dr. Beatrice Medicine, the Sioux anthropologist from Wakpala, gave a real good speech.

DIARY: DECEMBER 18, 1990

Survivors' Association members have been busy preparing for the Wounded Knee activities on December 29th.

I received calls from people who want to donate food. The Big Foot Riders will be providing the dinner on the evening of the 28th, and the Survivors' Associations will be providing the dinner on the 29th. Richard Garnier, Claudia Iron Hawk Sully's son, called to tell me that the Pine Ridge WKSA could only talk the Oglala Sioux Tribe into donating one buffalo, and asked me to deliver a message to Sam Eaglestaff to get more buffalo meat from the Cheyenne River Sioux Tribe since a big crowd is expected. When I arrived at Sam's daughter's house in Rapid City (where he is staying), Sam invited me to watch the documentary video called In the Spirit of Crazy Horse *moderated by Milo Yellow Hair, a piece based mostly on the book of the same name by Peter Matthiessen.*

CHRONICLE

In The Spirit of Crazy Horse was first published by Viking in 1980 and had wide appeal to middle American readers who found it to be astonishingly informative in that it revealed to them the notion that, perhaps, they couldn't trust their government; that, in fact, their president and government officials and even the Federal Bureau of Investigation might be capable of intentional wrongdoing. The book chronicled the 1973 shoot-out between Indians and FBI agents at Wounded Knee, the indictment of American Indians (including Leonard Peltier) on murder charges in the deaths of FBI agents, and the bitter struggle of the Lakotas with the United States for sovereignty. While all of this was no big news to Indians, they, too, had an interest in the book because of what it printed about local and regional indications of racism toward Indians which they felt had long been covered up by state officials, the media, and the general public.

The book is important because it said in print what many Sioux Indians had said to each other for some time; for example, that the man who

was then serving as attorney general of South Dakota and was to become
the governor of the state, Bill Janklow, had been accused by his baby-sitter,
Jancita Eagle Deer, of raping her while he was a "poverty" lawyer on the
Rosebud Indian Reservation, that is, the director of the Rosebud Sioux Legal Services Program. It is said to be an undocumented charge, challenged
vigorously by Janklow, but one believed by many Indians.

Mario Gonzalez, long a critic of some aspects of the American Indian
Movement, says the Matthiessen book glorifies AIM and he feels that Matthiessen's interpretation of the Black Hills Claim is largely fiction, a
figment of his own liberal imagination and what he has been told by his
AIM informants. For example, Matthiessen hardly mentions tribal governments except to condemn them and he entirely avoids discussing the
work done by Mario on the Sioux land claims. Mario rejects Matthiessen's
rationale, which makes it sound as though most of the progress on the
Black Hills Claim can be attributed to the American Indian Movement
and its militancy.[9] Mario considers Madonna Gilbert's assessment, quoted
rather extensively by Matthiessen, that urban Indian militants and their
white supporters changed Indian life on reservations forever by bringing
back culture and tradition, an exaggeration.

The book claims that Mario Gonzalez, who was then serving as a Rosebud Sioux tribal judge, had brought charges against Janklow on behalf of
the tribe and its citizens but that since Janklow is a white man, he was not
subject to tribal jurisdiction. It is inaccurate to suggest that Gonzalez
brought the charges, since judges only hear cases, they do not bring charges. Jancita Eagle Deer filed a petition to disbar Janklow from practicing
in tribal court through her Minneapolis, Minnesota, attorney Larry Lev-
enthal and his co-counsel tribal advocate (lawyer) Dennis Banks. The
book claims that Janklow refused to answer the summons and the BIA refused to deliver the subpoenaed file on the alleged rape. The fact is that
Janklow refused to appear at a "show cause" hearing scheduled by the
court on the disbarment petition and the BIA intentionally sent the police
investigation file to its area office at Aberdeen, South Dakota, to keep it
outside of the jurisdiction of the Rosebud Sioux Tribal Court. The BIA
was responsible for law enforcement on the reservation at the time, and
had custody of the file. All the tribal court could do was grant Eagle Deer's
petition to disbar Janklow from further legal practice in tribal court. The
tribal court, at the request of Eagle Deer's attorneys, also issued a misde-
meanor arrest warrant for Janklow based on sworn testimony presented
on Eagle Deer's behalf (since it was generally believed at the time that

tribal courts had criminal jurisdiction over non-Indians), but no arrest
was ever made. Janklow denied Eagle Deer's charges in the press and managed to keep the book on the underground circuit and prevent paperback
sales by filing a civil complaint in federal court for slander against the
publisher and writer, who took the book off the shelves for several years.

Janklow has become an adamant foe of Indian Nationhood and got the
state of South Dakota to spend thousands of dollars in the *Oliphant vs. Suquamish Indian Tribe* case, which subsequently held that tribal courts have
no criminal jurisdiction over non-Indians on the reservation. An investigation into this kind of state-to-state complicity in anti-Indian legislation
and litigation is long overdue.[10]

In 1979 Janklow, according to the Matthiessen book, "abolished South
Dakota's Department of Environmental Protection" because it had joined
forces with Indians in the Black Hills Alliance and, therefore, would be in
support of the Lakota land claim to the Black Hills. He was called an "Indian Fighter" by the media and some say this is his political power.[11]

In a final irony, Janklow, after several years in private practice in Sioux
Falls, was reelected in 1994 to an unprecedented third term as governor of
the state of South Dakota. In this second coming, he has been quoted in
the *Rapid City Journal* as believing that the tribes in South Dakota have a
"master plan" to get all of western South Dakota returned to them or to
repurchase it through their newfound casino wealth. He often blames the
tribes and their "untaxed" landbase for South Dakota's poverty problems.
Tribal economic interests, he says, will only take from all South Dakotans
and make everyone suffer.

Media statements by tribal leaders throughout the state indicate that it
is their belief that the antagonists to their interests are still in place, waiting for the opportunity to strike them down. Matthiessen's book records
the history which supports that belief.

DIARY: DECEMBER 28, 1990

*Called Marie Not Help Him to ask if there was anything I should do in
preparation for the ceremonies at Wounded Knee tomorrow. She informed
me that KILI Radio had just announced an Associated Press Release that
Russell Means, Dennis Banks, and members of the American Indian
Movement plan to take control of the mass grave and not let the news media participate in the ceremonial events. I told her that the mass grave is
not public property; it belongs to the descendants of Chief Big Foot's band.*

I suggested that she get on KILI Radio to make an appeal that everyone respect the dead and the mourners.

An Arctic cold front is moving in. Sam Eaglestaff called to discuss the possibility about moving the events from the mass grave to the Manderson School gym. "It will be hard on the elderlies and the children," he said, "and this is not supposed to be an endurance test for them."

Andrea Staritz, a free-lance writer for Neues Deutschland East German Radio 100 in West Berlin called for information. I gave her a complete update on our lobbying effort and the ceremonies that will take place at the massacre site tomorrow.

I have been asked to pick up people at the Rapid City airport, including David Bradley, Suzan Shown Harjo, and Oren Lyons.

Wilbur Between Lodges also called to inform me that John Steele will pick up the buffalo meat donated by the Oglala Sioux Tribe at the Clinton, Nebraska, meat locker and bring it to Pine Ridge.

CHRONICLE

As the time for the Wounded Knee Centennial Ride neared, there was not a member of the tribes anywhere who was not filled with anticipation and pride. Hundreds of men and women known by all of the people would ride the same trail as their relatives a hundred years before.

Reasons for the 1986–90 annual re-creation of that historic journey to Wounded Knee taken by the Minneconjous are many. Surely, they wanted to make a renewed effort to tell the stories that the people cherished, to say to one another what was truthful, to give their power and strength over to form an extended meditation on the idea of history, to summon up the spirits, to remember the words of White Bull: "Such a madness we had experienced," to remember Death and give it meaning.

DIARY: DECEMBER 29, 1990

My family and I left from my home in Black Hawk for Wounded Knee with Suzan Shown Harjo about 7 o'clock A.M. When we arrived at the mass grave site, Sam Eaglestaff was announcing over his portable P.A. system to a crowd standing near the south entrance of the Catholic Church located just north of the cemetery (where the mass grave is located).

Sam arrived before sunup to participate in the sunrise prayers that are held at the mass grave each year. The descendants of Chief Big Foot's band have held the December 29th sunrise prayers since the formation of the

Wounded Knee Survivors' Association (formerly Big Foot's Claims Council) in 1901.

It was extremely cold, yet everyone endured the cold in anticipation of the Big Foot Riders coming over the hill near Porcupine Butte. Many people were going into the Catholic Church to keep warm and then coming outside again. The riders finally arrived at 12:00 o'clock.

Many visitors had arrived by the time the riders arrived. Descendants of Chief Big Foot's band from the Pine Ridge and Cheyenne River Reservations were there. Representatives of the Oglala and Cheyenne River Sioux Tribal Councils were there. Indians from other tribes were there. Governor George Mickelson and his state delegation were there. The news media was there.

When George Mickelson attempted to go into the cemetery and visit the mass grave, Russell Means ran out and stepped in front of him, blocking his entry. Russell made some verbal threats. The governor decided to avoid a confrontation and walked back to the church. This confrontation troubled Sam, Claudia Iron Hawk Sully, Celane Not Help Him, Marie Not Help Him, Belva Hollow Horn, and other members of the Survivors' Associations. They felt that Russell was using the centennial ceremonies to get media attention for himself; that he had showed no respect for their dead relatives.

When Marie Not Help Him stated that she was going to confront Russell and tell him that he had no right to assume control over the mass grave since he is not a descendant of Chief Big Foot's band, Sam advised her to "let it go." He said that Russell lost the respect of Chief Big Foot's people, and he would now have to live with this shame for the rest of his life. This would be his punishment.

The Survivors' Associations decided to move the ceremonies to the Manderson School gym (located 11 miles north of the mass grave) after the confrontation between Governor Mickelson and Russell Means. At the gym, the agenda I drafted was followed. Several persons, including Governor Mickelson, gave speeches. I read the names of the Lakota men, women, and children killed in the massacre; when I concluded, I asked for a moment of silence in their honor.

Because some of the victims buried in the mass grave are my blood relatives, i.e., Dewey Beard's family, I imagined how terrible it must have been. To see unarmed men, women, and children run down by Custer's Seventh Cavalry and killed. Then, a few days later, to see our dead relatives stripped of the clothing and personal property by souvenir hunters and unceremoniously thrown into a pit by a civilian burial crew, one on

*top of the other, and buried. Celane told me that one person was still alive
when he was thrown into the grave and buried.*

*Clothing and personal property stolen from the bodies of our deceased
relatives can presently be found in museums and personal collections all
over the world. It is difficult to understand how people who call themselves
civilized and Christians could be so cruel and brutal.*

*Toward the end of the day, I was beginning to feel chilled, and ill. I told
my wife and children that I was ready to return home. We looked for our
passenger (Suzan Shown Harjo) to see what her plans were, but couldn't
find her. We asked Sam to tell her we headed back to Black Hawk.*

WORD SEARCHERS

Just before and even after the Lakota Memorial Riders had completed their
stunning commemoration of the murder of their relatives at Wounded Knee
one hundred years ago, the state's newspapers, filled with stories about Indians, told tales that constituted quite an unusual kind of positive news for
South Dakotans. There was a momentum, now, to interview Indians who
had, somehow, caught the imagination of the public again, in one of the cycles
of public interest in an otherwise forgotten people.

The *Sioux Falls Argus Leader*'s interviews with various spokespersons tried
to keep pace with the *Lakota Times,* which specialized in Indian news, and
other national and international journals and newspapers sent reporters and
photographers to Indian Country. Various articles were thought to be informative to a public which had spent years ignoring Indian lives.

The *Argus Leader* wrote:

> Wounded Knee—A century after her grandparents were shot at Wounded
> Knee, Celane Not Help Him still waits for an apology from the people who pulled
> the trigger.
>
> She claims the U.S. government murdered 300 Lakota Sioux warriors, wom-
> en and children under a [white] flag of truce on December 29, 1890.
>
> The U.S. Army has said the Sioux started the conflict.
>
> Now, the argument could be headed for Washington, D.C., under a bill being
> pushed by the Wounded Knee and Cheyenne River Survivors' Associations.
>
> They want an apology from Congress, a memorial at Wounded Knee and $10
> million for injuries and their ancestors' loss of life and property.
>
> "Nothing has happened in a hundred years," says Not Help Him, 61 year old
> Oglala. "They didn't come; they didn't say they were sorry. When we've asked for
> compensation in the past, they didn't think they had to."
>
> In 1939, Senator Francis Case, R-SD, introduced a bill seeking $1,000 for every

Big Foot Riders, December 29, 1990, 100th Anniversary of Wounded Knee. © 1990 by Don Doll. Used by permission.

man, woman, and child who died at Wounded Knee or survived the conflict. That failed. Sen. James Abourezk, D-SD, filed a similar bill in 1975, upping the compensation to $3,000 for each victim and survivor, and again it failed.

But Gonzalez, who has approached Sen. Tom Daschle and Rep. Tim Johnson about sponsoring the bill, is optimistic.

"To me, it's a no-lose situation," said Gonzalez. "Any normal-thinking congressman or senator would say, 'Hey, this is the centennial year at Wounded Knee.' And, there's no reason why non-Indian people should object to it in view of the fact that the Japanese got compensation."

Last year, Congress approved compensation for Japanese-Americans who were interned in camps on the West Coast during World War II.

Daschle and Johnson, both South Dakota Democrats, say they are still studying Gonzalez's draft legislation. While most of the $10 million is pegged for educational and cultural purposes on the Pine Ridge and Cheyenne River Reservations, Johnson says he has doubts about a bill that asks for that much money.

"It involves huge expenditures, and there are tribes all over America who could equally claim reparations for things that occurred 100 years ago," Johnson says.

"Frankly, we're at a time when it's hard getting money to hire doctors for hospitals, when our Indian colleges we have on the reservations are grossly underfunded, much less seeking funds of this magnitude.

"Then, adding to it the precedential value it has, it makes this bill an awfully tough sell on the whole."

As for the precedent of the payment to the Japanese, Johnson says, "I voted against that bill . . . of course, there's all sorts of arguments that some sort of reparations should be made. On the other hand, the federal government has been spending millions of dollars on Indian programs, much of it not very efficiently, for a long, long time."

Asked if the government wasn't obligated to make payments under its treaty agreements, the congressman says, "It isn't that the taxpayers haven't been making significant contributions all along to the Indian people."

Such talk irritates Gonzalez.

"It's been real frustrating because I don't think our senators have enough courage to really do what they should be doing," he says. "If Daschle and Johnson don't have enough courage to present this to Congress, then we'll probably have to get other sponsors."

Gonzalez distinguishes Wounded Knee from other Massacres in that he believes there is a legal basis for compensation and not just a moral one. The 1877 act says that the Sioux are protected in their rights of property, person and life, and the 1889 act extended those protections to all Indians living on the reservations, he says.

"There was an obligation of the U.S. to protect these people when they went on the reservation and they didn't," he says. "Some call it a Massacre. To me it is a mass murder because people were disarmed and they couldn't protect themselves."

In previous hearings on Wounded Knee compensation bills, the U.S. Army has argued against that assessment. In response to the Abourezk hearings, acting secretary of the Army, Normal R. Augustine, says undisputed testimony showed that the 1890 conflict began with an Indian firing the first shot and that a number of Sioux opened fire with concealed weapons.

While a number of officers testified after the battle [sic] that the troops might have been positioned to cause soldiers to fire upon themselves, "even if this were true, it would merely establish that shots which were fired . . . were spontaneous and uncontrolled and not the deliberate, intentional shooting of helpless persons," Augustine says.

Edgar High Whiteman, who testified in 1976 in Washington, D.C., says bodies of women and children found in the hills around Wounded Knee indicate they were hunted down and murdered.

"They shot and killed defenseless children, babies and women, and they took everything away from them," says High Whiteman, 80, of Oglala, whose mother survived the battle [sic]. "What the white man says sometimes their history is distorted. You know that."

Augustine countered by suggesting that those killed beyond the battlefield might first have been wounded in the camp area, or possibly hit by stray shots. He cites testimony indicating soldiers were ordered not to fire at children and women.

"Despite these precautionary efforts, it is apparent that individual excesses occurred," he says. "They were not based, however, on preconceived sentiments of malevolence. Instead, they were the actions of inexperienced, untested troops who were carried away in the heat of the battle [sic]."

"If that's so," Gonzalez asks, "then why were up to 23 Congressional [sic] Medals of Honor awarded to the U.S soldiers who fought at Wounded Knee?" By comparison, only three out of 63,000 South Dakotans who served in World War II won the same medals, according to former state historian, Will Robinson.

Herbert Hoover, a history professor at the University of South Dakota, says: "To me, medals of honor have nothing to do with valor. You give out medals of honor because you want to create an image. I suppose they gave out those medals to make people believe it was a noble thing."

"But it wasn't noble," says Gonzalez. "Three hundred women and children died. And an inventory of Wounded Knee survivors conducted by Standing Rock Reservation agent James McLaughlin in 1920 showed the Sioux lost $20,000 in horses, wagons, tipis and other personal property."

He quotes Gen. Nelson Miles, overall commander of the U.S. Army's Missouri Division in 1890, who said of Wounded Knee, "In my opinion, the least the government can do is make a suitable compensation."

Whether that happens in 1990 is something Johnson can't predict, Daschle hasn't decided and the Wounded Knee Survivors won't back down.

CHRONICLE

The Big Foot Memorial Ride to Wounded Knee in 1990 was exploited by
photographers worldwide. Many of the photos were quickly placed with
agents in places like Denver and Golden, Colorado; Omaha, Nebraska;
New York City; even as far away as Paris. Professional photographers from
all over the world placed the work through publishing agencies, which
made it virtually impossible for the Sioux people themselves to get access
to the photos without paying hundreds of dollars for their use.[12]

"Never forget that we come from the Earth," say the old people of the
Sioux. Yet, that idea has rarely been respected by outsiders, and the struggle of the Oyate to keep their homelands and live on them and with them
has never been the focus of America's telling of Indian stories. Indeed, the
rites and rituals of the foreign word searchers tell an Indian story that
comments on the reality of the territorial United States, not as a place with
thousands of years of history and culture, but as an experiment in a democratic way of life, barely two hundred years old, an experiment, Indians
say, based on the exploitation of resources by a government whose major
principles are theft and competition. Surely, the old people say, it will cease
to exist when the resources are done.

As for the Wounded Knee crime, in the plethora of present-day and
historical versions, the focus on "who fired the first shot?" and the question, "was it a massacre or was it something else?" have served to make
this historical event seem "inexplicable" to many who refuse to examine
the real social and political patterns that lie behind it. It is, of course, "inexplicable" to those who fail to understand the longing for what the Lakota warrior Crazy Horse called "the land on which the people walk."

When Indian history is made to seem inexplicable, the writers of it deliberately create fantasies (untruths) and look for scapegoats (savages). Under
these conditions, then, Wounded Knee is not interpreted as a national crime
against humanity for which someone must be indicted. It seems, rather, a
"mystery," a "paradox," and it produces a false kind of U.S. history in which
the perpetrators of crime can become blameless. What this has meant to a
lot of individual Indians and to many of the First Nations of this land is that
it is futile to appeal to any sense of justice and democratic principles in the
cases of atonement and reclamation. Apathy and despair and wholesale de-
basement of Indian communities are often the result.

An example of "inexplicability" in the history which precedes Wounded Knee is, of course, the so-called Custer myth and the Battle of the Little

Bighorn, which occurred more than a decade prior to the massacre. "Who was the man?" and "Why did it happen to him?" ask historians of Custer's life and times. "How did it happen? Why did he attack the Indians when he did? Who is the warrior who killed him? What are the savage codes of the warriors who killed him? Can Reno be blamed?"

None of these questions can be answered *satisfactorily*. Thus, the event is made to seem inexplicable, a "mystery," and Custer, himself, a "paradox," a hero or a fool, a seemingly contradictory figure—and these unanswerable questions take the place of those questions which might provide broader historical interpretation.

The truth of the matter may be that the defeat of Custer on the Montana prairie is imminently explainable. Very simply, he meant to wipe out the United Sioux, a superb military force, a nation of people who had signed solemn treaties with the United States of America as sovereigns and who, within a decade, began to understand the perilousness of the treaty process and were now desperate to defend themselves, their way of life, their homelands. If one grasps that basic fact, one can move on to understand the contemporary lives of the Lakota/Dakota people, their politics, their communal motives and actions.

The contrived inexplicability of Wounded Knee has contributed for too long to a historical and intellectual denial which has remained central to racial disharmony and inequality in a region where reconciliation is critical to the future lives of the people who live there. Legal precedent rises out of the way historical experience is interpreted; thus, out of the so-called incomprehensible Custer fiction comes the license for genocide and land theft. A mere fourteen years after Custer's timely death was deemed "mysterious" by the word searchers, the killing of unarmed Minneconjou occurred and another "mystery" was created. The unanswerable questions were asked: "Who fired the first shot?" "How did it happen?" "Was it 357 or 380 or 150 who died there?" By posing the unanswerable questions over and over again in a deliberate historiography an incomprehensibility is created that makes it impossible for earthly light to be shed on the Wounded Knee reality.

Meaning in our shared histories cannot continue to be obscured if this great experiment in democracy is to have a stable future. The slaughter of unarmed Indians at Wounded Knee is what white America has done. That deed represents, as some recent Indian historians have suggested, the sin at the core of the culture. It must be seen as a constant reminder of what white America might do again. It must be seen as the reason for oppressive

legislation, continued land and resource theft, as well as dangerous and inappropriate legal maneuvering in federal Indian policy.

There has never been a point in American history, so far, at least, when
the ultimate sacrifice of Indian lives for the "greater good" was not
justified by the word searchers. If the children and grandchildren of both
Whites and Indians in the United States are taught nothing else about our
concomitant histories, they must be taught that, for those who profess to
teach virtue know that the continuation of historical lies is the most dangerous of all human pursuits. During the period of 1990 and 1991, the legislative battle for a monument continued. It was, after all, a centennial period. The ride, led by the visionaries of the tribes intent upon
commemorating the journey, was a story in itself, a reminder that indigenous peoples all over the world, in protecting themselves and their histories, are protecting something that is precious to all humankind, the right
to possess memory and imagination.

The Lakotas found themselves in the national and international spotlight, and the possibility that the public might both assist and harm them
now became a realization. A study of alternatives requested by the WKSA
at the September 25, 1990, hearing was finally authorized by the Department of Interior. South Dakota tourism associations scheduled meetings
on the reservations in anticipation of making huge sums of money. Newspaper reporters and editors who wanted to become the new storytellers,
word searchers, and image makers of every kind converged on tiny ham-
lets where people lived hitherto unnoticed lives.

The WKSAs worried that the political reality of their quest for a monument might now be swallowed up in the tumult of a contrived story. They
knew better than most that the cult of personality in terms of Indian history often masked truths. They had seen it happen before, of course,
when, in 1973, a public appetite for Indians came into the homelands and
created an imagined "militant era" instead of understanding the events of
the time in terms of predictable political action. They saw the public producing the American Indian Movement media stars in the "spirit of Crazy
Horse" as foremost tribal spokespersons. They saw the events of that era
labeled "Wounded Knee II." Their relatives had seen the public create "the
most powerful Indian in the plains" in an 1880 epic of vast historical proportions at the same time the people's land was stolen. Now, they wondered, would Wounded Knee provide a spiritual universe for America's re-
demption while crimes against them went unavenged? In spite of the
publicity spotlight now upon them, the task for the Survivors' Associa-

tions and their tenacious attorney remained: how can we protect our history? how can we honor our deceased relatives? how can we keep from quarreling amongst ourselves? how can we sustain ourselves through the coming struggles for the sake of the children?

DIARY: DECEMBER 30, 1990

> *I had dinner this evening with my wife and Suzan Shown Harjo. During our conversation, Suzan indicated that she knew Senator Daniel Inouye, chairman of the SSCIA, was not happy about the final language in S.C.R. 153, and the deletion of the word "apology," asking, "isn't this a little weak?"*

DIARY: DECEMBER 31, 1990

> *After my wife and I took Suzan Shown Harjo to the Rapid City Regional airport to catch her plane to Washington, D.C., I called Paul Putz of the South Dakota Historical Preservation Office to discuss the Survivors' Associations' objections to the Wyss feasibility study. He admitted that the Wyss study does not include a memorial as such, and that the massacre site, itself, would be the memorial. I told him that the Survivors' Associations simply would not support any plan that did not include a memorial, and that it must be left to the descendants of Chief Big Foot's band to define what type of memorial will be placed at the mass grave site. I told him the Wyss study was outrageous and had very little input from the WKSAs. He became angry and defensive, saying that the WKSAs had sufficient input. I told him that my clients would never agree to the idea that the massacre site, itself, would be the memorial and that we needed to further deal with this matter. I suggested that we schedule meetings on the Cheyenne River and Pine Ridge Reservations to discuss the Wyss study with members of the Survivors' Associations.*

CHRONICLE

Volume 1—*Inventory of the Wounded Knee Feasibility Study*—was published November 30, 1988, and volume 2—*Preliminary Concepts*—was published September 15, 1990. These projects were sponsored by the Oglala Sioux Parks and Recreation Authority and funded with federal monies from the National Park Service and the Department of Interior, through the South Dakota State Historical Preservation Office. They were put together by Rapid City architects and design associates from Montana and Utah.

In the minds of the descendants of the survivors the intrusion of what
became the focus of the Wyss study soon became unacceptable. They said
it reflected views contrary to the goals of the Survivors' Associations,
which had in mind a kind of Vietnam War Memorial *with the names of the
victims enshrined on it,* not a memorial which excused the United States
for its crime nor a memorial which would take their land.

The "historical significance" of the Wounded Knee Massacre, as far as
the Wyss study was concerned, was said to be (a) that it was the last
conflict between the U.S. government and the Sioux Nation, (b) that the
Ghost Dance religion was eliminated from the Lakota Sioux, (c) that the
Sacred Hoop of the Sioux Nation was broken, (d) that the Indian people's
dream died, and (e) that the Wounded Knee site is considered the symbol
of the fight for freedom by all Indian Nations. Though Wounded Knee is,
in fact, the single most notorious Indian placename in the United States
and worldwide, the association members felt the Wyss study missed the
point. Various other narratives were provided by the South Dakota Historical Preservation Office, stories said to be "generally accepted" by both Indians and historians. Few agreed to the list cited above as the "most
significant" aspects of Wounded Knee. It was not a "conflict," they said. It
was a "crime," and they wanted that said.

In spite of wide Indian consultation, no mention of the criminal nature
of the killings at Wounded Knee by the American military appeared in
these thematic renderings nor was its connection to the theft of the Black
Hills focused upon. In the bibliography which followed there was not a
single reference to the work of Indians such as Vine Deloria, Jr., nor to any
of the oral histories of tribal storytellers which are now available in various repositories around the country. All citations were to white historians
and the story took on an attitude of benign objectivity.

Two controversies seem to have been inherent in the findings from the
beginning: first, the matter of "acquisition" of lands by the federal government, lands which have been tribal, "trust," deeded, and/or allotted over a
period of one hundred years but which must assume a new status during
the memorial building; and second, the single most important matter of
"interpretation."

The federally mandated procedure for "acquisition" of lands at the
Wounded Knee site is called "Condemnation of Allotted Lands by Indian
Tribes," and such lands would immediately become part of the "trust"
land holdings of the federal government. It seemed to many at the time of
this discussion, that this would be in direct conflict with the current effort

to have federal lands "returned" to tribal ownership status as the Black Hills case seeks to do. How the federal government has come to possess Indian lands has always been a matter of some anxiety for the Sioux Nation and for First Nations across the United States. So, the effort to "condemn" ownership and "acquire" title or lease would prove to be a very complex and controversial matter in the national monument project.

The National Park Service put out a release describing Zuni-Cíbola National Historical Park "leasehold agreement" *as a model.*[13] The language indicated: "A review of the draft leasehold agreement and the Park's legislation should clarify whatever misunderstandings. The intent of Congress was to provide the Zuni Tribe the authority to remain fully involved in the planning and management of the national historical park. It is anticipated that the Zuni people will take a major role in all park educational programs."

In the Zuni-Cíbola model, an advisory commission would be set up, and cooperative agreements would be provided for training tribal members. The Zuni Tribe would lease to the National Park Service (NPS) five separate parcels of land, total acreage of less than eight hundred acres. The lease would be for ninety-nine years, with a review every three years. The legislation would prevent payment of rent, but tribes would receive "significant economic benefits" such as employment and sales of goods.

As the Wyss study and the Zuni-Cíbola model became available to the general Lakota public, there seemed to be important and significant objections from various constituencies, and tribal discussions began anew at the local level. Sometimes the discussions were rhetorical, heated, and angry. At other times they were based on history. One great fear was that the grassroots people would lose control of the effort and it would be taken over by whites, scholars, and anthropologists, by the bureaucracies, by the federal and state governments whose main interest was, as it always had been, a whitewash.

As Gonzalez and Eaglestaff and others read and reread the documents and others like them being made available by the bureaucracies involved, they discussed the interpretive role of the proposed monument. Their own interpretation, they held, was critical.

The government report (in error) indicated that "the majority of the Wounded Knee Massacre Site is located on deeded lands as recorded in Fall River County, with various claims to ownership of some of these lands by families of Wounded Knee Survivors and possibly others." There was no critical discussion of this matter as a consequence of the failed and corrupt federal Indian policy of the era, nor any discussion of the Peace

Treaty of 1868, nor of the religious freedom issues involved. Thus, many observers felt that the history being utilized was, again, a history of denial.

It is in the tribes (Indian Nations) that our rights reside, you can hear the traditional philosophers of the Sioux saying in their conversations with one another. Thus, the ethical idea of the precedence of tribal, communally held lands over individually held lands was the part of the discussion. This matter quickly emerged as an argument of some substance when some tribal members began to assert their individual needs and concerns. The hated Allotment Act of the nineteenth century which broke up communal, tribal lands and changed life on the Plains forever was forgotten as a crime against the communal, tribal notion concerning land "ownership." The disagreements among tribal members on issues of this kind are long-standing. Some scholars, among them Michael L. Lawson who wrote *Dammed Indians,* have suggested that the Allotment Act (sometimes called the Dawes Severalty Act of 1887) was the single most devastating piece of legislation ever inflicted upon Indian Nationhood. In this case, one can see clearly the resulting land problems—checkerboarding, land loss, a fragmented land base, and heirship estates of fractionated interests so small as to be useless to a tribal economy or development.

DIARY: JANUARY 3, 1991

Sam Eaglestaff ended up in the IHS Hospital at Eagle Butte right after the Wounded Knee ceremonies. I am very concerned about his health. Time is running out for Sam, I think.

Tom Daschle (in an interview) said that he is making the national monument at Wounded Knee "his personal priority"!

Joe Horn Cloud called for a status report on our lobbying efforts. I gave him an update.

DIARY: JANUARY 13, 1991

Sam called and said he plans to attend the January 15 Survivors' Association meeting. He asked me to stop by his daughter's home and pick up the alternator for his vehicle, and bring it to Manderson (where his vehicle broke down). Out on the reservations this time of year it is difficult for Indian people to keep their vehicles in good running condition, especially for people like Sam, who do not always have access to auto parts.

The Wounded Knee Centennial Commission, which was organized to coordinate the 100-year anniversary activities for the last year, will be dissolved since its work is now completed.

DIARY: FEBRUARY 28, 1991

Irv Mortensen, superintendent of the Badlands National Park, indicates that a March planning meeting will be held in Denver, Colorado, to discuss the Wounded Knee study of alternatives, and NPS is putting together a list of people to serve as consultants. He requested permission to submit my name for the list even though some people involved in the project regard me as a "troublemaker." Nonetheless, he thought I truly represented my clients' interests. I gave him permission to submit my name.

The Wall Street Journal, *no less, is quoting from the Wyss feasibility study that the massacre site itself will be the memorial. I informed Neva Grant of the National Public Radio in Washington, D.C. (who had picked up the story) that the statement that the Survivors' Associations back this study is false. It appears that we must now engage in damage control and inform everyone that the Survivors' Associations do not support the study.*

DIARY: MARCH 14, 1991

Avis Little Eagle of the Lakota Times *called today to verify the* Wall Street Journal *article. I articulated the Survivors' Associations' position on the Wyss feasibility study for a corrective article.*

DIARY: APRIL 1, 1991

Assisted Marie Not Help Him with her testimony for the United Nations hearing on treaty rights violations held in Rapid City today. She testified on the 1890 Wounded Knee Massacre as a violation of human rights.

DIARY: APRIL 6, 1991

Under traditional Lakota government, individuals were selected to lead based on their proven abilities. Thus, the very best leaders were placed in positions of authority. These individuals practiced Lakota virtues of honesty, bravery, generosity, humility, etc. and maintained the utmost respect of the people.

Under the 1934 Indian Reorganization Act, tribal leaders are selected on a one-man, one-vote principle. Leadership is based on political campaigns in which candidates make promises they can't keep. Under the IRA governments, the worst people are often selected to lead because they develop the ability to tell people what they want to hear for votes even though they lack leadership qualities.

Under traditional government, a leader was required to take a neutral stance (despite his personal views) and was able to mediate intratribal disputes. Under the IRA governments, leaders are unable to do this since the system forces them to take a partisan stance on issues. They become part of the problem and are not able to mediate disputes.

Today, tribal leadership under IRA governments isn't based on the ability to lead, it is based on the ability to control people. Many tribal council members believe that they must be in control of every aspect of the lives of reservation people. They have become governments of the council, by the council, and for the council. Thus, some tribal council members want to seize control of the WKSAs' lobbying effort rather than work with the WKSAs to make the national monument a reality.

At a WKSA meeting in Manderson today we discussed two proposed resolutions which will be coming before the April 15–16 meeting of the Oglala Sioux Tribal Council which illustrates this point.

The most important resolution is called a generic resolution which councilman Mike Her Many Horses will present to place control of the Black Hills Claim, the proposed Wounded Knee legislation, and other unspecified items in the tribal council itself.

The WKSA will oppose the resolution since the proposed Wounded Knee bill involves the Minneconjou on the Cheyenne River Reservation, not just the Oglala Sioux Tribe. The resolution is inappropriate and will cause needless friction between the tribal council and the Survivors' Associations.

The WKSAs are also against the resolution because it fails to take into consideration the work we have done so far. It took the Survivors' Associations a considerable amount of time, energy, and money to build up support for the proposed legislation.

The second resolution asks for $100,000 to do a tribal study of the development of the Wounded Knee national park and memorial. This is proposed by Eddie Little Sky of the Oglala Sioux Parks and Recreation Authority which desires a P.L. 93-638 contract, to conduct a study.

The WKSA also opposes the second resolution since the $125,000 already appropriated for the NPS study of alternatives was a direct result of the WKSA efforts. A bill will not be passed by Congress without this study. There is no need for a separate tribal study.

At the meeting Claudia Iron Hawk Sully said that we should "leave well enough alone, since we already have a good relationship with the Cheyenne River and Oglala Sioux Tribal Councils, Wounded Knee District Council, and local groups. The last thing we need now is the division which this resolution is sure to cause. It will undermine relationships already established."

Belva Hollow Horn, treasurer of the WKSA, added that two identical, separate studies occurring at the same time would duplicate energy and costs. She said that the WKSA should not, however, "oppose the Parks and Recreation Authority in getting 638 monies to cover its costs and expenses in participating in the federal study."

CHRONICLE

The "638 monies" referred to here are funds made possible by P.L. 93-638, commonly known as the Indian Self-Determination Act of 1975, which can be applied for by tribal entities since the mid-seventies.[14] The Lyndon Johnson administration, when it set up the Office of Economic Opportunity legislation, began discussions concerning "self-determination." Johnson was the first president to highlight "self-determination" as a basic objective of his national Indian policy. He set up the National Council on Indian Opportunity, which lasted through the first administration of President Richard Nixon but was dissolved by President Ford in late 1973.

When the resolution was passed by the Oglala Sioux Tribal Council, word came from Clara Spotted Elk that Congressman Johnson, Senator Daschle, and Senator Inouye supported it and word went out that Gonzalez was being accused of "shooting from the hip" on the resolution in that it wouldn't cause that much damage.

It did what Gonzalez predicted, however, in damaging the relationships already established. Almost immediately, Melvin Garreau of the Minneconjou at Eagle Butte, in expressing his anger, threatened the outrageous act of having the bodies of the Minneconjou relatives exhumed and reburied on the Cheyenne River Sioux Reservation. The Grey Eagle Society, made up of elderly Lakotas from both tribes, began to gather to see how it would be best to confront the Oglala Sioux Tribal Council on the resolution.

Eddie Little Sky and others, when asked about the resolution, said that the main thing was to have the tribe dealing on a government-to-government basis, that it was a matter of sovereignty. He said that the Wounded Knee Associations would remain a part of it all, that it was not their intention to "take over" or take "the lead." He said he supposed he would catch a lot of "heat" but it had to be government-to-government dealings. There was an agreement that community meetings should be held at Red Shirt Table, Oglala, Slim Buttes, Wounded Knee, Manderson, Porcupine, Wakpamni Lake, Kyle, Wanblee, Pass Creek, LaCreek, and Sharps Corner. Since criticism against tribal governments is that they are notorious for being "mouthpieces" for the federal government, Little Sky's speech was met with skepticism.

DIARY: APRIL 18, 1991

The Oglala Sioux Tribal Council meeting today was interesting. No action was taken on the Cheyenne River Sioux Tribe's request that the Oglala Sioux Tribal Council rescind the resolutions. There were expressions of regret. Mike Her Many Horses said he was disturbed by statements that the Cheyenne River Sioux would even think of having the bodies removed. Charlie White Elk cautioned "patience," saying that the survivors are all of our relatives.

Duane Brewer, in a defiant mood, asked "Why should we start shaking in our shoes when another tribe [meaning the Minneconjous] starts threatening us?" He said no one would allow it. White Elk again called for patience, saying that it was not a matter of "shaking in our shoes," it was that we are traditionally seven council fires and must come together on these issues.

OST chairman Salway was very disturbed by the actions of the council. Gregg Borland, chairman of the Cheyenne River Sioux Tribe, backed the grassroots movement and was quoted in the Lakota Times *as saying: "The position of our Tribe is the same as the Wounded Knee Survivors' Association's position on the proposed legislation."*

CHRONICLE

As the Cheyenne River Sioux began public discussions, more hostilities were expressed. Terry Fiddler, a nationally known traditional dancer and tribal political activist, asked the questions which were on everyone's mind: "Why does Pine Ridge get a museum and Cheyenne River does not?" and "Why aren't there any *traditional* Indians on the Advisory Commission?"

In spite of some optimism of the moment concerning the overall project, open opposition from the Indian critics of the Wounded Knee legislation was at this time becoming public and it would serve to give the legislative components in Washington, D.C., never themselves entirely persuaded of the importance of the project, reason to delay and question. Valid concerns about the oppressive role of the National Park Service were at the center of the public controversy. Their employees and directors were all over western South Dakota, holding meetings in Indian and White communities alike. To some it seemed that the need or the legitimacy of the memorial on tribal terms was not the focus of the discussions, rather it was turning to tourism and economics.

The institution of the National Park Service came into existence in 1916. The bureaucracy known as the Forest Service was initiated in 1905 as a result of the expansionist policies of President Theodore Roosevelt. Both agencies have a long and troubling history of intervention and public service activities. They are often accused by the tribes across the country of taking Indian lands for the "public domain," giving out ecologically questionable leasing and grazing rights, "managing" tree farms and selling timber, building roads for logging, promoting widespread camping and tourist activities, and, in general, representing some kind of public interest to the detriment of the economic health of the Indian tribes from whom the land originates. In Sioux Country these bureaucracies are seen as supporting public activities which menace and ultimately destroy the spiritual places and activities and economies of tribal people.

In actual practice, these federal agencies, one in Agriculture and the other in Interior, are quite different. Though they have different mandates in the lexicon of federal interventions, their distinctions are often blurred in their dealings with Indians and their motivations are suspect.

If it was not the intent of the National Park Service and the Forest Service to become aggressor and enemy of tribal land possession, they have nonetheless acquired status and influence in Indian Country through the onerous "Indians do not own nor use the land anyway" concept. In this case, it becomes one of the many ironies of contemporary Indian life that the tribes are now forced to kowtow to the interests of the NPS and the Forest Service in achieving their goals, another example of the kind of colonial system which is at the heart of any tribal struggle.

By spring, 1991, when Wyss Associates had made the second volume of the study widely available and it had been examined for several months by many Indians, several "preliminary concepts" had emerged and were becoming the subject of much controversy, because they raised questions of "land acquisition" by the federal entities as well as of the nature of the "interpretive schemes" which seemed to be foremost in the minds of the planners.

Four alternatives were developed by Wyss, each plan to be preceded by a site-specific archeological investigation:

Concept A—NO ACTION provides no improvements to the deteriorating
infrastructures, and leaves in place those features that interfere with the
ability to educate the public about Wounded Knee.

Concept B—INTERPRETIVE AUTO-LOOP relocates existing roads, provides an orientation center remote from the actual massacre site; provides paved interpretive hiking trails on the site; and locates the
Wounded Knee memorial.

Concept C—INTERPRETIVE TRAILS relocates existing roads, provides an
orientation center outside of the preliminary landmark boundaries;
provides paved interpretive hiking trails on the site; and locates the
Wounded Knee memorial.

Concept D—ON SITE ORIENTATION CENTER provides an orientation
center and memorial with the closest overview of the massacre site but
separate from the cemetery; provides an optional interpretive auto-
loop; and relocates existing on-site roads.

Management options called for strictly enforcing the development of
existing zoning regulations at the site, as well as initiating negotiations between the tribal council and the National Park Service to address NPS
management with unspecified tribal "involvement."

♦

Almost immediately a vicious debate about the wisdom of any of the
plans took place in Indian circles. Many argued that the implementation
of any of the options in the plan would not only damage their right to interpret the massacre *as a crime of genocide* but would take the site itself out
of their jurisdiction and put it in the hands of federal governmental institutions and bureaucracies.

The future of the memorial seemed in jeopardy, and the conciliatory
language which was traditional of those who spoke for the seven council
fires of the Sioux took on a shrillness that could be heard throughout the
prairie hills.

PART 3

Wocowoyake
(True Stories)

(April 30, 1991–October 12, 1991)

When there is no longer that fit between worldview and
religion, between reality as it is defined and as it is lived
we have reactions ranging from millennial dreams to
violent revolution, all designed to reestablish a reasonable,
integrated life.

Alfonso Ortiz, Tewa anthropologist (quoted in *The Sacred:
Ways of Knowledge, Sources of Life,* ed. Peggy V. Beck, Anna Lee
Walters, and Nia Francisco, p. 166)

CHRONICLE

Another hearing before the U.S. Senate Select Committee on Indian Affairs would take place at Pine Ridge on April 30, 1991, but this time there would be perceptible differences, for now there would be Indian antagonists who added their objections to the dialogue.

The legislation, rewritten, is again submitted by the Wounded Knee survivor/descendant groups and their attorney, Mario Gonzalez. It is, again, draft legislation which would be circulated to Senate and House members.[1]

The process, like floes or glaciers during the Ice Age, moves relentlessly.

♦

American social scientists have made various studies of the weapons used by the truly powerless.[2] They seldom, however, discuss intertribal struggles for empty power with any degree of clarity. The Sioux, on the other hand, are quite familiar with these futile grabs for power and it has become obvious to them that no weapons are more divisive in the realm of tribal politics than those used by a diversity of opportunists (both Indian and White) who are familiar enough with tribal workings to lose no time in moving into the power vacuums which exist because of the failures inherent in modern Indian political infrastructures.

It is said that in traditional times, using traditional methods, the very best leadership was selected because the choice was always based on the person's ability to lead the people and have their confidence. During the modern era, tribes have adapted western-style governments under the IRA, in which the selection of leaders occurs under the one man/one vote principle. There are those who say this precept, while it may work for other societies, only causes chaos in tribal governments because it cares only about who wins and who loses, not about true consensus.

In addition, because there is little concrete federal or international support for the tribal governments formed in 1934 through the Indian Reorganization Act, and because there is always an impasse created during any negotiations (which confirms the suspicion that federal/state/tribal governments have about one another), there is often a power vacuum into which any interloper may come. Recently, there has been an international effort on the part of the Sioux Nation to develop treaty defense alliances and to organize defense strategies for treaty tribes in the United States, but even this effort has come up against the negative power of colonizing nations. These realities have made issues of legislation and development on native homelands ripe for internal dissension and conflict, all the while contributing to the weakening of struggling tribal governments. The crisis in Indian leadership can be confronted only if the legitimacy of tribal governments is acknowledged. As long as state governments choose to quibble over jurisdiction and as long as the feds continue as colonial holders of land, the crisis will only become more profound.

When Lakota and Dakota treaty and historical organizations which have existed for a hundred years are treated by state and federal officials as pariahs and by the media as circuses, any outside group may form, imitating and usurping the real tribal authority, however ineffectual they may be in the broader scheme of things. These outside, inchoate, and oftentimes self-serving organizations solicit funding from unwary sources, stretch the truth about their connections to legitimate tribal entities, create ideological responses that are often far removed from the cultural realities of the people, attempt to set policy, and, in general, create unnecessary chaos and unrealistic expectations.

During the early spring and summer of 1991, a group calling themselves the Black Feather Council made an attempt to seize power during what they viewed as a period of inactivity and uncertainty. Without tribal sanction, this council had presented arguments for sovereignty to the U.N. Working Group on Indigenous Populations in Geneva, Switzerland. Their official letterhead, claiming member bands and tribes as Hunkpapa, Oglala, Minneconjou, Itazipo, Oohenumpa, Brule, Sicangu, Yankton, Sihasapa, and Santee, read "Lakota, a Sovereign Nation Re-established at Bear Butte, July 14, 1991." Their address was given as Lakota National Organizing Committee, 638 E. Blvd., N. Suite B, Rapid City, S.D., 57701. Richard Grass,

Bernard Peoples, Chris Fire Thunder, and Tony Black Feather were said to be the spokespersons. Before the summer was over, the denunciation of this group would become front page news, and progress toward a memorial would be mired down in serious conflict. Author David Seals was active in this effort.

DIARY: APRIL 30, 1991

Today I attended the Senate Select Committee hearing on our proposed legislation at Pine Ridge. The Honorable Thomas A. Daschle presided. He began with the passive introduction, in which he glossed over the intentional killing of the unarmed men, women, and children of Chief Big Foot's band of Minneconjou. We all know that the soldiers of the Seventh Cavalry had hangovers the morning of the massacre, from the whiskey brought in by a trader for the purpose of celebrating the "capture" of Chief Big Foot, and that they were seeking vengeance for their defeat at the Battle of the Little Bighorn in 1876.

William Horn Cloud and Oliver Red Cloud were not on the list of witnesses invited to present testimony. During the hearing (when it was nearly finished) Oliver Red Cloud came up to me with an angry expression on his face and said that William Horn Cloud was being excluded from presenting testimony; that he should be one of the main people speaking. I communicated his comments to Marie Not Help Him and suggested that she ask Pete Taylor to place them on the agenda. Taylor agreed to allow them to present testimony.

Both William and Oliver spoke in English, an indication that their comments were mainly directed toward the public officials present. In the end, Horn Cloud gave supportive testimony but Oliver said "I'm against this." This kind of divisiveness has an adverse impact on people like Daschle who really don't understand that Oliver's opposition to our proposed legislation is based on his personal dislike for Celane Not Help Him and her daughter Marie (who support it).

Later, I called Melvin Garreau at Eagle Butte and reported to him on the proceedings, I told him that I was unhappy with Oliver Red Cloud's testimony. That he has no sense of history. That it was Chief Red Cloud who invited Chief Big Foot to Ridge in 1890 and failed to assist him when he was surrounded by the Seventh Cavalry, and now it is his great-grandson Oliver that is doing everything in his power to prevent Chief Big Foot's people from getting the U.S. government to atone for the massacre.

This was what Daschle said when he opened the April 30, 1991, hearing:

> According to accounts, in the course of attempting to collect the arms of Chief Big Foot and his band, *a shot was fired* [emphasis added] by an unknown person. Soldiers on ridges opened fire with their Hotchkiss guns. General panic ensued, and when the so-called Battle of Wounded Knee was over, more than 300 Sioux Indian men, women and children lay dead or wounded. Sixty troops were also killed or wounded, many by the fire of their own forces. There can be no question that the military forces lost control. It is entirely proper that the consequences be described as a massacre.
>
> Last year in the 101st Congress, both the Senate and the House of Representatives adopted a resolution, Senate Concurrent Resolution 153, expressing the *deep regret* of the U.S. of America to the descendants of the victims and survivors of the Wounded Knee Massacre and the respective tribal communities, and expressing the support of Congress for the establishment of a suitable and appropriate memorial to those who were so tragically slain at Wounded Knee. To facilitate consideration of such legislation, I join with the Chair of the Senate Select Committee on Indian Affairs, Senator Inouye, in a letter seeking comment on draft legislation prepared by counsel for the Wounded Knee Survivors' Association [*sic*] of Pine Ridge and Cheyenne River to establish a national park and memorial at Wounded Knee.

Daschle further stated: "The purpose of our hearing today is to consider the proposed legislation. We have an excellent group of witnesses and I'm pleased that as we open the hearing this morning we have the opportunity to call upon our leaders on two of the reservations: Harold Salway, the president of the Oglala Sioux Tribe of Pine Ridge, and Gregg Bourland, the chairman of the Cheyenne River Sioux Tribe in Eagle Butte."

Harold Salway's testimony was 100 percent supportive of the legislation. Gregg Bourland was not so supportive of the bill "*as is.*" He said that the Cheyenne River Sioux Tribal Council had a meeting and agreed to support the draft with a few conditions. Senator Daschle said that was understandable and when a new draft is presented it usually is subject to changes.

The dialogue went on:

> SENATOR DASCHLE   Let me ask any one of the panel members who is currently before the committee if they could explain the joint management agreement on the Badlands Park or the old Pine Ridge gunnery site. How does it work? Has it been a beneficial plan? Has it worked fairly well? What overall thoughts do you have on that?
>
> MR. GONZALEZ: Mr. Chairman. I would like to respond to that question. The joint management plan between the Oglala Sioux Tribe and the National Park Service resulted from a 1968 Act of Congress and before I get into that Act, I'll give you the background.

In 1942, the U.S. Department of Defense condemned an area in the northwestern part of the Pine Ridge Reservation. I think it is [48] miles by 12½ miles, for a gunnery range during World War II. Throughout the years many of the Lakota family members lobbied Congress to have their lands returned to them. Finally, in 1968, Congress passed an act which created what is now the south unit of the Badlands National Park, composed of both tribal lands and individually-owned lands. The former owners were given an option to either take life estates or [submarginal] lands off the gunnery range [but on] the reservation.

Once Phase I of that plan was completed, which was allowing former owners to obtain their life estates or take new lands on the reservation, then the act went into Phase II. Phase II is what is pertinent here today. Under Phase II, the act provided that the tribe and the National Park Service . . . enter into a cooperative agreement and, under that agreement, all of the Federal lands in the south [unit would be] transferred to the tribe, so that the south unit is now totally owned by the tribe.

Part of the agreement was that the lands would be jointly managed as part of the Badlands National Park. . . . It governs such things as hunting and fishing, the tribe would develop some of the [sites] with gate receipts from the park . . . which was additional income for the tribe to construct and maintain parks throughout the reservation. So there is a lot of benefit that has resulted from that agreement between the National Park Service and the tribe, and the proposal that we have submitted here today would be similar, in that the lands here would be totally owned by the tribe also. It would be different in some respects, in that you would have an advisory committee actually consulting with the Secretary of the Interior to manage it. But, essentially, it's joint management.

. . . .

SENATOR DASCHLE: Thank you for that explanation. Could you talk a little bit about the need for condemnation proceedings in a plan such as this? To what degree do you think condemnation is necessary? Is it essential? Is it a tool that would be helpful? Do you think it would be required?

MR. GONZALEZ: Yes, Senator. As you probably have noticed, Zuni-Cíbola doesn't have any provisions for condemnation, yet we inserted a provision for condemnation in our legislative proposal to give the Secretary of Interior some flexibility. There [are 40] acres of deeded land owned by nonmembers of the tribe and, hopefully, the Secretary will be able to purchase that tract and transfer title of that tract to the Oglala Sioux [Tribe], [a]nd then, lease it back from the tribe over a 99 year period with possible extensions of the lease.

. . . in the event that the owners of that tract do not want to sell, then the Secretary would have an option to initiate condemnation proceedings to ac-

quire [it]. It's a very indispensable part of the park. It's located right adja-
cent to the mass grave area to the south. And we, the Survivors' Associations, feel that the tract should certainly be included in the proposed park.

SENATOR DASCHLE: I have no further questions. If there are no further comments . . .

MR. GONZALEZ: Senator. We . . . request that Suzan Harjo be allowed to make
a comment for the record.

SUZAN HARJO: I'm from the Tsitsitas Hodulgee, Muscogee, Cheyenne and
Creek Nations, and I'm here as the representative, the Washington representative, of the Wounded Knee Survivors' Associations and I am privileged to
be here with this group.

I would like to comment on the Park Service written testimony, although
some of my questions have been answered in brief discussion with Jerry
Rogers. With all due respect to my friend here who gave some very interesting answers, I asked about the line here in the Park Service testimony saying
that Wounded Knee *ended the American frontier and signaled the transformation of Indian Sovereignty,* and, like a good administrator, he owned up to
the statement but said he had no idea where it came from.

CHRONICLE

It was difficult to say what if anything had changed since 1985, when the
people of the survivor/descendant organizations had started their work.
Much of what Senator Daschle had to say this day and what others have
had to say about this matter over the years characterizes the massacre (or,
in their terms, still a battle) as a "tragedy." And it is worth trying to understand the use of that term both literally and otherwise.

In the classical and literary sense, *tragedy* is drama which depicts a protagonist engaged in what is often called "a morally significant struggle." It
usually ends in the protagonist's ruin or death, out of which comes some
great human understanding. The "gods," of course, are involved. And so is
"Fate." Until the United States abandons her notion of white/Euro immigrant specialness and her truisms concerning the historical moral obligation
to dispossess Indians, it will be impossible for the Wounded Knee killing to
be analyzed appropriately or reflected upon in its horrific actuality.

One of the most important characteristics of tragedy is that events
must be outside of the parameters of "human" control. That's what makes
the cumulative events tragedy and not just a sad story. In tragedy things
happen that humans could not have known about, or done anything
about. In *Romeo and Juliet,* the Shakespearean tragedy that almost everyone has read, for example, Romeo doesn't have some vital information

about Juliet's scheme, the priest who is carrying that information, the message, fails to get the message to him (ah! fate!), and so Romeo kills himself because he mistakenly thinks Juliet is dead. Alas! Humans, you see, in accordance with this pattern, cannot control everything about their lives, thus, tragic events occur. And the gods, after all, must have respect from mere mortals because they can turn on you for reasons you cannot fathom.

This is the context in which the word *tragedy* is used in Indian history. The remarkable thing about this kind of history is that it releases everyone from responsibility except the gods. What Lakotas have argued throughout the century is that, on the contrary, human beings were, indeed, in control of events at Wounded Knee, that there was then and still is a policy inherent in the American philosophy toward them which has systematically denied them justice. It may at one time or another have been a policy of removal, or a policy of genocide, or a policy of assimilation, or a policy of dispossession. The argument is that there has always been such a thing as federal Indian policy, since before the first treaties were signed, thus, people and institutions can be held responsible to history. Lakotas point out that it was Custer's old command, after all, and the peace treaties had already been signed, and there was no state of war which existed at the time of the mass killing. These were things humans knew then and they know now. People are responsible, not the gods nor Fate, for Wounded Knee.

Listening to Senator Daschle's anachronistic rendering of the event was, therefore, painful for many in his audience.

In the document eventually published on this hearing, the language reads: "The events of December 1890 at Wounded Knee have in recent times taken on symbolic significance as representing the culmination of more than four centuries of cultural conflict. For some, it has been viewed as the final days of a great nation, the Sioux Nation, as well as the end of the American frontier and the transformation of Indian sovereignty. For others, it represents the loss of control over their lands and even their own destiny."[3] Though Harjo didn't follow up too much on this line of discussion, her initial comment here illustrated her deep distrust of the motives of the NPS, a distrust shared by the Sioux whom she represented.

HARJO (cont'd): My suggestion is that someone in the depths of the National Park Service has taken a look at the Canyon de Chelly National Monument in the Arizona agreement and the Zuni-Cíbola agreement, upon which the legislation before you is based, and has seen the difference in that a greater measure of . . . that the Zuni-Cíbola legislation would accord a greater measure of the exercise of Indian sovereignty jurisdictionally, as opposed to Canyon de Chelly legislation, which the Park Service cites.

I wanted to indicate our understanding of what the primary difference is in the Zuni-Cíbola legislation, in its joint-management scheme, and further, that, so that the ownership issue is absolutely clear. There would never be a question as to who owns this area, as there is a question, regarding Canyon de Chelly. So, the Zuni-Cíbola model in the legislation before you is the one that we would be most interested in.

On the issue of condemnation, we're very well aware that the Office of Management and Budget dislikes condemnation and always goes with the willing seller/willing buyer, unless it is Indian land, in which case there's always the willingness to condemn. We would suggest that this is one place where condemnation procedures do need to be entered into over the objections of the OMB.

CHRONICLE

Land ownership issues are rarely on the agendas at those meetings between Sioux Indian and White U.S. politicians; usually they talk about poverty and alcoholism, 638 contracts, and "tragedies" and the Mni Sose Water Rights Coalition. Thus, the rancor of the aerial "gunnery range" history remained largely unspoken and Daschle seemed unaware of the complications in that history. He seemed, like a lot of white South Dakotans, to know little of the questionable dealings of the U.S. government toward the Oglalas in a case which had long been a festering sore for the Sioux.

The initial "taking" of the Oglala lands for a World War II aerial gunnery range by the U.S. government (though there were plenty of white-owned unoccupied lands which could have been used) and the failure to return those lands after the war set the stage for a 1970 protest by tribal people which started on Sheep Mountain on the northern part of the reservation (and within the proposed south unit of the Badlands National Park). The history: shortly after the bombing of Pearl Harbor in 1941, the U.S. government needed "gunnery" training ranges and, finding the Oglala lands to be appropriate for their purposes (and being very handily a historical "trustee" of those lands), gave ten days' notice to tribal people to vacate their lands, sent bombers in to strafe tribal herds and buildings before they could be moved, and, in the wartime climate, pressed ahead with its perceived needs. One of those evicted was Dewey Beard (Iron Hail), the grandfather of Celane Not Help Him, by this time an old man, who had been a prime mover in the earlier monument development and a spokes-man for the people. He was also the last living survivor of the Battle of the Little Bighorn at the time of his death, and a survivor of the 1890 Wound-ed Knee Massacre.

It was said by the Indians that after they left their homes, white people from the Wall, South Dakota, area came in and ransacked them; and white cattlemen such as a man named Duhamel managed to get near free use of the range if they were willing to take the risk. Duhamel ran cattle there "at risk" for many years and, according to Indians, "got rich" enough to be-come a corporate giant in the radio/television industry in South Dakota. Not the first, of course, to build an empire using Indian lands, but one of the most successful, they said.

Leo Wilcox, a brother to Mario Gonzalez's mother, Geneva Wilcox Gonzalez, organized the 1970 protest against the National Park Service in-trusion into the return of these lands, and the failure to return lands even af-ter two or three decades. He, along with Richard Little, Birgil Kills Straight, Dode Brown, Everett Jordon, Eugene Trimble, and Mario (who was on sum-mer break between his first and second years of law school), staged the pro-test at Sheep Mountain. He later moved it to the more visible Mount Rush-more. Once that move was made, Red Power militants, particularly Lehman Brightman from California and the Bellecourt brothers from Minnesota (and cofounders of the American Indian Movement), came in and "took over." Three years later, in March, 1973, at the height of the Wounded Knee militancy, Leo Wilcox (by this time a member of the Sioux Oglala Tribal Council) was found dead in his badly burned automobile near the Chey-enne River on Highway 44 east of Rapid City. His death has never been ex-plained to the satisfaction of his relatives, who suspected foul play.

The Sheep Mountain episode is described by some as an indication that the Lakota people's protests concerning governmental policies started long before the American Indian Movement arrived on the scene, that the Oglala people were already activists trying to effect change and that the American Indian Movement doesn't need to take all the credit for articu-lating modern tribal resistances. This is important, they say, because the *tribal meaning* of such protests during that time was often lost when the urban-based AIM began to interpret change on Indian reservations, and when tribal meaning is lost or obscured, dangerous political splits occur. The joint management plan described here by Gonzalez was set in motion even though there was considerable tribal objection at the time and many believe it continues to be less than an ideal solution. Fear of land owner-

ship in the name of the federal government or trusteeship of tribal lands
continues to be a reality to the Lakota. All trust land is held in the name of
the United States in trust for the tribe or individual Indian owner. What is
feared is when the federal government confiscates or acquires Indian land
for itself; this land is not held in trust.

Also not discussed in front of the Daschle committee hearing was the
rumor throughout the Pine Ridge area that while the military used the site
in World War II, not only did they leave significant unexploded ordnance
but there was the possibility that the government had been engaged in unrecorded and untraceable dumping of hazardous wastes at the site. To this
day, the federal government retains ownership of a 3,000-acre area in the
former gunnery range. This area was not returned to the tribe in the 1968
act because it contained too much unexploded ordnance and was too dangerous to return and too expensive to clean up. In 1995, the Oglala Sioux
Tribe received a federal grant to start the cleanup of the whole gunnery
range including the 3,000 acres. It hopes the 3,000-acre area will be returned appropriately.

As far as the condemnation of the 40-acre tract of land needed for the
Wounded Knee memorial was concerned, no one wanted to get into discussion of federal policies and procedures (considered illegal by Indians)
which allowed such treaty-protected Indian lands to be taken over by
whites, purchased and traded and stolen in the past.

This hearing, which was held after the Centennial Ride but before the
National Park Service and the State Historical Society and the other white
governmental agencies had a chance to finalize their bureaucratization of
the legislation, was a moment of clarity nonetheless, because though some
subjects were not broached, many others were. Some people took the opportunity, since the hearing was held on their home turf, to say what they
truly thought, if not about history at least about philosophical matters:

> "I want to say a few words about parks," began William Horn Cloud. "The
> Park Service would take money and set up this park system. And you might say
> it's the same as buying a piece of land, like this 'Wounded Knee.' It would be
> set aside as a park. The same thing would happen to it, like the Pipestone in
> Minnesota, set aside as a park. And, now we can't go over there as we want to
> and dig rock for our pipe. It's controlled by the Park Service. And, then, toward
> the last, Congress wasn't satisfied so they come and took our Black Hills out of
> our hands. So, if we're not allowed the land, if they get lands from the public
> domain, they could build a park. But, we can't even get a piece of post from the
> Black Hills Park."[4]

Some listening to the old man's testimony may have wondered about what his true thoughts were. Their parents and grandparents told them how they had crept into the hills from the Pine Ridge Reservation, when Rapid City was just a hay camp, in the dead of night, to get just the right kind of tipi poles for their lodges, the right kinds of limbs for the sweat lodges. Sometimes it took several days and they hid out during the daylight hours to be sure no one caught them. They did the same to pray there and, of course, still do. Even today, the telltale cloths of red and black used in Lakota ritual are found by unknowing white hikers or hunters in the area.

They heard his prediction: "Pretty soon maybe this reservation will be established as a park and in time we'll be like those animals they have . . . bears . . . and the coyotes, and all those, they'll be behind a chain-link fence. That could happen to this generation."

William Horn Cloud was caught in the middle. Some close relatives like Celane Not Help Him considered him somewhat of a traitor for marrying into the Red Cloud family when it was the old chief who had, so the story goes, enticed Big Foot into his disastrous journey and then did nothing to help him. William now supported the efforts of the Wounded Knee Survivors' Associations at a local tribal meeting he attended but he would be influenced by others at other public gatherings. Oliver Red Cloud resented Celane and her daughter Marie for any influence they might have over William, and also for "talking bad" about the old Red Cloud relative. Some felt that Oliver's opposition to the monument was influenced by these old histories.

William Horn Cloud finished his speech and left it to his relative by marriage, Oliver Red Cloud, himself old and discouraged, to talk about control. Giving the impression as he always did that he spoke for everyone, Oliver said "today, a lot of people, people that don't have no right, no business, not involved. They go in front of us, and they don't respect us. I would like to go and dig up your mamas and your grammas . . . whoever. Dig the bones itself. I would think you don't like that. That's the way the Indian people are feeling. Leave them alone. It's happened. And the War Department won't apologize. They don't recognize or respect our bill. So, what's the use talking about it? Leave the people alone."

The people, often insecure about the Red Cloud legacy, listened tentatively. They thought about the story that the old Chief Red Cloud, once a leader of the people in the war against the whites, a defender of the people at the Hundred-Soldiers-Kill Fight in 1866, after many decades had passed invited his Minneconjou relative Big Foot to Pine Ridge Agency and then didn't help him, sitting in his warm cabin while the massacre occurred. Then, a year later, the chief and his son, Jack Red Cloud, collected money under the 1891 Indian Depredations Act[5] but the Big Foot people, what was left of them, considered hostile, were left on the prairie with nothing. The people, listening to the old men talk, were saying to themselves that for the past hundred years Wounded Knee Massacre descendants have been trying to get compensation and have a national memorial established and, they asked themselves silently, who is the main person speaking against them, opposing them when they are finally about to accomplish some of their goals? Great-grandson Oliver Red Cloud. Some of the people even said this aloud and there was, then, more silence. However, even those related to Oliver listened quietly to the accusations and finally admitted sadly that such things might need to be said at this time.

Harold Salway, articulate young president of the Oglala Sioux Tribal Council at this time, and a Red Cloud relative, was a lead witness at the hearings:

> In all humility, I am Akil Nujipi. The Oglala Sioux Tribal Council fully supports the legislative proposal developed by the survivors' associations to establish the Sioux Nation Park and Memorial. We take into consideration the historical impact it would have, not only here in the United States but, also, abroad. Internationally, we must reeducate the world about what the image of the Indian is truly about and the denigrations that have occurred throughout time. We have a place to develop and that legacy that must be told has to be developed from the minds of the people. . . . On the reservations, we have people of high caliber who know what the Lakota philosophy is and how it should be intertwined with the legislative effort.[6]

When John Yellow Bird Steele of Manderson (who would soon replace Salway and, later, be replaced himself by Wilbur Between Lodges as president of the tribal council) spoke, he said:

> First, we would like the site restored to its original condition, reroute the road back to where it was at the time the Massacre occurred. Then, there are these issues:
>
> 1. We must have the Oglala point of view. We know it was a mass murder by the government forces. We want that said.
> 2. If there are jobs we want Indian people employed, a better place for our children.

3. We have opposition to the National Park Service having any jurisdiction, and,

4. The need for condemnation, there is very definitely that need."

In 1979 I, along with at the time the councilman Melvin Cumings, the tribal administrator, had $40,000 set aside through HUD on land acquisitions within that 10 (ten) tract area, to acquire the 40 acres there. We almost had it done until someone saw dollar signs and inflated the price to $4 million and said that Crazy Horse was buried there and, you know how it goes. But, we cannot, on our own . . . we have tried . . . I honestly say that we've tried . . . to acquire that land and at this time it is a safety and health hazard for the community living there and it is a safety and health hazard for all the visitors coming in here.

Steele was referring to the fact that a 40-acre tract of deeded land was still owned by the Gildersleeves, the white family who owned a trading post that was much resented on the reservation. It was said to be a safety and health hazard because AIM burned the trading post down during the 1973 Occupation and the debris from the fire still littered the ground in 1991.

He went on to say:

A couple of years ago, I remember we put up a shade by the road and we invited all different types of people down there and with all that came a Mr. Paul Putz, from the South Dakota Historical Society. We didn't know it at the time but he was counting cars that came through there within an hour's period. He saw the importance of the site of Wounded Knee being a draw for all these visitors coming through there, and, so the State of South Dakota has now taken an interest in it.

Claudia Iron Hawk Sully spoke for the Sioux when she said: "We don't want our deceased relatives exploited by those people whose sole aim is to make money off the Massacre Site."

It was clear during this period of further testimony that the people wanted to protect themselves and their relatives and they wanted to protect their land claims. In the traditional way, they talked among themselves about how to do that. The old men, Horn Cloud and Red Cloud, and all of the others with a sense of responsibility for the defense of tribal life gave their opinion. At these times, it seemed no big thing that the people sometimes saw themselves quarreling and "turning away" and making it hard for each other. This was expected. But, more than anything, the people wanted their lives to have meaning through their own stories which promised nothing except the next beginning.

DIARY: MAY 2, 1991

> Marie Not Help Him called. We discussed Terry Fiddler's request to
> Daschle that a hearing of our proposed legislation be held on the Chey-
> enne River Reservation.
>
> Salway also called to say he was disappointed with Oliver Red Cloud's
> negative testimony. Both Cheyenne River and Pine Ridge WKSA members
> agree that a joint meeting between President Harold Salway, Chairman
> Gregg Bourland, and WKSA representatives should be scheduled for the
> purpose of generating unified support for a draft bill that satisfies every-
> one's concerns.

DIARY: MAY 3, 1991

> I had a long telephone discussion with Suzan Shown Harjo today. We
> agree that many people involved with Indian affairs look for negative
> things to say about other people (rather than praising their accomplish-
> ments). Milo Yellow Hair, for example, told Suzan that Oliver Red Cloud
> opposes the Martinez Bill (H.R. 5680). I know for a fact that this state-
> ment is false since I personally know the history behind both bills (I am
> the author of both bills). Oliver supports the Martinez Bill but is opposed
> to the Bradley Bill (S. 705).[7]
>
> Both bills propose to reconvey federally held land in the Black Hills to the
> Sioux tribes. The Martinez Bill, however, addresses compensation for articles
> 5 and 8 benefits under the 1877 Black Hills Act; the Bradley Bill does not. The
> Martinez Bill is actually an amended version of the Bradley Bill.
>
> Gerald Clifford and the Black Hills Steering Committee (and their sup-
> porters) blindly support the Bradley Bill and refuse to acknowledge its short-
> comings. These shortcomings can be illustrated by the following scenario:
>
>> The year is 2019. Economic power is shifting from the United States to
>> Asia. An extremely conservative government controls the United States
>> and is looking for ways to cut federal spending for Indian tribes. An Interi-
>> or Department official (or some other bureaucrat) gets an idea that fund-
>> ing to Indian tribes can be greatly reduced by limiting the scope of the fed-
>> eral government's trust responsibility to trust landholdings. The secretary
>> of the interior issues new regulations that cut funding to tribes for general
>> assistance grants and other benefits.
>>
>> A large Indian tribe in the Southwest is angered by the secretary's ac-
>> tion and initiates a civil suit under the Administrative Procedures Act to

restore these benefits, arguing that the United States has a general trust re-
sponsibility to provide these benefits under federal common law (court-
created law).

Since "trust responsibility" is a creation of federal common law, a con-
servative U.S. Supreme Court can eliminate it or restrict its application
with the stroke of a pen. The tribal suit reaches the Supreme Court and the
Court affirms the position of the secretary. The Court rules that no general
trust responsibility has ever existed which obligates the United States to
provide general assistance funds and other benefits to tribes, and tribes are
not entitled to these funds unless they can point to an express treaty provi-
sion or federal statute granting them such rights.

The Sioux tribes believe they are protected by articles 5 and 8 of the
1877 act. They immediately initiate a civil action in federal court to restore
funding for these benefits on the basis that Congress expressly obligated it-
self to provide these benefits under articles 5 and 8 of the 1877 act which
provide in pertinent part as follows:

> *Article 5: "In consideration of the forgoing cession of territory and [hunting]*
> *rights . . . the United States does hereby agree to provide all necessary aid to as-*
> *sist the Indians in the work of civilization; . . . Also to provide the said Indians*
> *with subsistence consisting of a ration to each individual . . . or in lieu of said*
> *articles the equivalent thereof, in the discretion of the Commissioner of Indian*
> *Affairs. Such rations, or so much thereof as may be necessary to continue until*
> *the Indians are able to support themselves."*

> *Article 8: "and Congress shall, by appropriate legislation, secure to them an or-*
> *derly government; . . . and each individual shall be protected in his rights of*
> *property, person and life."*

The Supreme Court agrees with the Sioux tribes' interpretation of the
1877 act, but rules against them on the basis that the 1877 act transformed
Sioux territory and hunting rights into article 5 and 8 benefits—including
general assistance grants and other benefits. A trust responsibility was im-
posed on the federal government by the 1877 act to provide these benefits
for as long as necessary for the survival of the Sioux.

But in 1951, the Sioux tribes filed a claim in the Indian Claims Com-
mission for monetary compensation for the territory and hunting rights
confiscated by the 1877 act, territory and hunting rights that were trans-
formed into article 5 and 8 benefits. The ICC award was settled by passage
of the Bradley Bill. Under section 22 of the Indian Claims Commission
Act,[8] all Sioux claims—including claims for article 5 and 8 benefits—were

extinguished when Congress transferred 1.3 million acres of federally held land in the Black Hills back to the Sioux tribes.

The Sioux tribes quickly come to the realization that they unwittingly relinquished their claims to the article 5 and 8 benefits when they allowed the Black Hills Steering Committee to talk them into lobbying the Bradley Bill through Congress. They gave up billions of dollars worth of article 5 and 8 benefits in exchange for 1.3 million acres of federal land. If they would have supported the Martinez Bill, they would have obtained the restoration of the 1.3 million acres of Black Hills territory to the Sioux tribes while preserving their rights to articles 5 and 8 benefits.

Suzan and I also discussed the need for a condemnation provision in our proposed legislation. Condemnation may be the only means of returning the 40 acres of deeded land owned by the Gildersleeve family to tribal ownership

CHRONICLE

Who owns land in and around the massacre site has been a major obstacle. The forty acres said to be owned by the white family, Gildersleeve, seems to be a symbol of land within the reservation borders which is for one reason or another owned by people who are not tribal members. There are many versions about the Gildersleeve matter. One story, about which there is much ambiguity, is as follows:

The Gildersleeves, a family of non-Lakota landowners who have hung around the Pine Ridge Reservation for several generations, owned and operated a store on the reservation for decades and possessed an enviable collection of Indian artifacts, much of which was destroyed during the "take-over" by the American Indian Movement in 1973. They are the owners of the forty acres discussed in the Wounded Knee monument project. How the land came to be in their possession is worth noting, though there is some controversy and much rumor concerning this history.

The Wounded Knee Trading Post and Museum was established by Clive Gildersleeve and his father in about 1930. Records show that in 1934, President Franklin D. Roosevelt *granted* forty acres of land to the Gildersleeves for the purpose of trading. This was, the Oglalas say, treaty-protected land, not up for sale or trade, land possessed by them. Clive and his wife, a Chippewa, (who, it has been said, is related to the AIM brothers from Minnesota, the Bellecourts), seemed to be accepted by the people but when they sold stock to Jim and Jan Czywczynski in 1968 and it seemed obvious that there was an effort to capitalize on the grim historical killing, there was almost universal opposition to the Gildersleeves from Indians across the country. They represented, it was said then, the worst kind of exploiters. The Gildersleeves and their partners were ambitious to begin what they called "America's first privately owned national park," and the Indians were opposed to such outright marketing of their history. AIM exploited this opposition during the seventies.

After the AIM burning and trashing of the property, Czywczynski was asked by a group including the Reverend Wesley Hunter, executive director of the South Dakota Association of Christian Churches, to make an estimate of the damages and he estimated $1,025,000. When asked how much it would take to buy the corporation outright, Czywczynski said he would sell for $2,500,000 with 30 percent down and guaranteed payment or cash. Indians considered this price and this response an example of the outright greed of white people on their lands. He now owns a motel across from the Reptile Gardens outside of Rapid City on Mt. Rushmore Road.

The 1930s period, just before the passage of the Indian Reorganization Act (1934) and the setting up of the IRA tribal governments as they are known today, was an era of extraordinary exploitation and degradation of native sovereignty. But this period of exploitation began during the allotment period, starting just prior to statehood in the northern plains, by ushering in a post-treaty era of land theft which allowed Whites to invade the reserved homelands many thought were protected by treaty. Much cheap Indian land was newly accessible, in much the same way "homestead" lands were available. White ownership of the lands around Pine Ridge and the massacre site had always been an irritation to the Oglalas and an insult to the sensibility of Oglala sovereignty for generations.

The Gildersleeve/Czywczynski corporation, to this day, is still hanging on to the land made available by the federal government, with the possibility of millions of dollars of profit when the land is eventually reclaimed by the Sioux tribe. It is another case of dispossession and the aftermath of a corrupt legal history. The Gildersleeve and Czywczynski families have lived in Reston, Virginia, Rushville, Nebraska, and in Hill City, just outside of Rapid City, South Dakota, since the Wounded Knee 1973–74 events, and have been thought of by the public in and around South Dakota as victims of the militant Indians of the era. They have been quoted in interviews as blaming "educated, outside Indians" for the plight of the locals, yet it is quite clear to most observers that the American Indian Movement's role in the event simply served to clarify the exploitative deeds of whites like the traders and cor-

porate organizers in and around Pine Ridge, which had gone on for many
decades. The source for much of this is Rolland Dewing's book, *Wounded
Knee: The Meaning and Significance of the Second Incident.*[9]

DIARY: MAY 6, 1991

> *Drafted a letter to Marie Not Help Him requesting that the Pine Ridge
> WKSA pay the $242.86 bill from the* Lakota Times *for printing the pro-
> posed legislation in the April 24 issue from monies it raised from the sale of
> bumper stickers. Marie indicated agreement. I have advanced the WKSAs
> costs for trips, the Panther productions project ($5,000) and other costs
> since I have been their attorney. The only way I will ever get reimbursed is
> if the compensation bill (not yet drafted and indefinitely on the back
> burner) is someday passed by Congress. That will be difficult since opposi-
> tion for the compensation bill is already being voiced by Francis He Crow,
> Leonard Little Finger, Emil Blue Legs, Alice New Holy and others. Most of
> this opposition has to do with petty jealousies and prejudices. Francis for
> example refers to me as a "Mexican." But, the truth is, my Indian lineage
> from Mexico carries with it much heritage and history of which I am very
> proud.*[10]

CHRONICLE

During the month of May, Lakota people had time to study the April 30
hearing testimony and it was at this time, also, that much effort on the
part of supportive survivor/descendant groups was put into getting the
stalled legislation going again. For some the time was well spent; for others
it was simply a time to muddy the waters.

Eddie Little Sky, representing the Oglala Sioux Parks and Recreation
Authority, had submitted testimony to the Senate Select Committee asking
that while he was making application for funding for a tribal feasibility
study, the legislation be put on hold. The prospect of holding up the legislation for at least two more years meant to the WKSA members more
damage to their bill. When Little Sky suggested that the legislation they
had been developing since 1985 might be "premature," they were angered.
Before the month was out, the tribal council passed a resolution withdrawing the Little Sky written testimony and another potential crisis and
delay was averted. The story is told here to illustrate the critical and unan-
swered questions of who is really in charge on Indian reservations. Indeed,
looking at the political workings of any of the First Nations in the country

suggests that underdeveloped governing systems (the result of historical colonialism and federal paternalism) create more problems.

Alex White Plume of the Big Foot Riders' Association (who later assumed Little Sky's position as director of the tribal Parks and Recreation Authority) was putting out brush fires in other times and places, in support of the legislation. He attended a meeting at Eagle Butte early in the month to try to influence the Cheyenne River Sioux council that its objections to compensation and condemnation in the bill would work to the disadvantage of the people in both tribes. Cheyenne River Sioux attorney Steve Emery, former council chairman Wayne Ducheneaux, councilman Terry Fiddler, and others continued to argue in opposition to those matters and, as might have been expected, their motives were thought by some to be self-serving.

Minutes of a meeting that gave some history of the situation, show that after the meeting there seemed to be more agreement:

1. The survivors of the massacre, including the Horn Clouds, Dewey Beard, and others raised money for a memorial and purchased one from Chadron, Nebraska. This was erected at the mass grave in 1905. Only the names of heads of household are on it and the relatives have always wanted a memorial which would have everyone's name on it. People of the Sioux Nation have talked of this for many decades and there is hardly anyone who isn't familiar with the wishes of the people.

2. The Wounded Knee Survivors' Association has pushed for the last hundred years for the relatives. Gonzalez told those at the meeting that Congress passed a Sioux Depredations Act in 1891 and everyone was paid for their losses surrounding the massacre except those people who actually survived. Chief Big Foot's people who managed to save themselves were considered "hostiles" and ineligible for compensation.

3. Four hearings have already been held: one in 1939 on H.R. 2535, actually introduced in 1938. This hearing was attended by the major spokesperson survivor, Dewey Beard, and resulted in a good record. (One witness stated that in one instance, an Indian was still alive when buried in the mass grave.) The second hearing was on Senator James Abourezk's bill, introduced in 1975, and another introduced the following year. These hearings created a very good record. The files are thick, important, and useful. The third hearing was held on September 25, 1990, as a result of the current efforts of the people, and the most recent was held on April 30, 1991.

If nothing else, these hearings produce the important evidence for eventual success with the project.

4. Gonzalez reviewed what organizations were/are involved and concluded by saying that he was encouraged. He reminded the group that in the early days of this effort, no one could even get Daschle on the phone to discuss the possibility, Johnson was fearful and unsupportive, and Pressler refused to even call it a massacre. If part of the function of such a memorial is to educate the people, Gonzalez told the group, no one should be discouraged because that is already happening.

DIARY: MAY 16, 1991

> Mr. Allen Hagood of the Denver office of the National Park Service stopped by today to inform me that a meeting of the "working committees" established as part of the NPS study of alternatives has been scheduled on the 23rd of this month at Wall, South Dakota. He said the NPS plans to hold several meetings around the state in order to "hear the voices of concerned citizens, Indian and White, about the future of Wounded Knee." Meetings will be held from June 17 to 28, two in Pine Ridge, one in Rapid City, one in Sioux Falls, and one in Pierre. He will hire an Indian stenographer to record the proceedings at each meeting.
>
> I told him that the Wyss study should be rejected because of lack of input from the WKSA members, and because it does not support the concept of a national memorial that is designed in accordance with the wishes of the descendants of the massacre victims. I told him the reason we find the Zuni-Cíbola Act attractive (as a model) is because ownership of land will always remain with the tribe; that title to land and easements are acquired in trust for the Oglala Sioux Tribe and leased to the federal government for a national park. If, down the road in time and circumstance, the park ceases to exist, it will remain Indian property. If title to land and easements are taken in the name of the United States (i.e., they become federally owned property) and the park ceases to exist, state politicians will make an effort to lobby Congress to transfer ownership of the park to the state of South Dakota. We would, again, become enmeshed in a conflict that will divide the Indian and non-Indian people of the region.
>
> I pointed out that this is exactly what happened to the Oglala Sioux Tribe with regards to Fort Robinson. In 1970 the tribe attempted to acquire Fort Robinson from the federal government, only to have the Nebraska congressional delegation intervene and have the federal facility transferred to the

state of Nebraska even though it is located within Lakota treaty territory and has important historical significance to the tribe (it is the site of Chief Crazy Horse's assassination in 1877). It is now called Fort Robinson State Park.

Hagood said he has no position on the WKSA's proposed bill because Congress does what it wants and NPS does what Congress wants. If Congress goes ahead and passes our proposed legislation, the study of alternatives in which NPS is presently engaged will become moot. But NPS is required to continue with the study unless Congress acts.

Hagood said that $33,000 has been transferred from NPS to the tribes to cover travel and per diem expenses of tribal members and officials that will be attending these meetings.

DIARY: JUNE 27, 1991

Melvin Garreau called to give me an update on the NPS meeting at Cherry Creek. He said that Francis White Bird of the governor's Indian desk office in Pierre, Paul Putz of the South Dakota Historical Preservation office in Vermillion, and DeeDee Rapp of the South Dakota Tourism office in Pierre attended and the meeting went well. He said there was some discussion of a meeting held about ten days ago at Pine Ridge in which Oliver Red Cloud again spoke very negatively about our proposed legislation. The purpose of this meeting was to "Study possible ways to manage the site of the 1890 Wounded Knee Tragedy."

Senator Larry Pressler (R-SD) has refused to nominate Phil Hogen[11] as the U.S. Attorney again. Hogen sided with the Cheyenne River Sioux Tribe on closing down illegal liquor establishments, mostly run by non-Indians, on the Cheyenne River Reservation. There has been a significant backlash from the non-Indian population on the reservation against Hogen, and, naturally, Pressler responds to this constituency.

DIARY: JUNE 28, 1991

Members of the Black Hills Sioux Nation Council (BHSNC), especially Reginald Bird Horse, have been unhappy with the current chairman's (Oliver Red Cloud's) refusal to call a meeting to elect new officers. They feel he wants to hold on to the position of chairman for prestige, so he can go to meetings and say he is the chairman of the eight Sioux reservations council—implying that he is head traditional chief of the Sioux Nation. They feel their organization is becoming ineffective in dealing with the Black Hills Claims because of Red Cloud's refusal to call meetings.

DIARY: JULY 3, 1991

Today President George Bush will visit Mount Rushmore. *My niece Misty Daniels, whose husband (Michael Daniels) was killed in Operation Desert Storm, has been cleared to make a presentation of gifts to the president on behalf of our family. She will also present an Oglala Sioux Tribal flag and a letter from the OST president regarding the need for the federal government to resolve the Vietnam War POW/MIA issue (as suggested by Vietnam War veteran Chuck Richards).*

CHRONICLE

There was not much participation by Indians at this fiftieth anniversary gathering for several reasons, one of them being that, to Indians, the "shrine of democracy" is mostly a tourist attraction. Indians have taken to calling the whole Rushmore thing "the desecration tour," especially since the whites have now gotten busy blowing up a mountain in the name of Crazy Horse, a project about which there is much ambiguity. Lakota spokeswoman Charlotte Black Elk has been a vocal critic.

Merlin Moore, an opera singer (now deceased, a victim of AIDS) and the son of the minister of the Christian Life Fellowship Church on the Rosebud Reservation, had been invited to sing the national anthem for the Bush visit. Moore had his name changed legally to White Eagle when he returned to the reservation and wore a white fringed buckskin coat when he performed. He became very popular with white audiences, as did his cousin Mary Moore, who has gone by the name Mary Crow Dog and worked with a white writer (Richard Erdoes) on her biography, *Lakota Woman*, which was published a year after the Bush visit. Later, Mary Moore called herself Mary Brave Heart and collaborated on her second book with Erdoes. These books were eventually made into the movie fare offered by the Ted Turner-Jane Fonda movie-making team as part of the millionaires' investment in what they call heritage projects. The books, which also have been used rather extensively in Women's Studies courses at many American universities, have generally been commented on negatively by Lakota women reviewers as exploitative and inaccurate. The *Lakota Times* and UCLA's *American Indian Culture and Research Journal* published several reviews.

The Bush visit to South Dakota went largely uncommented upon by the native enclaves in the state. His appearance at the so-called Shrine of Democracy, the Rushmore Memorial, in the sacred lands of the Sioux, was deemed by them a distasteful "tourist" and "political" event, in this essentially Republican state. George Bush's tenure in the White House, as far as Indians were concerned, was not expected to modify the region's implacable opposition to Indian needs in any way.

For much of the native population in the state, the carved faces of the U.S. presidents on Mount Rushmore are viewed as an insult to Indian history and to the discussion of democratic ideals.

There are probably no two figures in American history more exemplary of the Indian/White racial dilemma than Abraham Lincoln (1861–65) and Theodore Roosevelt (1901–9), whose faces accompany those of Washington and Jefferson on the carving.

Lincoln has always been well known to the Sioux but not for the Emancipation Proclamation nor even for the Civil War. He is infamous because on December 6, 1862, he signed an executive order that sent thirty-eight Santee Indian patriots to their deaths by public hanging in New Ulm, Minnesota, for their participation in defending their own homes against the whites in Eastern Dakota Territory.[12] Though this executive order has been purported by most white historians who have written on the matter to have been a compassionate act, since there were over three hundred Santee names on the hanging list and Lincoln reduced the number to thirty-eight, the Sioux have never been grateful. Nor do they dismiss a revealing fact of the racial history of that time: not one white southern rebel was hanged for his participation in civil rebellion though vicious murders and atrocities were probably as common in that event as in any native engagement.[13]

Some historians have wanted to dismiss this fact as merely a "double-standard," not racism. The Sioux believe it to be an act of racism which has always been at the core of America's treatment of them.

More significant, from any historiographer's point of view, perhaps, is the fact that it was during Lincoln's term that the dialogue on race relations in the United States was framed as Black versus White, relegating the indigenous people's struggle to the back burner, where it has been ever since.

At the turn of the century, when Sioux Indians, having survived a hundred years of out-and-out genocide, were living in poverty on their homelands, President T. Roosevelt euphemistically "opened up" (again, with a stroke of the executive pen) thousands of acres of treaty-protected lands in the Dakotas for White settlement in violation of every treaty ever written. In addition, through executive order, he declared a fifty-square-mile tract of Pine Ridge Reservation treaty-protected Sioux lands in Nebraska "public domain" lands. Roosevelt later amended his executive order to exclude 620 acres of that area for the "Pine Ridge School/Farm Project." That area is still part of the reservation homelands.

If Roosevelt had had his way, though, there would have been no tribal lands left to Indians. Communal lands were not restored during the Roosevelt era since it was his position that, as soon as possible, land should be wrested from the savages who "infested" it. Breaking up the homelands through theft was, as the Sioux well know, the intent of most of Roosevelt's dealings with them. He held the view that "The simple truth is that the Indians never had any real ownership of it [the land they occupied] at all."[14]

One can readily see why the head of Roosevelt is carved forever into the mountains of the Sioux homelands, for he gives rationale to stealing Indian lands under the guise of democratic virtues, a necessary tenet for those whites who continue to occupy the lands. Mount Rushmore and the Shrine of Democracy is, in fact, one of the most visited places in the United States.

Modern Indian thinking concerning this history, contrary to much of what is written and expressed in the popular media, is this: The Sioux do not quarrel with the fact that in the nineteenth century they signed treaties for peace and survival with the United States and reserved lands for themselves and their future generations. The point is that lands were later acquired by the United States through illegal actions. The Sioux believe in democratic ideals and recognize the treaty-signing as the history of their modern times.

Their expectation is that, as modern peoples who make up the First Nations of this land, who hold sovereign status as First Nations, they have a right to their treaty-protected lands and that theft of such lands, proven to have been stolen during specific governmental administrations by political criminals sitting in high places, will eventually be regarded as such.

They expect their stolen lands to be returned and their histories guaranteed, but they know, more than do most Americans, that such perfect solutions, while not impossible, require arduous determination and ethical thinking. Not only by Indians but by Americans of good faith as well.

To the Sioux, the faces on Mount Rushmore seem to exemplify the political criminality of the United States rather than the democratic ideals and virtues to which so much lip service is paid. Indians often refer to this monument as the "Shrine of Hypocrisy." For those who analyze historical

trends toward Indians, these presidents who are carved into Mount Rushmore are representative of four significant periods of oppression of minority and indigenous rights and populations.

DIARY: JULY 11, 1991

*Luke Duncan, chairman of the Ute Tribe, called today to invite me to a
Treaty Rights Organization meeting in Salt Lake City, Utah. Pine Ridge
Grey Eagle Society members plan to attend. The organization was established to protect the treaty rights of member tribes. The establishment of a
Treaty Rights Organization was originally suggested by Royal Bull Bear at
an intertribal meeting held at Rapid City. The Utah meeting will be held
in conjunction with a National Association of County Government meeting. Duncan believes that the tribes should issue a press release to voice
their opposition to the Association's stand against Indian sovereignty and
treaty rights.*

DIARY: JULY 12, 1991

*The remains of Lost Bird were brought from the West Coast and buried at
Wounded Knee cemetery (surrounding the mass grave). Arvol Looking
Horse from Green Grass, the keeper of the pipe and one of the leaders of
the Centennial Riders, will take care of the reburial rituals. The Oglala
Sioux Parks and Recreational Authority donated a buffalo to feed partici-
pants.*

DIARY: JULY 16, 1991

*Participated in a training session at the JTPA (Jobs Training Program)
office at Billy Mills Hall for Oglala Sioux Rural Water Supply System
project employees today.[15] At lunch, Paul Little, White Clay District councilman, said he heard a rumor that Ann R. Roberts, the great-grand-
daughter of John D. Rockefeller (who furnished some of the funding needed to bring Lost Bird's remains from California) was "ripped off" during a
sweat lodge ceremony. Her jewelry, which she was required to remove before she entered the sweat lodge, was stolen while she participated in the
ceremony.*

DIARY: AUGUST 9, 1991

*Allen Hagood sent me materials on the NPS "action committees." NPS has
established the following committees, viz.:*

1. *History/Cultural Resources/Interpretation*
2. *Economics/Tourism*
3. *Cooperative Models/Assistance Programs*
4. *Spatial Relationships*
5. *Public Involvement/Documentation*

Though the funding for the study on alternatives was initiated by the Survivors' Associations (by asking Jerry Rogers to request it at the 9/25/90 hearing in Washington, D.C.), and the study has to take place before our proposed legislation can be passed by Congress, WKSA members are becoming very concerned that NPS officials have their own vision and agenda of how the Wounded Knee Massacre site should be developed. They do not want the site to become something that is not theirs. The NPS officials are, at times, pushy and aggressive. WKSA members are beginning to feel that the tourism people and bureaucrats are losing sight of the goals and objectives of the WKSA. There is always a danger in that, especially in the case of the massacre site, which is regarded as sacred ground by the descendants of Chief Big Foot's band—not commercial property.

Hagood also asked me to respond to the following questions: (1) who are your clients? and (2) our anthropologist Larry Van Horn wants to know if there is a third [survivor] organization. Are there other [survivor] organizations?

CHRONICLE

As an example of the extent to which bureaucracies were organizing around the project, the National Park Service documents catalogue wide-ranging and diverse topics to be considered by various action groups of the Wounded Knee Study Team:

* Cultural, societal and spiritual Meanings.
* Breaking and Mending the Sacred Hoop.
* Lakota heritage and message to the nation and world.
* What happened at Wounded Knee, historic events and cultural trends.
* Ties between Wounded Knee, Bigfoot Trail, Stronghold Table.
* Heritage and commemorative movements.
* Historic Site Preservation and Memorialization.
* Interpretive Themes.
* Interpretive/Information facilities and Media.
* Socio Cultural and visitor impacts.
* Economic impacts.

- Visitor Projections.
- Travel Promotion, tour routes.
- Business potential, sales, concessions, private enterprises.
- Management unit staffing.
- Development Costs.
- Economic Feasibility Analysis.
- Financing Methods.
- American Indian/State/NPS/BIA models.
- Federal/State/Tribal/Foundation Assistance.
- NPS affiliated areas.
- NPS and State trail programs.
- Partnership and heritage corridor concepts.
- Suitability; analysis.
- Historic Site Preservation.
- Review Past Studies of NPS.
- Landownership and Boundaries.
- View shed analyses and threats to resource.
- Access and circulation, roads, trails.
- Facilities and utilities for administration.
- Development costs.
- Floodplain, T & E species, natural resources impacts.
- Organize feasibility analysis.
- Prepare/edit/review/print.
- Conduct project-related interviews with elders.
- Assess public input and keep team current.
- Design study document and Update.
- Produce production outline.
- Facilitate Heritage Forum

At the same moment that these regional plans were being made and timetables being created for accomplishment of specific tasks for the project, the quincentenary of Columbus's so-called discovery was nearing. It was just a few short months until 1992, which would mark five hundred years of Europeanization of the continent. Books were already appearing on the bookshelves, some which had been in the planning stages of research for many years. Historians were being interviewed, celebrations planned.

More than at any time in U.S. history, this historic occasion was being examined with a skeptical eye, and Indians, more than ever before, were being asked about their feelings on the entire matter. Mario, who had become a public spokesperson for Indian events, causes, politics, and issues in the last decade or so, was inundated with calls and contacts by local people and institutions who had spent years ignoring Indians, as well as by inquiries from all over the country.

DIARY: AUGUST 15, 1991

A reporter from the Rapid City Journal, *Bill Harlan, called for information regarding the quincentennial of Columbus's "discovery" of America. He asked what Indian people planned to do to commemorate the event. I told him to the best of my knowledge no "celebrations" are being planned.*

He wanted to know if I had read a new book by Tom Clancy called Sum of Their Fears, *a novel about the Middle East in which a Sioux Indian from South Dakota plays the role of a terrorist. When I told him that I had not, he said that Clancy is the novelist who wrote the best seller* The Hunt for Red October, *which was made into one of the outstanding movies of the year. He said that this book is also expected to be a best seller.*

In our discussions about book reviews, I mentioned that the book Badlands Fox *by a local Hermosa, South Dakota, author, Margaret Lemley, might be a good one for him to review for the* Journal. *This is a book about her father, a rancher who, for the most part, believed that the Indians brought about their own deaths. According to Margaret, he told her the entire story about all the Sioux Indians he killed during the Ghost Dance craze and "it is all true!" Harlan did not indicate an interest in reviewing it; he appeared to be more interested in the quincentennial celebrations.*

CHRONICLE

Later, Gonzalez contacted Renée Flood, a local white writer working on a book about Lost Bird, and, when the book *Badland Fox* was mentioned, she said she did the editing of that work. She said she had no great regard for the originator of the book, Mr. Lemley, and did not consider him a reliable historian.

When Cook-Lynn later contacted Lemley by telephone, Lemley said that the book was "self-published" either in 1990 or 1991 and that it was her opinion as it had been her father's that all these books "which say how bad the Indians were treated are just goddamned lies." When she was told that Cook-Lynn and Gonzalez were writing a nonfiction manuscript about history and politics she replied, "I suppose you're going to write another book about the 'poor, beleaguered redskins'"; and she said she objected to those books because "it was their own treachery that did them in," that "they had guns hidden under the skirts of their squaws and opened fire." The idea was that they deserved what they got at Wounded Knee. Her father, Pete Lemley, was apparently a member of Governor Mellette's "Home Guard" and was well known for telling stories of some of the atrocities of the period. She, as a dutiful daughter, wrote them down "as is."

When asked about reviews of her book she said they were "mixed." She couldn't recall the names of reviewers nor where the reviews had appeared.

Renée Flood's book on Lost Bird was accepted by Scribners' and she donated part of the proceeds from her first payment to three Wounded Knee organizations, as her way of trying to "right the wrongs" of history.

In further correspondence about *Badlands Fox,* Gonzalez heard from a William Coleman of Drake University, who wrote mainly to discuss two particular chapters in which Lemley discusses violence against the Ghost Dancers, using her father as the source. Coleman told Gonzalez: "In all my research I have never found any report in any newspaper of 75 Sioux Ghost Dancers being killed by the Mellette Home Guard, as Lemley mentions, and has been taken up by Flood. I think such a so-called 'victory' would have been in the headlines. Obviously, Lemley was enhancing his own memories about his bravery and his daughter was allowing him to do so without checking the real facts." Coleman added, "Lemley, to me, was a racist and a liar." Of much more interest to Coleman was this: "No one has made much of the fact that by all accounts I have located, no more than three young Indian men at Wounded Knee were armed when the firing started." Renée Flood, in her meticulously researched book on Lost Bird, quotes from Lemley's tape-recorded account. She says: "His account of the Home Guard ambush (12/16/1890) is a cowboy's unashamed narrative of the day he considered one of the most exciting of his life" (p. 52).

So much for local historians.

DIARY: AUGUST 24, 1991

Melvin Garreau called to let me know he won't be able to make it to the WKSA meeting at Bridger next week. I asked him if he was aware of the Sacred Pipe Ceremony scheduled for August 28, the day before our meeting. He said he was, and that Stanley Looking Horse just got out of the Fort Yates hospital and will be able to assist with the ceremony.

Garreau also said that he attended a meeting a week ago. Sam Eagle-staff was there and told him of a dream he had. In the dream he was advised that the pipe keeper is not doing right. "He seemed quite worried," Melvin said.

We discussed the activities of Tony (Buzzy) Black Feather, Garfield Grass Rope, and other members of an organization called the Sioux Treaty Council. They have been talking about taking the Sacred Calf Pipe away from the Looking Horse family. I told Melvin that Buzzy, Garfield, and other members of their organization are living in a fantasy world in regards to the Black Hills Claim and have illusions of grandeur; that they actually believe that they are the legitimate representatives (chiefs) of the entire Lakota Nation.

The Sioux Treaty Council consists of about a half dozen core members who espouse a "full blood only" mentality (although none of them are true full-bloods). They have virtually no support on the Sioux reservations but attend United Nations meetings in Europe and claim to be the official spokesmen for all the Lakota people.

The Sioux Treaty Council is supported by a David Seals, who wrote the book Powwow Highway *which was eventually turned into popular movie and video fare and who is involved in politics.*

CHRONICLE

To show just how far out of the mainstream of Indian thinking the press oftentimes can get, just a few months after this conversation and diary entry, in November, David Seals, who has claimed Indian heritage, published an essay entitled "The Lakota Nation: Another Breakaway Republic" for a New York–based journal ironically called *Lies of Our Times*. In the article, Seals exploited a black and white picture of the Big Foot Riders and said, among other things: "The Sioux Indians declared independence from the United States this summer. They claimed as their ancient territory an area larger than the Ukraine, based on 19th century strategic reduction Treaties that were easily ratified by the Senate, signed by a lame-duck President, and upheld by the Supreme Court in 1980."[16]

Essentially, this was Seals's story. He, it was rumored, was one of the major instigators of the episode which began in early July as people began to camp there. The story as recounted in the magazine suggests Seals's role was mere observer, reporter, interpreter:

At first a group of Lakotas took a few acres on their sacred mountain, Bear Butte, on the northern edge of the Black Hills.

There were only a few tipis and a couple of families fed up with the starvation and alcoholic genocide on the federally mandated reservations. Then, a few more Indians joined them, and set up a few more tipis, and took a few more acres of private land. Tensions flared with the local non-Indian "landowners."

An Indian-White "reconciliation council" erupted in anger over the Governor's intransigence. More indians moved into Bear Butte, explaining to startled TV reporters that "we might as well take the mountain since the Governor won't even talk about it." The Governor started calling the Chairmen "total failures," in their economic and political management of hundreds of thousands of acres of reservation lands in the state. They called him names back. More Indians and others moved onto Bear Butte still insisting that no weapons were allowed and that they were there only to pray and conduct ceremonies.

The controversy escalated into a full-fledged confrontation of grievances about those old dishonored treaties, and ultimately a number of treaty council groups of elders worked out a remarkable coalition . . . and formed a National Provisional Government headquartered at Bear Butte. On July 14th, after weeks of meetings and gatherings coalition members all came together and held a press conference announcing "total separation from the United States." Then, in true guerrilla fashion reminiscent of a classic Crazy Horse tactic, everyone scattered out across the prairie in four directions. By the next day, when the FBI and a few reporters came around, the camp was deserted.

Indians everywhere on the 70 million acres of the land are discussing this sovereign action and formulating detailed plans for the renewal of their nation. Two elders flew to the Hague in August to attend a General Assembly Conference of the Underrepresented Nations and Peoples Organization (UNPO). The *Guardian* and the *Independent* in London covered the conference with headlines like: Shadow UN Attacks Use of State Force.

Other alienated and "disenfranchised" nations like South Moluccas and Tataristan and the Australian Aborigines are also members of the UNPO. The Mohawk Nation has joined UNPO and recognized the Lakota Nation, as have native Hawaiians, Cherokees, the All Pueblo Indian Council, and the First Nations of Canada.

The Lakotas are setting up their seven Council Fires and Elder's Council as the National Provisional Government. They are re-establishing the twelve warrior societies, seven advisory committees to reform the educational and medical and environmental crises wreaked by the totalitarian one-party capitalist State, forming a Lakota Film Commission to make sure such travesties as *Dances with Wolves* are never allowed here again, setting up a liquor embargo, and issuing ID cards for all citizens of Lakota as their drivers licenses and passports.

In true traditional fashion they are talking to all tiospayes, clans [*sic*], and headmen and women about the renewal. By next spring they will be back at Bear Butte and in the Black Hills with much greater force and unity. Stay tuned.

No one showed up in the spring of 1992 except the tourists and those Lakotas (as well as Indians from other tribes) who go there to pray in the traditional manner. The event is discussed here to suggest that what is real and what is fiction in Indian Country is still a matter of some ambiguity. Since the militant era of the 1960s, an unsuspecting public and an uninformed press have accepted such interpretations of events by various writers with very little checking of the facts.

This kind of journalistic rendition of activity needs to be placed in the context of the modern tribal scheme of things so that people can understand the lack of authority inherent in such phenomena. While it is true that the Lakotas have always been made up of a number of bands (there is no anthropologically defined clan system in this culture) virtually acting independently of each other, today's young white and Indian activists with access to the media or publishing outlets arbitrarily get together and form the external symbolic groups by which the broader American public is informed of Indian business. It is a very haphazard, dangerous, and, ultimately, damaging way for the United States to understand indigenous political issues. For the public, there is little sense of the damaging distortion which occurs in the telling of the stories, for the internal social mechanisms and long-standing, even legal governing mechanisms in which the ethics of tribal life are held sacred are virtually ignored. The superficiality of these phenomena are bound to make them fail, but, in the meantime, confusion reigns.

This was just before Seals published his second novel about the Cheyennes, *Sweet Medicine,* in an Orion Press series, "The Library of the American Indian," which has since been discontinued. He is said to be a member of the American Indian Movement and founder of the Bear Butte Council and, at this time, lived in Rapid City, South Dakota. A *Denver Post* blurb on the jacket of *Sweet Medicine* says about his first work, *Powwow Highway,* "While I was laughing at the heroic fools who populate this book, I also realized how profound my realization: I am, I thought, on a journey with REAL Indians, perhaps for the first time in my life"—proof that the Indians of the American imagination take on a fantastical appearance, a far reach from the nature of Indian societies as they really exist.

There are some facts about current Sioux political organizations which may clarify this issue. In each case, the responsibility to make clear the function of history is inherent in the organizations which the Sioux Oyate have known throughout the decades. Since the 1970s there have been two major treaty organizations formally sanctioned by the tribes. All others simply make fraudulent claims to authenticity.

One important organization is the Black Hills Sioux Nation Council, which has a charter approved by the eight Sioux tribes involved in Dockets 74-A and 74-B (the Sioux land claims litigation). The tribal councils select three representatives to sit on the council. Edwin Red Door of Fort Peck, Montana, was chairman for many years and, presently, Oliver Red Cloud of Pine Ridge, South Dakota, is the chairman. The people in the early years of this decade were talking of electing new leadership so it is assumed this council will have continued influence in tribal politics and law.

The second organization is the Lakota Treaty Council, which was started by the Pine Ridge Reservation people after the 1973 Wounded Knee occupation. Its membership included Frank Fools Crow, Frank Kills Enemy, Louie Bad Wound, and Larry Red Shirt, all respected tribal leaders for many years, all now deceased. When Bad Wound and Red Shirt died in 1982, the council quit holding meetings. Birgil Kills Straight and Milo Yellow Hair, Oglala Nation citizens who have been members of the council from the beginning, still go to Europe now under that organization's name. Otherwise, the Lakota Treaty Council is thought by many to be defunct and might be regarded as simply a temporary spin-off from the 1973 occupation, unless Kills Straight and Yellow Hair decide to go back to its base membership, and start holding meetings on the reservation again, which they have the right and responsibility to do.

Another organization, the International Indian Treaty Council, is a nongovernmental organization (NGO) associated with the United Nations; it is under the directorship of Oglala tribal member Bill Means, a longtime leader of AIM who claims to be speaking on behalf of the people.

The arbitrary gathering at Bear Butte in 1991, then, as described by Seal, is viewed by many tribal people as an insult to the sober treaty council mechanisms which have been a part of the Lakota political experience historically. Such unsanctioned activity only confuses an already confused American public about matters which the Sioux regard as essential.[17]

The Black Hills Sioux Nation Council takes up matters as needed and is seen by the people as a vital, functioning entity, well established for many decades with the sanction of the tribes. Another smaller tribally sanctioned organization is Joe Walker's Yanktonai Treaty Council, in Fort Yates, North Dakota. This group, too, has much integrity and influence

within tribal enclaves. In addition, an organization called the United Sioux
Tribes Development Corporation, for many years headed by Clarence Sky
and incorporated by the state of South Dakota, is a political arm of the
tribal IRA governments since its board of directors consists of chairmen
from the participating tribal governments. It is viewed as ineffectual, dependent, and plagued by cronyism and corruption.

Perhaps one of the most influential organizations at the grassroots level
is the historical Grey Eagle Society, which some say started at Pine Ridge
in 1987. Others, however, claim it is much older and named after one of
Sitting Bull's brothers-in-law who was a war lieutenant for the Hunkpapas
in the late 1800s. Grey Eagle's sisters, Four Robes and Seen By Her Nation,
were two of Sitting Bull's four wives. One of Grey Eagle's sons, a boy in
1890, watched from a hiding place as his father helped police seize and kill
Sitting Bull. As a result, the boy became dedicated to the memories of both
men whose political lives ended so violently during that period. The
young Grey Eagle boy grew up and became the head of a tribal society
and, in 1953, it was some of his relatives who retrieved Sitting Bull's body
from Fort Yates for burial beside the Grand River. This group has been active in the Black Hills litigation for several decades. It has a long and documented history in politics. Others claim this organization is a relative
newcomer, having emerged during the 1950s as a Lakota-dominated voice
when Sitting Bull's burial place was being contested or in the 1980s when
the tribes were getting serious about land claims in the Black Hills. Some
claim there is reference to this society on very old hide paintings, largely
uninterpreted by non-Indian scholars. The Grey Eagle Society members
now say that it is used as a lobbying group for child-protection issues.

In spite of the corrupt and foolish claims of people and organizations
to leadership positions, then, and in spite of the uninformed public's
readiness to recognize any person speaking for Indians, tribal sanction and
consensus as well as Lakota/Dakota history and lineage remain requirements for legitimacy in leadership roles.

Using unnamed "elders" and exploiting such events as the historical
Big Foot Centennial Ride to advance a private vision is not unheard of; indeed, such things have been done since time immemorial by writers who
wish to make history. To explain the Lakota Nation as "another breakaway Republic," however, is probably considered by many as a dangerous
idea during this period when Indian Nations like the Sioux Nation seek to
define sovereignty and self-determination in accordance with the real his-

torical and treaty relationships they have had with other nations. Nationalism, as it is described in traditional societies and it is sought for the twenty-first century, is serious tribal business not to be tied inappropriately to popular culture nor to the works and imaginations of outsiders.

DIARY: AUGUST 28, 1991

When I talked to Sam Eaglestaff this evening, I was disheartened to hear that the Sacred Pipe ceremony at Green Grass did not go well. The Looking Horse family refused to display the pipe for the elderly Lakota who had gone there for prayers. Sam said that everyone was hungry, but had to sit in the heat and listen to many boastful speeches. He said that Oliver Red Cloud was there and insulted Avis Little Eagle (the Lakota Times *reporter) by calling her a "white woman" and asked who her father was. Later, Oliver threatened to go to the tribal councils and get resolutions to force Stanley and Arvol to "open up the pipe."*

There is also much consternation over the fact that non-Indians are being allowed by the Looking Horse family to participate in the Green Grass Sundance. Arvol Looking Horse, as keeper of the most sacred object of the Lakota people, has a responsibility to protect the pipe and traditional Lakota religion from exploitation by non-Lakotas. "Misuse of our religious ceremonies is what Stanley and Arvol must prevent; we can't allow our religious practices to be discredited," Sam said.

Pine Ridge Grey Eagle Society members (Royal Bull Bear, Joe Swift Bird, and Elaine Quick Bear Quiver) also attended the Green Grass ceremonies. They left before the ceremonies were completed to participate in a Senate Select Committee on Indian Affairs hearing chaired by Senator Tom Daschle at Dupree, South Dakota. After the hearing, they returned to Green Grass. Sam said that the mixing of political and religious matters was inappropriate. Sam ended our conversation by saying that Stanley and Arvol "will open the pipe" for non-Indians but not for the elderly Lakota.

There is also a Survivors' Association meeting scheduled at the Bridger powwow grounds in a few days. Agenda items include: a status report on our proposed legislation, a report on the Lost Bird project, a report on the National Park Service's public meetings, a financial report, appointment of Burdell Blue Arm as fund-raiser, and acceptance of a sculpture from Francis Jansen of Ventura, California, who wants to donate the sculpture to the WKSAs to honor the massacre victims. Also from September 16–20, the National Park Service Working Committee will be meeting in Pierre.

CHRONICLE

Complaints about the Sacred Pipe keeper noted here in 1991 began at this time to be vocalized in public forums. In 1995 a respected elder and noted Lakota anthropologist, Beatrice Medicine, wrote in the letters to the editor column of *Indian Country Today* that she was refused entrance to the Green Grass community by two non-Lakota female gatekeepers as she attempted to visit a relative. She had not known that a Sun Dance was in progress but was merely traveling and going about her personal business on the reservation on public roads. She said about Arvol Looking Horse, the Keeper: "Perhaps he should keep away from white audiences in universities and out of the beds of 'white women' who are his source of economic support." This comment by a respected Lakota elder (a female relative of Looking Horse's mother) was shocking to those who read it in the public forum. Yet, many others felt that the public behavior of a religious leader with a public reputation was damaging to the interests of Oyate and needed to be publicly addressed.

Many of the contemporary Sioux have expressed the opinion that the intrusion of Europeans and non-Lakota persons, and particularly white female persons, into the religious realm of modern Lakota life has become a harmful phenomenon which causes chaos in tribal communities and, more importantly perhaps, masks the different political and religious histories of Indians and Whites in favor of a false assimilation. This phenomenon of intrusion has justified the idea that the cure for historical racism and genocide in the modern world is to pray with the Lakotas in their own sweatlodges and ceremonials. Personal, sexual, and spiritual connectedness will, according to this vapid reasoning, make the mass killings and land thefts unimportant in the broader scheme of human endeavors and hopes.

A BRIEF REVIEW OF THE INTERNATIONAL FORUM

At the same time that the Big Foot Centennial Ride was occurring, and at the same time that the Wounded Knee memorial project was going forward, the leadership of the Lakota/Dakota/Nakota Nation at their sixth summit, under the direction of Gerald One Feather and Bill Means, passed a resolution supporting application for recognition by UNPO (Underrepresented Nations and Peoples Organization, based in the Netherlands). Such recognition would assist the Sioux in conflict resolution and human rights issues. While UNPO is the most recent political entity organized mostly around global environmental issues, it is the hope of some that it can assist in land claims and jurisdictional issues of sovereignty as well. Lakotas are members of the Four Directions Council. Milo Yellow Hair is the representative. Tribal nations have always felt handicapped because their conflicts are relegated to U.S. Senate committees and the House committee on interior and insular affairs only. Tribal councilmen have been heard to say about this arrangement, "It's a little like the fox guarding the hen house."

This international arena for the discussion of political matters is not new. In September and October of 1981, in fact, Gonzalez (with Russel Barsh and Larry Red Shirt) was on a speaking tour of Switzerland, Germany, Italy, and Austria in one of the early efforts to get political assistance from an international audience. It was the intention of the 1981 tour to bring to many European capitals the issues of stolen land and violence toward natives in the United States.

Of that time, Gonzalez has said, "that the United States must return the sacred Black Hills to the rightful owners, the Lakota people. No amount of money can compensate the Lakota people for their religious property. The Black Hills are not for sale."

In their discussions with European scholars and politicians, Gonzalez and Larry Red Shirt began to refute the cherished American ideal that justice is blind and always on the side of the deserving. When Indians went to Europe to find audience a decade ago, it was felt that this movement was essential to rethinking the relationship of law to government and politics.

By taking the Wounded Knee memorial legislation to Congress in the 1990s and by taking issues of sovereignty to international organizations a decade before that, Indian attorneys showed that the so-called legal reasoning used to legitimize the claims of the U.S. government vis-à-vis the indigenes must be reassessed.

In any serious discussion, Indian lawyers point out the following: There is a notion of purity and reliability when one speaks of "legal reasoning," a claim which politics often ignores in the pragmatic day-to-day activities of running government and getting things done. This is one of the ways that politics has gotten a bad name and is thought to have nothing to do with ethics or the development of a civilized world.

Traditional American Indian or even reservation politics is often inseparable from ethics (i.e., spirituality) which makes its reasoning virtually impossible for those outside of the religion to fathom. The connection one has to one's relatives and to others in the world is a religious matter to Indians. It is not just a pragmatic idea about how to live together. Because of a spiritual connection, political life in an Indian community often seems chaotic and incomprehensible to outsiders. A man cannot legitimately, in a political matter, "go against" an uncle who has a spiritual relationship to him, for example, for it is a religious matter. But, if he does so anyway (as is often the case for the sake of federal law or state mandate or some other outside rationale), he loses any influence he might have had in his own community. The immediate result is often passivity which, ultimately, turns to tyranny when someone or something emerges to fill the power/influence vacuum.

Indian reservation or tribal law, having been largely removed from the theory and philosophy and culture of the people and replaced by federal or white man's law is, at the close of the twentieth century, in a crucial state of transition. This has become clear to those involved in the Wounded Knee legislation (and the Black Hills Claims legislation), and this is what makes the current efforts so important. It is up to those presently engaged in tribal/white affairs in the United States to make sure that the vacuum serves ethical reorganization, not mere power plays for self-serving, racist purposes. Many believe that now, at the close of this century, the time for a "civilized society" to correct the errors of its past is upon us.

Thus, the continuing story the WKSAs tell at the close of the century, largely dismissed up to this point as a frivolous complaint, is as follows: the failure of the United States government to implement its legal commitment to justice and to the Sioux Nation resulted in land theft, the illegal "taking" of the Black Hills in 1877. This theft, known to both victim and thief, began a series of vengeful acts. The result has been an abiding mutual hatred. Out of this hatred came more criminal action illustrating another political truth, that when one national political crime is committed and no charges are filed, it begets another. Thus, a little more than a decade after the theft, hundreds of unarmed and white-flag-bearing Lakotas were killed by U.S. troops.

No one can any longer deny that racial hatred was one of the causes for that atrocity. The evidence is that there were no indictments of wrongdoing filed and the criminals have claimed their innocence.

The Wounded Knee Survivors' Associations say that "legal reasoning" must now insist that the "claims" of the thieves have been insupportable. "Legal reasoning" cannot accept as ethical the corrupt offering of money for stolen land and "regret" for "apology."

Such verbal digressions from day-to-day practice by Indian lawyers are probably not often available to the public. They take place in the privacy of Indian gatherings. It is in such privacy that almost everyone agrees that in an idealized model of the legal process, there are no obstacles to returning the stolen land(s) through a land reform package, nor are there obstacles to issuing a national apology to the native Sioux. Every Indian, of course, of any generation, hopes for such an eventual solution.

To be realistic, though, for a nation of colonizing capitalists like those in charge of the United States governing and financial institutions, to return stolen lands (or even to consider a dialogue with natives on land reform) and to apologize for the systematic theft which continues even today requires something beyond "legal reasoning." It requires an idealized model which will not rise out of the present historic denial. It requires that greed, a human trait which eats at the heart of the United States and is described in Christian theology as one of the "deadly sins" for which one is merely sent to Hell, be removed from the legal process through which the United States addresses its First Nations. How this is to be done is the challenge of our time, and, most certainly, requires new forums in which Indians may discuss and evaluate the historical contests with their colonizers. The mechanisms presently in place, according to the new historicism, are racist in origin and colonialistic in practice.

An Italian theorist, Antonio Gramsci, who was born one year after the Wounded Knee Massacre and died only three years after the United States government implemented what it now calls the Indian Reorganization Act on the homelands of its indigenous populations (1891–1937), used the concept of *hegemony* to explain that the "legal reasoning" of the West was based on a combination of force and consent which would result in a "sense of fatalism and passivity towards political action." One can hardly examine the ineffectual governments of the tribal nations of the United States and of the Sioux Nation in particular (domestic nations whose law-making powers have been usurped by Congress), without understanding the role of coercion in the reality of Indian/White relations.

"Hegemony," Gramsci said, appeared as a strong force (including a whole range of institutionalized and governmental structures and activities, schools, churches, family, etc.) which "worked in many ways to induce the oppressed to accept or 'consent' to their own exploitation and daily misery."[18]

Gramsci, because he helped found the Italian Communist Party, is not widely read in the schools attended by American Indians, nor anyone else in the heartland, perhaps. Some of his ideas, however, assist in understanding the systemic causes of institutionalized injustice toward colonized peoples, American Indians in particular.

The work of Gonzalez and members of the Wounded Knee Survivors' Associations may be made more understandable through examination of the work of scholars such as Gramsci because their efforts do suggest that a searching look at the conflicts and power struggles between the United States of America and the Sioux Nation are not isolated from the domain of national and international politics. It is the opinion of many native activists that moving the entire discussion of justice for Native Americans to an arena that is beyond the insular United States would place such conflicts into a broader moral context that could not help but be politically healthy.

Gonzalez has always expressed the belief that to place native views and knowledge and experience in a broader context must not be looked upon as "an exercise in futility" but rather as providing the necessary "paper trails" which will eventually bring justice for native peoples.

CHRONICLE

Reasons for the international connection in Sioux politics are manifold, but a major reason for Gonzalez's interest was the need to reassess the myopic and intentional misunderstanding of cause and effect that characterizes U.S. history. To be specific, the American public's effort to treat the theft of the Black Hills and the atrocity at Wounded Knee, which took place in a period of less than two decades, as though they are not causally connected has contributed to the continued subjugation of both peoples, Indian and White, in their relationship to one another.

The work of contemporary Indian scholars, then, in the international arena has been to contribute to the understanding of these historical events as they impact policies which concern the treaties and the land and the nature of life and death in a tribal society. The South Dakota governor, George T. Mickelson, was hardly a major political figure in the state when the international connection was made years ago, but his call for "reconciliation" between the races in the region some years later may have been a direct result of those efforts.

As early as September, 1981, when Oglala Sioux tribal attorney Gonzalez, accompanied by another attorney and a friend, Russel Barsh and Larry Red Shirt (a representative of the Lakota Treaty Council), went to Europe, the rewriting of the Indian/White conflict in the United States began to take on international significance. Gonzalez's three-pronged approach to the Oglala Sioux Tribe's strategy was (1) to exhaust legal remedies in the United States' judicial system by taking the claim for land restoration to the U.S. Supreme Court, (2) to exhaust international remedies in the United Nations by getting an advisory opinion from the World Court, and (3) to seek a legislative resolution of the claim in the U.S. Congress. As the three toured Europe,

Larry Red Shirt and Mario Gonzalez waiting to speak at a rally in Rheinfelden, Switzerland, September 1981.

pushing for support on the Black Hills Claim, anti–nuclear missile rallies were being held in Italy and Germany. The huge rally in Bonn was organized by the German Green Party, which was considered quite radical in the United States. Gonzalez decided that the Oglala Sioux Tribe (his client) should deal primarily with "neutral" countries like Switzerland, Austria, and Sweden in order to avoid being branded as "leftists," which was how all Indian activists were being described in those days.

When Petra K. Kelly, Germany's Green Party organizer, formed a closer coalition with her former party, the Social Democrats, and its leader Willy Brandt, however, Gonzalez contacted her through the Lakota's German support group and scheduled a meeting, requesting that the Greens support the Lakota in the Black Hills Claim. Gonzalez felt that the perception of the German Green Party being a radical leftist party was diminishing in the United States and that Petra could become a valuable ally in forcing the U.S. government to resolve the Black Hills Claim in a fair and honorable manner. A Lakota delegation led by Oglala Sioux president Joe American Horse met with Petra Kelly in the spring of 1984.[19] She agreed to submit the Black Hills Claim for debate in the German parliament. Kelly introduced the question of judicial fairness toward Indians to the German parliament in this way:

> Since the United States Supreme Court rejected the Lakota's suit for the return of lands in the Black Hills, which were confiscated more than one hundred years ago, the Lakota want to try to bring their case before the International Court of Justice. They need the support of United Nations member states.
>
> (1) is the government of the FRG willing to support the Lakota's concern at the UN General Assembly and if so, which way?
>
> (2) If not, which are the reasons of the Government's attitude, regarding the fact that the "working group" confirmed violations of the Lakota's human rights and that the FRG ratified the human rights convention.

The following is a translation of the German government's answer:

> At the present legal situation the Lakota do not have the possibility to take the Black Hills case to the World Court. Referring to Article 34, par. 1 of its statute only states can be a party. Moreover, the League of Nations decided in the 1920s that Indian tribes in the USA are an internal matter of the USA and not able to act in international law. The question, if the Lakota can ask for a return of the Black Hills is also considered as an internal matter of the USA, referring to the Supreme Court's rule in 1980 and the Court of Claims.

The question of how the government justifies its attitude, if it is not willing to support the case, though it signed the human rights convention, the answer is: At the first session of the Working Group representatives of the Lakotas presented their case and reproached human rights violations. The Working Group took this complaint into its report without any comment and without defining it as a violation of human rights.

Petra Kelly responded in this manner in a Sept 12, 1984, foreign affairs bulletin:

I would like to respond to this answer, which was very unsatisfactory, that Indian tribes such as the Lakota have a valid claim to a certain degree of statelike character and international legal status, despite the involuntary (if also peaceful) occupation carried on by the USA.

Of all States, the Federal Republic of Germany should be the last to advance such a theory, since under the Potsdam Agreements it was peacefully occupied by the USA itself. This occupation, which lawyers characterize as "fiduciary" or in the nature of a "trust," did not prevent the FRG from asserting that it was a State, although the occupation continued a long time. In fact, American Indians' claim to statehood has had in many respects stronger foundations. The Lakota have never surrendered or capitulated to the United States . . . there was no debellatio in the sense of International Law, as there was in the case of Germany in 1945. The Government of the FRG in 1949 was established by occupying powers (the Allied High Commission), while the Lakota to this day have a pre-Columbian form of government (the Wolakota or Common Council) which has survived the treaties, wars, and U.S. Occupation without material change.

If the FRG could be recognized as a State in 1949, although it remained under a fiduciary occupation since its capitulation, the Lakota, despite the fiduciary administration of their territories by the USA, can therefore also speak of statehood. If they are no more or less than a domestic affair of the USA, so, too, was Germany in 1949.

Now, on 20 March the Federal Government further replied: "Under the present system of law there is no possibility for the Lakota Indians to take the Black Hills Case to the International Court of Justice. Referring to Art. 341 of the Statute of the ICJ, only States can be admitted to the Court as parties."

While it is correct, as the Federal Government asserts, that "only States" can be "parties" in a contentious proceeding before the Court, the Court nevertheless can render an advisory opinion at the request of an authorized organ or specialized agency of the United Nations (Art. 96 of the Charter, Art. 65 of the Statute of the ICJ). Among others, the General Assembly, the Economic and Social Council, and UNESCO are entitled to apply for advisory opinions from the Court.

I would therefore like to ask, Minister Genscher, if the Federal Government, as a Member State of the General Assembly, ECOSOC and UNESCO, could not recommend a resolution to submit the legal status of the Black Hills to the Court?

As the State affected the USA would also have the right to appear (Art. 66 of the Statute of the ICJ) and, if the Court directs, international organizations may be asked to participate in the proceedings (Art. 66(2) of the Statute of the ICJ). The Organization of African Unity decided to serve in this capacity representing the Namibian people, when the Court examined their legal status within South Africa.

The international legal status of the indigenous peoples of North America has never been determined by an international court. The arbitral decision in the Cayuga case to which the Federal Government referred, has been superseded by developments in International Law and decisions of the International Court of Justice.

The International Court of Justice is competent to decide if the possession and continuing occupation of the sacred places of the Lakota in the Black Hills by the USA violates its obligations under the Charter of the United Nations and the International Covenant on Civil and Political Rights.

I would be very thankful to learn shortly, if and when the Federal Government will undertake the concerns of the Lakota Indians. At present a visitor from the Lakota Treaty Council is in the Federal Republic. It would be good if the Lakota could find someone to discuss their concerns with in a foreign capitol. If such an opportunity for discussion can be arranged in September, I would give you my thanks. /s/ Petra K. Kelly.[20]

◆

Much of Petra Kelly's formal request was embodied in a position paper prepared by Gonzalez's co-counsel Russel Barsh:

I. *Did the League of Nations settle American Indians' legal status?*

The Federal Government apparently relies on the Anglo-American Arbitration Tribunal, which in 1926 remarked that, "From the time of the discovery of America, the Indian tribes have been treated as under the exclusive protection of the power which by discovery or conquest or cession held the land which they occupied." (1) By its terms, this arbitration was only binding on the United States and Great Britain. It was not a decision of the League of Nations or of any other international body, but merely of an arbitrator appointed for a special purpose by those two States. The Indians were given no opportunity to participate.

The international legal status of Indian tribes was not directly at issue in the Cayuga arbitration. The Cayugas sold some land to Great Britain on the eve of the American Revolution. After the United States won its independence, this land ended up on the American side of the border with British Canada. Great Britain refused to pay for it, arguing that the obligation to pay passed, with the land itself, to the United States. This argument prevailed over the United States' view that the duty to pay arose from Great Britain's treaty with the Cayuga Nation, and not from ownership of the land.

The U.S. position was based on applying familiar rules of State succession to the Cayuga treaty. Britain was forced to contend that the rules of State succession did not apply to the Cayuga treaty, because it was not really a treaty and the Cayugas were not really a State. This continues to be the position of the United Kingdom on the legal status of its eighteenth-century treaties with Native Americans. (2) However proper this decision may have seemed in 1926 to the United States and Great Britain, it has long since been superseded by developments in international legislation and decisions of the International Court of Justice.

The most important change in international law since 1926 has been the emergence of the *right of self-determination* as a peremptory legal norm. (3) Since the adoption of the United Nations Charter, colonialism of all kinds has been abolished, and all States administering geographically and culturally distinct territories are under a positive legal obligation to decolonize. (4) Acquiring indigenous lands by force is no longer lawful, nor is continuing to occupy them solely an internal affair of the occupying power. The International Court of Justice has made it clear that the doctrine of *terra nullius* (i.e., acquiring title to natives' land by "discovery"), on which the Cayuga arbitration relied, is no longer an acceptable principle of international law. (5)

II. *Is the dispute over the Black Hills an internal affair of the United States?*
    Indian tribes such as the Lakota have contended that they retain a degree of State character and international status, notwithstanding the involuntary (albeit peaceful) occupation of their territory by the United States. Of all States, the Federal Republic of Germany should be the last to question this theory, since the FRG itself was occupied peacefully by the United States under the Potsdam Agreement. This occupation, which several jurists have characterized as "fiduciary" or in the nature of "trusteeship," (6) did not prevent the FRG from asserting itself as a State while the occupation continued. Indeed, American Indians' claim to Statehood are in some respects stronger. The Lakota never surrendered or capitulated to the United States . . . there was no *debellatio*, in the sense of international law, as arguably there was in 1945 for Germany. (7) The government of the FRG was established by the occupying power (the Allied High Commission) in 1949, moreover, while the Lakota people retain a pre-Columbian form of government (the *Wolakota* or Common Council) that has survived treaties, wars, and U.S. occupation without substantial change.

If the FRG could be recognized as a state in 1949 while subjected to a "fiduciary" post-surrender occupation by the United States, it follows that the Lakota, too, may assert State character notwithstanding the United States' "trusteeship" of their territory. The Lakota people are no more an "internal affair" of the United States today than the FRG was an internal affair of the United States in 1949.

III. *Can the International Court of Justice review the Black Hills Dispute?*

While it is true, as the Government of the FRG contends, that "only states may be parties" to contentious cases in the Court (Article 34.1 of the Court's Statute), the Court also renders advisory opinions at the request of authorized United Nations organs and Agencies (Article 96 of the Charter, Article 65 of the Court's Statute). Among others, the General Assembly, Economic and Social Council (8), and UNESCO are competent to request advisory opinions from the Court.

As a State Member of the General Assembly, ECOSOC, and UNESCO, the Government of the FRG could sponsor a resolution referring the legal status of the Black Hills to the Court. The United States would have a right to appear on its own behalf as a State affected by the proceeding (Article 66 of the Statute). The Court would also have discretion to invite international organizations to participate in the proceedings (Article 66.2 of the Statute). The Organization of African Unity used this provision to represent the Namibian people when the Court reviewed their legal status within South Africa. As a nongovernmental organization in consultative status (category 11) with ECOSOC, the Four Directions Council would have standing to represent the Lakota.

The Court has twice rendered advisory opinions on the legal status of indigenous peoples under colonial domination. (9) In the Namibia case, the Government of South Africa unsuccessfully argued that the controversy was essentially "political" rather than "legal" in nature. (10) Although the Court limits itself to "legal" questions, (11) it has always maintained that the interpretation of treaties, including the United Nations Charter, is inherently "legal" and justiciable. (12)

The Court is competent to rule on whether a State's municipal law is compatible with international law and the State's international obligations. (13) This may include determining the municipal constitutional authority of a State where international legal obligations are involved. (14) Whether a State has acted . . . within its borders and under its own laws . . . in accordance with its treaties and its international commitments is entirely within the Court's jurisdiction.

States waive the defense of exclusive domestic jurisdiction when they ratify international human-rights treaties. By acceding to the International Covenant on Civil and Political Rights, (15) the United States made its respect for human rights an object of international law. Under the Covenant,

Article 1

1. All peoples have the right of self-determination. By virtue of that right they freely determine their political status and they freely pursue their economic, social and cultural development.

2. All peoples may, for their own ends, freely dispose of their natural wealth and resources. . . . In no case may a people be deprived of its own means of subsistence.

Article 18

1. Everyone shall have the right of freedom of thought, conscience and religion. This right shall include freedom to have and adopt a religion or belief of his choice, and freedom, either individually or in community with others and in public or private, to manifest his religion or belief in worship, observance, practice and teaching.

2. No one shall be subject to coercion which would impair his freedom to have or adopt a religion or belief of his choice.

Article 27

In those States in which ethnic, religious or linguistic minorities exist, persons belonging to such minorities shall not be denied the right, in community with the other members of their group, to enjoy their own culture, to profess and practice their own religion, or to use their own language.

The religious-freedom provisions of the Covenant have been clarified by the United Nations' Declaration on the Elimination of All Forms of Intolerance and of Discrimination Based on Religion or Belief. (16) Article 6(a) of the Declaration refers to freedom "to worship or assemble in connection with a religion or belief, *and to establish and maintain places for these purposes.*" This contemplates the protection of religious shrines and sacred sites such as the Black Hills.

Is it appropriate for the FRG to question the United States' interpretation of its obligations under the Covenant? The FRG participated in the *Reservations* case, (17) which questioned whether States could ratify the genocide convention subject to conditions or reservations. Having already ratified the convention without reservation, the FRG was not directly affected by the Court's decision, but had an interest in *other states' observance of the same treaty.* The same considerations apply here. As a State Party to the International Covenant on Civil and Political Rights, the FRG has a legitimate interest in the uniform interpretation and application of this treaty.

Conclusions

The international legal status of North American native peoples has never been determined by an international court. The Cayuga Indians arbitration, on which the Government of the FRG relies, has been superseded by developments in international law and by decisions of the International Court of Justice.

The International Court of Justice is competent to determine whether the United States' seizure and continuing occupation of Lakota sacred areas in the Black Hills violates the United States international obligations under the United Nations Charter and the International Covenant on Civil and Political Rights. The matter may be referred to the Court by (inter alia) the General Assembly, ECOSOC, or UNESCO.

It would seem appropriate to ask the Government of the FRG:

Is it not true that under Article 96 of the United Nations Charter the General Assembly, of which the FRG is a Member, can refer questions of law to the International Court of Justice, including questions of the interpretation of the International Covenants on Human Rights and their application to particular situations?

It appears to be the view of the Government of the FRG that the human rights of native Americans are an internal affair of the United States. Is it therefore also the view of the Government of the FRG that the legal status of the FRG, which also has been subjected to a "fiduciary" occupation by the U.S., is an internal affair of the U.S.?

SUMMATION OF THE INTERNATIONAL EFFORTS OF THE LAKOTA/DAKOTA TRIBES IN THE LAST TWO DECADES OF THE TWENTIETH CENTURY

The efforts of Mario Gonzalez, Larry Red Shirt, Russel Barsh, and other Lakota delegates in the international arena (1981–84) accomplished the objective of making the Lakota/Dakota claim to the Black Hills an international issue. The eyes of the world have been on this claim since then. The Black Hills Claim now symbolizes Native American resistance to colonialism in North America.

The Indian Claims Commission award has grown from $102,500,000 in 1980 to over $470,000,000 in 1998, yet the Lakota/Dakota tribes continue to reject the award and demand land restoration and compensation for the denial of the "absolute and undisturbed use and occupation" of the Black Hills for the past 121 years as guaranteed under article 2 of the 1868 Fort Laramie Treaty. The Indian world, particularly, but everyone interested in justice, is watching to see how the Lakota/Dakota tribes resolve this matter; they are waiting to see if these tribes, who were never militarily defeated by the United States, will finally succumb to the yoke of absolute colonialism by accepting the green government checks that will constitute payment and extinguishment of title to the Black Hills.

The theft of Lakota/Dakota land and resources has always been the objective of the United States government. In the nineteenth century and the early part of the twentieth century, it took the form of military aggression and genocide. Today, it takes the more subtle form of theft through the Indian Claims Commission process.

Gonzalez's contribution to the Black Hills struggle in the last two decades of the twentieth century can be summarized as follows:

First, he initiated a civil action in United States District Court at Rapid City, South Dakota, on July 18, 1980, that enjoined and prevented the federal government from "paying" out the June 30, 1980, Supreme Court award to the Oglala Sioux Tribe, which would have, in 1980, constituted an extinguishment of Lakota/Dakota title to the Black Hills.

Section 2 of the Indian Tribe Judgment Funds Distribution Act of 1973 (87 Stat. 466) provides that "[w]ithin one hundred and eighty days after the appropriation of funds to pay a judgment of the Indian Claims Commission or the United States Claims Court to any Indian tribe, the Secretary of the Interior . . . shall prepare and submit to Congress a plan for the use and distribution of such funds." Since no use and distribution plan was ever prepared and presented to Congress by the secretary within 180 days, the secretary lost his authority to pay out the Black Hills Claim and cannot pay out the claim until Congress passes new legislation authorizing payment of the award.

Second, he helped focus international attention on the Black Hills Claim in the early 1980s by:

• lecturing at universities and city halls with Larry Red Shirt and Russel Barsh in several western European countries in 1981;
• filing interventions (complaints) On behalf of the Oglala Sioux Tribe with the United Nations Sub-Comission on the Prevention of Discrimination and Protection of Minorities in Geneva, Switzerland, in 1981, 1982, and 1983;
• working with Larry Red Shirt, Mike Her Many Horses, Joe American Horse, Fred Brewer, Milo Yellow Hair, and Birgil Kills Straight from 1982 to 1984 to petition the governments of Austria and Sweden to sponsor the Oglala Sioux Tribe in the World Court for the purpose of getting the court to issue an advisory opinion on the legality of the United States' confiscation of the Black Hills in 1877;
• working with Joe American Horse and other Lakota delegates in 1984 to get Petra Kelly to debate the Black Hills Claim in the German parliament.

Third, he drafted the proposed Bradley and Martinez Bills for the Sioux tribes that established the framework for the Lakota/Dakota tribes to obtain a legislative solution for the Black Hills Claim.

Fourth, he helped create an awareness among the Lakota/Dakota people (and Indian people in general) that the Indian Claims Commission process is "a sham" designed to clear title to Indian lands stolen in the nineteenth century.

Fifth, he convinced all of the Lakota/Dakota tribes to reject the Indian Claims Commission award for the Black Hills and to demand, instead, that their treaties be honored by the United States government and that the Black Hills Claim be settled in a fair and honorable manner.

The legal theories contained in federal court pleadings and briefs filed by Gonzalez in the 1980s, and in the Bradley and Martinez Bills, have helped place the Lakota/Dakota tribes in the best position to demand land restoration that they have been in since signing the 1868 Fort Laramie Treaty. It is now up to the current leaders of the Lakota/Dakota tribes to stand up and unify the Lakota/Dakota people and demand that the United States fulfill its treaty obligations and resolve the Black Hills Claim in a fair and honorable manner to ensure the survival of the Lakota/Dakota people into the twenty-first century, and beyond.

DIARY: SEPTEMBER 3, 1991

I worked today on the final report to the Peace Development Fund in Seattle, Washington, for the $1,000 discretionary grant it awarded the WKSAs to help pay for the video news release entitled "The 100th Anniversary of Wounded Knee." I personally advanced the remaining $5,000 needed for the production. This video was produced by Panther Productions of Atlanta, Georgia, and televised worldwide by satellite through Media Link. Sam believes that the production accomplished its purpose in gaining public support for our proposed legislation.

DIARY: SEPTEMBER 6, 1991

Melvin Garreau called and told me that the Cheyenne River WKSA would like to have some type of memorial built on the Cheyenne River Sioux Reservation, as well as at the massacre site (on the Pine Ridge Reservation). Our proposed legislation can be revised to accommodate that objective. As an example, a national historic trail could be established from Bridger, South Dakota (the starting point of Chief Big Foot's journey), with markers all the way to Wounded Knee. This is a concept which the public should support. A second national monument could also be established on the Cheyenne River Reservation. I suggested that we discuss the national historic trail/second monument concept at the next WKSA meeting.

DIARY: SEPTEMBER 8, 1991

Today I made copies of petitions that I received from Dr. Sally Wagner and Tillie Black Bear requesting that the U.S. government revoke the Medals of Honor awarded to the Seventh Cavalry for the murder of unarmed Lakota men, women, and children at Wounded Knee on December 29, 1890.[21] I mailed copies of the petition to the members of the South Dakota congressional delegation. The U.S. Army has used the medals to legitimize the massacre. The medals are, however, nothing more than an artifice to influence public opinion that the dastardly deed was justified, while the army's action was in fact the continuation and furtherance of the U.S. government's nineteenth-century policy of genocide against the Lakota people. A lot of U.S. history regarding Indian tribes has been glossed over and covered up in this manner.

I have great respect for Tillie Black Bear, for her effort and commitment to reassess Lakota history and tell the story about the Wounded Knee Massacre the way it actually happened. It was not just an unfortunate and unavoidable episode as described by non-Indian historians.

CHRONICLE

This diary entry was a reference to something that began almost a year prior, as indicated in the December 31, 1990, issue of *Newsweek,* which ran the following piece in its "Periscope" section:

> Tillie Black Bear of St. Francis, South Dakota, can't ignore the past. She is a Sioux Indian who is leading a drive to urge the federal government to rescind 30 Medals of Honor awarded to members of the Seventh Cavalry for their part in the Battle [sic] of Wounded Knee on Dec. 29, 1890. The battle [sic] was more of a slaughter in which soldiers fired on and killed some 300 largely unarmed Sioux. Black Bear is studying accounts of the battle [sic] to prove the cavalry was hardly courageous. Many Sioux think Wounded Knee symbolizes the near destruction of their culture, and feel that rescinding the medals would help heal wounds with whites. South Dakota Governor George Mickelson has refused to endorse Black Bear's campaign.

In four months the Medill News Service, with a Washington, D.C., dateline, would enter the discussion by putting out the following release: "Governor George Mickelson of South Dakota says the State won't get involved in efforts to take away 18 Medals of Honor awarded soldiers participating in the massacre of Indians at Wounded Knee a century ago." The governor's press secretary, Gretchen Lord Anderson, was quoted as saying:

"He [the governor] wants to concentrate his efforts on things that will happen, and that plain won't happen."

During the Mickelson-proclaimed "Year of Reconciliation," Tillie Black Bear, in asking that the state lend its weight to the effort to have those medals revoked, called attention to the shallowness of his proclamation. Black Bear said she would continue to pursue the matter through the tribal governments. Later, Black Bear, whose work in dealing with tribal social problems is well known throughout the network of national women's coalitions, was honored by President George Bush as one of his "points of light." Some considered it an ironic and cynical gesture on the part of President Bush. As some readers may recall, Bush's campaign effort to develop volunteerism by describing people of goodwill as "points of light" was criticized as mere politics. Eventually this volunteer project developed into a foundation and received *twenty-six million dollars in federal funding* in its 1995 budget, while the proposed monument at Wounded Knee, which asked for five million more in federal monies, went unfunded. There has been some question of the efficacy of the Bush Foundation and critics suggest that such empty gestures and considerable expenditures do nothing very substantial in alleviating injustice and poverty.

Mickelson, during the public exchange concerning the Medals of Honor, made it clear that he now added this issue to the list of unmentionable reconciliation topics. At the top of the list, of course, remained the Black Hills land restoration issue, which had been effectively silenced by governmental officials and the complicit media. These behaviors, as far as the Lakotas were concerned, gave credibility to their historical theory that the genocidal events and land thefts of the period are inextricably intertwined.

David Miller, then a history professor at Black Hills State University in Spearfish, South Dakota, and a leader of what had become known as the anti-Indian movement against the Black Hills Claim, provided information for non-Indian interests by making follow-up statements to the Medill News Service such as: "The Medal of Honor was cheaper in those days. I don't understand that the best way to proceed with this 'reconciliation' is to go after a bunch of fellows who were probably in battle [*sic*] for the first time."[22]

Pat Price of the *Minneapolis Star* telephoned Mario Gonzalez during this period and asked what the Black Bear request was all about. Gonzalez explained that petitions are a legitimate way for people, even Indian people, to express themselves politically and that the awarding of Medals of Honor to murderers under the guise of military action was, very much, an important issue. The *Star*'s information came from Harold Iron Shield, a member of the governor's reconciliation committee, who was circulating Black Bear's petitions in that city; and it became clear to everyone that the committee and the governor were on a divided course. It was only a matter of time before Indians would become more and more critical of the reconciliation movement, finally withdrawing from any further pretense. When they did, the already moribund movement fell into silence.

DIARY: SEPTEMBER 11, 1991

Spent a few days in Washington, D.C., this week. I had an interesting meeting today with Dave Simon, natural resource program manager of the National Parks and Conservation Association.[23] Simon was particularly interested in the written testimony presented by Renée Sansom Flood about South Dakota governor George Mellette's Home Guard at the September 25, 1990, oversight hearing on the 1890 Wounded Knee Massacre before the Senate Select Committee on Indian Affairs. The following is an excerpt from her testimony:

> During the month prior to Wounded Knee, from November 15 to December 25, 1890, there occurred a series of events which must be carefully examined in order to clearly ascertain the amount of and severity of the liability of the United States Government toward the Lakota living within the boundaries of the Pine Ridge Reservation.
>
> No state of war existed during this time. The Sioux were praying during the "Medicine Dance," or the "Dance to Christ." They did not call it the "Ghost Dance" as they do now. They were at various locations with bands split up in order to evade the intruders who had been constantly harassing them during religious activities. These intruders were mostly curiosity seekers who came to the ceremonies wearing metal jewelry and carrying guns which was forbidden. White teachers came close to the sweat lodges for the men, even looking inside and trying to stop the prayers. White people tried to stop the Ghost Dance because these religious practices differed from their own and because they felt the Ghost Dance doctrine, real or imagined, was a threat to them. The Lakota did not walk into the Catholic Church near Pine Ridge and stop the confession of the priest with his parishioner, which would have been more or less the same situation.
>
> Maj. General Nelson A. Miles, new commanding general of the division of the Missouri, was headquartered in Chicago during most of these recent troubles on the Reservation. His continued distance from the troubles contributed to the disorder because orders to refrain from using force against the Lakota were ignored by several officers under his direct command. In particular, the

renegade 8th Cavalry, Troops A and B under Captain Almond B. Wells which
had been stationed at Oelrichs, South Dakota, since April, 1890. Under Captain Wells was Lt. Joseph C. Byron, a young West Point graduate itching for an
opportunity for advancement, a slow process during peace time. During the
first and second week of December, Lt. Byron repeatedly asked for permission
to patrol across the Cheyenne River into the Pine Ridge Reservation, and permission was granted by Captain Wells.

This came to light when Edward Lemmon, a respected and wealthy rancher,
wrote the story of his life, and he had the courage to criticize what he considered highly improper actions on the part of the U.S. Army. In his book Boss
Cowman: The Recollections of Ed Lemmon, 1857–1946, he states:

> Soldiers and troopers were thrown all around the Indian Reservation in
> a loose cordon, with troop camps from ten to twenty miles apart. Wherever
> possible these camps were off the reservation and the troops had strict orders
> to stay off, too, but the orders were often disobeyed by both the troopers and
> the guards. One day Third Lt. Byron asked Major Wells for permission to
> reconnoiter with a dozen men. With Gus Haaser as guide, they went out to-
> ward the west end of Cuny Table. Byron wanted to see if he could get can-
> non within range of the Indian village, out there on the flat. On the way
> back they came onto a small band of Indians. Byron and his men intention-
> ally cut the band off from their own village and killed them all. If this had
> been known at headquarters [General Miles] it would have been a court
> martial case, so it was kept a secret.[24]

After the 8th Cavalry Massacre, Lt. Byron lined up his men and gave them
a talk that no one would ever forget. He said that if one of them ever told what
happened all of them would be court martialed, jailed or hung. The bodies
were buried but the guns and other weapons found were buried in a trench
apart from the corpses.

A nephew of one of the enlisted men who took part in this massacre now
lives in Sioux City, Iowa. His uncle told him the exact location where the guns
were buried but made him promise not to dig up the guns until after his death.
The nephew did as he promised and waited until the old man died. He then
went to the location where the guns were buried and dug them up. They had to
be cleaned up a good bit but he was able to sell all of them one at a time at gun
shows so as not to create suspicion. He went to his attorney and was told that
he might be indicted for selling confiscated government property if the U.S.
Army found out about the guns. Because of this risk, and because of his advanced age he fears an indictment and does not want to be identified by name.
He wants proof he will not be prosecuted before he will come forward. He cannot pay back the money he earned selling the guns as he has no source of income except Social Security.

*There are no known survivors of the 8th Cavalry massacre but it is known
that the band destroyed was part of Two Strike's village. The band consisted of
between twenty-five and seventy-five innocent people murdered by the United
States army during peace time on their own reservation. The home guards that
Ed Lemmon mentions in his book were a two part cowboy militia organized by
Col. M. H. Day out of Rapid City in early December of 1890.[25]*

*Flood has also documented other clashes between Lakota Ghost Danc-
ers and the Home Guard in 1890 that resulted in the killing of Lakota men,
women, and children, including the ambush and killing of the seventy-five
Ghost Dancers north of the Cheyenne River on the northwest corner of the
Pine Ridge Reservation (in which Pete Lemley participated) and murder
of a peaceful group of Lakota men, women, and children while they
camped on French Creek. These previously unknown atrocities show both
a pattern of an army out of control and a federal policy bent upon the
genocide of a race of people. If such documentation is reliable, history
books written by non-Indian historians will have to be revised to include
an ethnic cleansing (United States style), a history long denied but one
that is embedded in Lakota thought and narrative.*

Diary: September 15, 1991

*Elaine Quick Bear Quiver and her husband Charles stopped by my office
today to tell me about a buffalo pipe ceremony held at Joe Swift Bird's
home yesterday. Sam Eaglestaff came from Eagle Butte to participate in
the ceremony.*

*Elaine showed me a photograph of the pipe, which was made from the
leg of a buffalo and appeared to be very old. She said that Joe saw what
appeared to be an old bone partially buried in the dirt by the road that
leads up to his home. He dug it out of the ground and when he started to
wipe the mud off the bone he suddenly had a strange feeling and realized
that it was an old buffalo pipe.*

Diary: September 17, 1991

*Called Elaine Quick Bear Quiver. During our conversation she said that
she was inundated with telephone calls today from people wanting information about the buffalo bonepipe ceremony held at Joe Swift Bird's
home. A neighbor of Swift Bird told her that he saw a cloud above Swift
Bird's home that was in the shape of a pipe. She said that there were a few
people who doubt the authenticity of the pipe like Irma Rooks and Richard
Moves Camp (who did not participate in the ceremony).*

DIARY: SEPTEMBER 21, 1991

Today's meeting at Rapid City with WKSA members and Francis Jansen went reasonably well. Francis is a sculptress from Ventura, California, who contacted me several months ago about giving one of her marble sculptures, called "Transformation through Forgiveness," to the Wounded Knee Survivors' Associations.

Sam Eaglestaff (the president of the Cheyenne River WKSA) spoke and said that he had prayed that someone would listen to the WKSA, and "out of blue, Francis Jansen appeared and wants to donate a sculpture." He told Francis that the WKSA members wanted to meet with her informally so that she could articulate her reasons for making the gift; that subsequent meetings of the Survivors' Associations will be held to determine whether her gift should be accepted. The sculpture portrays a traditional Indian man transforming into an eagle.

Francis told WKSA members that she "feels an enormous sadness, that there are many tears on the land, a beautiful land, your land." She said that "the marble man was meant to stand to heal an old wound, so that a transformation can take place." She felt it should stand at a sacred place like the Wounded Knee Massacre site.

When True Clown, Sr., stood up to speak, Melvin Garreau interrupted and said that he wanted everyone to know that True's great-grandmother is a sister to Chief Crazy Horse. True said that members of his family met with Korzak Ziolkowski when he began building Crazy Horse Monument in the Black Hills and told him that they did not want their names included on the monument. He also talked about Crazy Horse's visions of the eagle and buffalo.

True also objected to language in our proposed legislation indicating that the massacre happened on the Pine Ridge Reservation. He said that we should be saying that the massacre happened in the 1868 treaty area. The 1889 act, which created the Cheyenne River and Pine Ridge Reservations, was passed by Congress on March 2, 1889. Since the massacre happened on December 29, 1890, it did in fact happen on the Pine Ridge Reservation.

The reference to the Pine Ridge Reservation in our proposed legislation was made for the purpose of justifying the Survivors' Associations legal claim for compensation for the loss of the lives and property of massacre victims, i.e., that the U.S. Army violated article 1 of the 1868 treaty and article 8 of the 1877 act when it entered the Pine Ridge Reservation without the permission of the Lakota people in 1890, and allowed its soldiers to murder Chief Big Foot's people and strip the clothing and personal items off their dead bodies. True is technically correct, however, since the United States has never obtained the requisite signatures of three-fourths of the adult male population necessary to subdivide the Great Sioux Reservation into six smaller reservations (and effectuate a cession of nine million acres of the reservation) pursuant to sections 16 and 28 of the 1889 act.

DIARY: SEPTEMBER 24, 1991

In a telephone conversation with Sam Eaglestaff this evening, he made a statement that surprised me. He said that Melvin Garreau, Burdell Blue Arm, and other members of the Cheyenne River WKSA are going to get the Cheyenne River Sioux Tribal Council to pass resolutions authorizing the bodies buried in the mass grave to be exhumed and moved to the Cheyenne River Reservation and revising our proposed legislation so that the national monument will be placed next to the bodies at their new burial site. He said that the Oglala Sioux Tribe can have Francis Jansen's sculpture and the historical site and national park at Wounded Knee.

I told Sam that I will have to take a neutral stand on the repatriation of the human remains in the mass grave since this is a spiritual matter that must be resolved by the descendants of Chief Big Foot's band. I also told him that Celane Not Help Him, my Indian grandmother, is against the removal of human remains to the Cheyenne River Reservation and I certainly don't want to be placed in a position where I am opposing her. Sam said he understood my position and suggested that I "just stay on the sidelines" and let the Cheyenne River WKSA take control of the matter.

The consequence of the Cheyenne River WSKA's proposed actions will destroy all the progress we have made in generating public support for our proposed legislation over the past six years. Even though I am an enrolled member of the Oglala Sioux Tribe and have been involved in Indian politics since the late 1960s, I still find it difficult to understand why Indian people are so hard to please. I have expended hundreds of thousands of dollars in attorney time and advanced over twenty thousand dollars in costs to make our proposed legislation a reality. If I resign as the attorney for the two Survivors' Associations it is very doubtful that either the Oglala Sioux Tribal Council or the Cheyenne River Sioux Tribal Council have enough commitment to carry on our efforts. So I feel compelled to continue with the lobbying effort even though there appears to be a complete lack of understanding and appreciation for the sacrifice that my family and I have made to make the national monument at Wounded Knee a reality.

*I called Marie Not Help Him and informed her of the Cheyenne River
WKSA's plan. She said: "I will personally oppose any removal of the bodies
back to the Cheyenne River Reservation. I don't think they should do
that." I told her that our lobbying effort is beginning to degenerate into an
intertribal dispute about who will get the most out of our proposed legislation and that the two Survivors' Associations should meet and resolve their
differences in a dignified manner.*

DIARY: SEPTEMBER 29, 1991

*Sam called to tell me that he received a call from William Horn Cloud. He
said that Horn Cloud wanted to discuss the national park and memorial,
and agreed that a joint WKSA meeting should be held at Cherry Creek
rather than at Wounded Knee. Sam also stated that everyone at Cheyenne
River agrees that the bodies in the mass grave should be exhumed and
moved to the Cheyenne River Reservation. He said they have a person
with a doctor's degree from Denver who is willing to assist the Cheyenne
River WKSA to identify the bones and that I should start amending our
proposed legislation to establish the national monument on the Cheyenne
Rover Reservation instead of at the Wounded Knee Massacre site.*

*I told Sam that I personally do not have a position on the repatriation
of the human remains in the mass grave to the Cheyenne River Sioux
Tribe if that is what the descendants of Chief Big Foot want. But I am
greatly concerned about the hard feelings that will be caused between the
Cheyenne River and Oglala Sioux Tribes. I told him that any attempt to
repatriate the human remains will subvert our lobbying effort and make it
extremely difficult to get our proposed bill introduced in Congress.*

CHRONICLE

The statement of the Minneconjou shows us the real dilemma that Indians
deal with every day in the modern political/legislative systems which now
encompass their lives. Since the beginning, this has been a struggle for
identity and against violence and it is so ironic that now, the distractions in
the process, itself, compound all the things that Indian people despise: divisiveness, factionalism, helplessness, resentment. The distance between what
they want and what is actually happening widens. If Indian people didn't
have to go to the U.S. government and beg for everything, they could live
good lives. A government process which has had as its major objective the
destruction of the Sioux Nation over the last six generations is not going to
allow the seventh generation real independence and sovereignty.

Part of the answer to our dilemma is that all legislation is political, so when legislation is used to settle matters which are essentially religious, no one should be surprised that it turns the world upside down. The challenge is to continue.

As the relationships which were essentially political worsened, September and October produced a series of activities which painted a bleak picture for those who, just a few months before during the Big Foot ride, had felt genuine understanding and cooperation on all sides. Not only was the "reconciliation" movement moribund as well as one dimensional but the intratribal discussion of the memorial itself was no longer an issue of national survival but of economics and tourism, exploitation, and jurisdiction. To Gonzalez, the legislation as it was originally envisioned seemed poised for collapse, ready to be taken over by the bureaucrats, and the debate had taken on a particularly vicious tone.

DIARY: SEPTEMBER 30, 1991

> While at Pine Ridge today, Alex White Plume gave me a copy of a new draft Wounded Knee bill which he obtained from Sara Yager (of Senator Daschle's office). It was labeled "first draft, for discussion purposes only." Immediately, I noticed a change in section 2(6) of the Daschle draft which provided that Congress expressed its "deep regret" for the massacre in Senate Concurrent Resolution No. 153. Our proposed legislation provides that Congress "apologize" for the massacre in Senate Concurrent Resolution No. 153. The WKSAs want to clarify Congress's intent in Senate Concurrent Resolution No. 153 by having Congress state unequivocally that it "apologizes" for the massacre in Senate Concurrent Resolution No. 153. I told Alex that Daschle omitted the word "apology" in his draft bill just as he omitted the word "apology" in the final draft version of Senate Concurrent Resolution No. 153.

DIARY: OCTOBER 3, 1991

> Marie Not Help Him and I talked today about the Cheyenne River WKSA's move to have the human remains in the mass grave exhumed and moved to the Cheyenne River Reservation. She said her great-grandfather, Dewey Beard, stayed on the Pine Ridge Reservation after the massacre to be near his family and many of his descendants currently reside on the Pine Ridge Reservation and are enrolled members of the Oglala Sioux Tribe. She said she wrote a letter to Gregg Bourland yesterday to express her views on removal of the bodies in the mass grave.

Marie Not Help Him's October 2, 1991, Letter to Gregg Bourland

Dear Mr. Bourland (Chairman of the Cheyenne River Sioux Tribe):

I am writing this letter to let you know of my position as far as the removal of the victims of the 1890 Wounded Knee Massacre from their grave at Wounded Knee.

From my understanding, the Cheyenne River WKSA is in favor of moving our relatives that are buried at Wounded Knee back to Cherry Creek. This is one of the items that will be discussed at the October 5, 1991 meeting to be held at Cherry Creek. Here are the points to consider before taking such an action: What happens if all the descendants do not agree to removal or even to disturbing the grave in any way? Will such action cause disunity, division, and fighting between the tribes and the survivor's associations? What about the legislation that is about to be introduced in Congress? Will that be lost and nothing done for another hundred years? Is the Cheyenne River Sioux Tribe ready to properly acknowledge and receive and welcome the remains? What are the benefits to the CRST in reburying the Big Foot Band?

In order to gain the support from majority of the descendants some assurances should be made: first, that *all* the remains be removed, not only from WK but from Pine Ridge and all other sites were Minneconjou are buried here on this reservation. Second, identification has to be made and that will be a severe task, and third, after the reburial, offer the descendants of the victims a chance to be enrolled, allocated, and to receive all the benefits, housing and employment. In order for myself and others to support any such action, guarantees must be made. /s/ Marie Not Help Him

Chronicle

This discussion of repatriation, which had gone on now for weeks, was not just idle speculation.

Many tribes had been involved in reclaiming their dead for some time. The Native American Grave Protection and Repatriation Act[26] was signed by President George Bush on November 16, 1990, and was recognized as a step toward addressing some concerns of native peoples across the country. The act stated that the ownership of human remains and cultural items was legally and morally in the hands of the "lineal descendants." Scientific and salvage excavations would be permitted under this act, and a case could be made that regional solutions to regional issues was required. If the remains of the Big Foot Band were to be used only for economic purposes and tourist interests, then the descendants, the argument went, could defend and honor their dead by removing them from any jurisdiction they felt was inappropriate. At the time the Wounded Knee removal discussion was going on, tribal groups all over the country were involved in good faith efforts with museums and other institutions for the return of items and bones, and inventories were culturally identifying remains, summarizing sacred objects, funerary objects, and objects of cultural patrimony. Indians on both sides of this issue knew what was at stake.

DIARY: OCTOBER 5, 1991

A very divisive meeting was held at Cherry Creek today. I advised WKSA members that if they decide to vote on exhuming the human remains in the mass grave and moving them to the Cheyenne River Reservation, they should first consider the fact that some of us have been working very hard for the past six years on proposed legislation to establish a national park and memorial at the massacre site. A decision to remove the remains could cause a split between not only the Cheyenne River and Oglala Sioux Tribes but also communities and families on both reservations for years. I also reminded them that our proposed legislation is very close to being introduced in Congress; that we are waiting for the National Park Service study on alternatives to be completed, on which Raymond Takes The Knife will make a report.

Burdell Blue Arm requested the floor for Walter Little Moon. Little Moon informed everyone that "people will lose their homes and there will be nothing left of Wounded Knee" if the WKSAs' bill is passed by Congress. He said that the bill allows the National Park Service to acquire "up to 1200 to 1600 acres" for a national park and "we don't appreciate it because it will include our homes." He said he could agree to forty acres becoming a national park but "as for moving people, we're willing to do what's necessary." Little Moon also said that "the general consensus is to bring the bodies [in the mass grave] back to Cheyenne River, they belong here."

Little Moon left the meeting before I could respond to his comments. I told everyone that people should read our proposed legislation before they draw conclusions; that the only land that will constitute the national park (under our Zuni-Cíbola model) is tribally owned land, which will be "leased" to the National Park Service for a park. No individually owned land will be used for the park, which can be as small as the Oglala Sioux Tribe wants it to be or up to 1280 acres in size. The ceiling on acreage is intended to give the tribe flexibility to develop a park that will be multipur-

pose and, in addition to the grave site, could include a site for Francis Jansen's sculpture and a site for a cultural heritage center/museum. Now, Little Moon will go the next meeting and continue to spread false information about our proposed legislation.

Avis Little Eagle of the Lakota Times *also made a very important statement. She said she was speaking "not as a newspaper reporter but as a Lakota woman." She told everyone that she had accompanied the Lakota delegation to California to exhume Lost Bird's remains and return them to Wounded Knee and it was an experience she would never want to go through again. She told everyone how difficult it was to participate in exhuming and moving Lost Bird's remains. She believes that some of the remains stayed behind in California, and she cannot get the images out of her memory. She cautioned people to think long and hard because exhuming and removing the remains of one's relatives is a horrifying experience.*

A motion was made by True Clown, Sr., seconded by Manson Garreau, to exhume and rebury the human remains in the mass grave on the Cheyenne River Reservation. The motion passed by a vote of 11 for and 2 not voting.

A few more people spoke, Delores Quilt, Ira Blue Coat, Burdell Blue Arm, and others. As the meeting ended, Sam responded to a question of whether this action taken by the Cheyenne River WKSA to exhume and move the human remains in the mass grave to the Cheyenne River Reservation would be presented to the Cheyenne River Tribal Council for its concurrence. Sam said he would make the presentation to the tribal council.

DIARY: OCTOBER 6, 1991

Melvin Garreau called this morning. He said he wanted to let me know why he left yesterday's Cheyenne River WKSA meeting before it ended. He said that the National Park Service study on alternatives has been completed; that he intended to make a report on it but Sam had it scheduled too far down on the agenda. He said the study already dealt with the issue of removal of the bodies from the mass grave to the Cheyenne River Reservation.

He said that the Cheyenne River Tribal Council appointed two people to represent the tribe in the NPS study and, now the study is completed, it will be presented to the tribal council. He said that may be able to offset the divisive results of yesterday's WKSA meeting at Cherry Creek when he makes the presentation and that "all the hard work that you did for the WKSAs, and the hard work that others did is now going to pay off. Out of

*51 projects, the Wounded Knee project is now prioritized right at the top.
The United States is finally coming around to doing something about
Wounded Knee."*

Melvin also said that the issue of exhuming and removing bodies came
up once before on the reservation when the federal government built Oahe
Dam. The white people forced them to rebury the bodies of their deceased
relatives because they would all be under water if they were not moved to
higher ground.

CHRONICLE

The criticism by many in the community of the role of the National Park
Service in this project is a function of fear and past tribal experiences. Collaboration projects with such entities have been notoriously one-sided
even though Indians themselves are now involved in their workings. Like
the white (and oftentimes black) scholars of South Africa who claim to
oppose apartheid but continue to do the intellectual work of institutions
set up by colonizers, the National Park Service in the United States, along
with the Bureau of Indian Affairs and the Bureau of Land Management,
usurp the authority of the tribes and more often than not fail in the defense of Indian lands and resources. Ninety percent of the federal lands in
the West are now under assault by states' rights interests, county suprema-
cists, militias of various sorts, technocrats, and industry as well as outright
racist groups who misuse the Constitution and settled Indian law for their
own interests. Federal lands are often protected lands held "in trust" for
Indian Nations by the United States and it is a historical fact that the federal government has not always stood up to such groups in the past nor
are they likely to in the future unless there is constant vigilance on the part
of Indian nationalists. A distinction is made between *federal land,* the legal
title of which is held in the name of the United States, and *Indian land,* the
legal title of which is held in the name of the United States *in trust* for the
Indian nation or individual Indian.[27]

DIARY: OCTOBER 9, 1991

*Sam Eaglestaff telephoned late this day to say he was called before the
Cheyenne River Tribal Council to explain the action taken by the WKSA
at Cherry Creek. He said True Clown, Sr., is trying to stop our proposed
legislation until it is revised to include a provision that will authorize the
removal of the bones from the mass grave at Wounded Knee to the Cheyenne River Reservation but the tribal council is opposed to stopping our*

lobbying effort. He said the tribal council informed him that the issue of repatriating the human remains at Wounded Knee must be separated from the issues involved in our proposed legislation. He also stated that the tribal council passed a resolution to support our proposed legislation "conditionally." I asked him what he meant, but he was evasive.

DIARY: OCTOBER 10, 1991

Belva Hollow Horn called this afternoon to tell me about a Wounded Knee sub-community meeting called by Walter Little Moon. She said that Walter was exciting everyone, that they are going to lose their land if Congress passes our proposed legislation. He said that people from other places are making decisions for local people, and he threatened to kill anyone who tries to move him off his land.

Belva said that people attending the meeting included Walter Little Moon's family, Verlene Ice, Pat Rowland, and Leola Hall. I asked her why Leola and Pat did not voice their opinions since they were both present at our May 9, 1991, meeting at the Alex Johnson Hotel at Rapid City and expressed their support for our proposed bill. Belva said that Claudia Iron Hawk Sully told Walter and his supporters that she was going to get a tribal court order to restrain them from spreading misinformation about our proposed bill.

Claudia Iron Hawk Sully also informed me that Walter Little Moon and his brother Ben George Little Moon are organizing a "land committee" to oppose our proposed legislation.

CHRONICLE

Keyapi (they say) stories are always interesting and they have been a way for the community to understand the importance of a common tribal history. Mario listened and recorded some of the following in his diaries. What follows here are excerpts from these community stories taken almost directly from his diaries.

Leola Hall, an Oglala woman, told the people at a Wounded Knee Community meeting that since the Big Foot Riders completed their journey some time ago there has been no more *wanagi* (ghost) talk up there around the Wounded Knee Creek area. "It's quiet," she told people, "No more gun shots. No children crying." She gave her thanks for that and said that she was worried about what was going on in community meetings, more recently; she said there is something missing, the spiritual element which has always been so much a part of communal narrative(s) and sto-

ries. She talked for a long time about a son-in-law of the hated Gildersleeves who ran the trading post for so many years, and how this son-in-
law was a BIA employee who went through the entire massacre site with a
Geiger counter and took many things from there in the 1960s, things that
were a part of the people's belongings. This has happened, she said, and
now there is the problem of how to protect ourselves, and that the national monument would do that for us.

People expressed their feeling that there were issues of vandalism on
reservation and federal lands which were not public knowledge and which
no one was doing anything about. Part of the reason for the hatred toward
people like the Gildersleeves on the Pine Ridge Reservation had to do with
this kind of vandalism. Unless the people would move to protect themselves legally and protect their relatives at Wounded Knee, more and more
outsiders would be coming in their vans, treasure seeking, picture taking,
manipulating, using, stealing. Recently, the owners of the Black Hills Institute of Geological Research, Inc., located at Hill City, South Dakota, had
come under criticism from the feds for taking dinosaur fossils from Indian
trust lands and Indians were very much interested in this case though
their opinions were not part of the major dialogue. These white men had
attempted to pay a mere $5,000 to an Indian rancher on the Cheyenne
River Reservation for an entire tyrannosaurus rex fossil, one which was
probably worth millions of dollars. Long and complicated criminal and
civil court cases ensued and most of the media covered the events with
much sympathy toward the culprits who possessed the fossil. White communities in western South Dakota were largely sympathetic, as well; yet it
was clearly a vandalism that the descendants of the victims of the massacre felt was not unrelated to the present memorial legislation and political
agenda.[28]

Leola told of a 1983 ceremony at Wounded Knee with medicine man
Vernal Cross and said the spirits of 396 of Big Foot's people came to that
ceremony for reconciliation. She admonished the Cheyenne River Sioux
people for saying the Oglalas have no feeling for them. She said "what
happened to your relatives also happened to us because we are your relatives." She said what is important is not that we accuse each other but that
we let the world know that the foundation of this country, the United
States of America, was built on the murder and genocide of our people,
and, unless people know that, believe it and act on it, our lives will continue to be pitiful. It was a powerful talk given by a woman who had history
in mind.

Eventually, as all Sioux stories go, they got to talking about genealogy. It started because of True Clown, Sr.,'s claim to be a descendant of Crazy Horse.[29] Sam Eaglestaff, his wife, Kathy (who is an Arapaho from Wind River, Wyoming), and Ellen In The Woods, over coffee, began an afternoon of storytelling at Mario's home at Black Hawk, South Dakota. It was said that Crazy Horse's father (Waglula, or Worm) had at least one brother and one sister (Big Woman). Waglula's name was Crazy Horse but he gave that name to his son who became famous in the defense of the Lakota homelands while he took the name Waglula. Some say that the Standing Bears descend from Big Woman.[30]

After Crazy Horse's real mother, Rattle Blanket Woman, a Minneconjou, left Worm, Worm married two sisters of Chief Spotted Tail, the famous chief of the Brules (Sicangu). Worm died on the Rosebud Reservation in his old age. The mystery is, what ever happened to Rattle Blanket Woman, Crazy Horse's real mother?

Elaine Quick Bear Quiver, who claims to be a descendant of one of Rattle Blanket Woman's sisters (Good Looking Woman), and Joe Swift Bird say that Rattle Blanket Woman ran off with her brother-in-law (Waglula's brother) and, in shame, hanged herself. That is why she ceases to exist in the tribal genealogies. It is a dishonor to run off with your brother-in-law, thus, suicide, in this case, would be a dishonor, too. So, people just excluded her from the tribal history. (It is different, of course, if your husband is deceased. In that case, you are encouraged to marry your brother-in-law, and it is part of the *tiospaye* way.) It was said here that Waglula and Rattle Blanket Woman had at least two children, the famous warrior Crazy Horse and a sister.[31]

Ellen In The Woods, a woman who is known to have a remarkable memory, had a different version about Rattle Blanket Woman, who is related to her, and it is a version she says she has heard since early childhood. She was told that Rattle Blanket Woman went by the Indian name, She Na Sna Wi, a quiet woman. Ellen said she was told that Rattle Blanket Woman caught her husband, Waglula, with another woman, and it was then that she hanged herself. This, of course, is an honorable way for a woman in such a position and she would have been, perhaps, revered for her courage.

Joe Swift Bird told Mario that the place Rattle Blanket Woman hanged herself is south of Wolf Creek in Nebraska where she was living at that time with Waglula. She hanged herself on a tree at the foot of the hill. Ellen went on to say that after Rattle Blanket Woman hanged herself her

son, Crazy Horse, grew up with his father and went back and forth between his father's and his mother's relatives. But he was unhappy.

Ellen said that she heard talk about Crazy Horse often in her home. It
was mentioned that Crazy Horse had a tall spotted horse after he became
famous. She remembers that a horse they had on their ranch when she was
young looked just like that, was taller than other horses, and had a habit of
running back and forth, back and forth. One of the older women in her
family would say, "It looks like Crazy Horse is back. There's his horse.
Look, she would say, ahitowan." Ellen said that Crazy Horse was a pipe
carrier and she knew that he was the way they talked about him, *canupa
yu ha*. Mario told her that he had heard one of the Grey Eagle Society
members at Pine Ridge say he was not a pipe carrier, but Ellen said that is
wrong and she doesn't know why they would say that.

The talk turned to the three Crazy Horse figures in Lakota history. Waglula, who used the name briefly before he gave it to his son; Waglula's
son, the warrior Crazy Horse or the one who became famous in history;
and, finally, the man who married the warrior Crazy Horse's half-breed
wife, a Larrabee girl, after his death. This man, it is said, simply used the
name Crazy Horse so that he could use his ration card and be recognized
by the federal government for supplies. This later Crazy Horse, it is said, is
Julia Crazy Horse's father and is buried in the Catholic cemetery at Wanblee, South Dakota.[32]

Quite obviously, in light of discussions like these, the question "*taku
iniciapi he?*" or "what is your name" is a sacred question which most often
means "who are you in relation to all the rest of us?" Thus, one's relatives
are diligently traced by ordinary people. The matter of personal history
and how it impacts tribal knowledge is a fascinating intellectual pursuit,
both casual and significant. The contemporary reality is never far from the
past, nor is it unconnected to the future.

When they got to talking about the burial place of Crazy Horse, a bit of
silence fell upon the group. Mario told them he had always heard stories
about Crazy Horse being buried in the Manderson/Wounded Knee area
but he was told by Robert Dillon, a son of Emily Standing Bear-Dillon,
that his remains were moved several times and the final burial site is east
of Wanblee. He recalled for them how he had also listened to Robert Burnette, a Sicangu politician of the 1960s and 1970s, now deceased, who told
about a man named Coffee being a relative to Crazy Horse and how he
would go visit the grave site. But, when he did, he would never tell anyone

where he went and he would not let anyone follow him. Burnette said he would head out walking, go north toward Norris from the community of Spring Creek on the Rosebud Reservation, and return the next day.

There is a tribal confidence in storytelling sessions like this one and they are happenings a person, in this busy life, is party to only rarely. Such discussions, for many, tell that the idea that Indians are just "wanderers" and "simple primitive berry pickers," and "followers" of the herd, are the worst kinds of stereotypes. The Sioux are, instead, a people with sophisticated notions about cultures and historical legacies.

These are the heroic stories of virtue, relatedness, failure, and triumph which tell the listener how it is to be a Lakota. The spectacle of emotional conflicts, setting, warlike deeds, love and duty, loyalty and failure, are the heroic tales told by grandmothers such as Ellen In The Woods and Elaine Quick Bear Quiver and many, many others throughout the communities, to describe nationalistic life sometimes passionately, sometimes impassively, sometimes neutrally as simple matter of fact.

WKSA members had been subject to both encouragement and disappointment during the slow-moving events of 1991 and thought that things were, in many ways, getting worse instead of better. They were concerned that members of the Wounded Knee sub-community (such as Tom Clifford and Anita Ecoffey) had begun circulating the following controversial document (called a position paper) based on a misunderstanding of the actual language of the proposed legislation, in order to ensure themselves a significant place at the discussion table, a discussion we all know will take place inevitably.[33] These are the people responsible for the round building that was being constructed near the mass grave against the wishes of the WKSA. The WKSA felt they intended to sell handicrafts at the building, profiting off the dead—the massacre site as commercial property mentality.

Position Paper

  1. The people of Wounded Knee are landowners and have a lifetime residency. The residency of the people in Wounded Knee community is perpetual, unlike the elected officers of the Tribe which exists from term to term and more than likely to change continually.
     The people of Wounded Knee community include descendants of Chief Big Foot and his people, and Tribal Members at the grassroots level. We feel our residence has been continually violated and ignored by all the outside individuals and organizations who tend to forget we are an *active, function-*

ing governing body of the Wounded Knee Sub-community. We are a recognized governing body under the Tribal Constitution with specific rights and responsibilities.

When the people voted to adopt the Howard-Wheeler Act of 1934, they established the right for communities to promote self-determination, specifically Article VI of the Tribal Constitution which states, "each community established under this constitution may undertake and manage local enterprises in furtherance of the purposes set forth in the preamble to this constitution . . . to establish a more perfect organization, promote the general welfare. . . ."

Wounded Knee Community has always been actively organized and has functioned as a governing body.

2. Wounded Knee Community is aware of the uniqueness of the Massacre Site and recognizes the sensitivity of the issue. The goals and objectives of the WKC has always been: to bring respect and dignity to the area which it deserves; establish a visitors center for interpretation of the site and provide a place for local Arts & Crafts persons to promote their products; create employment for local community first, then other district members.

3. The WKC helped initiate the feasibility study with the State Historical Society, which was conducted and completed by Wyss, Inc.

4. The WK district passed a resolution making the WKC the "Lead Agency" for all development in WKC. This resolution was never brought to the Tribal Council floor by our Elected Representatives for ratification.

5. The Wounded Knee Community is the only entity that began the process of development by starting construction of a visitor's center in 1988. The project is supported by District Council, OST Executive Committee, OST Tribal Legal Counsel, the people of the Wounded Knee Community, Bureau of Indian Affairs Superintendent, and the OST Chief Judge. The target date for completion is June 25, 1991. All materials and equipment are donated by Robert Clifford, all plans, design and labor is donated by the members of the community. Robert also donates his time and talents.

6. The Wounded Knee Community voted to support the goals of the WKSA to work with them and give input for any amendments or changes deemed necessary on the Survivors' legislation/bill.

7. The Wounded Knee Community demands that the OST Council rescind the Resolution introduced by Mike Her Many Horses and passed by the council. This Resolution places the OST Parks and Recreation Board in charge of any proposed development at the Wounded Knee Massacre Site.

The Wounded Knee Community would like to point out the fact that Mr. Mike Her Many Horses has violated the Tribal Constitution he has sworn to uphold, mainly Article VI, which gives the WKC the right to develop their own community.

The WKC would also like to point out the fact that Mr. Her Many Horses has never consulted with the Community Council or with the WKSA on any proposed Resolution assuming control of development in Wounded Knee. The WKC sees this violation as an act of deception on the part of Mr. Her Many Horses who was in no legal position to introduce such a resolution affecting the community.

8. WKC stands together on this issue and the people will be the ones who will continually reside in the WK sub-community, and for this reason, the WKC does not want anyone, elected or otherwise, to make important decisions on our behalf without first consulting with the WKC people.

9. The WKC hereby declares that any future projects that will have a profound impact on Wounded Knee, concerning development by any organization, Tribal, Private, or Religious, must consult with the WK people.

10. The WKC people go on record vehemently opposing any desecration or removal of remains from the Mass Gravesite.

11. The WKC at this time opposes any plans to support the establishment of a National Park at Wounded Knee because of the sacredness of the burial site. Many elders and community members feel the freedom to pay respects and offer prayers at the gravesite will be restricted or eliminated once the site is designated as a National Monument.

The WKC supports the establishment of a Memorial for the victims, as has been the intention from the beginning but has to reject any establishment of a Monument by the National Park Service System. Because designation as a "Monument" includes land occupation by the National Park Service, and the tribal land base continually declines, we feel a Monument will further erode our tribal landbase, and every inch of land left is valuable to our people and should remain as such, even though many elected and appointed people see otherwise.

12. WKC demands to be recognized and considered as a legitimate and integral part of any and all Planning and Development at Wounded Knee.

PART 4

The Imagined Sense and the Community as Tribal Nation

(October 13, 1991–April 24, 1992)

Father, I thought you said we all would live.

Sioux woman, Ghost Dance rider/singer at Grand River,
from the oral traditions, 1890

CHRONICLE

Colonized peoples, when all is said and done, face up to their lives within the colonizer's structure. This has been especially true for the Lakota/Dakota native peoples of the north plains whose images have been manufactured by the United States as savage and vanishing—or degraded or noble. The struggle for an appropriate accounting of the Wounded Knee Massacre, if it tells us nothing else, tells us that monuments are, after all, pedestals on which heroes and ideals are placed. Thus, the final decade of a century defined by the struggle for self-identity and self-protection, not only on the part of the Sioux Nation but on the part of the United States as well, has proven to be a period of enormous risk for indigenous peoples in this country. The question "Whose ideals will be placed on the pedestal?" will continue to be the quintessential challenge of our time.

Some believe that the Indian/White antagonists are poised, now as never before, at the crux of change. As South Africa is freed of white racism in its ruling class, and as the beaten, oppressed countries of Europe emerge from totalitarianism, no reasonable person can look at America's Indian Nations and believe in the rightness of the colonial structures of governance which still hold their lands hostage. Thinking people know that the first nations people of the United States must be free of the oppressive, systemic coercion of the white power structures. The story told here in the diaries of Mario Gonzalez reveals the dominance of white bureaucracies faced by the native people as they struggle to claim their own history from the usurpers.

This struggle poses questions which must be answered if we mean our concomitant futures to be successful. What happens to a people when government structures are used to influence them to reconcile themselves to white domination, theft, and murder? What is the meaning of a history written by others, and how can the people be rid of it? How may native nations and people who have been invaded by democratic capitalists be governed most effectively in the succeeding generations, especially when the native people still possess enormous tracts of valuable land and resources coveted by their invaders? How can the "trust" responsibility of the governing class of the United States toward its domestic nations-within-a-nation (a function of a haphazard history) be infused with integrity after centuries of greed and theft? How can native people thrive within and alongside their historical oppressors who are loathe to give up their self-serving dogma?

These questions are not rhetorical. They deserve answers. Today the Lakotas refuse, as they always have, the things most harmful to them in their relationship with the United States. In spite of everything, they will work to do what is right because everyone knows the old Dakota song:

> The great grandfather
> has said
> so they tell me
> "Dakotapi . . .
> be Americans"
> he says this
> but
> it will be impossible for me
> Dakota ways
> I like them.

This is a reminder that any nation of people connected by history and custom and spirit to specific lands and customs, as are the Indian Nations of this continent, will honor its ways and demand its birthright.

DIARY: OCTOBER 13, 1991

Today I reviewed the Wounded Knee Alternatives Study dated October 2, 1991, prepared by Greg Sorensen. It was sent to me by Larry Van Horn, cultural anthropologist for the Park Service. It is called "Notes, Planning Alternatives Meeting for Wounded Knee." This came out of the September, 1991, NPS Working Committee meeting at Pierre where two basic approaches to interpret the 1890 massacre were discussed:

> *1. Tell the story from both the Lakota and non-Indian points of view and let the visitors decide, based on the evidence, where to place the blame.*

2. *Tell the story from the Lakota point of view, recognizing that the non-Indian point of view has been widely written about and published for the past 100 years, while the Lakota point of view is virtually unknown.*

"Interpretation" of is an important issue to the members of both survivors' associations. Marie Not Help Him, Claudia Iron Hawk Sully, and Sam Eaglestaff believe that the interpretation of the massacre must be from the Lakota point of view since our notion of history (and heroism) has always been diametrically opposed to the non-Indians' interpretation. It is quite obvious that the National Park Service's interpretation of the massacre will be a continuation of the U.S. government's cover-up of its slaughter of unarmed Lakota men, women, and children in violation of article 1 of the 1868 treaty and article 8 of the 1877 Black Hills Act.

DIARY: OCTOBER 21, 1991

Sam called today to tell me about a telephone conversation he had with Claudia Iron Hawk Sully to raise money for both survivors' associations. He also informed me that he got a flu shot at the Eagle Butte Hospital today and was suddenly feeling weak. He asked if I could call him later because he needed to rest.

DIARY: OCTOBER 23, 1991

Today, I received a disturbing call from Kathleen Danker, an English professor at South Dakota State University in Brookings. She said that when she worked for the Nebraska State Historical Society Museum in Lincoln, she saw a baby's leg with its foot still in a moccasin. It was one of the souvenirs taken from dead bodies at the 1890 Wounded Knee Massacre. She broke down and cried on the phone—apologizing for her loss of composure. She was just a lab assistant, then, going to college, and did not know much about the Wounded Knee Massacre. She said the leg is in the Goffin Collection and the person who would know about it is Gail Christensen at the NSHSM. She said Goffin lived in Genoa, Nebraska, and had the collection for a long time; that there was a label on the leg indicating that it was picked up at the "Wounded Knee Battlefield." She said that Jim Hanson, who opposed the Pawnees in their repatriation efforts, also knows about the leg. I assured her that I would take the information to the survivors' associations.

Sam also called today. He said that the Cheyenne River Reservation

*District Council No. 4 is attempting to oust him as president of the Chey-
enne River Survivors' Association. District members believe that he and
Burdell Blue Arm (WKSA vice-president) received a lot of money when
they heard the news about Francis Jansen's donating her sculpture to the
WKSA on October 12, 1991, at the Howard Johnson Motor Lodge at Rapid
City.*

*I suspect that District Council No. 4's attempt to remove Sam as presi-
dent of the Cheyenne River Survivors' Association is based on an article
about Francis Jansen's sculpture that appeared in the October 6, 1991, edition of the* Vista-Ventura County Star Free Press. *The following solicita-
tion appeared at the end of the article: "The Wounded Knee Survivors' Association is seeking donations to finance the memorial museum and other
monuments at Wounded Knee. Contributors should send checks or money
orders to the Wounded Knee Survivors' Association, State Bank of Eagle
Butte, P.O. Box 10, Eagle Butte, SD 57625."*

*Melvin Garreau called to inform me that Larry Van Horn and Nola
Chavez, the NPS's landscape architect, would be going to Eagle Butte to
look at potential sites for a memorial on that reservation.*

CHRONICLE

The issue of raising money for various charitable reasons is a thorny one.
There are many organizations which take it upon themselves to ask for
money in the name of Sioux Indians. Indian people generally don't like
this sort of thing. There is a church-run school at St. Joseph's in Chamber-
lain, as just one of a dozen examples, which uses pictures of unnamed Indian children on brochures and says, "in the name of the poor little children, send money." There is much criticism in Indian communities of this
sort of thing. Many people think these institutions don't have the right to
make beggars of little Indian children.

DIARY: OCTOBER 29, 1991

*The weather report indicated that blizzard conditions exist across the state
of South Dakota.*

*Called Sara Yager to find out on what date our legislative proposal will
be introduced in Congress. She said that during her meeting with Knute
Knudson last Friday, he said the bill had to be "greased up" with the administration (Office of Management and Budget) before it could be introduced. She thought it would be introduced in mid-December if Congress is
still in session.*

Bill Harlan of the Rapid City Journal *called to tell me that in his conversation with Knutson, he was told that I had drafted a good bill and that it "comes close" to what the NPS "wants" at Wounded Knee. Since the purpose of our legislative proposal is to have Congress atone for the massacre, what the WKSAs want should be more important than what the NPS wants.*

Sam is preparing for the NPS meeting in Denver. He asked me if he should show the videotape of the last meeting with the sculptress Francis Jansen to NPS officials. Since the videotape contains footage with Walter Little Moon and Verlene Ice opposing our legislative proposal, I told him I thought it might be counterproductive to show it. It would only confuse them and create an erroneous perception that there is a lot of local opposition to our legislative proposal when in fact people like Walter and Verlene are a vocal minority.

CHRONICLE

Sam was invited to go to Denver to participate in what was called "a Lakota Cultural Review panel to evaluate the draft alternatives in the Wounded Knee Alternatives Study." Panel members included Ben Black Bear, Jr., Sam Eaglestaff, Calvin Jumping Bull, Luis B. Kemnitzer, Marla N. Powers, William K. Powers, and Reinhardt D. Theisz—three Lakotas, three white anthropologists, and a white professor. Reinhardt Theisz, a white man who came to the Rosebud Sioux Reservation in 1972 to teach at Sinte Gleska College and now is professor of communications and education at Black Hills State University (formerly Black Hills State College), has become an expert consultant in everything from Lakota music to tribal government to etymology. He wrote *Standing in the Light,* an ethnographic biography of the now-deceased Lakota singer Severt Young Bear, which has received positive reviews.[1] Luis Kemnitzer, who lives much of the time in San Francisco, is a well-known researcher in anthropology and teaches from time to time in that discipline at tribal colleges. The Powers couple continue to do research at Pine Ridge and are often in residence there during the summer months. For the Wounded Knee memorial project, they were recommended for hiring by DeeDee Rapp, a former employee of the South Dakota Department of Tourism who served on one of the NPS committees. They were hired as consultants to do the "Rapid Ethnographic Assessment" work suggested by Ms. Rapp and authorized by the NPS.

During this period, also, Francis Jansen promoted her sculpture by talking about fund-raising to cover the cost of transporting and erecting it at the massacre site. Her representative, Richard Rovsek, met with Secretary Manuel Lujan, who talked favorably about placing the art piece at the site. Sam Eaglestaff discussed the various controversies with Gonzalez, issuing the following October 28, 1991, statement concerning the gift to the Lakota descendants of the massacre victims:

Sculpture for Wounded Knee

Francis Jansen, a Hollander from Ventura, California, has donated a sculpture and called it "Transformation through Forgiveness." But, as president of the WKSA I think it means more than transformation through forgiveness. It represents the beauty of the LDakota people who never broke their treaty or promise to protect the Laws of the Land.

Our people realized that we are going to depend on our valuable resources someday. Chief Big Foot and his people died because a president and a general wanted to make a name for themselves. The entire Seventh Cavalry was wiped out at Little Bighorn as a result and it happened that a small band of Minneconjou people were the ones to pay the heavy price for the Seventh Cavalry's revenge. I believe that the mass murder victims should be left alone at the gravesite. The gravesite represents that these people died for the love of their people and the land that rightfully belongs to them.

I believe our younger generations should learn our beautiful Lakota traditions and that the world must see that the Lakota people were generous and sharing people. Divide and Conquer! That doctrine continues as we sit and argue over who is going to be speaking for the Lakota people, while the United States government is helping themselves to our resources. Someday soon they'll tell us that there are no more monies after all the resources are gone and the government will tell us that we are on our own to improve our health care, education, and tribal government. For those of you in the big cities, the slums are filled with unwanted people who will kill for a few pennies. This is where our coming generations are headed if we continue to argue among ourselves.

/s/ Sam M. Eaglestaff, Descendant.

Calls for unity have always been a part of the ceremonial discourse of the Lakotas and now, in the face of political dissension, Eaglestaff was eager to have a coming together.

The presence of white scholars is historical. Vine Deloria, Jr., the Sioux critic and scholar, first made this observation about Indian reservation life back in the late sixties when he wrote in his "manifestos" *Custer Died for Your Sins* and *We Talk, You Listen* that an Indian family was made up of father, mother, children, and the white anthropologist. It was taken up by the Santee folksinger Floyd Red Crow, who wrote "Here Come the An-

thros! Better hide your past away. Here come the anthros. On Another
Holiday!" (from his record/CD entitled *Custer Died for Your Sins,* put out
by Canyon Records).

While this was taken by some to be a humorous exaggeration, the evidence even today of the many scholars who have made their careers on
"living with the natives" makes the observation not quite so outrageous as
it first seems.

The presence of the white anthropologists William and Marla Powers,
therefore, on the NPS survey committees was particularly ironic since
their observations have sometimes been more "politically correct" than
truthful. Marla Powers's "Sex Roles and Social Structure," a chapter in
Oglala Women, for example, says this about indigenous Lakota sovereignty
and the ability of Sioux Indians to cope:

> The continuing myth that the men are in charge, makes it impossible for
> male leaders to really compete in a society free from the control of the United
> States government through agencies such as the Bureau of Indian Affairs.
>
> For example, though at Pine Ridge local government is strangled by petty
> bureaucracy to the extent that even minor decisions are difficult to make, tribal
> leaders travel to Washington, D.C., or write letters and resolutions to congress-
> men or even the President of the United States making *outrageous* demands.
> The tribal leaders who cannot control even the limited economy of the
> reservation . . . such basic necessities as gas stations and grocery
> stories . . . appeal to the federal government to *give them control* of the Black
> Hills with all their resources so that the Sioux can underwrite their own tribal
> programs. The goals of the tribe are global and therefore unrealistic and *all are
> destined to fail* [emphasis added].[2]

This, as it is written, gives the reader the notion that the Sioux are igno-
rant of and naive about the colonial situation on their homelands. Nothing could be further from the truth. As it is written, also, it intimates that
the Sioux want the government to "give" them the Black Hills. The reality
of the Sioux position on this matter is that the Black Hills were stolen
from the Sioux Nation by the United States government during its western
expansionist era (as acknowledged in a 1980 Supreme Court decision), and
the Sioux are insisting upon *land reform* as an economic necessity and a
moral deconstruction of historical racism and colonialism.

DIARY: NOVEMBER 3, 1991

*Picked up Sam and Kathy Eaglestaff at Rapid City Regional Airport this
morning. Sam said his vehicle was impounded while he was away (it is at*

*Ed's Towing Service and his keys and oxygen tank are in it). Sam asked me
to lend him some money to get it out of impoundment, since he was short of
cash. He said the NPS didn't pay him his per diem as he had anticipated.
NPS officials told him that his check would be mailed to him. I therefore
loaned him the money he requested to help him out of his predicament.*

*Sam gave me an update on the NPS meeting and said NPS will issue a
written report in about four months. He said the meeting was very educational and committee members advised NPS officials that they should give
deference to the wishes of the WKSAs rather than "do their own thing at
Wounded Knee."*

DIARY: NOVEMBER 4, 1991

*Received a telephone call late today from Dr. William Powers of Rutgers
University. He said that he and his wife, Dr. Marla Powers, have been
hired as consultants to write a "Rapid Ethnographic Assessment" for the
NPS and attended the meeting in Denver with Sam Eaglestaff. He said the
meeting resulted in narrowing down the alternatives to two: first, to create
a national park that would include both the Cheyenne River and Pine
Ridge Reservations and establish a Big Foot National Historic Trail between the two reservations; and, second, to integrate the Stronghold and
other historic sites under a joint management agreement and let the tribes
be funded directly to run them.*

*One of the things that Dr. Powers mentioned greatly concerns me. He
said that the National Park Service would like to acquire a solid tract of
land at Wounded Knee, up to 1600 acres which will include a buffer zone. I
informed him that this concept was suggested in an earlier draft of our
proposed legislation and omitted because of opposition from local people;
that under our current draft, only tribal lands will be "leased" to the National Park Service for a national park (based on the Zuni-Cíbola Act
model recommended by the NPS). No privately owned land is involved,
although the Oglala Sioux Tribal Council has the authority to zone the
area around the proposed park to prevent businesses from being established on privately owned lands.*

*I also expressed my concern about the lack of communication between
NPS and the WKSAs, like the meeting in Denver. I told him that I was unaware of the meeting or its purpose until I read Sam Eaglestaff's travel
voucher. Moreover, I told him that I was concerned about the manner in
which NPS officials are going to the reservations and holding meetings
without informing the WKSAs. Tribal, district, and community support*

on both reservations for our proposed legislation is fragile *since our May 9, 1991, meeting at the Alex Johnson Hotel in Rapid City (attended by representatives of the WKSAs, Wounded Knee District Council, Wounded Knee Sub-community Council, OST president Harold Salway, Suzan Shown Harjo, and me to reach a consensus on our proposed legislation).*

Powers also said Sam gave him a copy of the WKS bill and that this was the first time he learned of our work. That statement makes it apparent that the NPS officials have their own agenda on the massacre site and view the WKSAs and me as obstacles to achieving their goals.

Dr. Powers went on to say that the National Park Service had met with Bishop Chaput of Rapid City, who told him that local parishioners seem receptive to the NPS plans to make a national park at Wounded Knee. Bishop Chaput also said that the Catholic hierarchy does not want non-Catholics buried in a Catholic cemetery. The people in the mass grave were not Christians; they practiced traditional Indian religion and many of them were recent converts of the Ghost Dance religion. Dr. Powers also mentioned human remains of Indians from Florida that were buried (in a private cemetery) north of the massacre site a few years ago. He said that the Catholic church was all ready to come out and oppose it on the basis that they didn't want pagans buried in the cemetery.

I wondered how Bishop Chaput could justify his statement that the Catholic church does not want non-Catholics buried in the Wounded Knee cemetery when most of the people in the mass grave, perhaps all, were non-Christians! This reality has been the underlying rationale for the killing and wounding of the members of Chief Big Foot's band. The Christian nations could, with impunity, kill off non-Christians, these "pagans," indiscriminately and, in fact, the paganness of the original inhabitants of this continent precipitated millions of deaths *since the "discovery" of America by Christopher Columbus in 1492. At any rate, Dr. Powers said that Bishop Chaput's attitude is that the Catholic church will leave it up to the Wounded Knee Community to determine whether a national park should be established at the massacre site.*

Later, Sam called to tell me that Larry Van Horn of the NPS wants to meet with us tomorrow.

CHRONICLE

During this period, Gonzalez was not consulted by the bureaucracies concerning the "interpretive" function of the monument. Tribal people who were contacted conceded that they wanted "the Lakota side" to be the fo-

cus of interpretation but rarely was the content of that idea examined.
This discussion, then, served as a further reminder of how it is that Indian
histories have been made in isolation from tribal reality. By the churches.
By the bureaucracies. By the federal government. By scholars and bureaucrats. One current example, rarely talked about publicly, was the 1990 gesture by the U.S. Post Office of putting the picture of Sitting Bull on its 29-
cent stamp, along with ex-presidents, priests, feminists, and Elvis Presley
in the "Great American" series. *The truth is, Sitting Bull was never a United
States citizen either by choice or force. He was a Dakota nationalist throughout his long life and that reality was the reason for his assassination.*[3] The
way Indians eventually became citizens of the United States and, therefore,
Americans, was through the arbitrary passage of the Indian Citizenship
Act by the U.S. Congress in 1924 in violation of every treaty ever signed,
oftentimes over the objections of Indians themselves.[4]

The effort to obfuscate Indian history is a modern American compul-
sion, apparently, that cannot be resisted. While the exploration of the actual meaning of the relationship modern Indians would *like* to have with
the United States of America would be a fruitful area of inquiry, it has
never been part of the official discourse and it was only casually given
credibility during the monument legislation process. Colonialism, assimilation, imperialism, and oppression, it seemed, were as much a part of
contemporary Indian life as ever.

Matters of "interpretation" were to become even more of an issue as
the days and months wore on.

DIARY: NOVEMBER 13, 1991

*When I talked with Sam today in my office he wanted me to look at a "re-
lease" form which was sent him by Gary Rhine of KIFARU Productions
(located at 1550 California Street, Suite 275, San Francisco, California,
94109), along with a video copy of the production called* Wiping the Tears
of Seven Generations. *Mr. Rhine's November 1, 1991, cover letter to Sam
read as follows:*

Dear Mr. Eaglestaff:

Well, finally, after months of work, the documentary on the Bigfoot Memorial
Ride is done. Everyone who worked on this project sincerely hopes that you feel
it speaks for you and for all the people who participated in The Ride.

After watching "Wiping the Tears of Seven Generations" we need you to
sign the enclosed permission form so that we may begin to distribute the program to schools, librarys [sic] and educational television.

We will begin by sending viewing copies to all Lakota schools and educational institutions at no charge.

The program was shown at The Two Rivers Film Festival in Minneapolis and received very favorable reactions from those who saw it. It is scheduled to be shown at the American Indian Film Festival in San Francisco later in November.

If you have any questions, please don't hesitate to call, collect if necessary. In advance, thank you for your cooperation in returning the permission form as soon as possible.

Mitakuye oyasin [All my relations]

/s/ Gary Rhine

The personal release form read as follows:

> This will confirm that I have agreed to the photography of me by KIFARU Productions and its successors (hereinafter called producer) and that producer will own any and all rights in said photography of me photographed for the video program titled "Wiping the Tears of Seven Generations." This will permit producer to proceed with the said photography and I now waive, as to producer and its successors, assigns and licensees, all personal right and objections to any use to be made of me, my name and my personality, in connection with the use photography containing my photograph, for any and all motion picture, radio and television purposes, and performances thereof, accompanied by any narration and dialog whatever, and the publicity in connection therewith, and/or for any other trade and advertising purposes. I understand that in signing this release form, producer will act in full reliance on the foregoing permission.

Sam was asked to sign, give his address, and have his signature witnessed. He indicated that he did not want his interviews used for commercial purposes and that he would not sign the release form.

Marie Not Help Him also called and informed me that many people who are unhappy about the video interviews taken by Fidel Moreno who, she believes, sold the footage to Rhine. She said that several persons she spoke to did not want their video interviews to be used for anything except in support of our proposed legislation. That's the only reason they allowed themselves to be interviewed.

DIARY: NOVEMBER 14, 1991

Gary Rhine of KIFARU Productions called today and left a message on my telephone recorder. He said that I probably already heard of him and he wanted to talk to me about the release forms he sent to WKSA members. I was surprised to learn that he used the interviews without signed release

*forms. He said that he is trying to get Indians to feel good about the pro-
duction and feel like it speaks for them; he hoped that WKSA members
will go ahead and sign the release forms so they can keep sending the video
out to people. Rhine requested that I call him at my convenience.*

CHRONICLE

The historical use of Indians by photographers (and more recently videog-
raphers and filmmakers) has always been like the use of the landscape: unknown, nameless, free. Hundreds of thousands of photos of anonymous
Indians exist in America and Europe and in the archives of every library
and museum on the continent. The issue of "intellectual property rights,"
a term coined in the last couple of decades to talk about the inappropriate
manipulation of everything from economics to literatures and native
medicines, plants, bodies of knowledge, etc., had not been discussed much
by the Sioux up to this point but the flourishing of technology which
characterized the nineties has made this term a household word throughout Indian Country. In the end, Sam Eaglestaff did not sign the release
form because he thought it was a wrongful kind of manipulation, and, in
addition, many others did not sign either, but the production called *Wiping the Tears* went ahead and was eventually added to the plethora of documentaries utilized by commercial and scholarly outlets.

   This entire episode was complicated by the threat of a lawsuit by Renée
Sansom Flood against Fidel Moreno who, she said, sold Rhine tapes of a
Lost Bird segment of the production. Moreno is a member of the Yaqui
Tribe married to an enrolled Navajo. Flood said she had a book manuscript on Lost Bird accepted for publication and Moreno's production on
video was a violation of her right to tell the story. The spectacle of non-
Siouxan writers, filmmakers, and others fighting amongst themselves over
the Lakota story was not only unseemly. It was an example of the kind of
rush to exploit the so-called Indian story which has characterized the media from time to time.

DIARY: NOVEMBER 21, 1991

   *I received a packet in the mail today from Gary Rhine. Mr. Rhine's cover
   letter read as follows:*

      *You'll find a video cassette enclosed, of a one hour program concerning the Lako-
      ta tribe, known to the American culture as the Sioux. The program is entitled
      "Wiping the Tears of Seven Generations" and will be released in early 1992.*

The program was produced without the aid of any foundations, corporations, or governmental agencies. Instead, it was produced with my sweat, tears, savings, and credit. While producing the program, I also shot and acquired enough footage to produce several more programs on Native American people and their concerns for the preservation of their cultures. I have enclosed a description of the program series.

I am writing this letter today, Columbus Day of 1991, because at this point, I need help. I would like to release all the programs during 1992 to help counter the misinformation that will be generated by the Columbus Quincentennial Celebration. In order to accomplish this, I am offering concerned individuals and small special interest groups the opportunity of participating in this effort. Plenty USA, a non-profit relief organization, will be acting as a fiscal sponsor for the project, which will allow donations to be considered tax-deductible.

After you've viewed this tape and had a look at the written description of the series, if you'd like to talk, I would he honored to receive your call.

As the Lakota people say, All my Relations.

/s/ Gary Rhine

Other materials in the packet indicated that the series is called the "Native American Relations Series." The series is a grouping of one-hour documentaries that are available and advertised as "appropriate for the home video market." The titles are as follows:

1. Wiping the Tears of Seven Generations, the Bigfoot Memorial Ride, *directed by Gary Rhine and Fidel Moreno (Yaqui/Huichol);*
2. Inya Sa, the Blood of Our Ancestors, *directed by Robert Labatte (Sisseton Dakota);*
3. Grandfather Peyote, a Humble Way of Indian Prayer, *codirected by Thomas K. Cook (St. Regis Mohawk) and Gary Rhine;*
4. Running to Heal the Kinkyone, the Wilaki Ancestral Homelands, *directed by Jonathan Rosales (Chiricahua Apache);*
5. 500 Years of Fire, Native Holocaust in the Americas, *directed by Fidel Moreno;*
6. The Longest Walk, Protesting the Trail of Broken Treaties, *directed by Fern Mathias (Sisseton Dakota);*
7. The Red Road to Sobriety, *directed by Chante Pierce (Cherokee/ Cheyenne);*
8. Quanah Parker, the Last Comanche Chief, *directed by Phil Cousineau;*
9. The Story of Lost Bird, *directed by Fidel Moreno.*

*I also received another interesting letter in the mail, dated 11/20/91,
from Renée Sansom Flood, who, apparently, was another one of the recipients of Gary Rhine's video "packet." Her letter follows:*[5]

Friends:

Please read every single word in your fund-raising promotional packet. It looks to me like we might have been taken for a ride. I think a crude but more appropriate term would be that we got screwed!!

I do not see ONE WORD about future proceeds going to any of the Lakota or Dakota organizations involved in these films. If I am wrong, please let me know. I do see that Mr. Gary Rhine states that he owns these documentaries that he produced with his "sweat, tears, savings, and credit." To me that translates to his looking for funds worldwide and accepting the funds donated under false pretenses. If he said in this fund-raising packet that he was going to donate proceeds to Indian organizations represented, I might not have been as concerned as I am now.

How is it that Gary Rhine obtained the rights to these documentaries, films that chronicle the most religious and sacred event of our lives? Did he buy the film that Robert Labatte directed on the Sacred Pipestone Quarry and the Pipestone Run? Or did he pay Mr. Labatte to film the documentary?

Did Mr. Rhine buy the right to the documentary "Wiping the Tears of Seven Generations, the Bigfoot Memorial Ride." Or did he pay Fidel Moreno to film this most precious healing celebration?

In my case, I was told by Fidel Moreno that funds generated by HIS documentary would be donated to the Wounded Knee Survivors' Association and the Lost Bird Society. I believed him, but I didn't sign anything. In fact, I warned him that he couldn't use anything he filmed on Lost Bird without my signature on a contract. I never saw the contract. Because I am a researcher I watch things. . . .

Look at the name of the supposedly non-profit organization waiting to receive donations . . . Plenty, USA. Plenty what? Money? Blood? Our souls?

It has also come to my attention that copies of the film "Wiping Away the Tears" have already been sent out across the country for reviews and were sent to participants with an enclosed release form. Did anyone sign the release form?

Writers, directors, and producers who are sincere, share proceeds. They give back to the people whether it is proceeds from a book or a film. They let it be known up front before and later in writing when contracts are signed. In my own case ALL the proceeds from my books have gone to the Yankton Dakota. Ask Allen Hare at Marty about my dedication to the elderly of his tribe. He may tell you that I am a dingbat, but he will also tell you that I am a truthful, faithful dingbat who brings in money for his tribe. They have my books and *they sell them. So, I have a track record that goes back 13 years. I am married to a Yankton and have four Yankton children. That's why I am concerned about this matter and am bringing it to your attention.*

As I said, if I am wrong, PLEASE tell me. I see this fund-raising effort as un-professional and illegal. I have, therefore, as of this date, 11-20-91, initiated a class action lawsuit against Gary Rhine, KIFARU Productions, and Fidel Moreno. Those of you who wish to join in the suit can do so. Through my lawyers I can try to make Gary Rhine accountable for proceeds or stop his productions altogether. The content of his films may be beautiful but he must be held accountable.

First they sold ghost shirts and now they sell home videos. It is the same. That is how they got the Lakota and Dakota people to sign the treaties, they paid Indian people to go among you for signatures. Nothing has changed, except now they come with video cameras and slicker tongues. And the irony of it all is that we still believe them because we have good hearts.

Please respond as soon as possible regarding this matter. Mr. Rhine could already have raised a million dollars. You may turn on your TV tonight and see your grandmother telling of the slaughter of her family at Wounded Knee. Then we must suffer again the bloody remembrance because we allowed these people to take advantage of our pain.

If anyone signed the release forms sent out by KIFARU Productions, let me know. We still might be able to stop them from using them.

Please notice that Mr. Rhine signed his letter, "As the Lakota people say, All My Relations." Now he will have the opportunity to prove those words or eat them.

By the way, Scribner's Publishing Company has bought the hardcover rights to The Lost Bird, *my next book. We are negotiating for film rights. I understand Kevin Costner may be reviewing the story this week. Be assured my friends that you will share in the proceeds in everything I do. I always give back because you have taught me your ways and they are good.*

/s/ Renée Sansom Flood

DIARY: NOVEMBER 27, 1991

Dr. William K. Powers and Dr. Marla N. Powers stopped by today. They were returning to Pine Ridge from the National Park Service meeting held in Eagle Butte. Although Sam had already called and said he thought the meeting went fairly well, the Powerses' indicated that the people on the Cheyenne River Reservation are maximizing the conflicts at Pine Ridge and that they should tone this down.

They explained how they got involved with the NPS study of alternatives. They rented one of the houses behind Red Cloud Indian School and while they were there, an NPS meeting was being held at the school. They were told by Brother Simon that the people at the meeting, namely Allen Hagood of the NPS, Francis White Bird of the South Dakota governor's office, and Mike Kesby, an anthropologist, would like to meet them. They eventually were hired as consultants to do a "Rapid Ethnographic Assessment" of our proposed legislation—an assessment to see what reservation people think about it. They are attending both public and private meetings to get people's opinions. They do not believe that the NPS really understands Indian people.

An example they gave was that the NPS people were shocked when during a meeting in Wounded Knee Alex White Plume got up and said "I hate white people," and Gary Rowland said he would destroy everything the NPS established at the massacre site.

They wondered why I was not invited to the Denver meeting, as legal counsel to the WKSA, and as a person who has been involved in the legislation from the beginning. They again reiterated the fact that they had not been given copies of our proposed legislation, saying how helpful that would have been to those just coming into the discussion.

They said that the final NPS meeting for their involvement would be to vote on alternatives by March 9, 1992. Two alternatives are under consideration: (1) leave the bill as it is, or (2) plan a tribal park at both ends of the Big Foot Trail, one at Wounded Knee and one on the Cheyenne River, connecting the trail and managed by the tribes. They said that everyone is planning to have the Wounded Knee bill introduced in Congress in January or February.

They also said that many people DO NOT want the Francis Jansen sculpture, the private donation to the WKSA, to be at the grave site.

They also said that I should be at every meeting from now on because I am the author of the proposed Wounded Knee legislation and have been involved with the national monument issue "from the beginning." I told them that I do not know the reason why the NPS officials have not invited me to a single meeting regarding the study of alternatives; that I recall talking to Irv Mortensen, the superintendent of the Badlands National Park, when NPS was establishing its two committees, an advisory committee and a working committee. Irv told me that some NPS officials said that Mario Gonzalez is nothing but a troublemaker—apparently in reference to my representation of the Oglala Sioux Tribe in the Black Hills case and other land claims—but he was going to nominate me to be on the advisory committee anyway. I told them that I do not know if Irv made the nomi-

nation, or if the NPS officials' view of me has anything to do with NPS not inviting me to any of their meetings, but I will attend future NPS meetings if I am invited.

CHRONICLE

Some time later, DeeDee Rapp (formerly of the South Dakota Tourist Commission) said that the NPS ethnographic study was needed and she was the person who called for it since the elders did not participate very satisfactorily in the meetings which were called periodically. She said the NPS study team selected the Powers couple, that she herself drafted the contract, that the state hired them and the NPS reimbursed the state.

DIARY: JANUARY 2, 1992

Senator Tom Kerry, a candidate for president of the United States, will be at Pine Ridge this afternoon. At the request of Paul Valandra (a Rosebud Sioux tribal member), I drafted a position paper concerning our proposed Wounded Knee legislation and faxed it to Mr. Valandra. He will present it to Kerry.

DIARY: JANUARY 6, 1992

Royal Bull Bear, Joe Swift Bird, Reginald Bird Horse, Manson Garreau, and other Grey Eagle Society members met at the Billy Mills Hall today for the purpose of discussing the Black Hills Claim and other important issues affecting the Lakota people. Also attending were Gerald Clifford (coordinator of the Black Hills Steering Committee), Charlotte Black Elk, Terry Fiddler, and Ted Thin Elk.

This meeting was sponsored by the Oglala Sioux Tribal Land Committee.

After I got back to my office I got a call from Knute Knudson who was calling about Walter Little Moon and the Wounded Knee Land Owners' Association (that was recently organized to oppose our proposed legislation). He wanted to discuss their position paper opposing our proposed legislation, which was drafted by Tony Ramirez, Walter Little Moon's nephew.

DIARY: JANUARY 12, 1992

I received copies of materials in the mail today from Larry Van Horn which were sent to Greg Sorensen by Bishop Charles J. Chaput of the Diocese of the Catholic Church of Rapid City. Included was a letter to Mr. Sorensen from Bishop Chaput, which basically said that when he was in

Manderson, South Dakota, on January 1st he received a statement and po-
sition paper from Patrick Clifford, Chairman of the Wounded Knee Com-
munity, which made it clear that the parishoners absolutely did not want
the church moved or the cemetery touched. There does not seem to be any
interest at all in compromising on either of those issues.

I called Marie Not Help Him and read Bishop Chaput's letter to her.
She said (with disgust) that the Catholic church has no business getting
involved in our proposed legislation; that Father Croft gave the last rites to
the Lakota people who were killed in the massacre and he turned out to be
a government spy. The church seems to forget, Marie said, that the people
in the mass grave were not Christians and had no intentions of ever be-
coming Catholics. They had their own religion and were deliberately killed
for exercising their religious beliefs.

I also called Sam Eaglestaff and informed him of Chaput's letter. He got
angry and said that he would contact Monsignor Lentz in Washington,
D.C., and enlist his support for our legislative proposal. He said he was
disgusted with the Catholic church allowing people to be buried around
the mass grave; that there is barely enough room to walk around the mass
grave.

CHRONICLE

The Father Croft referred to here may be a Father Craft whose activities
during the period of the massacre at Wounded Knee have been briefly
chronicled in a far different light in a report from the Bureau of Ethnology: "The heroic missionary priest, Father Craft, who had given a large part
of his work among the Sioux, *by whom he was loved and respected,* had en-
deavored at the beginning of the trouble to persuade the stampeded Indians to come into the agency, but without success, the Indians claiming that
no single treaty ever made with them had been fulfilled in all its stipula-
tions" (emphasis added).[6]

This is another example of how those who tell the public stories get to
claim and define heroism. While that report printed a complete list of
officers and enlisted men who were killed or died of wounds or exposure
in connection with the massacre, dead Indians remain, for the most part,
unnamed in public writings. Even today, there is little public agreement on
how many Indians were killed there and what their names were.

Ollie Flying Horse Napesni of St. Francis, South Dakota, says that her
mother told her of a plan the Indians had of burning down Holy Rosary
Mission just two or three days after the massacre, a story which suggests

that not everything about the Catholic history there has been "loved and respected." The plans, so the story goes, did not materialize (mostly because many Indian children were in residence school there) but it is a narrative which says very clearly that the people at Wounded Knee were not then nor are they now unaware of the politico-religious mission of the Catholic Fathers and how devastating it was to the people. Gonzalez has in his possession an article by a white schoolteacher at Oglala Community School during that time and it is an admission that they kept the children in the school, using them as shields to protect themselves. In this article, Thisba Hutson Morgan describes her experiences on December 29, 1890, the day of the Wounded Knee Massacre, as follows:

> We were sixteen miles away but news of it rapidly reached us at the school. It was the noon hour and the children were scattered over the grounds at work and at play, awaiting their call to dinner, when the first runners from the battlefield [sic] reached the Agency. The children were the first to get the news and report it to us, because they could understand and interpret the sign language of the runners as they reached the knoll behind the school house, outstripping the Army couriers, swift though they were. The children were panic stricken as more news came in for many of them knew that their parents must have been in the fray [sic]. A few of them escaped in their excitement although it was a rule of the school that no one, teacher or pupil, should leave the grounds, which were enclosed by a high fence, without first reporting their business.
>
> We hurried them into the house, battening the doors and windows, and each of the twenty or more teachers stood guard in turn while the others tried to soothe and comfort the best we could the wailing, hysterical, fainting children who could hear those coming from the battlefield [sic] call to them to get away for they were going to shoot fire-arrows into the roof of the school house and burn it. The teachers soon sensed that their safety depended upon keeping the children in the school house as the Indians would not set fire to it so long as their children were inside. All during that afternoon of December 29th, I could see from my classroom windows a continuous stream of Indians coming from the north, passing southward to what was known as Loafer's Camp. An occasional shot could be heard. Mischief-makers brought tales that excited the young friendly braves. They began to council for immediate attack on the Agency by encircling it and striking from every side at once; but the calmer older warriors councilled for delay and the Agency was saved. Chief Red Cloud and his band had remained at the Agency, friendly to General John R. Brooke, then commanding, and helped repel those councilling to destroy it.[7]

In 1996 this historic church at Holy Rosary Mission which was at the center of such controversy did burn to the ground in an unexplained fire.

DIARY: JANUARY 15, 1992

Today I attended a tribal council meeting at Pine Ridge. During the noon hour, I had a discussion with Celane Not Help Him who told me that she was disgusted with Oliver Red Cloud and asked her uncle Royal Bull Bear why he listened to Oliver in opposing the Wounded Knee bill when Chief Red Cloud killed Chief Bull Bear (Royal's wife is a descendant of White Lance, who is a brother to Celane's grandfather Dewey Beard). Celane said that Chief Red Cloud didn't come to Chief Big Foot's rescue when he was being massacred at Wounded Knee.

Celane also criticized Oliver for getting a log house through a log house program administered by Reginald Cedar Face and funded by the Christian Relief Services. She said that Oliver got the first house, which should have gone to the most needy people on the reservation. She said that if Oliver is really a chief, he should give one of his two houses away to a needy person; that in pre-reservation days, the doorway to a chief's tipi was said to be "greasy" because so many people came to see him and he would give them things they needed.

Celane also asked about Suzan Shown Haro. Said she really respected Suzan because she was strong, understanding, and brave. She said a mother had to be brave in pre-reservation days.

As I was leaving the tribal council chambers I met Claudia Iron Hawk Sully in the hallway. She said she was lying on her couch at her home in Wounded Knee listening to KILI Radio when she heard me addressing the tribal council. She came to see me for an update on our proposed legislation. I told her that our proposed bill will probably be introduced in Congress by the South Dakota congressional delegation as soon as Congress reconvenes.

DIARY: JANUARY 26, 1992

Sara Yager of Senator Daschle's office in Washington, D.C., called to tell me that Senator Daschle will introduce our proposed legislation on February 7th.

DIARY: FEBRUARY 3, 1992

When I returned from a client's bankruptcy deposition today, I had a call from Suzan Shown Harjo who said that Daschle will not be introducing the our proposed legislation this Friday. Pete Taylor of the Senate Select

Committee on Indian Affairs told her that they cannot have the bill ready by then, that there is more work to be done on the amendments.

DIARY: FEBRUARY 20, 1992

Gary Rhine called today regarding Sam Eaglestaff's involvement in the "Wiping the Tears of Seven Generations" video. I informed him again that Sam wants his interview deleted from the production. Instead of assuring me that he would honor Sam's request, he said that Avis Little Eagle would be reviewing the video in the Lakota Times, *her review would most likely be positive; that maybe Sam will change his mind after he reads Avis's review.*

Sam is at the regional hospital in Rapid City. When I called him he said he was "up and around." I gave him an update on our proposed legislation and my conversation with Gary Rhine. Sam is getting weaker every day. He is now in a wheelchair and uses an oxygen tank. He says he will assist Renée Flood, who received $25,000 (as first half of advance) for her book on Lost Bird, with her request for assistance in disbursing some of the funds she wants to donate to Lakota organizations, the CR and PR Wounded Knee Survivors' Associations, as well as the Lost Bird Society which Marie Not Help Him established for Indian people (Lost Birds) adopted into non-Indian homes so they could find their lost relatives.

DIARY: FEBRUARY 28, 1992

While I'm in the midst of getting ready for a conference in Colorado, Elaine Quick Bear Quiver called me and told me she heard a rumor that someone had put black paint on the granite monument at the Wounded Knee mass grave. Joe Horn Cloud called a few minutes later about a KILI radio broadcast and a phone call from his brother William concerning this rumor. He wanted to know how to give a reward for information leading to the arrest and conviction of the person(s) responsible if, indeed, the rumor proves to be true. What else can go wrong?

DIARY: MARCH 3, 1992

Called Sara Yager and told her that I was very concerned that the South Dakota congressional delegation has not introduced our proposed legislation in Congress; that if it isn't introduced soon we will not be able to get it passed in the current session since it is a short session. She said that some people feel we should wait until May 15, 1992 (when the NPS circulates its final report) before it is introduced.

Elaine Quick Bear Quiver called. She said that Royal Bull Bear told her that the Pine Ridge Grey Eagle Society members are letting Oliver Red Cloud run roughshod over them and it has to stop. She said Oliver was going to the Red Cloud building to "chew some people out" and Royal told him not to go. Royal told her that his great-grandfather also signed the 1868 treaty "so he has just as much say about treaty matters as Oliver."

DIARY: MARCH 5, 1992

When I spoke with Joe Horn Cloud today he suggested that we should call for a federal investigation of the vandalism of the monument at the mass grave. He said tribal law enforcement officers have been unsuccessful in finding the vandals. All they can say is "too bad."

Sam's wife delivered a message from him. As she drove him back to the hospital, he asked her to have me check to see why the introduction of our proposed legislation is being delayed again. He wants to make sure that the proposed legislation is introduced before he gets too sick. She said the doctors don't know what is wrong with him; that he may have some kind of chemical imbalance. She is worried because he is now "sleeping all the time."

I drafted the following letter to Senator Daniel Inouye for Sam's signature (as per his request), viz.:

Honorable Daniel Inouye, Chairman
Senate Select Committee on Indian Affairs
838 Hart Senate Office Building
Washington, D.C., 20510

    Re: Wounded Knee Bill

Dear Senator Inouye:

Our attorney, Mr. Gonzalez, informed me that he faxed proposed amendments to the Wounded Knee bill to Mr. Pete Taylor on February 24, 1992, including recommendations made by the National Park Service. As you are aware, introduction of this bill has been delayed several times even though the National Park Service representatives agreed, at the hearing held at Pine Ridge on April 30, 1991, that introduction of the bill would not be dependent on completion of their final NPS report on alternatives.

I feel that it is imperative that the amendments be incorporated into the bill and that it be introduced immediately, since the current session of Congress is a short session and we need time to generate public support for the bill. Thank you for your prompt consideration and response.

/s/ Sam Eaglestaff

DIARY: MARCH 10, 1992

*I stopped by Rapid City Regional Hospital today to visit Sam. I was re-
lieved to learn that he had been released and returned to his home in Eagle Butte. I have the feeling that he does not have much time left. I am
saddened when I think about the many years that people like my friend,
Sam Eaglestaff, have been denied justice.*

DIARY: MARCH 13, 1992

*I called Pete Taylor today to express my concern about the delay in intro-
ducing our proposed legislation in Congress. I asked him if our proposed
legislation could be introduced prior to the release of the NPS final report
on May 15th, since members of the WKSAs feel that if the introduction of
our proposed legislation is delayed for too long a period of time, we will
not have a sufficient amount of time to lobby it through Congress. Taylor
agreed that it should be introduced as soon as possible and that we should
not have to wait until May 15th to get it introduced.*

*I also suggested that the language relating to the Big Foot Historic Trail
should be revised so the proposed legislation would authorize a feasibility
study to establish the Big Foot Historic Trail rather than attempt to authorize it without a feasibility study.*

DIARY: MARCH 17, 1992

*Called Sam today. His voice sounded stronger, but started to fade away
during our conversation. His wife Kathy got on the phone and explained
that Sam's doctor told him he had a TIA stroke, which he can get anytime
and causes him to lose his memory. He could also have a major stroke at
any time. She said her brother came over from Wind River and made some
Indian (Arapaho) medicine for strokes. They had a ceremony for Sam on
Saturday and are hopeful that the medicine will help.*

DIARY: MARCH 28, 1992

*Returned Renée Flood's call today. She asked if Sam Eaglestaff will be able
to attend the Indian Week powwow at Vermillion, South Dakota, on April
11th to receive the donation she plans to give the Cheyenne River WKSA
from the proceeds of her book* Lost Bird. *I told her that I spoke to Marcella
LeBeau and was informed that Sam had been transferred back to Rapid
City Regional Hospital, so I do not know if he is well enough to travel to
Vermillion to accept the donation.*

DIARY: APRIL 3, 1992

> *Pete Taylor called today to tell me that there will be a short congressional recess that will end around the 23rd of this month, so he wants to aim for the end of April to have our proposed legislation introduced in Congress. I drafted a memorandum to WKSA members to inform them of my conversation with Taylor and mailed copies to Theresa Two Bulls, Sam Eaglestaff, Marcella LeBeau, Melvin Garreau, Marie Not Help Him, Belva Hollow Horn, Claudia Iron Hawk Sully, Susan Shown Harjo, Alex White Plume, Richard Rovsek, Dr. Dwight Davis, and Francis Jansen.*

CHRONICLE

Mario Gonzalez, by profession a lawyer who has been trained to think of time and events in terms of progress and getting the job done, was unhappy with the uncertainty that as spring came along things could only get better, or else the business of waiting would set in, or, unfortunately, things could get worse. Who could say what?

He tried to keep a positive attitude because it is his belief that "persistence pays off."

Had he been a reader of poetry, he might have known that T. S. Eliot's commentary about April could help him through the next several weeks. Eliot said: "April is the cruelest month, breeding / Lilacs out of the dead land, mixing / Memory and desire, stirring / Dull roots with spring rain" (*The Waste Land*, 1921) Though some have said this important American poet expressed despair at the triviality and moral decay of modern civilization, something Gonzalez could also attest to, his real point was that the thunder told people to have hope in natural ceremonials. All Lakotas, including Gonzalez, know about thunder and ceremony and fields of hope.

As April began in 1992, then, there would be more delays in the struggle for the legislation which would develop a monument to the Sacred Dead at Wounded Knee.

Delays were brought on by the birth of a new tribal administration at the Pine Ridge Agency and this event would illustrate the inevitable contrast and continuation of the tribal struggle as well as the impact that political and bureaucratic tyranny has on tribal life.

The new tribal chairman, John Yellow Bird Steele, would head the Oglala Sioux government for the next term, at least, and in the process would become one of the major critics of the National Park Service plan to administer the Wounded Knee memorial.

Rarely in the history of this IRA tribe since 1934 has any chairman been elected for more than one term, the one exception being Dick Wilson (1972–76) during the American Indian Movement era. This is a fact which, when contrasted with the long-term, often lifetime leadership patterns known to have existed among the Sioux for centuries, is astounding. One of the reasons for such short-term leadership is that modern tribes and their officials are often seen as simply federal creatures whose main purpose is to administer federal Indian Affairs according to a Washington, D.C., set of guidelines and procedures.

While this may not have been the intent of the legislation (the IRA), it has been its effect. With the passing of one IRA administration on the tribal homelands, then, and the inauguration of another, the people would simply have to struggle on in anticipation or dread of the hand from which Steele would deal the cards of a tribal deck. This card game, some say, continues to be severely limited by an oppressive federal bureaucracy. Steele was later defeated and then, in 1996, joined the rare ranks of those chairmen who served again by being reelected by the people.

DIARY: APRIL 5, 1992

Melvin Garreau called to inform me that he resigned his position as tribal representative on the NPS team on the "study of alternatives." The reason he gave was that the Cheyenne River Sioux tribal chairman, Gregg Bourland, seemed to take the position that you have to be an elected official before you can represent the tribe on these matters. I told him I was sorry that he had resigned because we need more people from the communities to have input in the study.

We also discussed other matters, including the $2,000 to be donated by Renée Flood to the Cheyenne River WKSA from the Lost Bird book. I suggested that he attend the Indian Week powwow at Vermillion and participate in Renée's presentation of the checks to the WKSAs.[8]

DIARY: APRIL 6, 1992

Called Sam today. His daughter Kay Eaglestaff informed me that Sam started to go into a coma today so they took him to the Eagle Butte Hospital. He is recovering.

DIARY: APRIL 12, 1992

Called Renée Flood to hear how the presentation of checks to the WKSAs turned out. The checks were presented last night at the Indian Week pow-

*wow in Vermillion. Renée said that Alex White Plume attended and just
left for home. Sam Eaglestaff made it; he accepted the check on behalf of
the Cheyenne River WKSA and gave it to Burdell Blue Arm (their treasurer). She said that both Sam and Burdell spoke at the powwow, but Sam
had a fever so he and his family returned home early this morning. Burdell left about the same time.*

    *She also said that Claudia Iron Hawk Sully and Marie Not Help Him
were also there, and also left for home. Others in attendance included Suzan Shown Harjo and Kevin Locke.*

Diary: April 14, 1992

*Newly elected Oglala Sioux tribal president John Steele's inauguration is
set for today. I will not attend because of prior commitments, and because
I really have no personal desire to attend. I believe that tribal inaugura-
tions are a waste of time and money, especially when the money could be
better spent to provide services to Indian people who really need assistance.
I worked with Steele since the 1970s and I feel he lacks cognitive mobility
and will become a negative influence on our lobbying effort. Unfortunately, as tribal president, his views will carry a lot of weight with the South
Dakota congressional delegation and the Senate Select Committee on Indian Affairs, who have done enough foot dragging thus far.*

    *I had an interesting exchange with Pete Taylor today that illustrates
what I mean. When he asked how John Steele felt about the amended bill,
saying that he seemed to have negative feelings about the bill when he visited in Washington, D.C., after winning the election, I told him that John's
position was not as important as the tribal council's position, and that the
tribal executive committee's resolution (which acts on the behalf of the
tribal council when it's not in session) is the current position of the tribe
and it supports our proposed legislation In response, Taylor said rather
heatedly, "Oh, yes, his position DOES matter!" I responded by telling Taylor: "Haven't you heard? We have a democracy here on the Pine Ridge Reservation, not a dictatorship."*

    *Taylor then asked me if I knew what Steele's position was and I said I
didn't. All I know is that he was supportive of our proposed legislation at
the April 30, 1991, Senate Select Committee on Indian Affairs hearing at
Pine Ridge.*

    *I told Pete that I have over $20,000 in out of pocket expenses and over
$200,000 in attorney's time invested in our legislative effort, and that I*

wasn't going to allow that investment to go down the drain based on the whims of one individual, namely John Steele. I told him that I made a commitment to the WKSAs in 1985 to help them in getting Congress to atone for the massacre, and I intend to make the national monument a reality. I told him that I would, nevertheless, contact Steele and solicit his support but that, if necessary, I will ask the tribal council to reaffirm the tribe's support for our legislative proposal.

CHRONICLE

The federal bureaucracies bend over backwards to give IRA governments lip service and the illusion that they have power. However, when Sioux Nation politicians tell the bureaucracies to give back the land they stole, nobody pays the slightest attention. In the case of the Black Hills land reform issue, the tribes have said, *officially,* that they will not be paid off and "The Black Hills Are Not for Sale!!!" and John Steele, himself, has said it over and over. Since when does "his position" matter to the bureaucrats??? Only when it can cause controversy and conflict and delay!

DIARY: APRIL 15, 1992

Paul Little called this morning. He said that while he was attending the Steele-Lone Hill administration's inauguration yesterday, a man from the Yankton Reservation informed him that a large meeting is planned at Manderson today to oppose our legislative proposal, that these people are in favor of leaving the Wounded Knee site as it is today and oppose any type of development at the site. I responded that "protection" of the site is what our proposed legislation is all about. More and more tourists will be visiting the mass grave each year, and since we can't stop them, we better do something to protect the sacredness of the site.

DIARY: APRIL 20, 1992

I received a call from Belva Hollow Horn today. She said that a Wounded Knee District meeting was held this past weekend and Walter Little Moon, Oliver Red Cloud, and other opponents of our proposed legislation dominated the discussion. Joe Swift Bird tried to speak and every time he did, Oliver Red Cloud, who was sitting at the speaker's table, would stand up and interrupt. Little Moon allowed this to happen. Belva saw this as a strategy to keep Swift Bird from giving his opinion in support of our legislative proposal.

She also commented on the hypocrisy of Gerald and Pamela Ice and their followers who are opposing our proposed legislation, yet are engaging in their own private fund-raiser to raise $3 million to commercially develop the massacre site. *They appear to be treating the WKSAs as business competitors for the commercialization of the site, and completely misapprehend the position of the WKSAs that the religious and historic values of the site must be protected; that the WKSAs regard the site as sacred ground, not commercial property.*

DIARY: APRIL 21, 1992

Mailed the copy of the April 20th draft of the WK bill to Elaine Quick Bear Quiver (which includes the amendment requested by the Oglala Sioux Tribal Executive Committee). She told me that the Pine Ridge Grey Eagle Society supports our proposed legislation, but they are thinking of a smaller acreage for the park, like the 40-acre Gildersleeve Trading Post area. I told her that the mass grave will have to be included in any proposed park and it is located on the 40 acres the Catholic church returned to the Oglala Sioux Tribe north of Gildersleeves. I told her that the minimum size of the proposed park under the current version of the bill is 640 acres.

Elaine also said that Francis He Crow and Oliver Red Cloud recently got into a big argument. Francis asked Oliver who Jack Red Cloud's wife was; Oliver said he didn't know and Francis responded by saying "you should know these things, you're a Red Cloud." She said that as the argument intensified, Francis told Oliver he didn't know anything, including treaties. Oliver told Francis he didn't know anything and they both left.

I told Elaine that the Grey Eagle Society members should not be listening to Francis because he is irrational. He talks about kicking all the mixed bloods off the Pine Ridge Reservation and implementing P.L. 741 (which is actually the 1954 Ute Termination Act).[9] In the 1960s, someone on the Pine Ridge Reservation retyped the Ute Termination Act and inserted the words "Oglala Sioux" in place of "Ute" throughout the act. Francis and others who think like him now believe that the retyped version of the Ute Act (which circulated throughout the reservation) is actually an Oglala Sioux Termination Act.

DIARY: APRIL 22, 1992

Pete Taylor today informed me that our proposed legislation will probably be introduced in Congress during the first week of May.

DIARY: APRIL 24, 1992

My good friend and ally, Sam Eaglestaff, died today. His wife Kathy asked me to be a pallbearer. The funeral will be held at Eagle Butte, South Dakota, and burial will be at Black Hills National Cemetery near Sturgis, South Dakota. The Grey Eagle Society members will conduct traditional Lakota burial ceremonies at the cemetery.

THE FOLLOWING EULOGY FOR SAM EAGLESTAFF WAS PRESENTED BY MARIO GONZALEZ AT CHRISTIAN WAKE SERVICES HELD ON APRIL 28, 1992, AT THE CATHOLIC CHURCH IN EAGLE BUTTE, SOUTH DAKOTA

Since graduating from law school in 1972, I have worked with many Lakota people who have passed on to the spirit world. This has been one of the difficult aspects of working on the Sioux land claims and our proposed legislation to get Congress to atone for the 1890 Wounded Knee Massacre. And now Sam has joined those who have left us. The greatness of a Lakota person after his death is not determined by the amount of wealth he accumulated, or the type of personality he or she had. It's determined by what that person stood for. For example, Chief Crazy Horse was a great man because he was a patriot who was willing to lay down his life in defense of our homeland and way of life. Sam's greatness will be determined by what he stood for. Although I have known Sam for only a few years, I recognized many of the good qualities he possessed. He was a man who was close to his wife, children, and grandchildren. His existence revolved around them. I knew him as a Lakota man who possessed and practiced Lakota virtues. I knew him as:

a spiritual *man in both the Catholic religion and traditional Lakota religion*

a wise *man who showed wisdom in making difficult decisions*

a generous *man, especially to his children*

a humble *man who lived a simple lifestyle and was never arrogant toward other people*

a brave *man willing to stand up for the rights of the Lakota people and his tribe*

These are virtues that I greatly admire. They are virtues that we must teach to our children and grandchildren so they will become good citizens.

CHRONICLE

After the death of Sam Eaglestaff, Gonzalez, for the first time, began to
talk privately of the enormity of coming to grips with this historical legacy
of injustice. He felt more determined than ever to get the Wounded Knee
legislation passed by Congress.

Though Gonzalez and others in the movement to achieve a monument
to the Minneconjou dead felt enormously saddened at the loss of another
significant elder, they knew that the Lakota search for its own national
identity had to be continued.

April and May came and went and the prediction that the bill would be
introduced went with them.

Another year went by as bureaucrats dragged their feet and tribal people wrangled among themselves. This delay was seen by Gonzalez as a
function of the underdeveloped legal and political systems on the reservation and of the one-sided U.S. power structures.

Finally, in May of 1993, a meeting with Secretary Babbitt of the Department of Interior was held. While the secretary seemed enthusiastic, newly
elected OST president John Steele made a statement in opposition to the
legislation. He told Babbitt that the Oglala Sioux Tribe had to have complete control, more input and jurisdiction over the project, even though
individual Minneconjou tribal members (who were lineal descendants of
the Wounded Knee dead) and the Cheyenne River Sioux Tribe have an interest in the mass grave and in preventing commercial exploitation of
their dead.

Also, he said, "We will not give up any land."

That seemed to be taken as a kind of threat and the effect was that the
proposed legislation came to a standstill. It also may have been a misstate-
ment since the Zuni-Cíbola model recommended by the National Park
Service and utilized by the WKSAs in their proposed legislation did not
authorize a conveyance of title to Indian land to the National Park Service.

The May 13, 1993, special to the *Lakota Times* read:

> Porcupine, S.D.—The site sits forlornly on the hill, the cleansing winds of time
> blowing but unable to sweep away the tragedy that happened here.
> One hundred years after the Wounded Knee Massacre, the site is close to
> being recognized as the most deserving of places to erect a memorial for the
> victims killed here.
> But, on the eve of being introduced in Congress, the proposed Wounded
> Knee Memorial bill, lobbied by the WK Survivors' Associations for the last six

years, was referred back to the tribe for the approval of the newly elected President's administration.

Pine Ridge Tribal President John Steele, saying he was personally against the bill, broke a tie on the issue and referred the proposal back to the committee.

The council meeting was called at the request of the National Park Service to present three alternatives to the Wounded Knee Survivors' Association bill.

A study on alternatives is required before Congress can pass the bill. The study was presented by Badlands National Park Superintendent Irv Mortensen and Allen Hagood, Denver.

Several members of Wounded Knee District also appeared to support President Steele in his opposition to the bill, including District Chairman Tom Clifford, Bob and Anita Ecoffey and Walter Little Moon. Oliver Red Cloud also voiced his opposition to the bill.

Black Hawk attorney Mario Gonzalez, who has represented the Survivors' Associations since 1986, gave a historical background of the efforts to get Congress to atone for the 1890 Massacre. He said, in part,

In 1891 Congress passed the Indian Depredations Act. Under this Act, everyone was paid for losses associated with the 1890 Massacre except Chief Big Foot's People (Sitanka Oyate). Big Foot's people were denied compensation because they were considered "hostiles."

For the past 101 years the Survivors' Associations have been attempting to get Congress to atone for the massacre by compensating massacre victims and their families for their losses.

According to Mr. Gonzalez, a number of bills were introduced in Congress, some in the 1940's and 50's to pay $1,000 compensation to each victim or their descendants. "All of these bills failed in Congress because the U.S. Army would oppose them on the basis that the massacre was the fault of the Indians."

A pivotal meeting was called by Gonzalez a month later, on June 13, 1993, when he arranged an informational session to be held in Rapid City at the request of some WKSA members in order to deal with the conflicts posed by Oglala Sioux tribal chairman John Steele.

Using all of the "conflict resolution" skills he had learned in twenty years of legal wrangling about tribal affairs, he began by asking two questions: "Who are the identifiable groups to have final input?" and "What do they want?"

The Pine Ridge Wounded Knee Survivors' representatives were quick to respond. They wanted the right and responsibility to tell the story, to interpret the story, and, in the process of that they expected the secretary of the interior to appoint an advisory committee of native professionals and Big Foot descendants to design an appropriate monument. They also wanted protection for the site and an apology from the United States government for murdering their relatives on their sovereign homeland. And, finally, they wanted a cultural heritage center/museum located near the massacre site which would contain an archival repository for their historical collections.

The Cheyenne River Sioux Survivors' Association wanted to give support to all that development at the site; they also wanted a Big Foot Historic Trail and a cultural heritage center/museum development on their own reservation, and tribal (not state or federal) jurisdiction.

The Wounded Knee District Council wanted to preserve the land base and individual land ownership. Their representative, and the representative of *tribal governments,* John Steele wanted to talk about land ownership, public safety issues, jurisdiction and oversight services, preservation and conservation, and funding mechanisms. He insisted that tribal jurisdiction, i.e., Oglala Sioux Nation jurisdiction over the massacre site, was essential.

The American Indian Movement, little heard from publicly during the entire six-year period, wanted to be assured that the Interpretation would not be left up to "them/others"; that the Lakotas would be in charge of interpretation. Others, less dedicated to the organizations named but members of the tribes, wanted to make sure that there would be no "federal ownership," no "state ownership" of lands, and no possibility of that ever happening in the future.

The National Park Service wanted to be assured that this affiliated unit of the park system would "meet National Park Service standards." They wanted to offer advisory, technical assistance in management and would also assist in the financial role of the park system.

As this discussion ensued, state officials, mostly tourist development personnel, sat quietly and had little to add. This discussion would eventually go into another draft of the legislation (see appendix J). What this meant was that the Zuni-Cíbola model originally recommended by the National Park Service would not be the major organizational structure for this park; rather, a new model would emerge and this would be the first of its kind, a tribal memorial park which would be developed within the National Park Service structure. It meant, finally, that the Zuni-Cíbola model would not be part of S. 382, a bill that would have created a national park based on the 1988 Zuni-Cíbola Act.[10] Instead, it would have its own unique "national tribal park" developmental intent and structure crafted by the WKSAs based on the third alternative of the National Park Service's study of alternatives.

These clarifications made a difference and the discussion of the development of a new model for this kind of development seemed to bring the tribal concerns into the appropriate focus.

On February 9, 1995, two years later, the proposed legislation (S. 382) sought so long by the Lakota people was introduced in both houses of the United States Congress, a momentous event.

The largest newspaper in western South Dakota, the *Rapid City Journal,* announced it in this way on February 10, 1995:

Bill Sees Wounded Knee Park
Legislation Would Create Tribal Park

Washington—Federal legislation to establish Wounded Knee Park has the backing of South Dakota's congressional delegation and a national parks group.

Sens. Tom Daschle and Larry Pressler and Rep. Tim Johnson introduced bills Thursday, and the National Parks and Conservation Association praised their leadership.

"Wounded Knee is a site of true national significance to the American people," said NPC President Paul Pritchard. "It should be protected and preserved for future generations."

The Washington-based watchdog group is dedicated to protecting the national park system. NPCA has more than 450,000 members.

Marie Not Help Him, president of the Wounded Knee Survivors' Association, joined the call for a new park:

"This bill is a long time coming. It's important to have a proper and fitting memorial to those who perished at Wounded Knee. We need to protect and preserve the area not only to educate our own people, but national and international visitors as well. This is an important part of American history."

The Pine Ridge and Cheyenne River Sioux tribes, along with the National Park Service, would jointly manage the park.

Even so, at the time of writing this book there is the recognition that the fight for the monument has a long way to go before it is accomplished in all of its potential. Even should the legislation go forward immediately, there will be voices of dissent which will slow progress and it may be many years before the people see their homelands protected and their relatives honored and their history told as only they know it.

On that day of reading the news of the accomplishment in the mainstream northern plains press, though, the Lakotas were reminded that there is a special kind of history which is written by white men that focuses on the winners and losers, the beginning and the end, the quick and the dead.

Indian history, it seemed to many of them, had a different emphasis, and now, in the wake of this long struggle, they could describe it in their own terms as a victory over time, themselves, and an enemy so implacable that its wish to declare them extinct and irrelevant seemed eternal.

If Indian histories had any feature which distinguished them from other histories, they said to one another, it was the fact that it was based on the continuum, not the triumph nor the loss, not the beginning nor the end. Its central feature seemed to be the continuation, the discursive story which gives meaning to communal events, singular lives, spiritual values, and the remembered earth.

To those who had accompanied Gonzalez on this journey, the final breakthrough in the struggle was not surprising, nor was it unexpected. It had always been, some thought, just "a matter of time."

Many had been witness to the careful perseverance of all of them. On several occasions, they had seen Gonzalez demonstrate his "conflict-resolution" skills, not ordinarily thought to be a part of a lawyer's traits. Lawyers, the subject of derogatory jokes in American popular culture, are often accused of not only exploitation but, worse, aiding and abetting conflicts which then get out of hand. Gonzalez, to the people who know him well, represents the kind of lawyer who will go the last mile to resolve differences and do the right thing. For the sake of the people.

The Lakota knew, also, that this drama of a particular Indian life struggle in the United States was not meant to be the last word, that it might be a mere postscript, a codicil, a continuation of the long story. It would provide a brief, modern framework for the dialogue to begin in support of the Sioux longing for its nation-centered narrative to be told by its own people.

Following the announcement of the introduction of the legislation, the young Oglala Sioux lawyer would go into broader fields of activities.

In 1995 he was named the first recipient of the Distinguished Aboriginal Lawyer Achievement Award, given by the Native Law Centre of Canada, University of Saskatchewan at Saskatoon. This award was given not only because he represented the Oglala Sioux Tribe in the 1980 Black Hills Case, was the author of the Indian language of the Mni Wiconi Act of 1988 and the 1994 amendments to that act,[11] and was the author of two Black Hills bills which require the return of stolen lands, the 1987 Bradley Bill (S. 705) and 1990 Martinez Bill (H.R. 5680). It was given also because he represented the Oglala and Minneconjou in what many considered a lost cause, the struggle for a tribal historical legacy to be embodied in an appropriately proposed Wounded Knee monument. It was given, most of all, because he symbolizes all of the resistances of native peoples throughout this continent.[12]

Mario Gonzalez takes with him as he goes about his work the assurance of the Indian people who always say, "I don't know why non-Indians believe the Lakota are a conquered people. It is just being fought on another battlefield. We now battle the U.S. government in the courtrooms, the halls of Congress, and at the United Nations. The Lakota people won every major military engagement with the United States in the 1860s and signed a peace treaty with the United States in 1868. Although the U.S. Army violated that treaty by attacking Lakota people exercising their article 11 and 16 hunting rights at the Little Bighorn River in Montana on June 25, 1876, the Lakota defeated Lt. Col. George Armstrong Custer's Seventh Cavalry at that battle, and have been residing in peace on their reservations as they agreed to do in 1868.

Gonzalez's current view of the political relationship between the Lakota people and the United States can be summarized as follows:

He believes that the long-term and devastating federal Indian policy was articulated by Chief Justice John Marshall in 1823 in the case of *Johnson v. McIntosh*[13] where Marshall—in describing the doctrine of discovery—stated that Indian tribes are conquered nations and will, eventually, be completely assimilated into American society:

> The title by conquest is acquired and maintained by force. The conqueror prescribes its limits. Humanity, however, acting on public opinion, has established, as a general rule, that the conquered shall not be wantonly oppressed, and that their condition shall remain as eligible as is compatible with the objects of the conquest. Most usually, they are incorporated with the victorious nation, and become subjects or citizens of the government with which they are connected. The new and old members of the society mingle with each other; the distinction between them is gradually lost, and they make one people. Where this incorporation is practicable, humanity demands, and a wise policy requires that the rights of the conquered to property should remain unimpaired; that the new subjects should be governed as equitably as the old, and that confidence in their security should gradually banish the painful sense of being separated from their ancient connexions, and united by force to strangers.

Gonzalez believes that the conquest of the Lakota people is a state of mind; that the Lakota people will become a conquered people only when they start believing they are conquered and start acting like they are conquered.

He believes that if the Lakota people want to exercise their God-given right to survive on earth as a distinct culture and sovereign people, they must continue to demand fidelity to Lakota treaties, reject the sale of the Black Hills through the Indian Claims Commission process, demand a fair and honorable settlement for the Black Hills Claim and other Sioux land claims, and demand atonement for the 1890 Wounded Knee Massacre.

Epilogue

The proposed monument at Wounded Knee not only honors the Lakota dead. It honors the Lakota ideals of its own storytellers. A nation whose story has been under foreign domination cannot express its nationhood, and such a condition will not be tolerated by the men and women of the First Nations of America. All of the dramatis personae you have been introduced to here in this story know that there is much work to be done and that the struggle to throw off the yoke of colonial domination has many origins. The proposed legislation referred to here is an exemplar of the beginning of a new relationship with the United States, and if such a collaboration were to occur in the way the survivors/descendants envisioned it, the wounds of the last century could begin to heal and there could be a new trust between the peoples of this region in the next century.

In the case of the Sioux Nation, where very old cultural ideas about the people's place in a specific geography have flourished for centuries, references to the meaning of life are found in all of the songs, in the names of wise men and brave women, in the actions of poets and warriors. Many native texts cannot be attributed to a specific person. Others can and are told over and over and, finally, are written down by those who have been saved from oblivion. The significance of Alice Ghost Horse's story about the 1890 Wounded Knee Massacre, which Gonzalez places in the front part of his diaries, is that it is prelude to what has amounted to the death and subjugation of thousands of Indians. It lays bare the historical reality that the colonization and subjugation of the Sioux Nation has always been the object of the United States' relationship with them and it suggests that America's new people have a far journey before they can overcome the prejudice against Indians that seems

to be part of their own immigrant origins in this land. The story of this cen-
turies-long struggle clarifies the historical intent of the U S. executive branch,
the Congress, and the court systems which have played the seminal role in
adversely affecting the ability of the Sioux to govern their own lives. Two
colonizing concepts, namely, Congress's plenary power over Indian tribes and
manifest destiny (implemented through the doctrine of discovery), have
resulted in the development of an institutionalized and bureaucratized body
of law directed toward the destruction of Indian nationalism and sovereignty.
These concepts must be examined and disavowed if indigenous peoples are
to be free of discriminatory treatment not only in South Dakota but around
the country.

Anything that is said about the Wounded Knee Massacre (the essential
subject matter of this book), any discussion of spirituality, any oration or song
about death, any ideas about the cosmos, any political conversation, or any
tribal dealings of any kind have reference in the concept of First Nation sovereignty in specific homelands, otherwise defined as the freedom of self-government of indigenous peoples.

The Politics of Hallowed Ground is a modern accounting of the efforts of
ordinary people to make sense of colonial politics in our time and it follows
a paper trail as clear and unmistakable as the trail of blood left in the hills of
the Pine Ridge Reservation after the killing a century ago. The expectation
of the current effort narrated here is that crimes against humanity can be
acknowledged by their perpetrators, that official apologies can ensue, that
stolen lands and rights can be returned to tribal peoples, that colonization
and enforced assimilation can be identified as among the historical crimes
against humanity, and that the recognition of wrongful death can be more
than just an ache in the heart.

Appendixes

Introduction to the Appendixes

Mario Gonzalez

The real causes for the 1890 Wounded Knee Massacre lie not in the Ghost Dance, as many non-Indian historians have claimed over the years, but in the deliberate theft and unlawful occupation by the United States and its citizens of treaty-protected Lakota/Dakota lands. The argument which is at the center of the Wounded Knee Survivors' Associations' efforts to get Congress to atone for the massacre is that the theft of the Lakota/Dakota lands in 1877 and 1889 coupled with the terrible conditions that existed on the Sioux reservations in the late 1880s are the real causes of the massacre. The Sioux Indians were looking for salvation in a messiah that would save them. Thus, the Ghost Dance religion was merely a symptom of their plight in 1890, not the cause of the massacre.

The materials that appear in these appendixes are intended to give the reader a better understanding of the history of the Lakota/Dakota bands. The materials illustrate why the Sioux people do not regard themselves as a defeated, conquered people. The United States did not militarily defeat the Lakota/Dakota bands in the 1850s and 1860s, but instead entered into a treaty of peace at Fort Laramie in 1868. This treaty has governed the political relationship between the United States and Lakota/Dakota bands, although the United States has continually violated it by confiscating Lakota/Dakota territory in violation of article 12 of the treaty.

Today, the United States treats the Sioux reservations and the Lakota/Dakota tribes that occupy them as colonial possessions rather than sovereign people who have the right to self-government within their territories. Even though the United States recognized in article 8 of the Black Hills Act that the Lakota/Dakota bands would be guaranteed an "orderly tribal government," they have illegally allowed the state of South Dakota over the years to extend state and local government and jurisdiction over the Lakota/Dakota reservations. The Lakota/Dakota people currently regard their relationship with the United States as a government-to-government relationship based on treaties, not upon conquest.

Since 1980, the Lakota/Dakota people have expressed their desire to embark on a new relationship with the United States built on enforcing treaty obligations in a manner that will recognize and respect the Lakota/Dakota as a sovereign people and ensure their survival as native people. This new relationship can start with the building of a national monument at the Wounded Knee Massacre site to begin a process of healing the deep wounds caused by the 1890 Wounded Knee Massacre and by settling the Lakota/Dakota land claims in a fair and honorable manner.

Appendix A

Other Readings and Dates of Significance

1. Treaty of July 5, 1825 (7 Stat. 252) with the Sioune and Oglala Bands (7 Stat. 252). The successors of the Sioune Band (which included the Minneconjou in 1825) currently reside on the Cheyenne River Reservation. The Oglala Band currently reside on the Pine Ridge Reservation.

2. Fort Laramie Treaty of September 17, 1851 (11 Stat. 749) with the Sioux or Dahcotahs, Cheyennes, Arapahos, Crows, Assinaboines, Gros-Ventre, Mandans, and Arrickaras. The Sioux that signed this treaty are the Seven Teton Bands (the Lakota) and the Yankton Sioux (the Nakota). This treaty recognized title to 60 million acres of territory in the Sioux as follows:

ARTICLE V

The aforesaid Indians do hereby recognize and acknowledge the following tracts of country, included within the metes and boundaries hereinafter designated, as their respective territories, viz:

The territory of the Sioux or Dahcotah Nation, commencing the mouth of the White Earth River on the Missouri River; thence in a southeasterly direction to the forks of the Platte River; thence up the north fork of the Platte River to a point known as the Red Butte, or where the road leaves the river; thence along the range of mountains known as the Black Hills, to the head waters of the Heart River; thence down Heart River to its mouth; and thence down the Missouri River to the place of beginning.

3. Explanatory Memorandum: Indian Office Memorandum and related documents concerning ratification of the Treaty of September 17, 1851. Kappler, *Indian Affairs: Laws and Treaties*, vol. 4, pp. 1067–81.

4. Fort Laramie Treaty of April 29, 1868, with the Sioux—Brule, Oglala, Miniconjou, Yanktonai, Hunkpapa, Blackfeet, Cuthead, Two Kettle, Sans Arcs, and Santee—

and Arapaho (15 Stat. 635). This treaty (among other things) established peace between the United States and the Sioux bands, established a permanent reservation for the Sioux Indians (art. 2), restricted the manner in which the United States could obtain cessions of the reservation (art. 12), and recognized Sioux hunting rights outside the reservation (arts. 11 and 16) as follows:

ARTICLE I

From This day forward all war between the parties to this agreement shall forever cease. The Government of the United States desires peace, and its honor is hereby pledged to keep it. The Indians desire peace, and they now pledge their honor to maintain it.

ARTICLE II

The United States agrees that the following district of country, to wit, viz: commencing on the east bank of the Missouri River where the forty-sixth parallel of north latitude crosses the same, thence along low-water mark down said east bank to a point opposite where the northern line of the State of Nebraska strikes the river, thence west across said river, and along the northern line of Nebraska to the one hundred and fourth degrees of longitude west from Greenwich, then north on said meridian to a point where the forty-sixth parallel of north latitude intercepts the same, thence due east along said parallel to the place of beginning; and in addition thereto, all existing reservations on the east bank of said river shall be, and the same is, set apart for the absolute and undisturbed use and occupation of the Indians herein named, and for such other friendly tribes or individual Indians as from time to time they may be willing, with the consent of the United States, to admit amongst them; and the United States now solemnly agrees that no person except those herein designated and authorized so to do, and except such officers, agents, and employees of the Government as may be authorized to enter upon Indian reservations in discharge of duties enjoined by law, shall ever be permitted to pass over, settle upon, or reside in the territory described in this article, or in such territory as may be added to this reservation for the use of said Indians, and henceforth they will and do hereby relinquish all claims or right in and to any portion of the United States or Territories, except such as is embraced within the limits aforesaid, and except as hereinafter provided.

ARTICLE XI

In consideration of the advantages and benefits conferred by this treaty, and the many pledges of friendship by the United States, the tribes who are parties to this agreement hereby stipulate that they will relinquish all right to occupy permanently the territory outside their reservation as herein defined, but yet reserve the right to hunt on any lands north of the North Platte, and on the Replica Fork of the Smoky Hill River, so long as the buffalo may range thereon in such numbers as to justify the chase. * * * *

Article XII

No treaty for the cession of any portion or part of the reservation herein described which may be held in common shall be of any validity or force as against the said Indians, unless executed and signed by at least three fourths of all the adult male Indians, occupying or interested in the same; and no cession by the tribe shall be understood or construed in such manner as to deprive, without his consent, any individual member of the tribe of his rights to any tract of land selected by him, as provided in article 6 of this treaty.

Article XVI

The United States hereby agrees and stipulates that the country north of the North Platte River and east of the summits of the Big Horn Mountains shall be held and considered to be unceded Indian territory, and also stipulates and agrees that no white person or persons shall be permitted to settle upon or occupy any portion of the same; or without consent of the Indians first had and obtained, to pass through the same; and it is further agreed by the Untied States that within ninety days after the conclusion of peace with all the bands of the Sioux Nation, the military posts now established in the territory in this article named shall be abandoned, and that the road leading to them and by them to the settlements in the Territory of Montana shall be closed.

5. Act of March 3, 1871 (16 Stat. 544). This act signified the end of the treaty-making period in United States/Native American relations, according to the United States version of history. The act contained the following language: "No Indian nation or tribe within the territory of the United States shall be acknowledged or recognized as an independent nation, tribe, or power with whom the United States may contract by treaty; but no obligation of any treaty lawfully made and ratified with any such Indian Nation or tribe prior to March third, eighteen hundred and seventy one, shall be hereby invalidated or impaired."

This language was attached at the last minute to an appropriations bill because the House of Representatives wanted more say over Indian affairs, since treaties are negotiated by the president and ratified by the Senate. Legal scholars such as Felix Cohen have condemned this not only as an inappropriate way to make Indian law but as possibly unconstitutional. See Felix Cohen, *Handbook of Federal Indian Law*, p. 66.

6. Just after the Battle of the Little Bighorn, which was won by the Sioux military forces and their Cheyenne and Arapahoe allies on June 25, 1876, Congress enacted the Act of August 15, 1876 (19 Stat. 176, 192), which provided that "hereafter there shall be no appropriation made for the subsistence of the sioux, unless they first relinquished their rights to the hunting grounds outside the [1868 treaty] reservation,

ceded the Black Hills to the United States, and reached some accommodation with the Government that would be calculated to enable them to become self-supporting." The Manypenny Commission was commissioned under this act to travel to the Sioux reservation and obtain the requisite three-fourths of adult male signatures required to cede the Black Hills. The Sioux referred to August 15, 1876, Act as the "starve or sell" act.

7. The Black Hills Act of February 28, 1877 (19 Stat. 254). The Manypenny Commission circulated an "agreement" among the Sioux which would have ceded the Black Hills portion of the 1868 Treaty Reservation (Great Sioux Reservation). The commission was able to obtain only 10 percent of the adult male signatures. To resolve the "impasse," Congress enacted the agreement into law on February 28, 1877. The agreement became an act of Congress which confiscated the Black Hills without the consent of the Sioux in violation of article 12 of the 1868 treaty and the Fifth Amendment. Articles 5 and 8 of the 1877 act are of particular significance to the Sioux Nation's current defense of the Black Hills:

ARTICLE V

In consideration of the foregoing cession of territory and rights, and upon full compliance with each and every obligation assumed by the said Indians, the United States does agree to provide all necessary aid to assist the said Indians in the work of civilization; to furnish to them schools and instruction in mechanical and agricultural arts, as provided for by the treaty of 1868. Also to provide the said Indians with subsistence consisting of a ration for each individual of a pound and a half of beef, (or in lieu thereof, one half pound of bacon), one-half pound of flour, and one-half pound of corn; and for every one hundred rations, four pounds of coffee, eight pounds of sugar, and three pounds of beans, or in lieu of said articles the equivalent thereof, in the discretion of the Commissioner of Indian Affairs. Such rations, or so much thereof as may be necessary, shall be continued until the Indians are able to support themselves. Rations shall, in all cases, be issued to the head of each separate family; and whenever schools shall have been provided by the Government for said Indians, no rations shall be issued for children between the ages of six and fourteen years (the sick and infirm excepted) unless such children shall regularly attend school. Whenever the said Indians shall be located upon lands which are suitable for cultivation, rations shall be issued only to the persons and families of those persons who labor, (the aged, sick and infirm excepted;) and as an incentive to industrious habits the Commissioner of Indian Affairs may provide that such persons be furnished in payment for their labor such other necessary articles as are requisite for civilized life. The Government will aid said Indians as far as possible in finding a market for their surplus productions, and in finding employment, and will purchase such surplus, as far as may be required, for supplying food to those Indians, parties to this agreement, who are unable to sustain themselves; and will also employ Indians, so far as practicable, in the performance of Government work upon their reservation.

ARTICLE VIII

The provisions of the said treaty of 1868, except as herein modified, shall continue in full force, and, with the provisions of this agreement, shall apply to any country which may hereafter be occupied by said Indians as a home; and Congress shall, by appropriate legislation, secure to them an orderly government; they shall be subject to the laws of the United States, and each individual shall be protected in his rights of property, person and life.

The Fifth Amendment to the United States Constitution (1791) provides:

No person shall be held to answer for a capital, or otherwise infamous crime, unless on a presentment or indictment of a Grand Jury, except in cases arising in the land or naval forces, or in the Militia, when in actual service in time of War or public danger; nor shall any person be subject for the same offence to be twice put in jeopardy of life or limb; nor shall be compelled in any criminal case to be a witness against himself, nor be deprived of life, liberty, or property, without due process of law; nor shall private property be taken for public use, without just compensation.

8. Executive Order of January 24, 1882. This order was signed by President Chester Arthur and created a 50 square mile buffer zone south of Pine Ridge Agency in Nebraska to keep out the illegal liquor trade. Kappler, *Indian Affairs: Laws and Treaties,* vol. 1, pp. 864–65.

9. The Act of March 2, 1889 (25 Stat. 888). This act carved out six smaller Sioux reservations from what remained of the 1868 Treaty Reservation (after the illegal confiscation of the Black Hills). The six reservations are: Pine Ridge Reservation (sec. 1); Rosebud Reservation (sec. 2); Standing Rock Reservation (sec. 3); Cheyenne River Reservation (sec. 4); Lower Brule Reservation (sec. 5); and Crow Creek Reservation (sec. 6).

The act also authorized allotments on the reservations (secs. 8–12). Section 28 of the act provided "That this act shall take effect, only, upon acceptance thereof and consent thereto by the different bands of the Sioux Nation of Indians, in manner and form prescribed by the twelfth article of the treaty between the United States and said Sioux Indians concluded April twenty-ninth, eighteen hundred and sixty eight, which said acceptance and consent, shall be made known by proclamation by the President of the United States, upon satisfactory proof presented to him, that the same has been obtained in the manner and form required, by said twelfth article of said treaty; which proof shall be presented to him within one year from the passage of this act; and upon failure of such proof and proclamation this act becomes of no effect and null and void." The Sioux do not regard the 1889 act as a valid act of Congress since the signatures that were obtained by the Edmunds Commission were obtained through fraud and coercion and do not constitute the requisite three-fourths of the adult male signatures for a valid cession of the 1868 reservation under article 12 of the 1868 treaty. The Sioux tribes, therefore, still claim all land and water to the east bank of the Missouri River as provided in article 2 of the 1868 treaty.

Under section 2 of the 1889 act, the 50 square mile buffer zone created by President Arthur's 1882 executive order was included as part of the Pine Ridge Indian Reservation as follows: "*Provided,* That the said tract of land in the State of Nebraska shall be reserved, by Executive Order, only so long as it may be needed for the use and protection of the Indians receiving rations and annuities at the Pine Ridge Agency."

10. Presidential Proclamation of February 10, 1890 (26 Stat. 1554). This proclamation was signed by President Benjamin Harrison to verify that the three-fourths of the adult male signatures were obtained by the Edmunds Commission under section 28 of the 1889 act (which incorporated article 12 of the 1868 treaty) and that the act was therefore in effect. The Sioux contend that the presidential proclamation is void since the requisite three-fourths of the adult male signatures were never obtained.

The 1890 proclamation in regards to the 50 square mile buffer zone south of Pine Ridge Agency said: "That in pursuance of the provisions contained in section one of said act, the tract of land situate in the State of Nebraska and described in said act as follows; to wit: Beginning at a point on the boundary-line between the State of Nebraska and the Territory of Dakota, where the range line between ranges forty-four and forty-five west of the sixth principal meridian, in the Territory of Dakota, intersects said boundary line; thence east along said boundary-line five miles; thence due south five miles; thence due west ten miles; thence due north to said boundary line; thence due east along said boundary line to the place of beginning, same is continued in a state of reservation so long as it is needed for the use and protection of the said Indians receiving rations and annuities at the Pine Ridge Agency."

11. Executive Order of January 25, 1904. This order was signed by President Theodore Roosevelt and "restored" the 50 square mile buffer zone in Nebraska that was included as part of the Pine Ridge Reservation under the 1889 act to the public domain as follows: "It is hereby ordered that the tract of country in the state of Nebraska 'withdrawn from sale and set aside as an addition to the present sioux Indian Reservation in the Territory of Dakota' by Executive Order dated January 24, 1882, be, and the same hereby is, restored to the public domain." The 50 square mile area was then opened up to non-Indian homesteaders.

The January 25, 1904, executive order was amended by Executive Order of February 20, 1904, which provides as follows: "It is hereby ordered that the Executive Order of January 25, 1904, restoring to the public domain the tract of country in the State of Nebraska which was 'withdrawn from sale and set aside as an addition to the present Sioux Indian Reservation in the Territory of Dakota' by Executive Order dated January 24, 1882, is hereby modified and amended so as to permanently reserve from entry and settlement, and to constitute a part of the Pine Ridge Sioux Indian

Reservation in South Dakota, the section of land embracing the Pine Ridge Board-
ing School irrigation ditch and the school pasture, which when surveyed is supposed
will constitute sec. 24, T. 35 N., R. 45 W.; and said lands are hereby reserved and set
aside for said purposes."

The section of land in Nebraska restored to reservation status by the February 20,
1904, executive order is the only portion of the Pine Ridge Reservation that currently extends into the State of Nebraska.

12. The Act of May 27, 1910 (36 Stat. 440). This act opened up the unallotted lands
located in the southeastern part of the Pine Ridge Reservation ("Bennett County")
for settlement by non-Indian homesteaders. This act was passed by Congress without first obtaining the requisite three-fourths of the adult male Oglala signatures
necessary to constitute a cession under article 12 of the 1868 treaty.

13. Under section 9 of the Act of March 3, 1863 (10 Stat. 612), Congress declared
that the jurisdiction of the Court of Claims "shall not extend to or include any claim
against the Government not pending in said court on December 1, 1862, growing out
of or dependent on any treaty stipulation entered into with foreign nations or with
the Indian tribes." Thereafter, Indian tribes had to petition Congress for a special
jurisdictional act to have their treaty claims heard.

The Act of June 3, 1920 (41 Stat. 738), was a special jurisdictional act that provided the Sioux bands with a forum in the U.S. Court of Claims for adjudication of all
claims against the United States "under any treaties, agreements, or laws of Congress,
or for the misappropriation of any of the funds or lands of said tribe or band or bands
thereof." The act for the first time allowed the Sioux tribes to sue the United States
for violating their treaty rights. The Sioux filed the a claim for the Black Hills under
the act in 1923, alleging that the United States took the Black Hills without just compensation in violation of the Fifth Amendment. The claim was dismissed by the Court
of Claims in 1942 on the basis that it was not authorized by the 1920 act to question
whether the compensation afforded the Sioux by Congress in 1877, was an adequate
price for the Black Hills, and that the Sioux claim in this regard was a moral claim
not protected by the Just Compensation Clause of the Fifth Amendment. Sioux Tribe
v. United States, 97 Ct.Cl. 613 (1942), cert. denied, 318 U.S. 789 (1943).

14. The Indian Claims Commission Act of August 13, 1946 (60 Stat. 1049, 25 U.S.C.
70 et seq.). This act created a forum to hear and determine all tribal grievances that
had arisen previously. The Sioux filed their claims in the ICC as Docket 74. Docket
74 was bifurcated in 1960. Claims based on a "relinquishment" of Sioux land under
article 2 the 1868 treaty were designated as Docket 74-A and claims based on takings
of Sioux land in violation of the Fifth Amendment (including the illegal confiscation of the Black Hills and Sioux hunting rights) were designated as Docket 74-B.

15. Originally, tribal members were not citizens of either the federal or state governments. This position is illustrated in an 1868 opinion of the U.S. attorney general: "[T]he fact, therefore, that Indians are born in this country does not make them
citizens of the United States." 70 Op. Att'y Gen. (1856) at 746. The attorney general

pointed out that Indians must relinquish their tribal membership before they could become U.S. citizens.

The status of Indians was not changed by the adoption of the Fourteenth Amendment in 1868. The amendment was interpreted as not including members of the Indian tribes owing direct allegiance to their several tribes. 70 Op. Att'y Gen. at 746. Also see Elk v. Wilkins, 112 U.S. 94 (1884); United States v. Kim Ark, 169 U.S. 649, 693 (1898); Ozawa v. United States, 260 U.S. 178, 195–96 (1922). The only manner of gaining U.S. citizenship was to renounce tribal citizenship. Congress, however, had to accept such expatriation before it became effective. Elk v. Wilkins, supra; United States v. Holiday, 70 U.S. (3 Wall.) 406 (1866).

The legal status of Indians was modified in 1924, when Congress granted U.S. citizenship to tribal members without the loss of their tribal membership. See Act of June 2, 1924 (43 Stat. 253; 8 U.S.C. 1401[a]) which provided that: "all non-citizen Indians born within the territorial limits of the United States be, and they are hereby declared to be citizens of the United States." The grant was limited to federal citizenship.

It should be noted that the central purpose of the Fourteenth Amendment was to convey both federal and state citizenship on the "inferior and subject condition" of the Black people under the common law of the United States. Dred Scott v. Sandford, 260 U.S. (19 How.) 293 (1856). In *Dred Scott,* the Supreme Court explained that Indian governments were foreign governments, to distinguish Indians from Black people. The framers of the Fourteenth Amendment intended to accomplish the task of incorporating the Black people into the political society of the United States by an act of Congress, but finally realized that an amendment to the Constitution was the only way to guarantee such a result because of the history of slavery in America.

The first attempt to grant the Black people a right of citizenship was the provisions of the Civil Rights Act of 1866. The act provided that "[a]ll persons born in the United States and subject to any foreign power, excluding Indians not taxed, are hereby declared to be citizens of the United States; and such citizens, of every race and color . . . shall have the same rights, in every state and territory of the United States" (14 Stat. 27, ch. 31 sec. 1), reenacted in the Civil Rights Act of 1870 (16 Stat. 144, ch. 114, sec. 18, 42 U.S.C. 1981). This statute only conferred federal citizenship on Black people. The phrase "Indians not taxed" was excluded from this act.

"Indians not taxed" is a constitutional category excluded from political representation in the House of Representatives. U.S. Const., Art. 1, sec. 2, cl. 3. This provision had been interpreted to mean that Indians in a tribal relationship were not a part of the political community of the United States or the states or territories from which their reservation were exempted. See S. Rep. No. 268, Effect of the Fourteenth Amendment upon Indian Tribes, 41st Cong., 2nd Sess. (1870).

To ensure that Black people were granted both federal and state citizenship, the Fourteenth Amendment was passed. The amendment provided that: "All persons born or naturalized in the United States, and subject to the jurisdiction thereof, are citizens of the United States and the states wherein they reside." The Fourteenth Amendment was seen as a more secure form of political guarantee of citizenship than an act of Congress, which could be modified at any time by future congressional action.

Since passage of the 1924 Indian Citizenship Act, lower federal courts have held that the Fourteenth Amendment makes Indians citizens of the states wherein they reside. See, for example, Goodluck v. Apache County, 417 F. Supp. 13, 16 (D.C.Ariz. 1975).

Many contemporary Indians claim that the 1924 act is unconstitutional, since an act of Congress cannot change the status of Indians in the Constitution, and that the imposition of federal income taxes on them therefore constitutes "taxation without representation" since they have no direct representation in the U.S. House of Representatives.

16. The Indian Reorganization Act of June 18, 1934 (48 Stat 984, 25 U.S.C. 461 et seq.). This act is commonly referred to as the Wheeler-Howard Act and stopped the allotment of lands on reservations and extended the trust period on existing lands indefinitely (sec. 2) and authorized Indian tribes to adopt constitution and bylaws (sec. 16) and federal charters to conduct their business affairs (sec. 17). The Oglala Sioux Tribe adopted a constitution and bylaws under section 16 of the IRA which was approved by Interior Secretary Harold Ickes on January 15, 1936; the tribal constitution was amended in 1969, 1985, and 1997.

17. The Indian Self-Determination and Educational Assistance Act of January 4, 1975, commonly referred to as P.L. 93-638 (88 Stat. 2203, 25 U.S.C. 450 et seq.). This act, as amended, allows Indian tribes to (among other things) enter into P.L. 93-638 contracts with the Bureau of Indian Affairs and Indian Health Service for the purpose of administering the programs that these agencies provide for the tribes.

Appendix B

Brown Hat's Vision

Brown Hat (also known at Baptiste Good) was a Lakota who kept a traditional calendar known as a "winter count." The *Tenth Annual Report* of the U.S. Bureau of Ethnology (1888–89) contains the following account of his visit to the southern Black Hills in 1856:

"In the year 1856, I went to the Black Hills and cried, and cried, and cried, and suddenly I saw a bird above me, which said: 'Stop crying; I am a woman, but I will tell you something: My Great-Father, Father God, who made this place, gave it to me for a home and told me to watch over it. He put a blue sky over my head and gave me a blue flag to have with this beautiful green country. ***My Great-Father, Father God . . . grew, and his flesh was part earth and part stone and part metal and part wood and part water; he took from them all and placed them here for me, and told me to watch over them. I am the Eagle-Woman who tells you this.

"'The whites know that there are four black flags of God; that is, four divisions of earth. He first made the earth soft by wetting it, then cut it into four parts, one of which, containing the Black Hills, he gave to the [L]akotas, and, because I am a woman, I shall not consent to the pouring of blood on this chief house . . . , the Black Hills. The time will come when you will remember my words; for after many years you shall grow up one with the white people.' She then circled round and round and gradually passed out of my sight. I also saw prints of a man's hands and horse's hoofs on the rocks [here he brings in petroglyphs], and two thousand years, and one hundred million dollars [$100,000,000]."

Prints of a man's hands and horse's hoofs had significance in 1856. It was a message of death. A dying warrior would leave his bloody hand print on his horse to let his family know that he died in battle.

The message in Brown Hat's vision is a message of death to all the Lakota tribes. It says that the Lakota tribes, and their culture and governments, will cease to exist on earth if they allow the United States Government to force the $100 million ICC award on them in the Year 2000.

What Brown Hat's vision failed to foresee, however, was the determination of the current generation of Lakota to carry on the fight for the Black Hills, not in the battlefields, but through the White men's own legal institutions. It failed to reveal that the Spirit of Crazy Horse would still be alive in 1980, when the Lakota people rejected the $100 million award and declared that "the Black Hills are not for sale." The current generation of Lakota will never allow the U.S. Government to force the 100 million ICC award on them in the Year 2000.

(From Mario Gonzalez, "The Black Hills: The Sacred Land of the Lakota and Tsitsistas." Reprinted courtesy of *Cultural Survival Quarterly* [Winter, 1996].)

Appendix C

Written Testimony of Mario Gonzalez from the September 25, 1990, Senate Hearing

STATEMENT OF MARIO GONZALEZ, ATTORNEY, CHEYENNE RIVER AND PINE RIDGE WOUNDED KNEE SURVIVORS' ASSOCIATIONS AND OGLALA SIOUX TRIBE, SUPPORTING PROPOSALS TO ESTABLISH A MEMORIAL AND HISTORIC SITE TO COMMEMORATE THE EVENTS SURROUNDING THE 1890 INDIAN MASSACRE AT WOUNDED KNEE CREEK, SOUTH DAKOTA, IN THE HEARING OF SEPTEMBER 25, 1990, BEFORE THE SELECT COMMITTEE ON INDIAN AFFAIRS, U.S. SENATE, WASHINGTON, D.C.

Mr. Chairman, and honorable Members of the Committee, my name is Mario Gonzalez. I am an enrolled member of the Oglala Sioux Tribe and a descendant of Chief Lip's Band. I am appearing here today as the attorney for the Wounded Knee Survivors' Associations and the Oglala Sioux Tribe. I am honored to appear before the Committee to discuss events surrounding the December 29, 1890 Wounded Knee Massacre.

I am also related by blood to some of the victims and survivors of the massacre. Dewey Beard, the last survivor of the Battle of the Little Bighorn and an 1890 Massacre survivor, was a first cousin to my great-great-grandmother, Rattling Hawk. Dewey's real mother, Seen By Her Nation, and my great-great-great-grandmother, Jealous Of Her, were sisters.

One cannot understand what happened at Wounded Knee without understanding something about the Sioux people and their history.

The term "Sioux" should be distinguished from the word "Siouan," which refers to a linguistic stock that the Sioux are a part of. Other Siouan peoples include such Tribes as the Mandan, Omaha, Otoe, Winnebago and Osage. The Sioux refer to themselves as "Lakota," "Dakota," or "Nakota," depending on whether the "L," "D" or "N" dialect is used.

It is also important to understand that the term "Sioux Nation" has been used to refer to different entities at different times. According to the Indian Claims Commission, the Sioux people were divided into seven divisions:

1. Mdewakantons
2. Sissetons
3. Wahpakootas
4. Wahpetons
5. Yanktonais
6. Yanktons
7. Tetons

The Mdewakantons, Sissetons, Wahpakootas, and Wahpetons, or eastern Sioux, are sometimes referred to as "Santee" or "Mississippi" Sioux and speak with the "D" dialect. The Yanktonais also speak with the "D" dialect. The Yanktons speak with the "N" dialect and the Tetons with the "L" dialect.

The Tetons, or the western Sioux, were sub-divided into seven bands:

1. Blackfeet
2. Brule
3. Hunkpapa
4. Minneconjou
5. Oglala
6. Sans Arc (No Bows)
7. Two Kettle

The Teton Bands held aboriginal title to a vast territory west of the Missouri River in what are now the States of North and South Dakota, Nebraska, Kansas, Montana, Wyoming and Colorado. Much of this territory was held jointly with the Cheyenne and Arapaho Nations. The Big Horn Mountains were the western boundary. The Yellowstone and Missouri Rivers were the northern boundary. The Republican River was the southern boundary.

The Tetons, along with the Yanktonai, also held aboriginal title to a tract of territory consisting of at least 14 million acres east of the Missouri River in the States of North and South Dakota.

Aboriginal title is legally based on use and occupation of an area "for a long time." Only a sovereign nation can extinguish aboriginal title, either through conquest, purchase or otherwise. The Supreme Court has held that aboriginal title can be extinguished by the United States without payment of compensation.

Recognized title, on the other hand, is a grant of title from a European nation, or successor nation such as the United States. Many times tribal leaders ask, "How can the United States give us land that we already own?" But this is exactly what happens. Even though a tribe may hold aboriginal title to a territory, the United States can still "grant" the tribe title to the same area *under its laws.* And once it is recognized, it comes under the protection of the Fifth Amendment and can be acquired by the federal government only by purchase or eminent domain.

The 1851 Ft. Laramie Treaty recognized title in the Teton and Yankton Sioux to 60 million acres west of the Missouri River in the States of South and North Dakota, Nebraska, Montana and Wyoming.

During the 1860s, the United States attempted to build a road called the "Bozeman Trail" across the 1851 Treaty territory. This resulted in the Powder River War of 1866 through 1868, which culminated in the 1868 Ft. Laramie Treaty. Under the Treaty:

+ All war between the United States and the Sioux people, in this case, the Tetons, Yanktonai, and Santee Sioux, would "forever cease" and the United States pledged its honor to keep the peace;
+ The Sioux would deliver over to the United States bad whitemen, and Indians who commit wrongs or depredations upon the person or property of whitemen, blackmen or other Indians, to be punished according to its laws.
+ Sioux Nation title would be recognized to a 26 million acre reservation, commonly referred to as the "Great Sioux Reservation" and located primarily in the State of South Dakota west of the Missouri River, for its "absolute and undisturbed use and occupation," and only persons authorized by the United States would be permitted to pass over, settle upon or reside on it.
+ All country north of the North Platte River and east of the summits of the Big Horn Mountains, namely, the 34 million acres of unceded 1851 Treaty territory and aboriginal title territory beyond the 1851 Treaty boundaries would be held and considered "unceded Indian territory," and no white person or persons would be permitted to occupy the same. The treaty also provided that the Sioux would relinquish the right to permanently occupy the areas outside of the Reservation boundaries, but could hunt on them so long as the buffalo ranged on these lands so as to justify the chase.
+ That no cession of lands held in common on the Great Sioux Reservation would be valid unless signed by at least 3/4 of the adult male Sioux occupying or interested in the Reservation.

In 1874 the United States Army planned and undertook a military expedition into the Black Hills portion of the Great Sioux Reservation. The expedition was led by Lt. Col. George Armstrong Custer, who sent out glowing reports of gold. This led to an invasion of the Hills by white miners and settlers in violation of the 1868 Treaty and created intense pressure on Congress to open the Hills for settlement. The influx of miners and settlers into the Hills increased when President Grant refused to enforce the Treaty and remove these trespassers.

In the winter of 1875 and 1876, most of the Sioux were residing on the Great Sioux Reservation, keeping the peace they promised to maintain under the 1868 Treaty. Others were exercising their hunting rights with their Cheyenne and Arapahoe allies near the Big Horn Mountains. Contrary to the terms of the Treaty, the Commissioner of Indian Affairs sent instructions to the hunting parties that if they did not return to the Great Sioux Reservation by January 31, 1876, they would be declared "hostile." The Sioux were under no legal obligation to return and could not return because of the weather. They were attacked, but defeated General Crook at the Battle of Rosebud and annihilated Lt. Col. Custer at the Battle of the Little Bighorn on June 25, 1876.

The U.S. violated Articles 11 and 16 of the 1868 Treaty by attacking the Sioux while they were exercising their right to hunt near the Bighorn Mountains. Although some refer to the Battle of the Little Bighorn as a "massacre," it was clearly a battle in which the Indians were defending their families against an egocentric Indian fighter who planned to capitalize on the event and become President of the United States.

The United States Government resented its defeat at the Battle of the Little Bighorn. The Battle, therefore, marked the beginning of a course of dishonorable dealings by the federal government with the Sioux people to [get] revenge [for] Custer's defeat. This course has continued down to the present time.

On August 15, 1876, Congress passed an appropriations bill, often referred to as the "starve or sell" bill, which provided that no further appropriations would be made for the subsistence of the Sioux under the 1868 Treaty unless they gave up the Black Hills and reached an accommodation with the United States that would enable them to become self-supporting. To accomplish this cession, Congress requested the President to appoint a commission to negotiate an agreement with the Sioux to buy the Hills.

The 1876 Commission, however, could not obtain the requisite number of signatures required by Article 12 of the 1868 Treaty, so Congress took matters into its own hands and enacted the proposed "Agreement" into law on February 28, 1877. This enactment confiscated the Black Hills, the 1851 Treaty lands, and hunting rights recognized under the 1868 Treaty.

It is important at this point to explain the importance of hunting rights. To survive, the Sioux people had to depend on buffalo for food, clothing and shelter. Other game animals were often scarce and too hard to kill. The buffalo, however, were a steady food supply until they were slaughtered by buffalo hunters with the encouragement of the federal government.The Powder River War was fought because the United States was interfering with buffalo migrations by putting a road across 1851 Treaty territory, the so-called "Bozeman Trail." The importance of the buffalo to the Sioux cannot be overemphasized. This is illustrated by Chief Spotted Tail's insistence that hunting grounds on the Republican River be protected in the 1868 Treaty.

Beginning in 1882, the Government attempted to reduce the remainder of the Great Sioux Reservation by creating six smaller reservations and having the Sioux cede the remaining 9 million acres. Congress supposedly accomplished this objective through the Act of March 2, 1889. However Section 28 of the Act provided that the Act would not go into effect until signed by at least 3/4 of the adult male Sioux interested in the reservation and proclaimed by the President. Since each Band of Sioux was a separate, distinct sovereign, Section 28 should have been interpreted by the U.S. as requiring 3/4 adult male signatures of each Band. This view is corroborated by the fact that Section 16 requires 3/4 of the adult signatures of each Band to constitute a release of title to each other's reservations.

The United States has never obtained the requisite 3/4 adult male signatures required by Section 28 of the 1889 Act, even under its own interpretation of that Section. Moreover, the Federal Government used coercion and fraud to obtain most of the signatures it managed to get. Many whitemen married to Indian women were allowed to sign as Indians and take allotments under the Act as Indians, even though Congress clearly denied them such rights earlier on August 9, 1888. Many of them dressed up as Indians for that purpose. Some persons signed twice. Many Indians under the age of 18 were allowed to sign. Some Indians signed after they were provided alcohol. But, worst of all, many Indian men were not allowed to leave the agency until after they signed, only to return home and find their gardens dried out. The President nevertheless issued a Proclamation verifying that the requisite number of signatures were obtained. Everyone has been forced to live under its provisions since 1889. The Supreme Court has termed the taking of the Black Hills in 1877 as the most "ripe and rank case of dishonorable dealings" in the nation's history. History will someday show and prove that the taking of 9 million acres of Sioux lands under the later 1889 Act was even more rank and dishonorable.

In the late 1880s, a Paiute Indian named Wovoka had a vision that was explained to a Sioux delegation in 1889 consisting of Kicking Bear, Short Bull and others, that if they did a certain ritual dance, the Indian people would be united with deceased relatives, the buffalo would return and the whiteman would disappear. Kicking Bear's delegation brought the prophesies contained in Wovoka's vision back to the Sioux reservations.

A terrible drought occurred in both 1889 and 1890. There were epidemics that caused death in many families. The beef rations promised by the 1889 Crook Commission were reduced. The reduction of beef rations was a violation of Article 5 of the 1877 Act that provided that, *in consideration for the confiscation of the Black Hills and Sioux hunting rights, the U.S. would provide all aid necessary for civilization and subsistence rations, or the equivalent thereof for as long as necessary for the survival of the Sioux.* This provision was continued in Section 19 of the 1889 Act.

Because of the theft of their lands in 1877 and 1889, and the terrible conditions that they lived under in 1889 and 1890, many Sioux looked for salvation in the Ghost Dance religion. The dance was a pacifist religious movement, but white settlers living near the reservations misinterpreted it as an Indian uprising. Indian agents also became alarmed and asked for military intervention and protection. The Sioux in turn became alarmed at the whites and donned Ghost Shirts to protect them from the bullets of the whitemen. This created great tension, which was exacerbated by what is called yellow journalism depicting the Sioux as bloodthirsty savages.

A boundary dispute between the newly created Rosebud and Pine Ridge Reservations also played a part in the events that occurred in 1890. The 1889 Act placed the Rosebud/Pine Ridge boundary at the mouth of Blackpipe Creek, about 15 miles east of Pass Creek. Chief Lip's band of Wazhazha had already settled on the east side of Pass

Creek when the 1889 Act went into effect. Because the U.S. regarded them as Rosebud Indians, they were informed that they had to move to the Rosebud Reservation.

Lip's people didn't want to move, since they had already devoted much time and energy on developing their homes and lands. They therefore demanded to be placed on the Pine Ridge census rolls. According to tribal elders, when Lip heard that General Miles was coming to Pine Ridge Agency, he decided to visit him to request assistance in resolving the boundary dispute. Other Rosebud Indians, who were concerned about the arrival of troops at their agency, attempted to convince Lip to join them in making a stand against the U.S. Army in the badlands. Lip ignored them and eventually established a temporary camp on Wounded Knee Creek near Pine Ridge Agency. Other Indians headed for the badlands and became part of the Ghost Dance camp.

There were also many clashes in 1890 between white cowboys, the U.S. Army and Indians that resulted in the massacres of Indian people. The following are three examples:

• The State of South Dakota took matters into its own hands. Governor Mellette sent hundreds of guns and ammunition to Rapid City to arm a cowboy militia he created, known as the "Home Guard." In early December, 1890, this militia devised a plan to kill Indians and collect depredation monies. They picked their best riders to cross the Cheyenne River onto the Pine Ridge Reservation and shoot at the Ghost Dancers. When the Ghost Dancers followed, they were ambushed and 75 of them were killed and scalped. The scalps and ghost shirts were taken to Chicago where they were displayed and sold.

• A small band of Indians were also killed by the cowboy militia in early December, 1890, on French Creek. The band had gone to Buffalo Gap to hunt at the ranch of a friendly whiteman they knew. They were greeted with a gun. They were unaware of the events that were transpiring around them. They sensed something wrong and attempted to leave. Because their horses were tired, they had to make camp on French Creek and were massacred in a surprise attack the next morning. One young woman managed to escape to tell the story. The U.S. Government had a duty under Article 8 of the 1877 Act to protect the Indians, but failed to hold the State of South Dakota responsible.

• The United States Army was also guilty of a massacre in early December of 1890. Troops A & B of the 8th Cavalry under Capt. Almond B. Wells was stationed at Olrichs, S.D. Wells allowed Lt. Joseph C. Byron to enter the Pine Ridge Indian Reservation and massacre a small band of Indians under Chief Two Strike on Cuny Table with Cannon fire. All the Indians were killed. This incident appears to have been covered up by the United States Army for the past 100 years. The property of the Indians was buried and the soldiers of the 8th Cavalry were sworn to secrecy, so that even General Miles, the overall commander at Wounded Knee in 1890, may not have been aware of it.

The above incidents are documented in the Renee Sansom Flood Collection at Vermillion, South Dakota.

Eventually, over half of the U.S. Army surrounded the Sioux reservations to protect settlers. Orders were sent out by the Army to arrest the Sioux leaders. Agent James McLaughlin sent the Indian police to arrest Chief Sitting Bull on the Standing Rock Reservation. On December 15, 1890, Sitting Bull and members of his family were killed. Members of Sitting Bull's band sought refuge with Sitting Bull's half brother, Chief Big Foot, at Cherry Creek on the Cheyenne River Indian Reservation.

Fearing for the safety of his band, Big Foot evaded arrest and sought refuge with Chief Red Cloud on the Pine Ridge Indian Reservation. Red Cloud had extended an invitation for Big Foot to come to Pine Ridge and help make peace between the whites and Indians. Big Foot's band endured great hardship on its way to Pine Ridge. The Band was intercepted at Porcupine Butte on December 28, 1890, by Major Samuel Whiteside. Big Foot surrendered and was taken to Wounded Knee Creek where he and his followers were fed and allowed to set up camp.

The Wounded Knee Massacre occurred the next day. Although the U.S. Army has attempted to shift the blame for the massacre to the Sioux, it was in actuality caused by the actions of the 7th Cavalry, whose members were intent on getting even for Custer's defeat at the Battle of the Little Bighorn in 1876.

Colonel James Forsyth assumed command of the 7th Cavalry at Wounded Knee on the eve of December 28, 1890. A barrel of Whiskey was brought into camp by an Indian trader. Officers, including Forsyth, and soldiers got drunk celebrating the capture of Big Foot. Some soldiers even tried to get Big Foot that night, but were stopped by the guards. This caused the surrounded Indians to become uneasy. Some of them understood English and knew that the soldiers were up to no good and were out for revenge.

Among the drunken soldiers was their drunken interpreter Philip Wells. Wells was part Sioux, but hated the Sioux for killing his father. He was known as a bad interpreter and was especially disliked by Big Foot's people.

On the morning of December 29, 1890, Forsyth ordered the disarming of Big Foot's band. The men were separated from the women and children. The soldiers were abusive to the Indian men during the disarming, pointing empty guns to their heads and pulling the triggers. The weapons were stacked in a pile near the Indians. The Indians, understandably, were reluctant to relinquish their weapons, although the majority of them did.

During the disarming, a scuffle occurred between some soldiers and a man called Black Fox, which some say, resulted in an accidental discharge of a rifle. Fighting immediately broke out on both sides and a massacre of Big Foot's people ensued. A few of the Indian people who were still armed fired back while others attempted to retrieve their weapons from the pile of guns. Some Indians engaged the soldiers in hand-to-hand combat, including Dewey Beard, who killed four soldiers.

Big Foot's people attempted to escape by rushing into a nearby ravine. Many soldiers died in their own crossfire. Soldiers chased and killed Indian women and children for as far away as two miles from the camp site. When it was over, about 356 members of Big Foot's band were killed or wounded. Approximately 30 soldiers from the 7th Cavalry died with them.

The slaughter of Big Foot's Band was caused in large part by the fact that the 7th Cavalry officers and interpreter, Wells, were drunk. Much of the basis for the Army's version of the 1890 Massacre was Wells's eye witness account, but his veracity was highly questionable. In all likelihood, Wells glossed over the whole affair to coverup his own ineptness as an interpreter and to cover for his friends.

Evidence also exists that when the bodies of the soldiers killed in the Massacre were exhumed in 1905 for reburial, their bodies were remarkably preserved due to the high concentration of alcohol in their bodies. This documentation can be found in the Renee Sansom Flood Collection at Vermilion, South Dakota.

The callousness of the 7th Cavalry is evident from their gruesome conduct as they buried the Indian dead, posing for photographs and jumping on the piles of bodies to pack them down into the mass grave. The soldiers were buried immediately. The Indian people were not buried, as indecent a burial as it was, until five days after the massacre, on January 3, 1891. At least one of Big Foot's people is known to have been buried alive, and with the knowledge of the overseers of the burial party.

Later that year, Congress passed the Sioux Depredations Act of 1891 to compensate the so-called "innocent victims" of the 1890 Massacre and the Ghost Dance troubles for their losses, including white people and churches. Everyone but the Indian victims of the 1890 Massacre were compensated.

My clients, the Cheyenne River and Pine Ridge Wounded Knee Survivors' Associations, have tried for years to get Congress to atone for the 1890 Massacre. Several bills have been introduced in Congress over the years, but all failed. The Survivors' Associations nevertheless continue in their quest for justice.

On March 13, 1917, General Miles stated in a letter to the Commissioner of Indian Affairs that: "[i]n my opinion, the least the Government can do is to make a suitable recompense to the survivors who are still living for the great injustice that was done them and the serious loss of their relatives and property—and I earnestly recommend that this may be favorably considered by the Department and by Congress and a suitable appropriation be made." And again, in an April 12, 1920, letter to the Commissioner, Miles reiterated his position by stating that "[t]he present time seems a most favorable time for the government . . . to atone in part for the cruel and unjustifiable massacre of Indian men, women and children at Wounded Knee on the Red Cloud Reservation." The General was hardly innocent of the heinous acts committed against the Sioux Indians at Wounded Knee, but at least he was man enough to admit his mistakes and urge the federal government to do likewise.

The Wounded Knee Survivors' Associations have been developing proposed legislation which would have Congress: (1) make a formal apology to the Sioux people for the 1890 Massacre: (2) establish a national monument and memorial at the Massacre site; and (3) compensate the descendants of the Indian victims for the killing or wounding of their relatives in the form of benefits, i.e., educational benefits and multi-purpose buildings, plus direct compensation for property confiscated by the Army. In 1921 Inspector McLaughlin, whose wife was Philip Wells's first cousin, inventoried most of the property taken from Big Foot's people and found its value to be $20,000.00.

It is my belief as that the Wounded Knee Massacre and indeed the massacres perpetuated by the 8th Cavalry and Governor Mellette's cowboy militia, are more than just moral claims. They are legal claims which only Congress can resolve.

It is questionable whether the military forces had a right to be *on* the Sioux reservations in 1890. The federal government certainly breached its promise to maintain peace with the Sioux under the 1868 Treaty. It also failed to follow the extradition procedures outlined in the 1868 Treaty when it attempted to arrest Big Foot on the Pine Ridge Reservation.

In 1890 the federal government also had a duty to *protect* the persons, lives and property of the Sioux Indians under Article 8 of the 1877 Act and the Fifth Amendment. It presently has a duty to *compensate* the Indians for their losses under the Fifth Amendment and the 1868 Treaty which provided that if persons "subject to the authority of the U.S. shall commit a wrong upon the person or property of the Indians, the U.S. will . . . reimburse the injured person for the loss sustained."

I urge this exemplary Committee to start the process to atone for the 1890 Wounded Knee Massacre by initiating legislation to accomplish the objectives of my clients. Thank you for your kind attention.

Appendix D

The Forced Reduction of the Great Sioux Reservation

From 1978 to 1988, Mario Gonzalez served as one of the founding directors of the Indian Law Resource Center in Washington, D.C. During this period of time, the Indian Law Resource Center assisted Mario with research on Lakota/Dakota history for cases he was working on. A January 8, 1980, report prepared by Robert T. Coulter, Curtis G. Berkey, and J. David Lehman is printed below by permission of the Indian Law Resource Center, to give the reader a better understanding of how the United States government used fraud and coercion to force the Lakota/Dakota people to agree to carve up the Great Sioux Reservation (created by article 2 of the 1868 Fort Laramie Treaty) into six smaller reservations and relinquish the remaining 9 million acres of the reservation to the United States in 1889.

THE FORCED REDUCTION OF THE GREAT SIOUX RESERVATION:
AN EXAMINATION OF UNITED STATES–SIOUX NATION RELATIONS
DURING THE PERIOD 1868–1889

This paper recounts the history of efforts of the United States to acquire a major portion of the Great Sioux Reservation. The United States purports to have acquired over 11 million acres of the Reservation in conformity with Article 12 of the Treaty of 1868, which required the consent of three-fourths of the adult male Sioux to any land cession pursuant to the Act of 1889. But the historical record shows that the Sioux did not freely and voluntarily consent to the cession.

The paper focuses on the period 1868–1890. Section One explains how the consent provision came to be included in the 1868 Treaty and then traces its application during the various abortive attempts to reduce the land area of the Great Sioux Reservation. Section Two discusses the Act of March 2, 1889, under which over 11 million acres of Sioux territory were ostensibly ceded to the United States. That part also examines closely the work of the Crook Sioux Commission and explains the methods it used to coerce the Sioux into ostensibly making a cession to which they were initially unanimously opposed. A documentary appendix accompanies the report.

The purpose of this study is to compile and analyze the relevant historical and legal data relating to the Act of 1889, its legal implementation, and the loss of Sioux lands which resulted from it. Our purpose is to determine, as far as possible, from this data, whether the loss of Sioux lands under the 1889 act was lawful.

SECTION I

The 1868 Treaty of Fort Laramie

The Fort Laramie Treaty was signed over a period of a half year in 1868 by various chiefs and headmen of the Sioux Nation and members of the Indian Peace Commission on the part of the United States. The major provisions of the Treaty are:

1. The restoration of peace between the Sioux and the United States;
2. The setting aside of a permanent reservation "for the absolute and undisturbed use and occupation" of the Sioux, encompassing all of the present-day state of South Dakota, west of the Missouri River, to which the Sioux were to move;
3. Withdrawal of the United States from the Powder River and Bighorn Countries, and abandonment of the United States forts along the Bozeman Trail;
4. Recognition by the United States of unextinguished Indian title to the Powder River and Bighorn Countries, and
5. A pledge by the United States to provide subsistence to the Sioux for four years at various points on the Missouri River, to which the United States hoped the Sioux would move.[1]

Article 12 of the treaty establishes requirements for negotiations concerning future land cessions, and reads in pertinent part:

> No treaty for the cession of any portion or part of the reservation herein described which may be held in common shall be of any validity or force as against the said Indians unless executed and signed by at least three-fourths of all adult male Indians occupying or interested in the same.[2]

The reality of what was understood about the treaty and what was considered central to the treaty was quite different from the language used in the written text which was exclusively in the English language. When the commissioners of the Indian Peace Commission convinced the chiefs and headmen of the Sioux bands to sign the treaty, virtually no attention was given to the consent provision in Article 12. The commissioners claimed to have read and explained all the articles of the treaty,[3] but the attention of both parties was on issues other than the consent provision of Article 12. To the Commission, the main purpose of the treaty was to clear a right-of-way for white settlers through the Platte River country. To do this, it wanted assurances that the Sioux would remain at peace and remove to a permanent reservation.[4]

The Indians were interested in other issues. They ignored, misunderstood, or were not told of the provision concerning removal to a permanent reservation.[5] To them the major issue was the abandonment of the forts along the Bozeman Trail. The concessions that the United States gave, including provisions and ammunition, were not seen as payment for a promise on their part, but as an attempt at appeasement of the Sioux by the United States.[6]

The record of the negotiations preceding the signing of the treaty contains no mention of the consent provision. This small section of the treaty was ignored in the interminable councils which usually degenerated into discussions of secondary issues.

Likewise, there is no record of how Article 12 got into the Treaty of 1868. To understand the reasons for the inclusion of Article 12, it is necessary to understand the shift in the United States' Indian Peace Policy.[7]

The Indian Peace Policy was the product of a reform movement led by such men as Commissioner of Indian Affairs, Nathaniel G. Taylor. A deeply religious man, Taylor believed the resolution of the problem of continued warfare on the plains lay not in military conquest but in extending the olive branch to the Indians. More and more easterners began to regard the U.S. military and avaricious whites, not the Indians, as the true cause of the bloodshed. Incidents such as the Sand Creek massacre and the Fort Fetterman disaster convinced federal legislators of the need for a change in the military policy toward Indians. Consequently, on July 20, 1867, Congress authorized a Peace Commission composed of eminent reform-minded civilians and military men, headed by Commissioner Taylor, to make peace with the Indian Nations in the West.[8]

The task of the Commission, in its own words, was to "conquer by kindness." Adopting a philosophy that it was less expensive and more humane to feed the Indians than to fight them, the policy was designed to make the Indians dependent on the United States and docile. The great task of bringing civilization to the Indians could then begin.[9]

One part of the philosophy of the Commission probably explains the reason why Article 12 is found in the Treaty of Fort Laramie. The reformers rejected the old method of treating with the Indians. Treaties were traditionally negotiated in an atmosphere of bribery and elaborate gift-giving. Disadvantageous terms were agreed to by the chiefs through the use of bribes. Many members of the tribe had no say in the outcome. The Commission believed that the Indians would keep the peace if presented with a treaty that was just and that proceeded from a spirit of equality.[10] It is therefore rather ironic that the Indians who signed the Treaty of 1868 were no more aware of what they were signing than were the Indians "in the bad old days."[11]

To summarize, Article 12 of the Treaty of 1868 was probably a child of the idealistic rhetoric of the Indian Peace Commission. During the negotiations leading to the signing of the treaty, the issue of consent to future land cessions was totally ignored. However, during the decades, 1870–1890, this consent provision would frequently resurface in the debate over the reduction of the Great Sioux Reservation.

Cession of the Black Hills

When gold was discovered in the Black Hills in 1874, white miners and settlers began pouring into Sioux territory. When the Sioux refused to negotiate a sale or lease of the Black Hills, President Grant ordered the Army not to enforce the provision of the 1868 Treaty prohibiting non-Indians from entering Sioux territory. Congress then declared a halt to treaty-guaranteed rations until the Sioux agreed to sell.[12] An "agreement" to sell was reached in 1876 with less than 10% of the Sioux consenting. Ignoring the fact that the provision in the 1868 Treaty requiring the consent of three-fourths of the adult males to any land cession was clearly violated, Congress implemented the terms of the agreement in the Act of February 28, 1877 and the Black Hills were lost.

The acquisition of the Black Hills by the United States did not satisfy the white settlers' hunger for Indian land. As white settlements grew to the east and west of Sioux Territory, United States officials increasingly came to view the Sioux Reservation as a barrier to the advancement of white civilization. Most officials regarded the acquisition of more Sioux land as an inevitable result of an inexorable process.[13] The increasing white population coincided with a dramatic decrease in the buffalo herds, forcing many Sioux into dependence on the United States for food and clothing.

The Edmunds Commission

By 1880, pressure was increasing for a cession of more land by the Sioux. The white settlers of Dakota, not satisfied with their capture of the Black Hills, wanted more land to accommodate new settlers. Two railroad lines through Dakota were forced to stop at the Missouri River, unable to enter Sioux country. To the whites the Great Sioux Reservation was an island of savagery, a block in the path of civilization that should be reduced or eliminated.

A strange coalition of Dakota politicians and landgrabbers, and eastern reformers led the fight for the reduction of the Great Sioux Reservation. The Dakota politicians were well aware of the problems the consent provision could cause them. In response to this problem, they developed a pragmatic theory to use in evading the consent provision. They reasoned that the "Agreement" of 1877, in which the Sioux Nation was stripped of possession of the Black Hills, provided precedent for ignoring the consent provision. This agreement had been made with only a handful of chiefs and headmen, and yet the same agreement was ratified by both houses of Congress as valid, despite Article 12. The Dakota politicians argued that the implication of this congressional action was that Article 12 was, in effect, repealed. And besides, they continued, Article 12 referred only to future treaties, and since 1871, the United States no longer made treaties with Indian tribes. They further argued that the consent provision of Article 12 could not apply to agreements.[14]

In 1882, the political climate seemed favorable for a division of the Great Sioux Reservation into smaller reservations, with the surplus lands given to white settlers. The Republican Administration of President Arthur did not seem particularly predisposed to defend the rights of the Sioux Nation. Secretary of Interior, Henry M. Teller from Colorado was known to be sympathetic to the land-hungry settlers of the West. As a westerner, he understood that to Dakotans, the Great Sioux Reservation was an obstacle to the economic progress of the territory.

On August 7, 1882, at the instigation of Congressman Richard Pettigrew of Dakota, a rider was placed on a sundry civil expense appropriations bill during the final hours of the first session of the forty-eighth Congress. The amendment provided $5,000 to enable the Secretary of Interior "to negotiate with the Sioux Indians for such modification of existing treaties and agreements with said Indians as may be deemed desirable by said Indians and the Secretary of the Interior."[15] Any agreement made would not take effect until ratified by both houses of Congress. The amendment slipped through Congress in the rush of the close of the session with barely a second notice.

Secretary Teller did not waste any time in appointing a commission of men who knew how to extract an agreement from the Sioux. Appointed to the head of the commission was Newton Edmunds, a former governor of the Dakota territory, and a major advocate for the division of the Sioux Reservation. The other commissioners were Peter Shannon, a former judge from Dakota and James Teller, a brother of the Secretary.

On September 16, 1882, the Commissioner of Indian Affairs, Hiram Price, wrote a letter of instructions to the newly-appointed Sioux Commission. In the letter he quoted the twelfth article of the 1868 Treaty and emphasized that it was necessary to obtain the consent of three-fourths of the adult male Sioux to any land cession as provided by the twelfth article. As to the question of whether the provision required three-fourths consent of the adult males of the Sioux Nation as a whole, or three-fourths of each separate band, the Commissioner apparently interpreted the provision to mean the former.

> I may say here for your information that no one of the bands composing the great Sioux Nation has a several interest in the lands within the reservation. They are held in common by the whole nation. You will explain to the Indians their rights under the treaty of 1868 and the agreement of 1877 . . . and advise them that no action will be taken without their consent, as provided in the treaty of 1868.[16]

Edmunds and Shannon were upset at the position taken by Commissioner Price. They desperately wanted to obtain a land cession from the Sioux and they knew it would be difficult, if not impossible to obtain the consent of three quarters of the adult male Sioux to any such cession. They wanted their instructions changed and wrote the reasons for their opinion in a long letter to Commissioner Price. At the same time they wrote the letter to Price they also sent a telegram to Secretary Teller, knowing that they could expect a better reception to their request from the Secretary than the Commissioner.

The telegram, dated October 2, 1882, reads as follows:

We respectfully submit that there should be a modification of the instructions as regards the signature of three-fourths of all adult male Indians. Article 12 only refers to a treaty *per se;* it was ignored in the agreement of 1876 and 1877, and the consent of the chiefs and headmen was deemed sufficient. The act of February 28, 1877 was passed with Article 12 of the treaty in full view and Congress did not find any infraction of the latter. The great reservation was very largely diminished by the agreement and act of 1877 by the consent of the chiefs and headmen only, and does not this furnish ample precedent? Is not article 12 virtually repealed? We deem it next to impossible, as at present advised, to get the signatures of three-fourths.[17]

The Secretary of Interior wasted no time in giving his assent to the Commissioners' proposition. On October 3, 1882, Commissioner Price answered their telegram saying that the Secretary had directed that the instructions of the Commissioners be modified so as to only require the obtaining of the signatures of the chiefs and headmen.[18] The Secretary, with full knowledge of the law, had chosen to blatantly ignore a provision of a ratified treaty between the Sioux Nation and the United States.

The Edmunds Commission, armed with this major concession, now moved into Sioux country to gain the land cession they so much desired. Their first stop was at the friendly Santee Agency, the only agency outside the Great Sioux Reservation, and which accordingly had little interest in its division. While at Santee, the Commission drafted an agreement by which the different bands of the Sioux Nation were to agree to take separate reservations to which the bands would hold exclusive title. The remainder of the Great Sioux Reservation, some 11,000,000 acres, would be opened to white settlement. Incredibly, the major part of the compensation for this cession would be 25,000 cows and 1,000 bulls.[19]

The Commission easily convinced the Santee Sioux to agree to these terms. Now with a draft agreement in hand, the Commission went to the Great Sioux Reservation. Here, the Edmunds Commission faced massive initial opposition at each of the six agencies. However, the commissioners were exceedingly clever in methods of persuasion and intimidation. The Commission used three primary arguments. Their first tactic was to lead the Indians to believe that they were only giving their consent to setting up six separate reservations around each of the agencies to which the separate tribes of the Sioux Nation would have exclusive title. The benefits of having separate title were highly touted. Little or nothing was said about the fact that in the process the Indians would be giving up half of their land to the United States. The second tactic was to leave behind the threat that if the agreement was not signed, the U.S. government would be powerless to stop the flood of settlers from entering the reservation and the Indians could stand to lose all of the lands. The Commission also threatened that the Sioux would be removed to Indian territory in Oklahoma if they did not sign. The final tactic was to lead the Indians at the different agencies to believe that the government already had enough signatures and that if they would not join in giving their assent to the agreement they would be "left out in the cold."[20]

Even with this combination of threats and misrepresentations, the Commission only succeeded in getting about 450 signatures from the whole Sioux Nation.[21]

However, the Commission could not take time to attempt to get more signatures. They were under pressure from Washington to return the agreement as soon as possible for ratification in Congress. In November, 1882, a Democrat, Grover Cleveland, had been elected President and with him the Democrats had regained the upper hand in Congress. After March 1883, the agreement would face serious resistance in a Congress hostile to the previous administration. Already news had begun to leak in the east of the flagrant abuses of the Edmunds Commission. It was important to push the agreement through Congress before these allegations had gained more currency. Under these circumstances the Edmunds Commission concluded they had received a sufficient number of signatures of Sioux leaders.

The Failure of the Edmunds Commission

Once the agreement reached Congress, the congressmen in favor of dispossessing the Sioux tried the same tactic that had worked so well in giving the Sioux Commission its original authorization. They attached approval of the agreement for the division of the Great Sioux Reservation as an amendment to a sundry civil appropriations bill, HR 7595.[22] The House had already given approval to the bill when the Senate took up debate on the measure late in the night of the final day of the session. Secretary Teller had the lame duck President Arthur waiting outside the Senate chamber, ready to sign the bill into law. However, the Senate did not rubber stamp the House version of the bill. Senator Henry Dawes of Massachusetts called the attention of the Senate to the obscure amendment to H.R. 7595 which, if passed, would have dispossessed the Sioux of half of their land:

> I want to show to the Senate one single proposition which it is proposed by the House of Representatives that the Government will stop unless the Senate will ratify. Here is a solemn treaty we entered into with the Sioux Nation, by which we covenant to them that—
>
> > no treaty for the cession of any portion or part of the reservation herein described, which may be held in common, shall be of any validity or force as against the said Indians unless executed as signed by at least three-fourths of all adult male Indians occupying or interested in the same.
>
> Here is an agreement (i.e., the Edmunds Commission Agreement) entered into by the chiefs and headmen alone, without regard to the other members of the tribe, and an alternative is presented by the House of Representatives that the Government shall stop unless the Senate will agree with them in violating a solemn treaty entered into by us with the Sioux Indians. That is one of the propositions that they propose to us the alternative here tonight in the last hours of the

session, that unless we will do this great wrong and violate this treaty obligation, whatever of necessity for the Government there is in this bill shall be lost: Sir, I would rather see the Government stop all its functions than to be forced by such an operation as this into violation of a solemn treaty entered into by the Government with these Indians.[23]

Senator Dawes forced the amendment back to conference committee where it was amended so as to force the Secretary of the Interior to go back to the Great Sioux Reservation and obtain the necessary three-quarters consent as provided in the Treaty of 1868.

The amendment reads:

For the purpose of procuring the assent of the Sioux Indians as provided by Article 12 of the Treaty between the United States and the different bands of the Sioux Nation of Indians made and concluded April 29, 1868, to the agreement made with said Sioux Indians transmitted to the Senate February 3, 1883, by the President, with such modification of said agreement as will fully secure to them a title to the land remaining in the several reservations set apart to them by said agreement . . . $ 10,000.[24]

On March 14, 1883, Commissioner Price reappointed Edmunds, Shannon, and Teller to return to Sioux Territory and obtain the necessary three-quarters consent as directed in the Act of March 3, 1883.[25]

The Commission did not regard the obtaining of the signatures as a matter of great moment. As they said in their final report of December 31, 1883:

The obtaining of the signatures of three-fourths of the adult male Indians, as required was regarded by us as a work of detail merely, involving no new or special negotiations, but rather the clerical work of taking the names of such of them as, following the example of their leaders, might be willing to sign. It called for visits to the scattered camps and villages, and could be done, it was thought, as well by one person as by several, and at less expense of time and money.[26]

For this task the Commission chose Reverend S.D. Hinmon, who had been the official interpreter of the Commission and was skilled at inducing the Sioux to put their mark on a paper.[27]

This time however, the Sioux Commission had more eyes on it. Senator Dawes of the Senate Committee on Indian Affairs followed with particular interest the negotiations in the Sioux Country. In July, 1883, Dawes was informed of several serious charges of fraud against the Sioux Commission and he wrote the Secretary of Interior inquiring into the matter. Dawes had received substantiated charges that:

1st. That a large part of the Indians were made to understand, not that it was a treaty parting with a large tract of land (11,000,000 of acres), but only a treaty separating the different bands, and conferring title to these lands in separate divisions of the existing reservation.

2nd. That at one or two of the agencies, the Indians were given to understand that in the event of their not signing the agreement they would be deprived of homes and farms without compensation, and if need be, removed by the military.

3rd. That the names of *children,* some as young as a year old, have been appended to the treaty to make up the necessary three-fourths of "adult males."[28]

Based on these allegations, to which he received no satisfactory answer from Secretary Teller, Senator Dawes and his Senate Indian Affairs Committee formed a special sub-committee to investigate the condition of the Sioux Indians in general and the events surrounding the Agreement of 1883 in particular.[29]

In December 1883, the Sioux Commission reported back to the Secretary of the Interior. In their report they stated: "Being unable . . . to prosecute further the work of obtaining signatures with any hope of present success, we return the agreement herewith without change. . . ."[30]

The Commission argued that according to Departmental instructions of a year ago, the signatures of the chiefs and headmen only had been necessary; that they felt sure that the signers had been authorized by the people; that the agreement had been approved by the President and thus should be ratified by Congress.[31]

But the Edmunds Commission now faced serious problems from Senator Dawes' investigating committee. During the fall of 1883, the committee was in Sioux Territory taking testimony from the agents, interpreters and the Sioux themselves on what had transpired during the two visits of the Edmunds Commission the previous year. Their final report documented in 400 pages the fraud that had taken place.[32]

In the report, issued in January, 1884, the committee addressed itself to the question of three-quarters consent.

The conclusion of the committee, however, without reflection upon the integrity of purpose by which the commission was actuated, is nevertheless irresistible that few, if any, of this large body of Indians were aware that the agreement brought to them by this commission for their assent would result, not only in the dismemberment of the nation itself and the erection of separate reservations, but in the cession to the United States of one-half of this great domain guaranteed to them by treaty stipulation for all time, unless three-fourths of their adult males should consent in writing to the disposal of any part thereof.

Arguments drawn from the desirability of such a cession, from its supposed advantages to the Indians themselves . . . do not seem to the Committee to have any weight or place against the expressed stipulation of this Government that

No treaty for the cession of any portion or part of the reservation herein described which may be held in common shall be of any validity or force as against the said Indians, unless executed and signed by at least three-fourths of all adult male Indians, occupying or interested in the same.[33]

The Committee recommended that the agreement made by the Edmunds Commission not be ratified by Congress. Commenting on the Commission's failure to comply with the Act of March 5, 1883, the Committee said, "This committee do not find in their failure to comply with this express enactment any justification for disregarding a plain treaty stipulation."

Although the Senate Committee rejected the methods of the Edmunds Commission, it did not reject its ultimate goal—the division of the Great Sioux Reservation. However, the Committee wished to cloak this goal in the guise of helping the Sioux.

> The Committee are therefore of the opinion and recommend that the agreement as submitted to Congress should not be ratified in its present form. They are, however, of the opinion that substantially the same results are attainable in strict conformity to our treaty obligations to these Indians, and in a manner that will result largely, not only to the benefit of these Indians, but to the public advantage. . . .
>
> The Committee have therefore prepared and recommend the passage of a bill, the legal effect of which will be to create separate reservations for the Indians receiving annuities and rations at each of the existing agencies upon the Great Sioux Reservation, and will cause to be ceded to the United States a large portion of that reservation, amounting to between nine and ten million acres. It provides for the experiment of making herders of such of these Indians as are fit to take suitable care of herds, and further for a fund of at least $1,000,000, to be held permanently in the Treasury to the credit of these Indians, the annual interest of which at five percent, to be devoted to the civilization, education, and training of these Indians for self-support and citizenship in such manner and by such methods as from time to time shall be deemed most wise and efficient by the Secretary of the Interior.[34]

The bill also provided for allotment in severalty as soon as the Indians in the opinion of the Secretary were far enough advanced.

Regarding the consent issue, the committee was explicit. "The bill is made dependent upon its acceptance by the Indians of the Great Sioux Nation, in conformity with the requirements of the twelfth article of the Treaty of 1868."

This bill, S.1755, recommended by the Senate Committee on Indian Affairs was passed by the Senate and received a favorable committee report from the House.[35] However, the bill failed to make it to the floor of the House for a vote and thus, S.1755 died.

The Edmunds Commission scandal had an effect on all subsequent attempts to divide the Great Sioux Reservation. The fraud and threats perpetrated by the Commission were so blatant that even Congress could not ignore them. Because of the revelations contained in the Dawes Report and the resulting scandal, a new emphasis was, at least temporarily, placed on the consent provision of the 1868 Treaty. Indian rights organizations, particularly the National Indian Defense Association, became more vigilant to ensure that subsequent bills would contain a consent provision. And perhaps most important, all of the commissions that would later attempt to gain the consent of the Sioux to the division of the Great Sioux Reservation would have to contend with the legacy of the Edmunds Commission and the resulting increased mistrust of the Sioux.[36]

The Sioux Bill of 1888

Congress did not pass another bill for the division of the Great Sioux Reservation until 1888. This five year lapse could be due to the failure of the Edmunds Commission. It could also be due to the lack of active support from the Cleveland administration which was much less sympathetic to the faction of Congress that wanted to dispossess the Sioux of their lands and make dirt farmers out of them. And besides, the attention of the Indian reformers was occupied by a much larger project— the General Allotment Act of 1887.

The idea of the division of the Sioux Reservation did not die, however. And in 1888 a concerted effort was made in Congress to effect its passage. The first version of the bill (H.R.7315) provided in Section 23 that:

> The agreement made by the Sioux Indians under the act making appropriations for the sundry civil expenses of the Government approved August 7, 1882 and said agreement (i.e. the Edmunds Commission agreement) certified to Congress by the President February 3, 1883, is hereby approved, ratified, and confirmed, subject to all of the modifications, qualifications and conditions prescribed in this act.[37]

This provision was merely a clever means of getting around compliance with the consent provision. The only similarity between the 1882 Edmunds agreement and the proposed Sioux bill of 1888 was that they both provided for the division of the Great Sioux Reservation into six small reservations, one for each Sioux agency. Under the Edmunds Commission agreement, the only compensation to the Sioux for almost 11,000,000 acres of land was to be 25,000 cows and 1,000, bulls. The 1888 Sioux bill applied the General Allotment Act to the Great Sioux Reservation, with the "excess" lands to be bought by the United States at 50¢ an acre. The money was to be put into a fund in the U.S. Treasury for the benefit of the Sioux. Congress, of course, was to be the sole arbiter of what was beneficial to the Sioux. The bill also extended for thirty years the educational benefits of the 1877 Agreement and provided for the supplying of farm implements and animals to all those Indians who made a selection of land in severalty.[38] In their ignorance of the Sioux, most congressmen felt sure that the increased educational benefits and the allotment provision would be all that was needed to persuade the Sioux to gladly sign. In reality, these "benefits" were to be a major block to the success of the Commission.[39]

When the House Committee on Indian Affairs reported back H.R.7315 to the House on March 7, 1888, it recommended that Section 23 be replaced by an amendment which read:

> That this act shall take effect only upon the acceptance thereof and consent thereto by the different bands of the Sioux Nation of Indians, in manner and form prescribed by the twelfth article of said treaty between the United States and said Indians concluded April 29, 1868: *Provided;* that it shall not be necessary to procure the assent or signatures of those Indians who have been at open war with the United States or engaged in open hostilities against the people thereof since the making of the agreement between the United States and the Sioux Nation of Indians in 1876 . . . [40]

During the debate on H.R.7315 on the House floor an amendment was made to strike out the proviso concerning the formerly hostile Sioux. The amendment was accepted and the Senate also approved the same language concerning consent.[41]

For the important task of obtaining the consent of the Sioux to the proposed agreement, the Secretary of the Interior chose R.H. Pratt, a man well-known in Indian affairs as the superintendent of the Carlisle Indian School. Most congressmen and Indian reform groups highly approved the choice of Pratt to head the Commission. Here was a man who knew the Indian, a man known as the Indians' friend.

Unfortunately, the reformers were wrong in assuming that the Sioux would be equally impressed by this "friend of the Indians." All they saw was an arrogant man who tried to bully them and treated them like they were his students.[42] The Commission failed miserably at their first stop at Standing Rock. Here they met with massive resistance from all quarters of the Sioux community. So strong was the opposition that most Sioux refused to take copies of the Act, fearing the Commission might construe it as acceptance or consent.[43] No amount of persuading would help, and the Commission left Standing Rock with only a handful of signatures. After only a few weeks the Commission realized that they would never obtain enough signatures, even if the response at the rest of the agencies would be overwhelmingly positive. The Commission had to acknowledge defeat.[44]

The Commission was followed back to Washington with newspaper reports of alleged official misconduct on the part of the Commission. The *New York World* reported that it had received information that the Sioux Commission, having failed to get the Indians to sign the agreement to surrender half their reservation, "are now resorting to threats, telling them that if they do not sign the agreement soldiers will be sent to drive them from their reservation to some other, and that in such a contingency they will lose their lands and get nothing."[45] Other newspapers echoed these charges. The Commission's own report recounts how the Commissioners reminded the Sioux that their future would be "problematical and uncertain" if they refused to accept the Act.[46] Significantly, the Commissioners hinted that the continued receipt of rations, guaranteed by the Agreement of 1876, was tied into acceptance of the Act.[47] Congressman Morrill submitted a resolution that these charges be investigated, but the resolution was never passed.[48]

Report of the 1888 Sioux Commission

Upon their return to Washington, the Sioux Commission wrote a strongly-worded report blaming the Commission's failure on the influence of the chiefs and half-breeds.[49] The Commission charged that influential half-breeds opposed the reduction of the reservation from motives of self-interest. "They want large bodies of land which cost them nothing on which to pasture their vast herds of cattle and horses. Necessarily also, they will exercise a great control over Indians when questions between the Government and Indians arise."[50] The Commissioners also attributed their failure to the perception of the Sioux people, historically verified since then, that the Act was "inspired solely by those who wished to possess themselves of more of the Indians' land, and so as framed wholly in the interests of the Government as against themselves."

As for the chiefs, they are characterized by the Commission as reactionaries, opposed to all progress, who held back the more progressive Indians by "the bondage of tribal relations." According to the Commission, the chiefs' main consideration is "how best to postpone the day when their people shall be free to act for themselves."

Ideally, the Commission saw the consent provision of the 1888 Sioux bill as a means "to break the control of such leaders by securing to the whole people the right to vote as guaranteed to them in their treaty of 1868." However, the Commission's experience in Sioux country demonstrated the opposite. The Commission was forced to admit that they saw little chance of convincing three-fourths of the Sioux to sign any agreement for the division of the Great Sioux Reservation:

> It is due and proper that we should say that if the consent of three-fourths of the male adult Indians is required in order to effect the sale or cession of any considerable part of their territory, in our opinion any negotiations or any terms that would meet the approbation of Congress and the people of the United States will fail of success. This opinion is maturely formed from our experience . . . Under the most favorable circumstances and with even the most extravagant offers of compensation we believe that more than one fourth of these Indians would object and refuse to sign a deed of cession. It therefore remains to be considered whether wise, just, and humane legislation for these people solely as the wards of the Government, and not through consultation, with them as independent people or communities whose assent to measures for their good is required, shall be enacted or enforced.[51]

Simply put, the opinion of the Commission was that the Sioux were an obstinate block to the progress of civilization, and that they could not even be prevailed upon to give their consent to measures for their own good. The Commission's recommendation was to impose white civilization on the Sioux. The means for this were to be:

(1) the immediate survey of the reservation; (2) required allotment of the lands in severalty; (3) required attendance for the children in government operated schools; (4) withholding of rations, annuities and all benefits under former treaties until all requirements were complied with; and (5) refusal to recognize the chiefs as competent leaders.[52] In the event Congress again required the consent of the Sioux, the Commissioners advised the next Commission to ignore the chiefs and focus on individuals because the chiefs' control over the tribe had a "pernicious effect" on the work of the Commission.[53]

SECTION II

Congress Passes New Sioux Bill

The report of the 1888 Commission, issued on December 13, 1888 had a considerable effect on a new bill for the division of the Great Sioux Reservation, reported out of the House Committee on Indian Affairs one month later, on January 5, 1889.

The new bill was much like the bill of the previous session. One exception was that it provided for giving the Sioux a higher price for their lands; $1.25 an acre the first three years after the land was thrown open to settlement, 75¢ the next two years and 50¢ an acre there after, instead of the flat 50¢ an acre price under the old bill. The new bill also upped the amount in the improvement fund from one to two million dollars.[54]

The most significant difference, however, was that the new bill, as recommended by the House Committee, contained no consent provision.

The committee admitted that under the Treaty of 1868 (which the committee preferred to call an "agreement") the consent of three-fourths of the adult male Indians was required to validate any cession of land on the reservation. However, the committee pointed to the failure of the previous year's Commission as proof of the inadvisability of inserting the consent provision in the new bill. The committee recited the charges of the Pratt Commission, that the average Indian was completely under the control of a few "arrogant and self-conceited chiefs," and was unable to vote for his own true interests. The chiefs in turn, according to the committee report, were under the control of a few squawmen (white men married to Indian women) who were reaping huge fortunes from the common property of the Indian. In the eyes of the committee the chiefs were also under the influence of several railroad companies in whose interest it was to keep the Great Sioux Reservation closed to settlement. The report specifically mentioned the Northern Pacific Railroad in this regard. Faced with this array of influences united to defeat any measure for the advancement of the Indians, and mindful of the opinion of the honorable Commission, that no bill, however liberal, would receive the sanction of three-fourths of the Indians, the committee reasoned that it would be imprudent and damaging to the Indians' true interest to risk a second attempt to gain the consent of the Indians.

Now the question is, shall we resubmit this great national question to these igno-
rant savages, and resort to old methods to secure their so-called consent? Shall
this great Government resort to the red-blanket dicker with its own wards, and
chief bribery, to secure their so-called consent; or shall we resort to the strong arm
of the military, and with our glittering bayonets, overawe and scare them into so-
called consent? The one would be dishonest and demoralizing. The other cow-
ardly and unmanly. Or shall we pursue an open, candid and sincere course?

It is the candid and honest opinion of your committee that this Government
should treat these Indians and their property as the children or wards of the nation, and deal with them as a humane father would with his child . . . Therefore
we recommend that the bill pass, and that the Government proceed at once to
survey these lands, allot to each family all the land required under the law, and
that of the best for agricultural and pastural purposes.[55]

The committee then attempted to justify their reason for ignoring an express treaty
stipulation.

The treaty of 1868, which requires three-fourths of the adult male members of the
tribe to consent to sale or cession of any part of their reservation, has been violated in several respects by both the Government and the Indians.

According to the committee, the Indians had failed to fulfill the treaty provision concerning keeping the peace, taking lands in severalty, and becoming capable of self-
support. The committee also cited the 1877 Agreement as a precedent for ignoring
the consent provision. By implication, the committee argued that since the Treaty
of 1868 had already been violated so often, the treaty was as good as abrogated.

On February 4, 1889, Representative Samuel Peel of Arkansas, Chairman of the
House Committee on Indian Affairs, called up for consideration on the House floor
the bill to divide the Great Sioux Reservation.[56] As the debate began, the opinion of
the committee on the consent issue was challenged by Representative Charles Hooker
of Mississippi. Hooker reminded the House that the Sioux bill passed during the
preceding session of Congress had required the consent of the Indians. "What, Mr.
Chairman," Hooker asked, "is the changed condition of affairs which makes it necessary now to pass a bill without a provision requiring the consent of these Indians?"
Hooker answered his own question:

Nothing apparently. It is a fact notorious that the commission was to obtain the
consent of the Indians in conformity to the treaty we made with these Indians
twenty years ago that they should retain possession of what remained to them of
their immense territory, that it should never be taken away from them except
under the form prescribed in that Treaty of 1868. Now, the bill of the last session
of Congress complied with that provision of the treaty and required as a prereq-
uisite the consent of the Indians themselves.

A commission was sent out and it failed to obtain the consent of the Indians. The gentleman from Arkansas (Mr. Peel) says that it failed because a certain chief stood in advance of the Indians and would not allow the commission to obtain their consent. We understand these Indians transact all their business through their chiefs, that their chiefs speak for them, that they assume to know the sentiment of the Indians better than anyone else.

Certainly it comes with bad grace from a government which conceded this question of ownership to ask that that stipulation of the treaty should be departed from; that now, driven by stress of weather, being unable to obtain the consent of the Indians by means of a commission you propose to do it without their consent.[57]

Congressman Peel argued that conditions necessitated ignoring the consent provision of the 1868 treaty:

I understand the rule to be that the guardian has the right to enlarge or increase the estate of the ward, but not to diminish it. Now, if our treaty with these wards contains a clause the execution of which would be to their detriment, shall we insist on doing them this damage? In our report we state our belief that where the execution of a clause of a treaty with these people would operate to their benefit we ought to adhere to it; but if such a course would be injurious to these uneducated, almost savage people who find it impossible to comprehend their own condition and the future that awaits them—if they are controlled or influenced by others, and are not acting under their own free will, and we find that carrying out that clause literally would continue these people in a state of savagery, the question is, should a government like ours adhere to the execution of such a provision.[58]

Representative Nelson of Minnesota added his opinion that he could conceive of only one method of gaining the consent of the Sioux: "If we would put into this bill or into some other bill a large corruption fund for the purpose of bribing the leading chiefs, giving them a large bonus, we should no doubt secure a formal approval of this treaty." Congressmen Cutcheon and Perkins added their assent to this statement.[59]

Further consideration of the bill was postponed until the evening of February 6 when the full House discussed the bill, section by section. Congressman Hooker offered an amendment concerning the consent issue:

That this act shall take effect only upon the acceptance thereof and consent thereto by the different bands of the Sioux Nation of Indians, in manner and form prescribed by the twelfth article of the said treaty between the United States and said Indians, concluded April 29, 1868 . . .[60]

Evidently Congressmen Hooker and Peel had come to some agreement in the interim between the two debates on the Sioux bill, for the Chairman of the House

Committee on Indian Affairs offered no resistance to the amendment. After some debate, the amendment was agreed to and the bill passed.

The Sioux bill as passed by the House was brought before the Senate later that month. The debate was led by Senator Dawes of Massachusetts.[61] In the Senate, the consent issue was not even debated and the Senate approved the same language for Article 28 as was contained in the Hooker amendment. Thus, despite the gloomy predictions by the 1888 Commission on the likelihood of Sioux acceptance of a new Act to reduce the Great Sioux Reservation, Congress included an identical consent provision in the 1889 Act.[62]

The Secretary of Interior appointed U.S. Army General George Crook to head the new Commission. General Crook spent over three months in the summer of 1889 attempting to persuade the Sioux to accept the Act.[63] According to official records, 4,363 adult males out of 5,678 eligible Sioux signed to accept the Act, thus ostensibly satisfying the three-fourths requirement.[64] As discussed below,[65] here is strong evidence that many of the authenticating marks on the document used to collect signatures were not genuine and that many Sioux whose names were listed as signifying approval may not have actually signed to accept the Act. For the purpose of discussing the work of the Commission, this report assumes the signatures were genuine.

In light of the dismal failure of the 1888 Commission, it is surprising that only one year later a different Commission successfully obtained the consent of three-fourths of the adult male Sioux. The terms of the 1889 Act were somewhat more favorable to the Sioux,[66] but this fact does not explain the Commission's success because the opposition in 1888 was not based primarily on objections to the terms of the Act. Rather, the Sioux rejected the 1888 Act because of a more fundamental objection to relinquishing more land. The number of acres to be given up did not decrease in the 1889 Act. Why, then, did the 1889 Commission succeed where the 1888 Commission had failed?

The Work of the Sioux Commission of 1889

The Commissioners perceived their task to persuade the Sioux to accept the Act rather than merely explaining its terms in a neutral fashion. They knew that the Sioux had overwhelmingly rejected a similar Act one year earlier and they expected to meet stiff opposition. They were aware that the Act greatly favored the United States and that the Sioux had become increasingly suspicious of any proposal involving a loss of land. The Secretary of the Interior and the Commissioner of Indian Affairs gave the Commissioners very little advice about how to accomplish their goal. They did, however, instruct the Commissioners to carefully choose interpreters so the Act would be "fully and fairly explained to their satisfactory understanding."[67] More important, the Commissioners' instructions emphasized the urgent necessity of removing this "barrier to free communication and commerce between eastern and western portions of Dakota."[68] The Commissioners spent the entire summer of 1889 working to per-suade the Sioux at the various agencies to accept the Act.

Rosebud Agency

The Commissioners first visited the Rosebud Agency because they believed the influential chiefs there were less likely to oppose the Act.[69] The official record shows that only 21 out of 1,476 eligible Sioux at the Rosebud Agency refused to accept the Act.[70] Yet the Commission reported very strong initial opposition, especially among the influential chiefs.[71] Significantly, the official report of the Commission and the official transcript of the council meetings do not satisfactorily explain how this opposition was overcome.

At Rosebud, the methods and tactics the Commission employed at almost every other agency were first revealed. Accepting the advice of the 1888 Commission, the Commissioners adopted the policy of bypassing the tribal chiefs and working instead with individuals.[72] Commissioner Crook was particularly suited for this strategy because he had used many of the Sioux warriors as scouts in his previous military campaigns against the Sioux Nation.[73] Consequently, a large part of the Commission's work occurred in private meetings off-the-record.[74]

The issuance of beef for feasts and the suspension of the rules against dancing were important parts of the Commission's strategy.[75] This was a deliberate attempt to create a receptive atmosphere for the Commission and the Act. In addition, the Commission made extensive use of the mixed bloods and white men married to Indian women, who generally favored the Act. Some were apparently paid for their assistance.[76] Equally important was Commissioner Crook's written assurance that the rations would not be reduced and the Sioux treaties would remain in force if the Sioux accepted the Act. Apparently this personal pledge persuaded many to sign.[77] But the key to the Commission's success at Rosebud lies in the practice of the Indian agent of refusing to allow those who opposed the Act to return home from the agency.[78] Thus, many Sioux may have signed to accept the Act believing they would be kept against their will at the agency if they refused.

Even the official record reveals there may have been attempts to threaten and intimidate the Sioux into accepting the Act. Commissioner Crook depicted the advance of white settlers onto the Sioux Reservation as inevitable and stressed the powerlessness of the Sioux or the President to prevent it.[79] Crook portrayed the Act as the last chance the Sioux would have to ensure their survival, leaving the distinct impression that the Sioux had no real choice.[80] He predicted that Congress would unilaterally take more Sioux land without their consent if they refused to accept this Act.[81] At one point in the discussions, Crook raised the possibility that the treaty-guaranteed rations might be affected by the intransigence of the Sioux.[82]

The significance of these representations were quite apparent to the Sioux. At the third council meeting, Agent Spencer reported that one chief had been telling his people that all the tribal members were being forced to sign the acceptance form.[83]

One week after the meetings started, Chief High Hawk reported hearing rumors that those who refused to sign to accept the Act would be disarmed and deprived of rations.[84] Although Commissioner Crook denied this report during the same meeting, only 250 were in attendance so many others may have signed with the belief that the rumor was true.[85] It is impossible to determine from the official record the number of Sioux who signed thinking their rations would be cut off if they refused.

Finally, there is some secondary evidence that the Sioux at Rosebud were bribed into accepting the Act.[86] Whatever the means, the Commission succeeded in two weeks in turning unanimous opposition to the Act into nearly unanimous acceptance.

Pine Ridge Agency

At Pine Ridge the Commission encountered its strongest opposition, led by Chief Red Cloud. The Commissioners reported that the Indian Defense Association had organized the resistance, which included an agreement among certain influential chiefs to reject the Act.[87] In fact, the opposition was so strong that the tribal government had ordered that no one speak to the Commission.[88] To overcome the opposition the Commissioners worked diligently in private meetings with individuals, enlisted the aid of the mixed bloods and white men, held large feasts and succeeded in obtaining 684 signatures in favor of the Act while 622 rejected it.[89]

Commissioner Crook's tactic of patiently working with individuals is recounted in his diary entry for June 19, 1889:

Tuned different Indians up. Got a good many signatures by different younger Indians who were made to see that they must think for themselves, and in this way it is breaking down the opposition of the old reconstructed chiefs.[90]

Attempts were also made to win the support of certain chiefs considered "progressive" by the Commission. American Horse was apparently persuaded to accept the Act by Commissioner Crook's threat at a private meeting that the Sioux would lose all their lands if they rejected the Act.[91] Once these chiefs decided to accept the Act, the Commissioners tried to use their influence among individuals to win further support.[92] The method used to gain the approval of the more traditional chiefs was not so subtle—Captain Pollock, one of Crook's officers, offered to provide Red Cloud, Little Wound and Young Man Afraid of His Horse $200 each to make a feast for their bands if they would accept the Act.[93] All refused the offer.

During the public council meetings, the Commissioners repeated the themes that apparently were so persuasive at the Rosebud Agency. The inevitable illegal occupation of Sioux territory by white settlers and the likelihood of a Congressional taking were clearly expressed by Commissioner Foster:

Settlements are made on the east by the whites up to the river and on the west beyond the reservation. It does not take much sense to see that the white man is going to break through this wall. Unless this act is accepted . . . these Senators and

Representatives from Dakota will influence the Congress to get through there in some way.[94]

Another device used at Pine Ridge, as well as Rosebud, was to exploit the Sioux perception of the Commissioners as powerful men with great influence in Congress and with the President. The Sioux had many complaints unrelated to the terms of the Act which they hoped the Commission could address after their return. The Commissioners suggested that their influence would be enhanced if they were successful in their mission and, therefore, they would be useful to the Sioux in addressing their complaints only if the Sioux accepted the Act.[95]

The Commissioners again raised the possibility of reduced rations if the Sioux continued to resist the efforts of the Government to "civilize" them and rejected the Act. The consequence of rejecting the Act was unmistakably clear:

> He is responsible for his own family, and if he decides wrong and hereafter he and his children get hungry, the chiefs or those who advised him against what was right, can not feed him, for they will have nothing to give. (Commissioner Crook).[96]

Finally, there is some evidence that at Pine Ridge the Commission may have attempted to influence the voting by issuing beef and other rations.[97]

Lower Brule Agency

At Lower Brule the Commission met with initial resistance from Chief Iron Nation, but "after several conferences the adherence of this chief was secured."[98] While the official record does not reflect the substance of these meetings, other records reveal that Iron Nation was persuaded to accept the Act by the personal promise of Commissioner Crook that the Lower Brule Sioux would be resettled on lands of the Rosebud Reservation if the lands of their reservation were taken by whites.[99] One writer has asserted that the number of promises made to the Sioux by the Commission during these meetings amounted to bribery.[100] With the support of Iron Nation secured, the Commissioners easily obtained the consent of nearly all the Sioux at Lower Brule.[101] Nevertheless, the Commissioners repeated their prediction that "whether you agree to it or not, a hole so to speak will be made through this reservation from the eastern to the western portions of the State of Dakota."[102] Beef rations for feasts were again issued during the meetings.[103]

Crow Creek Agency

The Commission spent only five days at the Crow Creek Agency, meeting a well-organized group of opposition led by the most prominent chiefs.[104] The Commissioners reported obtaining signatures of slightly more than half of the eligible adult males.[105] Yet the official count appended to their Report shows that 248 out of 305 eligible males signed in favor at Crow Creek.[106] Commissioner Crook reported in his diary on July 9, two days before the Commission left, that he had obtained 101 signatures, but that the principal chiefs had refused to sign.[107] These discrepancies are not explained in the official report and we have not found any other records which explain them.

In the council meetings, the familiar themes were repeated. The Sioux were told bluntly that "Congress will take this matter into its own hands" if they refused to accept the Act.[108] There is additional evidence that the Commissioners attempted to circumvent the authority of the chiefs and reach individuals directly.[109] When it became clear that many Sioux did not understand the Act, the Commissioners suggested holding private, off-the-record meetings where the influence of the chiefs would not be as great.[110] Beef rations were again issued.[111]

Commissioner Crook became somewhat pessimistic about the chances of success, writing to his Aide-de-Camp Kennon that "[T]his has been one of the worst experiences with Indians. We have met a different problem at each place and this is the most difficult one yet as this bill makes a very unjust discrimination against them. I can't tell what the outcome will be yet . . . "[112]

Cheyenne River Agency

At Cheyenne River, the Commission was faced with almost unanimous opposition.[113] After a week of "persistent work," which included numerous private conferences with individuals, the opposition apparently began to break down. The Commissioners again emphasized the probability of unilateral taking of land by Congress,[114] the inevitability of white settlers overpowering the Sioux,[115] and the necessity of adopting white civilization.[116] But the Commission's tactics at Cheyenne River were not limited to oral arguments. Feasts were held and dancing was again allowed.[117]

Commissioner Crook requested the Secretary of War to send Major G.M. Randall to Cheyenne River to assist the Commission.[118] Major Randall appeared at the council meetings in full military uniform.[119] The unmistakable message was that the Sioux would have to deal with the United States Army if they refused to accept the Act. Also important in the Commission's strategy at Cheyenne River was the policy of holding the Sioux at the main camp until they decided to accept the Act.[120] Despite the Commission's efforts, the Sioux at Cheyenne River were determined to oppose the Act. At one point in the council meetings, the Sioux began a filibuster to prevent any decision from being made. When Commissioner Crook ordered the signing to begin, Black Fox moved to prevent anyone from signing. Crook responded by threatening to call in the military to protect those who wanted to sign.[121]

Even in the official record, there is evidence of intimidation and bribery. In the transcript of the meeting held on July 20, 1889, the following statement of a Mr. Cook, identified as a lieutenant of police, is found:

And also you have tried to coward us, and see us in parts which has been spread among the Indians. That is the reason why there is a good many of us who do not sign. . . . And some words you tried to frighten us and some words you tried to please us.[122]

In the opinion of Mr. Cook, many Sioux signed in favor of the Act out of respect for and deference to the Commissioners:

> A great many don't understand the bill, but merely that you spoke to them, to see them, and they came here merely to sign this bill to please you, and were cowed down.[123]

Mr. Cook also reported hearing about certain adult males being offered money by unidentified outside parties to sign in favor of the Act.[124] Commissioner Crook disclaimed all knowledge and association with such activity.[125]

The Commission obtained only 300 signatures out of 749 eligible adult males, but the rolls were left with Agent McChesney and Major Randall, who succeeded in running the total to 620 within two weeks after the Commission left.[126] No record of the methods they used has been found.

Santee Agency

At Santee, the Commission obtained nearly unanimous consent with very little resistance,[127] but the usual predictions about loss of land and the futility of resistance were made by the Commissioners.[128]

Standing Rock Agency

Upon arrival at Standing Rock, the Commissioners found that the Sioux there had agreed among themselves to reject the Act.[129] Believing that it was futile to try and change the minds of the chiefs, the Commission concentrated on persuading individuals to accept the Act in disregard of the chiefs' position.[130] The Commission eventually obtained the signatures of 803 of the 1,121 eligible adult males.[131] They explained their success in these terms:

> For a time the task seemed almost hopeless, but persistence prevailed and interest was awakened. As soon as the question became debatable, the situation changed and success was secured. In this connection it is but due Agent McLaughlin to say that his assistance was invaluable.[132]

This official explanation does not adequately explain the success of the Commission in overcoming the opposition. Perhaps many were persuaded by the prediction of the Commissioners that white settlers would "make a hole" through the Reservation if the Sioux refused to accept the Act.[133] The taking of Sioux land by Congress was again portrayed as certain if the Sioux persisted in defeating attempts to obtain their consent.[134] The Commissioners stressed that it was in the best interests of the Sioux to remain on friendly terms with the Government, on whom they greatly depended for food.[135] The dependency of the Sioux on the Government was reinforced several times throughout the week of meetings by the issuance of beef rations by the Commission.[136]

The assistance of Agent McLaughlin was indeed invaluable to the Commission. At Standing Rock, Chief John Grass led the opposition to the Act. The Commissioners believed, correctly, that many individuals would support the Act if John Grass could be persuaded to accept it. This task was McLaughlin's responsibility, since he had lived among the Sioux for 17 years and apparently had gained their trust and confidence.[137] McLaughlin knew that a majority of the Sioux opposed the Act, but he considered it his "business to get them into another state of mind."[138] As he put it years later: "Grass and the other chiefs must be gotten into line."[139] On July 29, McLaughlin met surreptitiously with John Grass and persuaded him to accept the Act. McLaughlin describes their meeting in these words:

> I told him that if the act was not concurred in, a worse thing might happen: that legislation might be enacted which would open the reservation without requiring the consent of the Indians; and I labored with him until he agreed that he would speak for its ratification and work for it. When he said that, I knew that the matter was settled and the concurrence of the Indians assured . . . [140]

McLaughlin even helped Grass prepare his speech for the next council so as to recede "from his former position gracefully."[141]

Hyde asserts that the Commission also attempted to break down the opposition by telling the Sioux at Standing Rock that the Commission had obtained sufficient signatures at the other agencies so that those of the Standing Rock Sioux were not needed.[142] Hyde claims that this obviously false statement prompted many Sioux to sign out of fear of being deprived of benefits under the Act if their names did not appear in the final list of signers.[143]

Whatever the method, the Commission obtained 673 signatures before it left Standing Rock.[144] Upon checking the total number of signatures, the Commission discovered they did not have the signatures of three-fourths of the adult male Sioux. Word was sent to Agent McLaughlin to obtain more signatures from the Standing Rock Sioux. He subsequently brought the total to 803 out of 1,121 eligible males.[145]

General Observations

There is some evidence that the Sioux were not fully informed of the provisions of the Act. While the Act was explained at the public meetings, there is at least one aspect of the Act on which the Sioux appear to have been misled. Section 17 provided that three million dollars would be deposited in the U.S. Treasury to the credit of the Sioux Nation as a "permanent fund." The same section further provided that the United States would be reimbursed out of the fund for money expended under other sections of the Act for the benefit of the Sioux. Section 22 provided that the money accruing from the sale of the nine million acres released to the United States would be used to fund this "Permanent fund" and to reimburse the United States for "all necessary actual expenditures contemplated and provided for under the provisions of this Act . . . " These sections were never adequately explained to the Sioux.[146] It is, therefore, probable that they thought the proceeds of the sale of land would accumulate as an addition to the "permanent fund." The official record contains no evidence that the Sioux understood that money set aside for them in one part of the Act would be used to reimburse the United States for expenditures for them in other parts of the Act.

The Commissioners decided to allow the mixed bloods and white men who had married Indian women to vote to accept the Act. The Sioux strongly objected to allowing these groups to participate.[147] The Commission argued that all white men married to Sioux women were entitled to vote because the Treaty of 1868 incorporated them into the Nation.[148] Commissioner Foster told the Sioux at Pine Ridge that these white men would be allowed to vote, but he falsely assured them that these votes would not be counted until a court determined their rights.[149] The Appendix to the official Report of the Commission shows that votes of at least 93 white men were counted.[150] The unofficial tally of votes, made during the Commission's meetings, shows that votes of 109 white men were counted.[151] Moreover, one writer has asserted that 147 white men and mixed bloods were allowed to sign in favor of the Act at Pine Ridge,[152] although the official count shows that no white men voted and only 47 mixed bloods there accepted the Act. The official record shows that the votes of at least 184 mixed bloods were counted, while the unofficial count lists this number at 168.[153] Regardless of the exact number of white men and mixed bloods who accepted the Act, it is clear that the Commission would not have obtained the signatures of three-fourths of the adult males without the votes of these groups. It obtained only 206 more votes than necessary to meet the statutory requirement. Even under the official count, the votes of the mixed bloods and white men number 277.[154]

In light of the abundant evidence of fraud, coercive tactics, and the radical and sudden change in the attitude of the Sioux toward the Act, it is especially important to scrutinize closely the procedures used in taking signatures and the genuineness of signatures and authenticating marks. The Commissioners were given lists of eligible adult male Sioux and told to hold open councils to which all eligible Sioux would be invited. The Letter of Instructions to the Commissioners gave them unlimited discretion in establishing procedures for taking signatures: "Beyond these general instructions I rely upon your wisdom and fidelity and leave the details of the work to your good judgment and discretion."[155] The official transcript of the proceedings reveals that the Commissioners did not have a consistent procedure. At some agencies, signatures were taken in a separate building used especially for that purpose. In any event, no record was made of the actual signing procedure, so nothing is known of the safeguards, if any, that may have been employed to ensure authentic signatures.

Only a very few adult males appear to have actually signed the acceptance form or to have otherwise made an authenticating mark. Judging from the similar appearance of the "signatures" on the only acceptance form our research has located, almost all the authenticating marks were made by one or two persons at each agency.[156] Assuming this document is the original acceptance form, it is almost certain that most of the signatures of the Sioux are not genuine. However, it is possible that the document is not the original acceptance form, but rather a copy of the original or a compilation of names of those who signed the original. No evidence has been discovered which would support either of these possibilities.

The entire process of obtaining the consent of the Sioux is suspect because no procedures for ensuring the genuineness of signatures were established. The lack of well-defined procedures is especially significant in light of the fact that the Commission was not acting as a neutral and unbiased agent for the collection of signatures. Any process which rests in the same body the responsibility to persuade a group to accept an Act of Congress and the duty to obtain their written consent is inherently suspect.

Secondary Accounts

Numerous secondary accounts of the Commission's work confirm the conclusion that the Sioux were coerced into accepting the Act. In 1890, the Supervisor of Education for the Sioux wrote to the Commissioner of Indian Affairs that "the people were bribed and threatened into signing the Sioux Bill and by no means consented to it voluntarily."[157] Responding to a request for his opinion of the reasons for the Sioux outbreak of 1890–91, General Nelson Miles wrote to Senator Dawes: "While the Indians were urged and almost forced to sign a treaty presented to them by the Commission authorized by Congress the government has failed to fulfill its part of the compact . . . "[158] General John M. Schofield wrote to Senator Dawes in 1890 that the Sioux problem could not be solved until Congress fulfilled the "treaty obligations which the Indians were entreated and coerced into signing."[159] Bishop Hare, an Episcopal missionary who was present during the Commission's proceedings,[160] had this opinion of the Commission's method: "Commissioners with such a business in hand have the devil to fight, and can fight him . . . only with fire, and many friends of the Indians think that in this case the Commission, convinced that the acceptance of the bill was essential, carried persuasion to the verge of intimidation."[161] The monthly journal of the Episcopal Mission at the Santee Agency, a newspaper which favored the division and allotment of the Great Sioux Reservation, contained the following report in the September, 1889 issue:

No doubt but charges of bribery will be made against the Commission. Such charges were made before the Commission had been at work a week at Rosebud Agency. The charges may be true. Congress voted $25,000 to defray the expenses of the Commission in getting the signatures necessary. The Commission spent their money, so far as gaining their point was concerned, wisely. They engaged men to work for them. If these men were signers themselves, mixed-bloods of influence, that did not prevent the Commission from getting and using such influence. The moral effect of the methods used was not the best. Sabbath desecration, dancing, feasting, and participation in Indian customs by the Commission were indulged in too freely to give the Indians an idea of the best civilization.[162]

Thus, even those who favored the break-up of the Great Sioux Reservation admitted that the Sioux were not treated fairly.

Summary

In 1868, the United States solemnly guaranteed in a treaty that no future cession of any part of the Great Sioux Reservation would be valid unless executed and signed by at least three-fourths of all the adult male members of the Sioux Nation. The history of relations between the Sioux Nation and the United States during the period 1870–1890 is the story of how the United States violated the letter and spirit of this treaty provision in order to obtain over 11 million acres for its citizens.

In 1877, Congress ratified an agreement for the cession of the Black Hills which clearly and unequivocally violated the terms of the 1868 Treaty. Congress approved an obviously fraudulent agreement to which only 10% of the Sioux had consented. Beginning in 1880 enormous pressure developed to acquire more land within the diminishing Great Sioux Reservation. Massive Sioux opposition to relinquishing their lands defeated an effort by the Edmunds Commission in 1882 to obtain Sioux consent to a cession of a large area of Sioux territory. Despite using fraudulent methods, the Edmunds Commission only obtained the approval of 450 out of over 5,000 eligible adult male Sioux. A second attempt in 1888 to secure the consent of the Sioux also failed because of strong Sioux opposition.

The United States finally succeeded, after ten years of trying, in acquiring a major portion of the Great Sioux Reservation. The Act of March 2, 1889 divided the Reservation into several smaller, separate reservations and conveyed the remainder to the United States. Ostensibly, the consent requirement of the 1868 Treaty was satisfied. However, as one writer has noted, "it seems incredible that the Sioux . . . could be so united in opposition to the agreement, yet approve it by an over whelming majority of 4,463 out of 5,678 eligible to vote."[163] It is impossible to determine from the historical records exactly what persuaded individual Sioux who were initially opposed to the Act to ultimately decide to accept it. But as the preceding narrative amply demonstrates, the Crook Commission was not prepared to take "no" for an answer. It was clearly determined to obtain, by whatever method, the signatures of three-fourths of the adult male Sioux. Among the methods the Commission used to coerce the Sioux into accepting the Act were attempts to convince them of the inevitability of a unilateral Congressional taking of Sioux land if they rejected the Act; feasts and dances intended to create a favorable disposition toward the Act and the Commission; bribery or attempted bribery; threats and intimidation; extensive use of the mixed bloods and white men who generally favored the Act; hints of reduced rations if they rejected the Act; personal promises from the Commissioners of future help in exchange for acceptance of the Act; working directly with individuals in disregard of the authority of the chiefs; forcing some Sioux to stay at the Commission meetings until they agreed to accept the Act; and private lobbying with certain influential chiefs, especially at Standing Rock and Lower Brule. Thus, the Sioux clearly did not freely and voluntarily consent to the Act of 1889 as required by Article 12 of the 1868 Treaty.

Notes

1. For primary source material on the Treaty of Fort Laramie *see, Proceedings of the Great Peace Commission of 1867–1868,* edited by Vine Deloria, Jr. and "Report of the Indian Peace Commissioners," *House Executive Document 97,* 40th Cong. 2d Sess., Congressional Serial Set Number 13.

See also, George E. Hyde, *Red Cloud's Folk,* Norman: University of Oklahoma Press, 1937 at 162–167.

2. 15 Stat. 635 (1868).

3. *Proceedings, Id.* at 173–176 gives an account of Red Cloud signing the Treaty of Fort Laramie and states that the various articles and provisions of the treaty were fully explained on two separate occasions.

4. Francis Paul Prucha, *American Indian Policy in Crisis,* Norman: University of Oklahoma Press, 1975 at 16.

5. According to Hyde, *Red Cloud's Folk* at 169, "Red Cloud said in 1870 that he was told that the treaty was an agreement to restore peace and trade, nothing more, and many of the chiefs bore him out. They said that the treaty had not been read to them."

6. *Id.* at 166.

7. For a good overview of the Indian Peace Policy, see Prucha at 16, 23.

8. 15 Stat. 17 (1867).

9. "Report of the Indian Peace Commissioners" at 4.

10. *Id.* at 16.

11. Hyde *Red Cloud's Folk* at 168.

12. 19 Stat. 176, 192 (1876).

13. Letter from U.S. Indian Agent McGillicuddy to Commissioner of Indian Affairs:

I have no doubt but that it is merely a question of time—and a very short time— that the Indians will have to give up the region referred to.

14. For example, *see* Newton Edmunds to Commissioner of Indian Affairs, September 26, 1882, and Edmunds to the Secretary of Interior, October 10, 1882, in *Senate Executive Document 70,* 48th Cong., 1st Sess., Congressional Serial Set Number 2165. Similar sentiments can be seen in *House Report No. 533,* 50th Cong., 1st Sess., Congressional Serial Set Number 2599 at 3. *See also,* George E. Hyde, *A Sioux Chronicle,* Norman: University of Oklahoma Press, 1956 at 136. Hyde's book is not extensively documented so we have not been able to verify many of his assertions. How-

ever, some of his assertions are corroborated by the official account of the Commission's work and by Crook's diary, as will become apparent. Hyde lists as his sources "the usual official sources," contemporary newspaper accounts, and interviews with eyewitnesses. Preface at XV.

15. 22 Stat. 302, 328 (1882).

16. *Senate Executive Document 70* at 5.

17. *Id.* at 8–9.

18. *Id.*

19. A copy of the proposed agreement is in *Senate Executive Document 70* at 34–35. In Article I, the Indians purportedly acknowledge "the right of the chiefs and the headmen of the various bands at each agency to determine for themselves and for their several bands, with the Government of the United States, the boundaries of their separate reservations." Article IV contains the provision concerning the cows and bulls.

20. Actual transcripts of the councils were not kept by the Edmunds Commission, although *Senate Executive Document 70* contains some information on the proceedings. The abuses of the Edmunds Commission are documented in the "Dawes Report," *Senate Report* 283, 48th Cong., 1st Sess., Congressional Serial Set Number 2174.

21. The signatures obtained at the various agencies are in *Senate Executive Document 70* at 36–41.

22. Hyde, *A Sioux Chronicle* at 137.

23. 62 *Congressional Record* 3678, March 2, 1883.

24. 22 Stat. 602, 628 (1883).

25. *Senate Executive Document 70* at 48.

26. *Id.* at 57.

27. Hyde, *A Sioux Chronicle* at 137. Hinmon had been the interpreter for the Peace Commission of 1868, and a commissioner himself in 1876.

28. *Senate Executive Document 70* Part II, 48th Cong., 1st Sess., Congressional Serial Set Number 2165 at 1–2.

29. Joint Resolution, March 2, 1883.

30. *Senate Executive Document 70* at 59.

31. *Id.* The Commissioners argued:

Our agreement was signed by nearly all the chiefs and headmen, in numbers largely in excess of that ever before secured by any treaty or agreement with these Indians. In every instance we were fully satisfied that the signers were authorized by their people, by whom they had been deputed, in their own councils and after their regular and long-established customs, to act for them, and in submitting the agreement to you we regarded it, as we still do, as fully executed by the Indian people both in law and in fact.

32. *Senate Report No. 283*, 48th Cong., 1st Sess., Congressional Serial Set Number 217. At page v the committee makes its strongest statement about the lack of popular support for the agreement in Sioux Country:

The conclusions of the committee are that at the present time the Sioux Nation is practically unanimous in its opposition to the proposed agreement. Indeed the committee did not find, among all these Indians at the different agencies, and called into council by their agents, more than one or two Indians whose opposition to this agreement is not now outspoken and decided . . . Of the few Indians who signed the agreement most of them claimed that they did not understand it at the time. Quite a number of them assert that they were directly misled.

33. *Id.* at vii.

34. *Id.*

35. *House Report 1724,* 48th Cong., 1st Sess., Congressional Serial Set Number 2258.

36. Hyde, *A Sioux Chronicle* at 150.

37. 89 *Congressional Record* 1840, March 7, 1888.

38. *Id.*

39. Hyde, *A Sioux Chronicle* at 144.

40. 89 *Congressional Record* 1841, March 7, 1888.

41. For the full legislative history of the 1888 Sioux bill on the floor of Congress, see *Congressional Record,* 50th Cong., 1st Sess., at 1836, 1842, 1971, 2203, 2296, 2300, 2371, 2451, 2576, 2922, 2990, 3117, 3141, 3608. The debates are at 1836–1842, and 2296–2300.

42. Hyde, *A Sioux Chronicle* at 189.

43. *Senate Executive Document 17,* 50th Cong., 2d Sess., Congressional Serial Set Number 2610 at 5.

44. Hyde, *A Sioux Chronicle* at 190–194.

45. *See, House Miscellaneous Document 576,* 50th Cong., 1st Sess., Congressional Serial Set Number 2570.

46. *Senate Executive Document 17* at 5.

47. The Sioux were told that implementation of the ration provisions of the 1876 Agreement was dependent on compliance with their promise in that Agreement to take allotments and begin farming. The Commissioners suggested that the United States might enforce the allotment provision if the Sioux refused to accept the Act. *Id.*

48. *House Miscellaneous Document 576.*

49. The report of the 1888 Sioux Commission is in *Senate Executive Document 17,* 50th Cong., 2d Sess., Congressional Serial Set Number 2610. The report includes the commission's explanation for their failure, their recommendations, transcripts of the councils and correspondence. The report, issued December 17, 1888, is 293 pages long.

50. *Id.* at 27.

51. *Id.* at 21.

52. *Id.* at 20.

53. *Id.* at 22.

54. *House Report 3645,* 50th Cong., 2d Sess., Congressional Serial Set Number 2673. The bill was numbered H.R.11970.

55. HR 3645 at 3.

56. The legislative history of H.R. 11970 on the floor of Congress is in the *Congressional Record*, 50th Cong., 2d Sess. It was introduced in the use at 564, debated in the House at 1492, 1578, passed House at 1903, referred to Senate Committee on Indian Affairs at 1965, reported out of committee at 2139, debated in the Senate at 2283, unconcurred by the House at 2332, reported out of conference committee at 2476, passed by both houses at 2528, 2646, and signed by the President at 2723.

57. 100 *Congressional Record* 1493, February 4, 1889.

58. *Id.*

59. *Id.* at 1496.

60. *Id.* at 1580, February 6, 1889.

61. 101 *Congressional Record* 2283, February 25, 1889.

62. 25 Stat. 888, 889 (1889).

63. The other members of the Commission were Charles Foster, former Governor of Ohio and William Warner, former congressional representative from Missouri and then Commander in Chief of the Grand Army of the Republic, a veteran's association. *Report and Proceedings of the Sioux Commission, Senate Executive Document 51*, 51st Cong., 1st Sess., 1890, Congressional Serial Set Number 2682. (hereinafter cited as *Report of the Commission*)

64. *Report of the Commission* at 8. (Letter from Secretary of the Interior Noble to President Harrison, January 30, 1890.)

65. *See infra* at 41–42.

66. The Act of 1889 doubled the acreage of each allotment; provided that allotments would not be compulsory without the consent of the majority of the adult members of the tribe; increased the "permanent fund" in the U.S. Treasury from $1 million to $3 million; and increased the price of ceded land from $.50 per acre for the entire area to a sliding scale structure of $1.25 per acre for land disposed within three years after the effective date of the Act, $.75 for lands disposed within the following two years, and $.50 per acre for land disposed thereafter. 25 Stat. 888 (1889).

67. *Report of the Commission, Appendix, Exhibit B*, letter of Instructions, May 20, 1889, at 36.

68. *Id.* at 40.

69. *Report of the Commission* at 16.

70. *Report of the Commission, Appendix, Exhibit A.*

71. *Report of the Commission* at 16.

72. At a meeting held on June 7, 1889, a Mr. C.P. Jordan said:

I know it is not the intention of the Government to allow any small party of Indians in accordance with your old-time custom to control the action of the majority as a tribe. *Report of the Commission* at 48.

73. Martin F. Schmitt, ed., *General George Crook, His Autobiography*, Norman: University of Oklahoma Press, 1960 at 286.

74. *See* Diary of General George Crook, Military Research Collection, U.S. Army Military History Institute, Carlisle, Pennsylvania.

75. George E. Hyde, *A Sioux Chronicle,* Norman: University of Oklahoma Press, 1956 at 202.

76. *Id.* at 203, 206.

77. *Id.* at 206.

78. *Id.* at 208. Hyde is the only writer who reported this practice. We have found no evidence to corroborate this claim.

79. *Report of the Commission* at 58.

80. Mr. C.P. Jordan depicted the Act as the final solution to all Sioux problems. At the first Rosebud meeting, he said the Act was "the last opportunity to make yourselves rich and happy." *Id.* at 48.

81. *Id.* at 51.

82. *Id.* The use of threats of cutting off rations to gain concessions from the Sioux has a long history. It was used most successfully in 1876 following the failure of the Sioux Commission of 1875 to persuade the Sioux to cede the Black Hills. In the report of the 1875 Sioux Commission they recommend, "the plan here suggested, or some other to be adopted by Congress, should be presented to the Indians as a finality, and with it they should be told that its rejection will have the effect to arrest all appropriations for their subsistence in the future, and all supplies not absolutely required by the Treaty of 1868." (From the "Annual Report of the Commissioner of Indian Affairs" at 693, in *House Executive Document 1,* 44th Cong., 1st Sess., Congressional Serial Set Number 1680.) Congress concurred with this suggestion. (See note 12, supra.) A similar threat was used by the 1888 Sioux Commission. (*See* note 47, *supra.*)

83. *Id.* at 55.

84. *Id.* at 60, 64.

85. *Id.* at 61.

86. Hyde reported that a missionary paper called the *Word-Carrier* said in its September, 1889 issue that "money was given and promises were made that Indians would be given certain favors if they supported the land agreement." Hyde at 208.

87. *Report of the Commission* at 18.

88. Hyde at 213.

89. Crook's diary recounts eight days of private meetings. *See* note 32, supra. Hyde asserts that the mixed bloods and white men were counted on to bring in small groups of Sioux before the Commission. Hyde at 213. For the official tally at Pine Ridge, *see Report of the Commission, Appendix, Exhibit A.*

90. Diary of General George Crook, note 74, *supra.*

91. Hyde at 216.

92. Commissioner Crook described his method in his diary entry for June 21, 1889:

Had a big council this afternoon in which American Horse, Bear Nose and a couple of others made speeches in favor of the Bill for the first time . . . American Horse's Band commenced signing—I had coached Bear Nose.

93. Letter from Commissioner Crook to Commissioner Foster, August 27, 1889, reported in Schmidt at 288 and Hyde at 218.

94. *Report of the Commission, Proceedings* at 74.

95. *Id.* at 66, 95. Commissioner Foster said:

Now, an Indian can see that we can be useful to you only contingent upon our success . . . And if we do succeed . . . every just complaint you have made will be redressed.

96. *Id.* at 85.

97. *Id.* American Horse explained the effect issuing beef had:

Here back during the council whenever you tell them you are going to give them any beef or hard bread they are anxious and feel that good that they get right up and give a big yell. *Id.* at 96.

Crook's diary shows that 57 cattle were used for feasting at Pine Ridge. Diary of General George Crook, note 74, *supra.*

98. *Report of the Commission* at 19.

99. Hyde at 219. Crook wrote in his diary on July 3, 1889:

. . . after strong talking by Governor Foster and myself they were finally induced to sign today but not until I made many personal pledges of my help in the future. . . . Diary of General George Crook, note 74, *supra.*

100. Hyde at 219.

101. Only 17 out of 314 eligible adult males rejected the Act at the Lower Brule Agency. *Report of the Commission, Appendix, Exhibit A.*

102. *Report of the Commission, Proceedings* at 131.

103. *Id.*

104. *Report of the Commission* at 20.

105. *Id.*

106. *Report of the Commission, Appendix, Exhibit A.*

107. Diary of General George Crook, note 74, *supra.*

108. *Report of the Commission, Proceedings* at 146.

109. *Id.* at 149.

110. Commissioner Foster said:

Oftentimes in a little private conversation some matter may be better understood than it can be in these full meetings. *Id.* at 145.

Commissioner Crook held a private meeting with White Ghost the day he arrived and apparently succeeded in gaining his support. Diary of General George Crook, July 5, 1889, note 74, *supra.*

111. *Report of the Commission, Proceedings* at 143.

112. Crook to Kennon, July 8, 1889, in *George Crook Papers,* University of Oregon Library, Eugene, Oregon.

113. *Report of the Commission* at 20.

114. *Report of the Commission, Proceedings* at 175.

115. *Id.* at 152, 158.

116. *Id.* at 153, 155.

117. Hyde at 220.

118. Diary of General George Crook, July 10, 1889, note 74, *supra.*

119. Hyde at 221.

120. Hyde at 220. We have found no corroborating evidence of this.

121. Diary of General George Crook, July 18, 1889, note 74, *supra.* Hyde also reports that Crook threatened to call in troops if needed. Hyde at 224.

122. *Report of the Commission, Proceedings* at 177.

123. *Id.*

124. *Id.*

125. *Id.* Crook apparently thought he used these reports to his advantage. He wrote in his diary on July 20, 1889:

Had a council in which one of the police tried to bully us in which the tables were turned on him which materially weakened the opposition.

126. Hyde at 225. See also Schmitt at 287–88. *Report of the Commission, Appendix, Exhibit A.*

127. 334 out of 347 eligible males accepted the Act at the Santee Agency. *Report of the Commission, Appendix, Exhibit A.*

128. *Report of the Commission, Proceedings* at 125.

129. *Report of the Commission* at 21.

130. *Id.*

131. *Report of the Commission, Appendix, Exhibit A.*

132. *Report of the Commission* at 21.

133. *Report of the Commission, Proceedings* at 189.

134. *Id.* at 200, 206, 207.

135. *Id.* at 200.

136. 15 head of beef were issued on July 26 and 15 on July 30. Diary of General George Crook, note 74, *supra.*

137. James McLaughlin, *My Friend the Indian,* Boston: Houghton Mifflin Co. at 273 (1910).

138. *Id.* at 281.

139. *Id.* at 284.

140. *Id.* at 284–85.

141. *Id.* at 285.

142. Hyde at 226.

143. *Id.*

144. Diary of General George Crook, August 6, 1889, note 74, *supra.*

145. *Report of the Commission, Appendix, Exhibit A;* McLaughlin at 288.

146. Only at Pine Ridge, Cheyenne River, and Standing Rock were attempts made to explain the reimbursement provisions. At Pine Ridge, Commissioner Warner mentioned the reimbursement provision but did not explain that the money would

be reimbursed out of the proceeds of the land sales. *Report of the Commission, Proceedings* at 74. The best explanation, given by Commissioner Foster at the Cheyenne River Agency consisted of the following:

> Now when the Government gets the 8 million (from land sales)—if it gets it, it will take out of that 8 million, the 3 million that it first puts to your credit. It takes out also what it pays for cows and mares and agricultural implements and what is left is added to the 3 million that was first set apart for the Indians. This will leave . . . in our opinion about 5 million on interest for fifty years. *Id.* at 160.

At Standing Rock, Commissioner Foster only mentioned that the $3 million must be "refunded" to the United States, but he did not say from what source the money would come. *Id.* at 192. The operation of section 22 resulted in the Sioux "owing" the United States over $1½ million by 1910. The area ceded under the 1889 Act was 9,277,634 acres, for which the Sioux were credited with $5,332,295 in the Treasury. However, the United States made almost $7 million in "reimbursable expenditures." Letter from Commissioner of Indian Affairs R.G. Valentine to Rep. Charles H. Burke, March 12, 1910.

147. *Report of the Commission, Proceedings* at 93–94, 184–184.

148. *Id.* at 93, 173.

149. *Id.* at 94.

150. *Report of the Commission, Appendix, Exhibit A.*

151. Irregular Shaped Papers No. 68, Record Group 75, National Archives, Washington, DC. This tally reveals that several white men who signed were officially listed as mixed bloods in the final report.

152. Hyde at 219. No source is cited in the text to support this assertion. The official count does, however, contain many signers with English names but no Sioux name. Almost all of these are listed as members of the Oglala Band of the Sioux Nation.

153. Note 114, *supra.*

154. Commissioner Foster later recognized that the Commission would have been unsuccessful if the signatures of the mixed bloods and whites had not been counted:

> In fact I am of the opinion that the necessary three-fourths of signatures required by the treaty of 1868 have not been affixed to the late treaty unless those of the mixed bloods and squaw men are accepted and included. Letter from Foster to Secretary of the Interior, December 13, 1892, Irregular Shaped Papers, No. 115 Record Group 75, National Archives, Washington, DC.

There were other minor voting irregularities. At Rosebud, three women and eight males under age 18 were permitted to sign. Irregular Shaped Papers No. 68, note 151, *supra.*

A possible area for further research concerns the method used to determine the number of eligible adult males. Hyde asserts that the population figures were altered in order to reduce the number of eligible Sioux, but I have found very little corroborating evidence of this. Hyde at 228. The Commission of Indian Affairs Report for 1889 lists the number of males over 18 years of age at the Rosebud Agency as 1,783 whereas the Commission put the number at 1,476. *Commissioner of Indian Affairs Report for 1889,* at 161. Comparisons for the other agencies follow:

	Sioux Commission	1889 Commissioners' Report
Crow Creek	305	291
Cheyenne River	749	752
Lower Brule	314	291
Pine Ridge	1,366	1,330
Standing Rock	1,121	1,132

155. *Report of the Commission, Appendix, Exhibit B* at 44.

156. Irregular Shaped Papers No. 68, *supra,* note 151.

157. Letter from Elaine Goodale to Commissioner of Indian Affairs, December 18, 1890, Special Case 188, Record 75, National Archives, Washington, DC.

158. General Nelson Miles to Senator Dawes, December 19, 1890, reprinted in James Mooney, *The Ghost-Dance Religion and Wounded Knee,* New York: Dover Publications, 1973 at 835.

159. General John M. Schofield to Senator Dawes, December 19, 1890, reprinted in Mooney at 836.

160. Diary of General George Crook, June 2, 1889, note 74, *supra.*

161. Bishop Hare to Secretary Noble, January 7, 1891, reprinted in Mooney at 840–42.

162. *The Word Carrier,* September, 1889, Vol. 18 at 22.

163. Robert M. Utley, *The Last Days of the Sioux Nation,* New Haven: Yale University Press, 1963 at 52.

Appendix E

Chronology of Events Leading Up to
the 1890 Wounded Knee Massacre

July 5, 1825, Treaty with Sioune (now Cheyenne River) and Oglala Sioux Tribes: The United States agreed in article 2 to take the Sioux Indians under their protection.

April 29, 1868, Fort Laramie Treaty: The parties agreed in article 1 that all war between them would forever cease and pledged their honor to keep the peace; that the United States would reimburse the Indians for wrongs and loss of property committed by persons acting under federal authority and that the Indians would extradite bad men on their reservation to the United States. In article 2, the parties agreed that the Sioux reservation would be held for their absolute and undisturbed use and occupation; in article 12, that no cession of the Sioux reservation would be valid without the signatures of three-fourths of the adult males interested in the reservation; in articles 11 and 16, that the Sioux had the right to hunt in the Bighorn Mountains and area north of the North Platte River.

February 28, 1877, Black Hills Act: In article 1 Congress confiscated the Black Hills portion of the 1868 Treaty Reservation (7.3 million acres) without the consent of three-fourths of the adult male Indians as required by the 1868 treaty. This was also in violation of the Fifth Amendment, since the Sioux Nation acquired vested title to the land under U.S. law. In article 5 Congress promised that, in consideration for the land and hunting rights confiscated, it would give the Sioux Indians all aid necessary for civilization and subsistence rations (or the equivalent thereof) for as long as necessary for their survival. In article 8, Congress agreed that the Indians would be subject to the laws of the United States, thereby extending the protections of the First Amendment to freely exercise their religion and of the Fifth Amendment rights to the protection of real and personal property. In the same article, Congress promised that each Sioux Indian would be protected in his rights of property, person, and life.

Fall, 1883: Last Sioux buffalo hunt took place.

1888: Indian-issue beef herds on the Sioux reservation were decimated by anthrax.

January, 1889: Wovoka, a Paiute Indian in Nevada, arose from the dead (recovered from scarlet fever) after a total eclipse of the sun. Some say he learned of the eclipse through an almanac and planned his resurrection to correspond with that event. Word of his resurrection spread throughout Indian country. His prophecy was that if Indians believed and sang and danced to certain ritual songs, the buffalo and deceased relatives would return and the non-Indians would be covered by a new layer of earth. This event is recorded in history by some who say that an Indian messiah and the Ghost Dance were born.

March 2, 1889, Act of Congress: Congress agreed in article 28 that the act will not go into effect unless agreed to by three-fourths of the adult male population of Indians as required by the 1868 treaty but used fraud and coercion to acquire the signatures, calling Indian males to the agencies and not allowing them to return home until they signed and allowing underaged Indians and non-Indian males married to Indian women to sign in violation of the law. The president proclaimed the act although the required signatures were never obtained. The United States thus acquired an additional nine million acres of the 1868 treaty reservation by this method.

The 1889 act also divided the 1868 treaty reservation into six smaller reservations. Indians living on each reservation could not leave their reservations without a pass from the Indian agent.

Remainder of 1889: The United States agreed not to cut the subsistence rations obligated under article 5 of the 1877 Black Hills Act if the Indians agreed to the 1889 act but went back on their word and cut the rations by 50 percent as soon as they secured the purported signatures. This created famine and death on the Sioux reservations. There were also grasshopper plagues and a terrible drought, resulting in the loss of gardens.

Mid-summer, 1889: Spoonhunter, an Oglala married into and residing on the Wind River Reservation, sent a letter to his nephew Kicking Bear, living on the Cheyenne River Reservation, telling him about Wovoka and the Ghost Dance. Kicking Bear, an Oglala, was married to Woodpecker Woman, niece of Chief Big Foot.

Fall of 1889 and spring of 1890: A Sioux delegation consisting of Kicking Bear, Short Bull, and others traveled to Nevada to see Wovoka and returned to teach the Ghost Dance to the Sioux. The earth's rejuvenation was promised for the spring of 1891, with the coming of the green grass.

May 29, 1890: Indian agents were not too concerned about the Ghost Dance until Charles L. Hyde, a citizen of Pierre, South Dakota, wrote a letter to the secretary of the interior stating that he had reliable information from a Pine Ridge Sioux at the Pierre Indian School that the Sioux were planning an outbreak.

Summer of 1890: The Ghost Dance caught on with the Sioux because of the extreme conditions they were living under. White people living south and west of the Sioux reservations became alarmed and believed an Indian uprising would occur. Black Elk invented the Ghost Shirt. Indians gathered at the Strong Hold, a natural fortification on the northern part of the Pine Ridge Reservation.

October 20, 1890: Agent Royer of Pine Ridge Agency requested six to seven hundred troops at Pine Ridge to restore order.

November 13, 1890: President Harrison directed the secretary of war to assume military responsibility on the Sioux reservations to prevent an outbreak. Indian leaders were ordered arrested until the Ghost Dance passed.

November 20, 1890: The *Rapid City Journal* reported that Sioux were on the warpath. Yellow journalism everywhere added to the excitement.

November 22, 1890: Governor Mellette, the first governor of South Dakota, created the "Home Guard," a cowboy militia to guard homesteaders along the west edge of the Pine Ridge and Cheyenne River reservations. They were armed with hundreds of guns and a great deal of ammunition.

December, 1890: The South Dakota home guard engaged in two of their own massacres. The guard sent its best riders to the Pine Ridge Reservation to shoot into the Ghost Dancers at the Strong Hold. They led the Ghost Dancers into a trap and killed and scalped seventy-five of them. They also massacred several wagons full of Sioux on French Creek, who were visiting non-Indian friends at Buffalo Gap.

December 15, 1890: Chief Sitting Bull was murdered by federal Indian police when they attempted to arrest him at his home on the Standing Rock Reservation. Agent McLaughlin supplied them with a barrel of whiskey to give them enough courage to make the arrest. Sitting Bull's followers fled to seek refuge with his half-brother, Chief Big Foot.

December 28, 1890: Chief Big Foot, fearing arrest and the risk to his band, headed south to the Pine Ridge Reservation. Chief Red Cloud had already invited him to come to Pine Ridge and help make peace. Major Whiteside and his Seventh Cavalry intercepted Chief Big Foot and about 356 of his followers at Porcupine Butte and escorted them to Wounded Knee Creek. The campsite was already settled, with Mousseaux's store and several log houses located there. That evening Colonel Forsyth arrived and assumed command. The Indians were surrounded and harassed all night. A trader from Pine Ridge brought a barrel of whiskey and the officers and troopers got drunk celebrating Big Foot's capture.

That night some drunken troopers attempted to drag Big Foot out of his tent. Indians who could understand English heard talk of getting revenge for Custer's defeat. Some officers attempted to see if guns possessed by the Indians were taken from the Little Bighorn battle and if they were old enough to have been at the battle.

December 29, 1890: Colonel Forsyth attempted to disarm Chief Big Foot's band. The women and children were separated from the men. The soldiers were very abusive. Big Foot was sick with pneumonia and flying a white flag of truce next to his tent. The Indians were almost completely disarmed and completely surround-ed by the soldiers. When the soldiers attempted to take the rifle of a deaf mute, it discharged and the soldiers opened up on the Indians. About three hundred of Big Foot's band were killed. About thirty soldiers also died, many in their own crossfire. Some women and children were found as far as two miles away, gunned down by soldiers.

January 3, 1891: A burial party picked up the bodies of the dead Indians, about 146, still left on the massacre site after a raging blizzard swept through the area. They dug a mass grave and buried the dead without ceremony. At least one Indian is said to have been buried alive.

Appendix F

The Wounded Knee Death List

These are some of the names on the Wounded Knee Death List. Many more than this perished. Many more survived.

It was never about who was right or who was wrong.

It was always about the deliberate genocide of a people by the European invaders of this continent who called themselves Americans.

It was always a crime against humanity.

♦

This is an incomplete list of Big Foot's Oyate, those who died and those who lived. (Oral historians of the Lakotas say there were at least four hundred persons in the Big Foot Band.) The list may be filled with errors, but it is reprinted here as a memorial to those who paid the price of being Lakota in America. Many more stand still in the memory of their relatives. The names of those killed are followed by K; the names of those who were wounded but survived are followed by W. If there is an S by the name, it means that person survived, miraculously without injury, and became among the first native repositors of the knowledge of what happened at the killing ground.

This list was compiled by Richard E. Jensen and first published in "Big Foot's Followers at Wounded Knee," *Nebraska History*, 71 (Winter, 1990). We have adapted it slightly.

♦

"Woyaka Channi Wicooyake"—the beginning of the story

Afraid Of Bear *K*
Afraid Of Bear, young *K*

Afraid Of Enemy *W*
   wife, Brown Eyes *W*
   son, Scaring Hawk *W*
   daughter, Good (Pretty) Spotted Horse *S*
Afraid Of Hawk, Richard *S*
Afraid Of Left Hand *S*
Afraid Of Nothing Bear (Bear Fool) *K*
Afraid Of Tomahawk *Deceased before Wounded Knee*
   wife, Bone *S*
   son, Yellow Horse *S*
   daughter, In Front *S*
Appears Twice *K*
Arousing Squirrel *K*
   mother *K*
Ashes *K*
   wife, Bear Gone *W*
Audacious Bear *See* Industrious Bear
Ax *See* Brown Sinew
Back Bone *S*
   wife, Stands Looking *S*
   son?, White Hawk *S*
   son?, Big Boy *S*
   son?, King Boy *S*
Bad (Bear) Woman *W*
   son *K*
Bad Boy *S*
Bad Braves *K*
Bad Hand *See* Wing
Bad Owner Without Rope *K*
   wife *K*
Bad Spotted Eagle *K*
   wife, White Woman *K*
Bear Comes And Lies *K*
Bear Don't Run *K*
   wife, *S*
   daughter, Head Woman *K*
   son, Pawnee Killer *K*
   daughter, Farms At The River *S*
Bear Lays Down *K*
   wife *W*
Bear Parts (Cuts) Body *K*
   wife *S*
   son *K*
Bear Runs In The Woods *S*

Bear Sheds His Hair (also called Shedding Bear) *K?*
   wife *S*
   daughter, Red Buffalo (also called Red White Cow) *K*
   son, Trouble In Front *K*
   son, Runs Behind (also called Last Running) *K*
   mother-in-law *K*
Bear Skin Vest *K*
   wife, *W*
   daughter *K*
Bear That Shoots *K*
   mother *K*
Bear With Small Body *K*
   wife *K*
   son, Takes Away Enemy *K*
   son, Smokes Walking *S*
   son, Enemy *S*
Bear Woman *S*
Bear Woman *K*
Bear Woman (indicating a Bear Woman, Edith and 2 daughters) *S*
Beard, Dewey *W*
   wife, Wears Eagle (also called White Face) *K*
   son?, Thomas *K*
   baby, Wet Feet (also called White Foot) *K*
Benefactress *K*
Big Foot (also called Spotted Elk) *K*
   wife, Sinte-chigela (also called Small Tail) *K*
   daughter, Brings White (also called White Horse Woman) *K*
Big Foot, young *S*
Big Skirt (Shirt) *K*
Big (Loud) Voice Thunder *K*
   wife *K*
   child *K*
Billy Woman *W*
Bird Shaker *See* Brown Bull
Bird Wings *K*
Birds Afraid Of Him *S*
Birds Belly *K*
Black Bugle *S*
Black Crow *S*
Black Flutes *K*
Black Fox (Coyote) *K*
   wife, Brown Hair *S?*
   daughter, Brings White *K?*

Black Fox, Julia *S*
   mother *S*
Black Hair *S*
  wife *K*
  son, Joseph *S*
  son *K*
  son *W*
Black Hawk *K*
  wife, She Bear (also called Cheyenne Woman or Comes Out) *K*
  daughter, Weasel Bear (also called Weasel) *K*
Black Moon, Philip *See* High Back
Black Shield *S*
  daughter Pretty White Cow *K*
Black Thunder *S*
  wife Plenty Young Birds *S*
Black (American) White Man *S*
  daughter *S*
Black Zebra *S*
Blind *K*
Blind Man *S*
  wife, Day *S*
  daughter, Red Eagle *S*
Blind Woman (also called Woman Without Sight) *S*
  son?, Kills The Fair *W*
Blue American *K*
Blue Arm, Charles (Charley) *S*
  brother *K*
  brother *K*
  sister-in-law, Brings Her *S*
  sister-in-law *K*
Blue Cloud, Joseph *S*
Blue Hair *W*
Blue Whirlwind *See* Spotted Thunder
Blue Wing *S*
Bo Blue *K*
Break Arrow With Foot *K*
Bring Her Home *S*
Brings Choice *K*
Brings Earth To Her *K*
Brings It To Her *S*
Brings Many *S*
  daughter, Brings Yellow *S*
Brings Plenty *W*

Brings The Dirt *S*
Brings The Woman *K*
Brings White Horses, Mrs. *S*
    daughter *K*
Broken Arm *K*
Broken Arrow *K*
    wife *K*
Brown *K*
Brown Beaver *See* Elk Woman
Brown Bull *K*
    wife *K*
    son, Bird Shaker *K*
Brown Ear Horse *K?*
Brown Hoops (Hoop) *K*
    son *K*
    daughter *K*
Brown In Ears *K*
    son *K*
Brown Leaf *K*
Brown Sinew *W*
Brown Turtle *K*
    wife, Shot The Eagle *S*
    mother, First Born *K*
Brown Woman *K?*
    Yellow In Ear *S*
    Kills (The) Fair *S*
Buckskin (Bells In) Breech Clout *K*
    wife, Young Prairie Chicken *S*
Bull Man *S*
Burnt Thigh *K*
Cannu *K*
Cast Away And Run *K*
Catches The Boat *S*
    brother *S*
Charge [?] Near The Lodge *K*
    wife, Iron Horn Woman *S*
Charge At Them *K*
    mother *K*
Charger *K*
Chase In Winter *K*
Chief Dog *See* Dog Chief
Chief Woman *K*
Close To Home, Louis *K?*
    wife *S*

daughter, Brown Girl *S*
son?, Deserts Him *S*
Clown *K*
Comes Crawling *S*
Comes Crawling Woman *S*
Comes Home With Red *S*
Comes Last *K*
Comes Out Alive Woman *S*
Confiscate Arrow *K*
Corn, Frank *S*
Cottonwood *See* Hair Pipe
Courage (Courageous Bear) *K*
    wife *K*
    Fat *K*
    George *K*
Cow Buffalo Horn *K*
    wife *S?*
    son, Peter *W*
Crane Pretty Voice *S*
    wife, Rock (Woman) *S*
    daughter, Lost Bird *S*
Crazy Bear *K?*
Day *W*
Deaf *K*
Dependable *W*
Different Woman *S*
Disturbs Ahead *K*
Dog Chief (Chief Dog) *S*
    wife *S*
    child *S*
Drops Blood, Mrs *K*
    son *K*
    son *K*
Eagle Hawk Bear or Hawk Bear *K*
    wife, Eagle Hawk Woman *W*
    daughter *K*
    daughter, Haketawin *S*
    son *K*
Eagle Shape *S*
Eagle Wing (Wing Eagle) *K?*
    wife, Her Roan (Red) Horse *S*
Elk Creek *K*
    wife *K*
Elk Saw Him *W*

Elk That Looks *S*
   wife *S*
   daughter, Good Pipe *K?*
   daughter, Kills Enemy *S*
Elk Woman *S*
   son?, Brown Beaver *K*
   daughter?, Beaver *K*
Enemy Afraid Of Him *S*
Fast Wolf *S*
Fat Bear, mother of *K*
Fat Hips *S*
Feather Earring *K*
   son *K*
Feather Man *K*
First *K*
Fish Boy *W*
Flying Hawk *K*
Fool Bear *S*
Frog *W*
   wife (Mary) *S*
   daughter, Ones Call *K*
   son, Hunts to Death (Alfred) *S*
Gets A Fight *S*
Ghost Dog *K*
Ghost Bear *S*
Ghost Horse *See* Horses Ghost
Goes To War *S*
Goggle (Eye) Eyes *K*
   Fair Woman *K*
   Thunder Boy *K*
   Pretty Woman *S*
   Blue Spotted *K*
Good Bear *S*
Good Bear, old *K*
Good Bear, young *K*
   wife *K*
   son *K*
Good Enemy *K*
Good Hand *S*
Good Hawk *K*
   wife *K*
Good Land Woman *S*
Good Natured Woman *S*
Good Thunder (Sits Straight) *S*

Good White Cow *S*
Grease Leg Bone *K*
Grey *S*
Grey Hand *K?*
   wife *S*
   son, George Randall *S*
Grey In Eye (Eyes) *K*
Grey Owl Woman *S*
Grey Thunder *K*
Ground Horn Woman *S*
Hair Pipe *S*
   wife, The Hawk *S*
   son, Cottonwood *K*
   son, Starts The Horse *K*
   daughter, (Her War) Bonnet *S*
Handsome *K*
Happens *K*
Hard To Kill or Young Bear *S*
   wife, (Her) Elk Tooth *S*
   mother *K*
Has Scarlet *K*
Has The Bell *K*
Hat *K*
   daughter, Makes Presents *K*
Hawk, The *S*
Hawk Bear *See* Eagle Hawk Bear
Hawk Feather (Shooter) *See* Shoots the Hawk Feather
Hawk Flying *K*
Hawk Woman *S*
He (Male) Crow *K*
   wife *W*
   son, Jackson *S*
He Eagle *See* Male Eagle
Heart Of Timber *K*
Help Them (Helps Em Up) *W*
Helper, Simon *S*
Her Brown Faced Dog *S*
Her Cedar *S*
Her Eagle *S*
Her First *S*
Her Good Cloud *K*
Her Neck *S*
Her Room *S*
Her Sacred Blanket *K*

Her Shell Walks *S*
Her White Horse *S*
Her Yellow *S*
High Back *W*
   brother, Black Moon *S*
   brother, White Dog *K*
   sister, Brown Ear *K*
   mother *S*
High Hawk *K*
   wife, Bear Woman *K*
   son, Long Woman *W*
   daughter? *K*
   son, James or Kills In A Hurry *W*
   son, Alex or Kills Twice *W*
   son, Jonah or Scout *S*
   daughter *S*
   daughter, Only Man *S*
   daughter, Red Cow *S*
His Crow *S*
His Fight *K*
His Two Lance *S*
His War *S*
His Wounded Hand *K*
   wife *K*
   son, Daniel Blue Hair *W*
   daughter *K*
Hits Her On A Run *S*
Holds A Woman *W*
Hollow Horn Woman *S*
Hollow Teeth *S*
   son?, Uses His Feet *S*
   son?, Left Hand *S*
   son?, Runs Away With Horse *S*
Holy Bone *W*
Holy Comes *S*
Horn Cloud *K*
   wife, Yellow Leaf *K*
   son, William (Enemy) *K*
   son, Sherman *K*
   son, Joseph *S*
   son, Daniel (Warrior) *W*
   daughter (niece?) Pretty Enemy (Her Horse) *K*
Horse Nation *S*

Horses Ghost *K?*
    wife, Her (Good) Shawl (née Mrs. Courage Bear) *S*
    son, White Horse *K*
    son, Warrior *S*
    daughter, Alice Kills Plenty (Alice Dog Arm) *S*
Howling Elk, later called Many Holes *W*
    son, Sammey *W*
Hunts Alone *K*
Hunts The Enemy By Night (Hunts the Enemy) *S*
I Shot The Bear *K*
    wife, Her Mind *S*
    daughter, Kills Straw *S*
    son, Enemy *S*
I Shot The Hawk *K*
    Loose (Loves) Her Shawl *S*
Important Man *K*
    wife *K*
    daughter, White Cow *S*
Important Woman *S*
In A Cow's Horn *S*
    wife *S*
Industrious, Lawrence *See* Long Feather
Industrious Bear *K?*
    wife, Smoke Woman (Small Leg Woman) *S?*
    son, Frost On Her *K?*
    son, Poor *K?*
    daughter, Face *W*
    daughter, Big Woman *S*
Iron *S*
Iron American, Mrs. *K*
Iron Eyes *K*
    wife, Plenty Horses *K*
    son, Iron Eyes, Albert *K*
    Guy Buffalo *S*
    Has A Dog *K*
    Pretty Woman *K*
    Red Shirt Girl *K*
    White Day *K*
    son of White Day *K*
Iron Hail *See* Beard, Dewey
Iron Lavatta, Annie *W*
Joining War *S*
Jumps Good *S*
    wife, Red Beaver *S*

Kill Her White Horse *S*
Killed His Choice *S*
Killed The Bear *S*
    wife *S*
    son, Kills Against *S*
Kills *K*
Kills Assiniboine *K*
Kills Close to Lodge, Bertha *W*
Kills Crow Indian *K*
Kills First or Killed First or Kills Him First *K*
    wife, Holy Woman or Wakan *W*
    son, Wounded In Winter *K*
    son, Leon *S*
    daughter, Shoots The White *K*
    daughter, White Mule *K*
    daughter, Mary *S*
Kills In Bush *K*
    wife, Shawl Over Head *S*
    son, Mad *K*
    daughter, Hand *S*
Kills In The Middle *S*
Kills One Hundred *S*
Kills Seneca *K*
Kills Tincup *K*
Kills Two *S*
Kills (Killed) White Man *S*
    wife *W*
    son, Harry or Little Warrior *S*
    son, Makes Him Mad *S*
    daughter, Runs Off With Horse *K*
Kills Who Stand In Timber *K*
    wife *K*
Knife, Nellie *S*
Knocked In The Head *S*
Kyle, Charles *K*
    wife *S*
    child *S*
Lap, Mrs. *K*
LaPlant, Jack or Frank *S*
Last Man *K*
Last Talking *K*
Leg *K*
Light Hair *K*
Liking *W*

Little Bear *S?*
Little Body Bear *K*
   wife *K*
   son *K*
   daughter *K*
   son *S*
Little Bull *W*
Little Cloud *S*
   wife *S*
Little Elk *K*
   wife *K*
Little Eyed Woman *S*
Little Finger, John *W*
Little Water *S*
   wife, White Face *S*
   daughter, The Voice *S*
   Light Hair Girl *S*
   Whip *S*
   Sacred Blanket *S*
   Animal *S*
   Not Stingy *S*
Little Wound *S*
Liver Gall *S*
Lives In Iron *S*
Lives Reckless *S*
Living Bear *K*
Living Bull, Helena *S*
   son *S*
Lodge Knapkin *K*
Lodge Skin *K*
Log *K*
   wife *K*
Lone Child *K*
Long Bull *K*
Long Bull *S*
   wife, Badger *K*
   daughter, Weasel *K*
   daughter, Helen *S*
Long Feather *S*
Long Holy *S*
Long Medicine *K*
Long Woman *See* High Hawk
Looking Elk *W*
   wife, Lydia *W*

Looks Back (Looks Her Back) *W*
Lost Bird *See* Crane Pretty Voice
Made A Stand *S*
Made Him Long *S*
Made To Stand *K*
Made To (Makes Him) Shoot *S*
   wife *S*
Male Eagle *K*
   wife, Roan Horse Woman or Short Woman *K*
   daughter, Runs After Her *K*
   son, Edward or Warrior *K*
   son, Two Arrows *K*
   daughter, Comes Home With Red *S*
   daughter, Many Brothers *S*
Man Himself *S*
Mangy Elk *K*
Medicine Woman *See* White Man
Mercy To Others *K*
Minniconjou *K*
Missed *S*
Mousseau, Mrs *See* White Man
Moves Over, Alice *W*
Mule's daughter *K*
Mustang Elk *S*
Near Lodge *K*
Nest *K*
No Ears *K*
No Name *S*
Not Afraid Of Lodge (Camp) *K*
Not Go In Among (son of Hailing Bear and Her Good Medicine, who seem not to
   have been at Wounded Knee) *K*
On The Ground, Mrs. *S*
   daughter, Roan Woman *S*
   son, Red *S*
   son, Guide *S*
One Feather *K*
   son *K*
One Skunk *S*
   wife *W*
Owl King Mrs. *K*
   son, Edward or Fast Boat *W*
   son *K*
   son *K*
   daughter *K*

Pass Water In Horn (Use Horn For Toilet) *K*
Peaked *K*
Picket Horse *K*
Picks and Kill *S*
Pipe On Head, James *S*
   mother, Runs On *S*
   sister *K?*
Plain Voice *K*
Pretty Bear *K*
   son, Cub Bear *S*
Pretty Bold Eagle *See* Three, Henry
Pretty Hawk *K?*
   wife *K*
   baby, Whitewoman *K?*
Pretty Shield *S*
   wife *S*
   daughter, Her Shawl *S*
   daughter, Yellow Eyes *W*
Pretty Voice Elk *K*
Produce (From) *K*
Put Away Moccasins *W*
Quit On Him *S*
Rattles *K*
Rattling Leaf *K*
Really Woman's Son *K*
Red Belly *S*
   Brings Yellow *S*
   Stands Up For Him *S*
Runs Off With Horses *K*
Red Eagle *K*
   wife, (Her) Black Horses or Her Gall *W*
   daughter, (Her) Eagle Body *K*
   daughter, Cedar Horse *K*
   daughter *S*
Red Ears Horse *K*
   sister *K*
Red Finger Nail Woman *S*
Red Fish *K*
   wife *K*
Red (Scarlet) Horn *K*
   son, Good Scarlet Horn *S*
Red Horn Bear *S?*
Red Juniper *K*
Red Other Woman *K*

Red Shell *K*
Red Stone S?
Red Water Woman *K*
Roots Its Hole *K*
Rough Feather *S*
Run As Though His Hair Fussed *W*
Running Hawk, George *S*
Running In Lodge *K*
Running Standing Hairs *K*
   wife *K*
   daughter *K*
Runs After *K*
Runs After It *S*
Runs Around Lodge *W*
Runs Fast *S*
Sack Woman *W*
   son, White Cowboy *W*
Sacred Face *K*
Sacred In Appearance *K*
Scabbard Knife *K*
   wife *K*
Scares The Bear *K*
   wife, Yellow Bird Woman *K*
   grandchild *K*
   grandchild *K*
Scarlet Calf *K*
   son *K*
   son *K*
Scarlett Otter *K*
Scarlet Rotation *S*
Scarlet Smoke *K*
Scarlet Tipi Top *S*
Scarlet White Buffalo *K*
Scatter (Scatters) Them *K*
Scout *S*
Scout Tent *S?*
Sees The Bear *S*
Sees The Elk *S*
Seventeen, Patrick *S*
Shakes The Bird *See* Brown Bull
Shaving Bear *K*
   wife *S*
   four children *K*
Shell Necklace *S*

She Wears Eagle *S*
Shot At Accurately *K*
    son *K*
Shoot The Bear *See* I Shot The Bear
Shoots The Bear, George *K*
    wife *K*
Shoots (With) The Hawk Feather *K*
    mother *K*
Shoots The Right *K*
    son, Bad Wound *K*
Shoots Straight *K*
    wife *S*
    child *S*
Short Hair (Close Haired) Bear *K*
    wife *S*
    three children *K*
Shot Him Off *S*
Shot In Hand *K*
Shows His Cloud *S*
Sinew Belly *S*
Singing Bull *K*
    wife *K*
    son, Ha-shi-ta *K*
    grandson, later called James Red Fish *S*
    granddaughter, Scarlet Coat *K*
Sits Poor, Frank *S*
Sits Straight *See* Good Thunder
Slippery Hide (Slicks His Hide) *K*
Sloha main (Slohamani) *W*
Small Like (Bodied) Bear *K*
Snow Over Her *S*
Sole Of Foot *S*
    wife, The Ring *K?*
    daughter, The Browny *S*
Spotted Bear, John *S*
Spotted (Speckled) Chief *K*
Spotted Eagle *S?*
    wife, Good Horse S?
Spotted Elk *See* Big Foot
Spotted Elk (no. 2) *K*
    wife *K*
    son *K*
    son *K*
    son *K*

Spotted Thunder *K*
 wife, Blue Whirlwind *W*
 son, White Buffalo Boy *W*
 son, Spear *W*
 son, Pretty Boy *S*
Squirrel Bear *S*
Standing Bear, Chief *K*
Standing Bear, Mr. *K*
Standing Elk *S*
Stands A Showing *W*
Stands For Himself *S*
Stands With *W*
Steals A Running Horse *W*
Stinking Foot *S*
Stone Hammer, Mrs. *K*
 baby *K*
Stops Her Horse *S*
Strike Scatter *K*
 son *K*
Strong Fox (Tea) *K*
 wife *K*
 son, The Guide (Quick) *K*
 daughter, Brown Horn *K*
Strong Tea *K*
 wife *K*
Successful Spy *K*
Sun In The Pupil *K*
 wife *K*
Sunka Yatapi *W*
Swift Bear *K*
Swift Bird *K*
 wife *K*
 son *K*
 son *K*
Swift Dog *W*
Tail Hair *S*
Takes (Away) The Bow *K*
 wife *S*
 daughter *S*
 son, George Blue Leg *S*
Takes The Buffalo *S*
Takola Washaka *K*
 wife, Yellow Leaf Woman *K*
 child *K*

Tattooed *S*
Three, Henry *K*
Thunder *K*
Thunder Hawk Woman *K*
To Laugh *K*
Touches The Ground *S*
Trotter *K*
Trouble *K*
Trouble In Front *See* Bear Sheds His Hair
Trouble In Love, Mrs. *K*
Twin Woman *K*
Two Arrows *See* Male Eagle
Two Lance *S*
Unintentionally Brave *K*
Unties Shoestring *S*
Up To His Waist *K*
    wife *K*
    son, Important Man *K*
Used For Brother *K*
Waki-he-he-le *S*
    daughter *S*
Walking Buffalo *W*
Walking Bull *K*
    wife *K*
Walks Red *K*
    son, Chief Boy *K*
Walks With Circle *S*
War Is His *K*
Warrior *See* Horn Cloud and Male Eagle
Warrior *S*
Water Snake *K*
Wears Calf's (Calfskin) Robe *K*
    wife *S?*
    son, Chases And Kills *S*
Wears Fur Coat *S*
Wears Yellow Robe *S*
Weasel *K*
Weasel Bear *K*
   Louise *W*
Whip *K*
Whirlwind Bear *K*
Whirlwind Hawk *K*
    wife *K*
    daughter *K*

daughter *K*
daughter *K*
son *K*
son *K*
White American *K*
White Beaver Woman *K*
White Bull K?
    wife, Clown Woman *K?*
    son, Blue Horse *S*
    daughter, Pretty Hair *K?*
White Cow Comes Out *S*
White Eagle *S*
White Face Sun *K*
White Face Woman *S*
White Feather *K*
White Hair *S*
White Hat *K*
White Horse *S*
White Lance *See* Horn Cloud
White Man *K*
    wife, Medicine Woman *W*
    son *K*
    son *K*
    daughter *K*
White Man *K*
    wife, Never Misses It *W*
White Wolf *K?*
White Woman Hand *S*
Wicaka-badeea *K*
    wife *S*
Wild Man *S*
Wind K?
Wind In Guts *S*
Wing *K*
    son *K*
Winter *K*
Without Robe *K*
Wolf Eagle *K*
    son, Good Boy *K*
Wolf Ears, Edward *K*
    wife *W*
    son, White *K*
    son, Feather Enemy *K*
    daughter, Medicine Lake Girl *K*

Wolf (Dog) Skin Necklace *K*
    sister, later Mrs. Takes The Hat *S*
    daughter, Scarlet Woman *K*
    mother, Naki-he-he-la *S*
Wood Shade *K*
    wife *K*
Wounded Both *S*
Wounded Hand *K*
    wife, Comes Out Rattling *K*
Wounded In Winter *See* Kills First
Yell At Them *S?*
Yellow Bird *K*
Yellow Buffalo Calf *K*
Yellow Bull *K*
    wife, Humming *K*
    daughter *K*
    daughter *K*
    five grandchildren *K*
Yellow Hair *W*
Yellow Robe *K*
Yellow Turtle *K*
Yellow Woman *S*
You Can Eat Dog *S*
Young Bear, Henry *See* Hard To Kill
Young Calf *K*

Appendix G

List of Claims Paid under the Sioux Depredations Act

| 52D CONGRESS, | SENATE. | EX. DOC. |
| 2d Session. | | No. 93. |

IN THE SENATE OF THE UNITED STATES.

LETTER

FROM

THE SECRETARY OF THE INTERIOR,

IN RESPONSE

To Senate resolution of February 21, 1893, relative to claims of friendly Indians for depredations committed during the Pine Ridge disturbance.

FEBRUARY 27, 1893.—Referred to the Committee on Indian Affairs and ordered to be printed.

DEPARTMENT OF THE INTERIOR,
Washington, February 27, 1893.

SIR: I have the honor to acknowledge receipt of Senate resolution of the 21st instant, in the following words:

Resolved, That the Secretary of the Interior be directed to furnish to the Senate the following information:

(1) The number and value of claims presented by friendly Indians arising from depredations committed during the late Indian disturbance at Pine Ridge, S. Dak.

(2) A statement of the amount allowed on each claim, and whether paid to claimant in person or to an agent or attorney, and, if so, the name of such agent or attorney.

(3) A full statement as to the disbursement of the $100,000 appropriated by Congress for the settlement of such claims.

In response thereto I transmit herewith copy of a communication from the Commissioner of Indian Affairs reporting upon the inquiries specified in the said resolution, together with the original official report of Special Agent James A. Cooper, who disbursed the sum appropriated by Congress for payment of the claims indicated.

Owing to the great pressure upon the clerical force of the Indian Bureau, it has been found impossible to supply copy of Special Agent Cooper's report within the limit of the present Congress, and therefore the original document is forwarded with request that, when printed, it may be returned to the Department files.

I have the honor to be, very respectfully,

GEO. CHANDLER,
Acting Secretary.

The PRESIDENT OF THE SENATE.

2   CLAIMS OF CERTAIN INDIANS.

DEPARTMENT OF THE INTERIOR,
OFFICE OF INDIAN AFFAIRS,
Washington, February 25, 1893.

SIR: I am in receipt, by your reference of the 23d instant for report, of the following resolution of the United States Senate, adopted February 21, 1893:

Resolved, That the Secretary of the Interior be directed to furnish to the Senate the following information:

(1) The number and value of claims presented by friendly Indians arising from depredations committed during the late Indian disturbance at Pine Ridge, S. Dak.

(2) A statement of the amount allowed on each claim and whether paid to claimant in person or to an agent or attorney, and, if so, the name of such agent or attorney.

(3) A full statement as to the disbursement of the $100,000 appropriated by Congress for the settlement of such claims.

In reply to the first inquiry I have to say that appropriation of $100,000, for the settlement of claims growing out of depredations committed by hostile Indians, not only embraces losses by friendly Indians, but also by whites properly residing on the reservation at the time of the hostilities.

The investigation of the claims was committed by this office to Special Agent James A. Cooper, who, after a patient and thorough investigation, submitted a report to this office embracing the claims of 754 persons, the total amount claimed by them being $201,455.64. The special agent found that ten of those presenting claims were either hostile at the time of the outbreak at Pine Ridge or that the property for which they claimed payment had been subsequently recovered by them, and the number of claimants was, therefore, reduced by him to 744; he also found that only $110,976.58 of the amount above mentioned as a total of the claims was substantiated by proper evidence.

The above amount of $110,976.58, which was considered by the special agent to be due the various claimants, was further reduced by a deduction of 10 per cent, in order to bring the amount allowed within the appropriation made by Congress. Deducting 10 per cent, the amount to be paid was $99,880.23. It having been decided by the Department that the expenses incident to the investigation of these claims and the payment of the amount appropriated should be paid from the appropriation, it became necessary to make a further reduction of 1½ per cent, which was accordingly done, leaving the amount as finally determined $98,383.46. The report of the special agent, showing the above several amounts in detail, was approved by this office and forwarded to the Department, with the recommendation that it receive the approval of the Department, which approval was accordingly granted.

The report of the special agent, above referred to, was submitted to this office in duplicate, and it was the purpose of the office to retain one copy in the office, and forward the duplicate copy to the Treasury Department, for its information and examination in connection with the accounts of Special Agent Cooper, who subsequently paid the amounts due the several claimants, as shown in the said report. In view, however, of the near approach of the close of the present session of Congress, and the delay incident to the copying of this report, it has been considered advisable to forward the duplicate copy of said report, under the assumption that when it reaches Congress it will be printed, and that one of the printed copies can be compared with the original in this office, and sent to the Treasury Department in lieu of the duplicate copy referred to, which is transmitted herewith.

CLAIMS OF CERTAIN INDIANS. 3

As hereinbefore stated, there were 744 approved claimants embraced on the roll as submitted by Special Agent Cooper, the net amount to be paid them being $98,383.46.

After Special Agent Cooper returned to the field for the purpose of making payment to these claimants, he discovered that by an oversight the claim of Mrs. Jennie Whelan had been omitted from the list submitted by him and approved, and upon his calling the attention of the office to the matter authority was obtained from the Department for the allowance of her claim to the amount of $62.05, which amount was paid her in the final disbursement of the funds in question.

The Senate resolution asked, in the second place, for a statement of the amount allowed on each claim, and whether paid to claimant in person or to an agent or attorney, and, if so, the name of such agent or attorney.

In reply to this question I have to say that the answer to the first question covers a portion of this, viz, a statement of the amount allowed on each claim.

In reply to the inquiry as to whether the money due on these claims was paid to claimants in person or to agents, attorneys, etc., I have to say that Special Agent Cooper, who prepared the roll, was directed to make the payment, and the receipts filed by him in this office show that in every case, with the exception of two, the money was paid to and receipt taken from the claimants themselves. In the two cases in question one was where the husband had died after the claim had been presented, and the money due was paid to his wife; and the other, where the claim was in favor of a woman who died before payment was made, and the money in that case was paid to her husband. There are two other cases on the roll where the claims were not in favor of individuals, but of churches which had sustained losses during the hostilities, and the money in those cases was paid to the representatives of the churches.

No payment whatever, as far as shown by the receipts in this office, was made to any agent or attorney for any claimant.

There are nine persons on the rolls whose allowed claims amount to $736.61, who, for various reasons, were not paid by Special Agent Cooper, but their money was returned to the United States Treasury, where it remains to their credit, to be paid at some future time.

As to the third request of the resolution, for a full statement as to the disbursement of the $100,000 appropriated by Congress for the settlement of such claims, I have to submit the following statement:

Amount paid claimants by Special Agent Cooper	$97,708.90
Amount in the United States Treasury for Nos. 24, 153, 325, 473, 506, 572, 588, 594 and 621 (pay roll of Cooper)	736.61
Amount paid by Special Agent Cooper for clerical assistance, interpreters, traveling expenses, express charges on funds, telegrams, etc.	1,554.49
Total	100,000.00

The Senate resolution above referred to, together with a copy of this report, are herewith inclosed.

Very respectfully, your obedient servant,

R. V. BELT,
Acting Commissioner.

The SECRETARY OF THE INTERIOR.

4   CLAIMS OF CERTAIN INDIANS.

[Abstract L.—Claims.]

Abstract of depredation claims investigated by James A. Cooper, special U. S. Indian agent, for depredations committed by hostile Indians during the winter of 1890–'91 at the Pine Ridge, Rosebud, Cheyenne River, Standing Rock, and Tongue River agencies, showing the amount claimed, the amount allowed by Special Agent Cooper, and the 10 per cent reduction required to bring the total amount to be paid within the appropriation of $100,000, and 1¼ per cent reduction to cover expenses incurred in making investigation and payment as directed in office telegram dated February 17, 1892.

No.	Name.	Amount claimed.	Amount allowed.	Less 10 per cent.	Amount recommended, less 1½ per cent.
1	Fast Horse	$591.50	$474.50	$427.05	$420.65
2	Alex Adams	241.50	186.45	167.81	165.29
3	Iron Crow	2,089.25	1,096.06	986.46	971.67
4	Lame Dog	68.00	68.00	61.20	60.29
5	Louis P. Mousseau	1,297.25	530.30	477.27	470.12
6	Edwin Livermont	273.50	150.50	135.45	133.40
7	Yellow Eyes	239.75	215.10	193.59	190.70
8	Samuel Deon	147.00	97.50	87.75	86.45
9	Bear Eagle	165.50	125.85	113.27	111.58
10	Red Eagle	296.50	167.10	150.39	148.14
11	No Braid	1,031.50	585.45	526.91	519.01
12	Medicine Dance	109.00	102.50	92.25	90.87
13	Manuel Romero	195.00	153.00	137.70	135.64
14	Iron Horse	373.75	179.26	161.34	158.92
15	Capt. Geo. Sword	209.00	125.00	112.50	110.82
16	Fire	358.30	51.24	46.12	45.43
17	Ghost Bear	56.50	48.50	43.65	43.00
18	Afraid of Bear	341.65	152.20	136.98	134.93
19	John O. Rourke	730.25	441.43	397.29	391.34
20	Little Wolf	304.75	248.40	223.56	220.21
21	Juan Maestos	170.00	150.00	135.00	132.98
22	Hairy Bird	452.50	117.40	105.66	104.08
23	Black Elk	321.00	198.50	178.65	175.98
24	Red Nest	152.80	82.00	73.80	72.70
25	Roacher	177.00	160.25	144.23	142.07
26	Rocky Bear	259.40	178.30	160.47	158.07
27	Little Dog	359.25	201.25	181.13	178.42
28	Many Wounds	46.10	22.75	20.48	20.18
29	Yankton	303.25	176.69	159.03	156.65
30	White Blanket	110.55	80.75	72.68	71.60
31	Chasing Hawk	215.50	164.95	148.46	146.24
32	Henry Jones Eagle Horse	169.50	100.45	90.41	89.06
33	Spotted Elk	141.00	110.55	99.50	98.02
34	William D. McGaa	1,595.50	722.40	650.16	640.41
35	Not Afraid of Pawnee	199.00	105.99	95.40	93.98
36	George Harvey	131.50	85.00	76.50	75.36
37	Black Whirlwind	9.50	5.50	4.95	4.88
38	One Feather	383.00	178.50	160.65	158.25
39	Joseph Brown, jr	58.50	30.00	27.00	26.60
40	John Hard Ground	191.65	116.28	104.66	103.10
41	Joe Smith	122.00	49.27	44.35	43.69
42	Bad Hair	86.00	42.50	38.25	37.68
43	Moon Bear	29.45	14.61	13.15	12.95
44	Little Bear	60.35	57.38	51.65	50.89
45	Hunts his Horses	73.15	46.80	42.12	41.49
46	Little Bull	191.25	67.83	61.05	60.14
47	Owl Bull	176.90	149.40	134.46	132.45
48	Woman's Dress	48.75	23.50	21.15	20.84
49	Henry Red Shirt	80.80	56.33	50.70	49.95
50	Goes in Center	177.50	89.90	80.91	79.70
51	White Deer	1,164.00	732.60	659.34	649.46
52	Little Cloud	47.00	20.90	18.81	18.54
53	Crazy Horse	437.35	433.65	390.29	384.44
54	Little Wolf	180.00	95.00	85.50	84.23
55	Loves War	101.00	51.50	46.35	45.66
56	Eagle Bull	267.25	161.72	145.55	143.37
57	Mrs. High Back	174.50	134.90	121.41	119.60
58	Peter Comes Again	240.80	118.85	106.97	105.37
59	Louis Hawkins	315.95	162.05	145.85	143.66
60	Peter Bissinnette	404.00	115.68	104.12	102.56
61	White Wolf	351.00	105.45	94.91	93.49
62	Richard Stirk	1,008.00	360.90	324.81	319.95
63	Between Lodges	196.05	117.00	105.30	103.73
64	John Conroy	271.50	236.25	212.63	209.45
65	Iron Bull	403.25	245.80	221.22	217.91
66	Elk Voice Walking	23.00	19.00	17.10	16.85
67	Looks Twice	261.85	176.60	158.94	156.56
68	Black Spotted Horse	30.35	20.71	18.64	18.34

CLAIMS OF CERTAIN INDIANS. 5

Abstract of depredation claims investigated by James A. Cooper, etc.—Continued.

No.	Name.	Amount claimed.	Amount allowed.	Less 10 per cent.	Amount recommended, less 1½ per cent.
69	Jack La Point	$255.00	$150.00	$135.00	$132.98
70	Running Shield	18.60	9.25	8.33	8.21
71	Geo. Colhoff	1,637.45	1,079.11	971.20	956.64
72	Torn Belly	238.30	52.40	47.16	46.45
73	Holy Tail	82.70	69.73	62.76	61.83
74	Face	398.25	157.15	141.44	139.33
75	Yellow Wolf	121.70	94.85	85.37	84.10
76	Oliver Morrisette	145.75	95.50	85.95	84.66
77	Fire Thunder	328.00	201.88	181.70	178.97
78	Grass Cutter	65.00	25.00	22.50	22.17
79	Bird Necklace	294.25	232.90	209.61	206.47
80	Bull Bonnet	849.75	50.55	45.50	44.82
81	Marrow Bone	66.50	25.41	22.87	22.54
82	Steve Ameoitte	66.00	43.20	38.88	38.30
83	Pretty Weasel	281.50	126.50	113.85	112.15
84	Mrs. Jarvis	1,045.50	516.94	465.25	458.28
85	Plenty Hermaphrodite	181.35	132.38	119.15	117.37
86	Charging Enemy	215.15	170.20	153.18	150.89
87	Bear Stops	88.75	62.45	56.21	55.37
88	Big Turnip	119.50	76.85	69.17	68.14
89	Shoulder	262.25	113.95	102.56	101.03
90	Kills Hundred	272.55	190.15	171.14	168.58
91	Hard Heart	168.00	122.00	110.70	109.05
92	Revenger	69.10	56.22	50.60	49.85
93	Kills the Cow	370.90	284.48	256.04	252.30
94	Calico	307.25	223.20	200.88	197.88
95	Bab Cobb	197.00	141.50	127.35	125.45
96	Swift Bird	121.50	64.80	58.82	57.45
97	Cloud Shield	829.00	382.30	344.07	338.91
98	Hand	145.50	130.75	117.68	115.92
99	Cheyenne Butcher	147.75	110.85	99.77	98.27
100	Mrs. Josephine Cuny	641.70	357.97	322.18	317.35
101	Thomas Tyon	126.76	85.20	76.68	75.53
102	Horse Bear	90.50	78.10	70.29	69.24
103	Lucy B. Arnold	25.00	25.00	22.50	22.16
104	Mitch Armijo	1,200.00			(*)
105	Running Eagle	225.25	167.75	150.98	148.72
106	Two Dog	106.25	80.45	72.41	71.33
107	White Bear	238.60	139.90	125.91	124.03
108	Enos Ghost	146.00	106.40	95.76	94.32
109	Chas. Plume	158.00	139.00	125.10	123.22
110	David Little Spotted Horse	42.25	27.00	24.30	23.94
111	Yellow Hair	106.50	68.50	61.65	60.73
112	Grant Red Hawk	321.00	234.50	211.05	207.88
113	High White Man	125.00	106.75	96.08	94.64
114	Clear	81.75	46.60	41.94	41.31
115	Little Cloud	52.00	41.50	37.35	36.79
116	White Bear	187.25	142.30	128.07	126.15
117	Sam Smith	232.00	179.75	161.78	159.36
118	Running Jumper	139.50	101.50	91.35	89.98
119	Black Deer	169.75			(†)
120	Thunder Beard	334.75	178.10	160.29	157.89
121	Whirlwind Man	156.00	140.00	126.00	124.11
122	Little Dog	215.50	181.25	163.13	160.68
123	Red Shell	86.50	74.35	66.92	65.92
124	White Elk	187.70	84.90	76.41	75.27
125	Peter Richards	668.75	411.30	370.17	364.62
126	Walking Bull	67.50	30.55	27.50	37.09
127	Strike with Nose	133.00	56.00	50.40	49.65
128	Standing Bull	259.25	112.37	101.14	99.61
129	Ribbs	209.50	140.50	126.45	124.55
130	Mrs. Red Elk	105.50	90.50	81.45	80.23
131	Country Traveler	148.15	97.65	87.89	86.57
132	John Bird Head	164.75	107.00	96.30	94.86
133	Big Mouth	70.30	48.30	43.47	42.82
134	Phillip F. Wells	1,440.80	856.85	771.17	759.60
135	Turning Bear	223.00	174.55	157.10	154.74
136	Standing Soldier	356.25	199.00	179.10	176.41
137	Chas. Lone Wolf	204.50	129.05	116.15	114.41
138	Singing Bear	105.00	82.75	74.48	73.36
139	Coming Ghost	213.00	146.50	131.85	129.88
140	No Dress	226.10	168.90	152.01	149.73
141	Distribution	544.55	320.45	288.41	284.08
142	Iron Tail	160.00	91.00	81.90	80.68
143	Mrs. Louise Pablo	1,658.00	890.00	801.00	788.98
144	Stands Up	421.65	195.85	176.27	173.63
145	William Brown	312.00	194.00	174.60	171.98
146	Julia Patton	351.55	160.45	144.41	142.24

* Recovered. † Hostile.

6.

CLAIMS OF CERTAIN INDIANS.

Abstract of depredation claims investigated by James A. Cooper, etc.—Continued.

No.	Name.	Amount claimed.	Amount allowed.	Less 10 per cent.	Amount recommended, less 1½ per cent.
147	Mrs. M. A. Means	$114.00	$39.55	$35.60	$35.07
148	Silas Red Dog	164.00	69.50	62.55	61.61
149	Eagle Louse	521.25	228.37	205.54	202.46
150	Whistler	95.75	53.90	48.51	47.78
151	Black Hill	59.50	37.75	33.98	33.47
152	Little Horse	54.25	54.25	48.83	48.10
153	Bear Track	75.00	55.00	49.50	48.76
154	Little Hawk	479.00	145.30	130.77	128.81
155	Two Eagle	95.00	70.00	63.00	62.05
156	Big Head	183.50	102.45	92.21	90.83
157	Little Soldier	371.00	89.62	80.66	79.45
158	Yellow Wolf	448.50	119.10	107.19	105.58
159	Black Feather	525.50	97.05	87.35	86.04
160	Weasel Bear	478.00	189.00	170.10	167.55
161	Howling Horse	251.50	157.10	141.39	139.27
162	Blue Horse	571.00	358.45	322.61	317.76
163	Julian No Flesh	386.30	214.85	193.37	190.47
164	Red Ear Horse	388.50	349.15	314.24	309.53
165	Back	771.00	145.50	130.95	128.99
166	Chase In Sight	126.50	84.40	75.96	74.82
167	Eagle Horn	92.00	65.50	58.95	58.07
168	Medicine Tail	119.05	106.12	90.11	88.76
169	Joe Kettle Coat	364.50	217.70	195.93	193.00
170	John Long Dog	190.50	102.40	92.16	90.78
171	Black Coyote	258.85	197.22	177.50	174.84
172	Little Wolf	198.00	131.50	118.35	116.57
173	Singing Bear	28.00	18.50	16.65	16.40
174	John Bissonette	151.25	92.25	83.03	81.78
175	Lick	162.00	45.90	41.31	40.69
176	White Face Horse	107.20	37.10	33.39	32.89
177	Horned Horse	89.25	81.25	73.13	72.03
178	Newton Big Road	171.00	152.60	137.34	135.28
179	Black Road	180.70	63.75	57.38	56.52
180	White Horse	231.00	197.60	177.84	175.18
181	White Calf	178.00	120.50	108.45	106.82
182	Good Weasel	40.50	39.00	35.10	34.57
183	Bears Foot	175.00	84.00	75.60	74.47
184	Scabby Face	192.00	122.00	109.80	108.16
185	Thunder Tail	296.25	238.75	214.88	211.66
186	Chase In Winter	131.00	112.00	100.80	99.29
187	Stinking Bear	161.00	70.25	63.23	62.28
188	Jeff Blue Bird	66.00	55.00	49.50	48.76
189	Fast	134.50	39.60	35.64	35.11
190	Long Soldier	151.50	79.50	71.55	70.48
191	Afraid of Hawk	600.25	....	....	(*)
192	Pacer	61.15	51.42	46.28	45.59
193	Wooden Leg	111.00	71.00	63.90	62.95
194	Cross Dog	98.65	79.75	71.78	70.71
195	American Bear	314.00	100.50	90.45	89.09
196	Iron White Man	153.50	96.34	86.71	85.41
197	Apple	27.00	2.00	1.80	1.78
198	Red Hair	33.10	31.95	28.76	28.33
199	Standing Soldier, No. 2	295.25	233.95	210.56	207.40
200	Sleeping Bear	262.00	190.00	171.00	168.43
201	Thunder Hawk	118.75	88.62	79.76	78.57
202	Red Weasel	181.85	110.60	99.54	98.04
203	Horse Running Ahead	107.75	91.30	82.17	80.94
204	Red Blanket	1,112.00	217.75	195.98	193.04
205	Corn Man, Sr	1,132.00	126.32	113.69	111.99
206	Rock Mountain	230.50	144.20	129.78	127.84
207	Moccasin Top	114.50	94.35	84.92	83.65
208	Paints Yellow	310.00	153.25	137.93	135.87
209	Two Face	148.50	107.90	97.11	95.65
210	Standing Bear	180.00	150.00	135.00	132.97
211	Mrs. Bowman	44.50	31.00	27.90	27.49
212	Pawnee Leggin	13.00	13.00	11.70	11.53
213	Short Horn	113.10	94.00	84.60	83.33
214	Mrs. Z. A. Barker	895.90	509.30	458.37	451.50
215	Black Wolf	114.10	508.51	45.77	45.09
216	Julia Ecoffey	680.00	470.00	423.00	416.65
217	Guy Belt	201.25	94.15	84.74	83.47
218	Charging Wolf	135.50	113.17	101.86	100.33
219	Deer Woman	155.00	120.00	108.00	106.38
220	Fly	62.50	48.45	43.61	42.96
221	Yellow Boy	140.75	91.00	81.90	80.67
222	Red Hawk, sr	214.50	105.60	95.04	93.61

*Hostile.

CLAIMS OF CERTAIN INDIANS. 7

Abstract of depredation claims investigated by James A. Cooper, etc.—Continued.

No.	Name.	Amount claimed.	Amount allowed.	Less 10 per cent.	Amount recommended, less 1½ per cent.
223	Gives Away Alone	$150.35	$146.30	$131.67	$129.70
224	Corn Man	939.00	69.00	62.10	61.17
225	Dearly	63.00	49.75	44.78	44.11
226	W. C. Smoot	56.25	31.50	28.35	27.93
227	Blue Shield	139.50	70.75	63.68	62.73
228	M. S. Foutch	370.85	252.45	227.21	223.80
229	Afraid of Eagle	200.00	116.60	104.94	103.37
230	Mrs. Bissenette	58.75	26.75	24.08	23.72
231	Gap	25.00	13.50	12.15	11.97
232	Owl Eagle	190.00	130.00	117.00	115.24
233	Charles Giroux	202.75	124.82	112.34	110.66
234	Mrs. Kate Gibbons	2,765.30	1,188.95	1,070.06	1,054.01
235	John Bouyer	14.00	12.00	10.80	10.64
236	William Sires	102.05	57.19	51.48	50.71
237	Brown Eyes	440.00	272.00	244.80	241.13
238	Standing Bear	29.20	19.10	17.19	16.93
239	Clown Woman	34.25	24.50	22.05	21.72
240	A. W. Means	91.00	81.00	72.90	71.81
241	Running Bear	120.50	68.10	61.29	60.37
242	Alexander Baxter	77.00	43.00	38.70	38.12
243	Black Whirlwind	37.50	28.15	25.34	24.96
244	Bill Walks Under Ground	193.65	166.50	149.85	147.61
245	Peter Ladeaux	180.25	61.75	55.58	54.75
246	American Horse No. 2	750.25	401.60	361.44	356.02
247	Amelia Gleason	75.00	60.00	54.00	53.19
248	Beaver Monteau	394.00	133.00	119.70	117.91
249	Shoots the Ghost	202.50	150.60	135.54	133.51
250	Gray Grass	140.00	117.50	105.75	104.17
251	Loafer Joe	543.50	382.20	343.98	338.83
252	Julia Kocer	239.00	208.10	187.29	184.48
253	Cut Hand	223.75	55.95	50.36	49.61
254	Blue Hawk	92.00	34.20	30.78	30.32
255	Fay Running Horse	123.65	86.25	77.63	76.46
256	Medicine Horse	104.50	69.75	62.78	61.84
257	Blind	198.50	135.00	121.50	119.68
258	Joe Bisnette	245.40	169.40	152.46	150.17
259	Foam	88.75	69.75	62.78	61.84
260	Samuel Broken Rope	216.30	132.55	119.30	117.51
261	Good Lance	154.40	125.20	112.68	110.99
262	Part Rope	257.25	204.60	184.14	181.38
263	Jonas Holy Rock	90.50	39.00	35.10	34.57
264	Joe Bush	80.25	59.70	53.73	52.93
265	John Graham	126.50	114.00	102.60	101.06
266	Henry Spotted Eagle	126.00	80.00	72.00	70.92
267	White Beaver	94.00	84.25	75.83	74.70
268	Shield	172.00	172.00	154.80	152.48
269	The P. E. Church Society	1,017.00	1,013.00	911.70	898.03
270	Julia Siers	321.30	150.75	135.68	133.65
271	Fire Lightning	52.45	32.25	29.03	28.59
272	Charging Shield	940.16	391.11	352.00	346.72
273	Jacob White Eyes	45.00	40.00	36.00	35.46
274	Thos. American Horse	90.00	60.00	54.00	53.19
275	Bull Bear	163.00	66.00	59.40	58.51
276	Parts His Hair	18.00	14.00	12.60	12.41
277	Red Eagle	392.65	156.75	141.08	138.96
278	No Neck	362.00	142.75	128.48	126.55
279	Hawk's Wing	98.75	37.00	33.30	32.80
280	Iron Shell	107.50	83.25	74.93	73.81
281	Kills in Winter	82.00	76.50	68.85	67.82
282	Fast Thunder	1,901.70	1,102.45	992.21	977.32
283	Black Bear	157.50	153.60	120.24	118.43
284	Under the Baggage	105.25	85.07	76.57	75.42
285	Big Wolf	76.09	36.80	33.12	32.62
286	Roan Horse	40.50	33.20	29.88	29.44
287	Two Bull	217.75	146.75	132.08	130.10
288	Six Feathers	454.90	309.65	278.69	274.51
289	Bob Tail Horse	8.95	5.10	4.59	4.52
290	Black Chicken	61.00	28.25	25.43	25.05
291	Hollow Horn	73.00	51.74	46.57	45.87
292	Real Hawk	101.90	101.40	91.26	89.89
293	Big Road	229.75	64.95	58.46	57.58
294	Rib Man	61.00	28.75	25.88	25.50
295	Royal	237.00	125.75	113.18	111.48
296	Red Cloud	682.50	396.60	356.94	351.59
297	Chas. Cuny	1,595.00	1,380.00	1,242.00	1,223.37
298	Moves Her Lodge	328.50	125.60	113.04	111.34
299	Mrs. Little	77.50	47.87	43.09	42.44
300	Runs Against	141.25	62.25	56.03	55.19

8   CLAIMS OF CERTAIN INDIANS.

Abstract of depredation claims investigated by James A. Cooper, etc.—Continued.

No.	Name.	Amount claimed.	Amount allowed.	Less 10 per cent.	Amount recommended, less 1¼ per cent.
301	Mrs. Lizzie Kern	$1,034.75	$558.90	$503.01	$495.46
302	Long Woman	85.75	64.50	58.05	57.18
303	Black Horse	239.00	215.00	193.50	190.80
304	Alexander Le Buff	151.00	113.00	101.70	100.18
305	Little Moon	135.00	120.00	108.00	106.38
306	Sophia White Cow	252.50	192.45	173.21	170.61
307	Struck by Crow	150.50	132.85	119.57	117.78
308	Crazy Ghost	105.25	71.50	64.35	63.38
309	Frank Young	245.00	164.00	147.60	145.39
310	Henry Crow	120.00	80.00	72.00	70.92
311	Hubert Bisnotte	120.00	90.00	81.00	79.78
312	High Chief	146.00	78.00	70.20	69.15
313	Bell Ear Ring	41.00	26.90	24.21	23.34
314	John Conttier	25.00	20.00	18.00	17.73
315	Whetstone	170.00	160.00	144.00	141.84
316	Geo. R. Brown	60.00	45.00	40.50	39.89
317	Sarah Hunter	246.85	95.15	85.64	84.36
318	Mrs. Phil Hunter	248.80	140.97	126.88	124.98
319	Frank Feather	234.25	43.00	38.70	38.12
320	Red Cloud, jr	59.00	50.00	45.00	44.32
321	Bad Yellow Hair	361.50	202.95	182.66	179.92
322	Little Bull	373.25	95.50	85.95	84.67
323	Kills Alone	240.00	147.00	132.30	130.31
324	Moses Red Kettle	60.00	35.00	31.50	31.03
325	Bear Robe	160.00	124.00	111.60	109.93
326	Iron Wing	40.00	20.00	18.00	17.73
327	Little Bull	229.00	113.75	102.38	100.84
328	Dog Ghost	152.00	80.40	72.36	71.27
329	Three Stars	235.50	68.00	61.20	60.28
330	Chasing Bear	285.25	238.35	214.52	211.30
331	Plenty Antelope	65.00	40.00	36.00	35.46
332	Willie Three Star	87.15	71.55	64.40	63.43
333	Shinning Ground	1,448.90	743.40	669.06	659.02
334	Eagle Horse	70.00	49.50	44.55	43.88
335	Bear Looks Back	90.00	75.00	67.50	66.49
336	Charlott Chausse	245.00	115.00	103.50	101.95
337	Kills Ahead	36.50	20.50	18.45	18.17
338	Little Shield	120.60	80.00	72.00	70.92
339	Young Man Afraid of His Horses	1,222.85	320.85	288.77	284.44
340	Red Fly	100.25	65.90	59.31	58.43
341	Running Hawk	990.00	720.00	648.00	638.28
342	Pacer	195.00	135.00	121.50	119.68
343	Clown Horse	412.25	239.05	215.15	211.92
344	Fool Head	112.00	82.35	74.12	73.01
345	Nellie Shinning Ground	547.00	304.25	273.83	269.73
346	Mrs. Jessie Craven	1,581.00	804.35	273.92	269.82
347	Crow Likes Water	60.50	31.50	28.35	27.92
348	American Horse	5,252.50	1,714.40	1,542.96	1,519.82
349	Red Horn Bull	49.25	....	....	(*)
350	Amanal Arcunia	50.00	40.00	36.00	35.46
351	Red Star	394.00	221.70	199.53	196.55
352	Black Sheep	747.50	510.75	459.68	452.78
353	Ground Morrison	894.00	243.50	219.15	215.86
354	Z. Z. Morrison	570.00	....	....	(†)
355	Red Owl	105.75	73.50	66.15	65.16
356	Mrs. L. George Charger	223.50	163.20	146.88	144.68
357	Chas. Janis	502.50	95.70	86.13	84.84
358	Edgar M. Keith	363.55	205.68	185.12	182.29
359	Breaking In	86.50	79.75	71.78	70.71
360	Fast Elk	500.05	321.70	289.53	285.19
361	Shut Close	113.65	76.00	68.40	67.38
362	Short Bull	153.50	102.05	91.85	90.48
363	Eagle Elk	13.75	7.15	6.44	6.34
364	Yellow Bird	1,898.55	1,282.25	1,154.03	1,136.72
365	Henry Janis	285.00	40.00	36.00	35.46
366	Long Cat	74.00	57.55	51.80	51.12
367	Kills Brave	111.00	50.00	45.00	44.32
368	Two Lance, jr	27.75	25.75	23.18	22.83
369	He Bear	749.25	348.70	313.83	309.13
370	Good Ball	474.00	104.50	94.05	92.64
371	Big Crow	338.25	16.75	15.08	14.85
372	Keeps Battle	99.00	67.00	60.30	59.40
373	Kills in Winter	136.00	116.50	104.85	103.28
374	Spotted Horse	597.50	228.92	206.03	202.94
375	Walking Elk	84.75	59.25	53.33	52.53
376	Clayton Brave	100.75	40.00	36.00	35.46
377	Bad Heart Bull	209.85	179.90	161.91	159.48

         * Hostile.   † All recovered.

CLAIMS OF CERTAIN INDIANS. 9

Abstract of depredation claims investigated by James A. Cooper, etc.—Continued.

No.	Name.	Amount claimed.	Amount allowed.	Less 10 per cent.	Amount recommended, less 1½ per cent.
378	Dirt Kettle	$50.00	$29.50	$26.55	$26.15
379	Baptist Poirier	4,868.05	2,473.85	2,226.47	2,193.07
380	Thick Bread	171.50	108.65	97.79	96.33
381	Henry Twist	70.00	70.00	63.00	62.05
382	Foolish Woman	166.00	120.85	108.77	107.14
383	Dog on Butte	55.00	23.25	20.93	20.62
384	Mrs. Few Tails	315.75	203.40	183.06	180.31
385	Bad Moccasin	210.00	143.50	129.15	127.21
386	Spotted Eagle	520.00	158.00	142.20	140.07
387	Joseph Knight, jr	375.35	233.55	210.20	207.05
388	Amos Ross	7.00	5.00	4.50	4.44
389	Smoke	178.50	157.00	141.30	139.18
390	John Sitting Bear	230.00	170.00	153.00	150.70
391	Mrs. Long Wolf	651.40	156.90	141.21	139.09
392	L. Fisher	271.35	170.35	153.32	151.02
393	Yellow Boy	105.50	89.25	80.33	79.13
394	William Vlandry	236.05	138.65	124.79	122.92
395	Red Elk	59.00	46.50	41.85	41.23
396	Arapahoe	161.00	127.15	114.44	112.72
397	James Grass	166.25	54.45	49.01	48.27
398	Young Iron	45.80	31.45	28.31	27.89
399	Brave Heart	160.75	153.25	137.93	135.87
400	Presbyterian Board of Foreign Missions	1,095.00	1,083.55	975.20	960.57
401	Charging Bear	80.75	61.75	55.58	54.75
402	White Mouse	95.00	43.50	39.15	38.56
403	Young Bad Wound	42.50	30.50	27.45	27.04
404	John La Deaux	70.00	....	....	(*)
405	No Water	888.00	225.00	202.50	199.46
406	Flat Iron	217.75	167.00	150.30	148.05
407	Lone Dog	622.25	69.65	62.69	61.75
408	White Bird	1,593.95	416.95	375.26	369.63
409	White Whirlwind	128.00	78.00	70.20	69.15
410	Chas. A. Eastman	15.00	15.00	13.50	13.30
411	Wind Shawl	87.50	86.00	77.40	76.24
412	Big Bend	86.00	64.20	57.78	56.92
413	Takes Enemy	114.75	76.90	69.21	68.17
414	Horse Goes Out	85.75	39.82	35.94	35.31
415	Broken Leg	111.00	67.35	60.62	59.71
416	Whirlwind Bear	120.00	80.00	72.00	70.92
417	Jumping Eagle	32.00	32.00	28.80	28.37
418	Chief	70.00	49.50	44.55	43.88
419	Chase Close the House	302.25	217.75	195.98	193.05
420	Sound Sleeper	100.50	60.25	54.23	53.42
421	Tongue	215.85	196.60	176.94	174.29
422	He Dog	254.25	147.90	133.11	131.11
423	Red Bear	96.00	50.40	45.36	44.68
424	Gall	64.70	36.62	32.96	32.47
425	Goes on the Center	12.00	6.00	5.40	5.33
426	Iron Cloud	108.00	98.00	88.20	86.87
427	Wounded Bear	104.25	79.75	71.78	70.71
428	Stands First	113.00	102.80	92.52	91.14
429	Pretty Elk	27.00	17.85	15.89	15.66
430	Bear Runs in the Woods	113.80	81.50	73.35	72.25
431	Pumpkin Seed	1,084.50	297.50	267.75	263.74
432	Joseph Richards	486.00	375.00	337.50	332.44
433	Charging Alone (or Chases Alone)	125.95	111.30	100.17	98.67
434	Kills the Bull	329.20	150.32	135.29	133.26
435	Alfred Shield	101.50	68.25	61.43	60.51
436	Knife Chief	77.00	35.55	32.00	31.52
437	Chief Eagle	44.50	42.75	38.48	37.90
438	Red Beet	10.00	....	....	(†)
439	Crow Woman	58.70	53.60	48.24	47.52
440	Scabby Woman	55.50	52.50	47.25	46.54
441	Shell Woman	38.00	18.75	16.88	16.63
442	Little Bald Eagle	185.50	133.75	120.38	118.57
443	White Hawk	205.25	191.00	171.90	169.33
444	White Cow Man	98.75	98.75	88.88	87.55
445	Joseph Merriville	791.00	416.75	375.98	369.45
446	William Twiss	723.00	167.00	150.30	148.05
447	William Bird Head	95.00	85.00	76.50	75.45
448	Alexander Medicine Elk	45.00	30.00	27.00	26.59
449	Red Paint	180.00	125.00	112.50	110.81
450	Sounding Side	113.00	56.50	50.85	50.09
441	Red Shirt	824.00	264.00	237.60	234.04
452	Brave Heart	160.85	92.80	83.52	82.27

*Recovered stock.   †Hostile.

10   CLAIMS OF CERTAIN INDIANS.

Abstract of depredation claims investigated by James A. Cooper, etc.—Continued.

No.	Name.	Amount claimed.	Amount allowed.	Less 10 per cent.	Amount recommended, less 1½ per cent.
453	Jack Red Cloud	$1,446.95	$1,198.65	$1,078.79	$1,062.61
454	Crazy Bear	93.45	67.32	60.59	59.68
455	Afraid of Hawk	143.75	126.10	113.49	111.79
456	Frank Bear Nose	113.00	70.00	63.00	62.05
457	Breast	165.00	110.00	99.00	97.51
458	Iron	130.00	110.50	99.45	97.95
459	Cedar Face	30.00	20.00	18.00	17.73
460	Old Horse	55.00	34.00	30.60	30.14
461	Saves the Bears	145.70	98.75	88.88	87.55
462	Big Foot	90.25	38.25	34.43	33.91
463	Alex Seluin	109.00	79.00	71.10	70.03
464	Plenty Bear	64.50	32.00	28.80	28.37
465	Mrs. Clement Davis	675.90	278.05	250.25	246.50
466	H. E. Brown	106.37	104.05	93.63	92.25
477	John M. Sweeney	135.45	90.90	81.81	80.59
468	Spotted Cow	24.10	15.90	14.31	14.09
469	George Fire Thunder	74.20	60.00	54.00	53.19
470	Big Owl	97.35	56.80	51.12	50.36
471	Bank	101.25	100.50	90.45	89.09
472	Mrs. Plenty Wolf	403.04	108.09	97.29	95.83
473	Lucy Day	91.45	26.55	23.90	23.50
474	Flying Hawk	390.50	128.85	115.97	114.23
475	Good Thunder	79.00	39.05	35.15	34.62
476	Bird Eagle	210.00	180.00	162.00	159.57
477	James Lone Elk	92.50	42.05	37.85	37.29
478	Joseph Marshall	174.00	149.00	134.10	132.09
479	Red Feather	100.50	73.85	66.47	65.47
480	Placado Luhan	110.00	95.00	85.50	84.22
481	Chief Eagle	128.50	94.35	84.92	83.65
482	B. L. Condelario	391.25	234.00	210.60	207.44
483	Strikes Plenty	175.25	151.60	136.44	134.39
484	Albert Burning	168.10	111.35	100.22	98.72
485	Eagle Pipe	360.00	180.00	162.00	159.57
486	Shell Boy	119.00	96.00	86.40	85.10
487	Kills Himself	120.25	87.60	78.84	77.66
488	Ettie Bingham	964.50	269.05	242.15	238.52
489	Rock	44.50	38.50	34.65	34.13
490	Badger	115.00	80.00	72.00	70.92
491	Stabber	125.00	93.00	83.70	82.45
492	Yellow Bull	53.00	31.90	28.71	28.28
493	Catching Bear	146.00	120.00	108.00	106.38
494	Yellow Thunder	649.00	107.10	96.39	94.94
495	Broken Arm	458.00	54.00	48.60	47.87
496	Yellow Bear	276.00	253.35	228.02	224.60
497	Kills Enemy	45.00	15.00	13.50	13.30
498	Little Wound	608.50	418.50	376.65	371.00
499	Standing Elk	121.50	58.35	52.52	51.73
500	Poor Elk	493.50	329.50	296.55	292.10
501	Red Willow	67.00	44.00	39.60	30.20
502	Two Crow	185.00	96.80	87.12	85.81
503	Black Hawk	595.00	25.00	22.50	23.16
504	Young Dog	160.00	125.00	112.50	110.81
505	Poor Bear	203.25	152.85	137.57	135.51
506	Top Bear	148.00	89.50	80.55	79.34
507	Conquering Bear	62.00			(*)
508	Last Horse	197.00	139.00	125.10	123.22
509	Eagle Elk	210.00	190.00	171.00	168.43
510	White Rabbit	557.45	373.60	336.24	331.20
511	White Bull	138.75	102.25	92.03	90.65
512	Tramped by Mice	93.50	77.50	69.75	68.71
513	Millie White Cow	33.25	23.50	21.15	20.83
514	Nellie Whetstone	44.25	30.20	27.18	26.77
515	Grass	147.00	97.75	87.98	86.67
516	Peter Shangrau	667.50	197.00	177.30	174.64
517	Brings Plenty	141.00	72.85	65.57	64.59
518	White Feather or Plume	58.75	38.25	34.43	33.91
519	Mrs. Brewer	67.40	46.90	42.21	41.58
520	Frank McMahan	115.00	75.00	67.50	66.49
521	Her Holy Shawl	127.50	90.40	81.36	80.14
522	Mrs. Armigo	580.00	240.00	216.00	212.76
523	Allico Pallardy	436.25	247.50	222.75	219.41
524	John Rooks	50.00	40.00	36.00	35.46
525	Thunder Bear	172.70	131.45	118.31	116.54
526	Slow Bull	135.00	47.40	42.66	42.02
527	Blue Horse	40.00	40.00	36.00	35.46
528	Bear Comes Out	18.00	12.70	11.43	11.26
529	John Rondo	211.25	122.25	110.03	108.38
530	Goes Out Bad	243.00	200.00	180.00	177.30

* Hostile.

CLAIMS OF CERTAIN INDIANS. 11

Abstract of depredation claims investigated by James A. Cooper, etc.—Continued.

No.	Name.	Amount claimed.	Amount allowed.	Less 10 per cent.	Amount recommended, less 1½ per cent.
531	Bear Eagle	$36.50	$58.25	$52.43	$51.64
532	Chas. Turning Hawk	665.90	333.65	300.29	295.79
533	Kill Bear	104.00	80.50	72.45	71.36
534	Frank Galigo	368.00	106.00	95.40	93.97
535	Too Too	436.00	267.75	240.98	237.37
536	White Cow Chief	347.25	186.45	167.81	165.30
537	Jumping Eagle	81.00	54.50	49.05	48.31
538	His Whirlwind Horse	426.75	277.10	249.39	245.65
539	Alfred C. Smith	102.05	100.05	90.05	88.70
540	Little Soldier	10.50	10.00	9.00	8.86
541	Shot in the Eye	302.75	162.95	146.66	144.46
542	Mrs. Twiss	69.50	46.55	41.90	41.28
543	Little Elk	53.00	48.00	43.20	42.55
544	Hollow Wood	401.00	181.50	163.35	160.90
545	Fast Whirlwind	99.50	61.55	55.40	54.57
546	Mrs. Allman	107.50	55.10	49.59	48.85
547	Old Eagle	88.30	41.05	36.95	36.40
548	Patrick Star	394.00	262.90	236.61	233.06
549	Thomas Crow	213.35	182.60	164.34	161.87
550	John Lee	86.00	6.00	5.40	5.33
551	William Shangrau	477.50	173.25	155.93	153.60
552	Little Bear	266.00	133.00	119.70	117.91
553	Slow Bear	1,588.10	914.85	823.37	811.02
554	White Belly	81.00	62.35	56.12	55.28
555	Red Bear (Cheyenne)	182.25	115.50	103.95	102.40
556	Red Rabbit	35.00	35.00	31.50	21.03
557	Eagle Heart	37.75	27.25	24.53	24.16
558	Lone Wolf	240.75	134.45	121.01	119.19
559	Mrs. Red Crane	238.00	82.30	74.07	72.96
560	Eagle Hawk	174.00	119.75	107.78	106.17
561	Returns From Scout	101.55			(*)
562	Red Bear (Ogalalla)	59.00	49.00	44.10	43.44
563	Flesh	253.00	168.00	151.20	148.93
564	Henry Standing Bear	380.00	220.00	198.00	195.03
565	Foot	39.50	27.00	24.30	23.94
566	Lone Bear	148.25	114.25	102.83	101.29
567	Red Sack	400.00	139.10	125.19	123.31
568	Edgar Fire Thunder	107.25	45.50	40.95	40.34
569	Makes Enemy	115.06	64.00	57.60	56.74
570	Thunder Bull	655.95	254.90	229.41	225.97
571	Red Blanket	22.00	9.05	8.15	8.03
572	A. L. Fredrick	60.00	40.00	36.00	35.46
573	James F. Asay	160.00	150.00	135.00	132.97
574	Allice Two Elks	25.00	20.00	18.00	17.73
575	War Bonnet	704.00	233.50	210.15	207.00
576	Swimmer	105.00	40.00	36.00	35.46
577	White Hawk	295.00	155.20	139.68	137.59
578	Straight Forelock	56.00	56.00	50.40	49.64
517	White Eyes	589.00	242.40	218.16	214.89
580	Black War Bonnet	151.00	82.00	73.80	72.70
581	Abe Summers	95.00	80.00	72.00	70.92
582	Eagle Elk	329.50	42.25	38.03	37.45
583	Chas. Richards	111.50	70.00	63.00	62.06
584	James Richard	40.10	23.65	21.29	20.79
585	Nick Janis, jr	150.00			(†)
586	Knee	205.30	150.25	135.23	133.20
587	Whirlwind Bear	102.50	53.75	48.33	47.65
588	Mrs. White Wing	46.80	36.60	32.94	32.45
589	Running Above	29.50	10.00	9.00	8.87
590	Two Men	227.25	162.70	146.43	144.23
591	William Black Bear	361.75	314.25	282.83	278.59
592	Mrs. Blind Man	223.25	135.47	121.93	120.11
593	Mrs. Adams	211.00	136.00	122.40	120.56
594	Hawk (Cheyenne)	221.25	180.20	162.18	159.75
595	Kills in Woods	68.00	20.00	18.00	17.73
596	Hawk Head	282.00	130.00	117.00	115.24
597	Blue Heart	55.00	55.00	49.50	48.76
598	Real Bull	8.60	8.20	7.38	7.28
599	Lone Elk	77.05	61.20	55.08	54.25
600	Cherry Stone	69.80	42.40	38.16	37.59
601	Thomas Mills	146.00	146.00	131.40	129.43
602	W. R. Jones	760.00	760.00	684.00	673.74
603	John Grass	65.00	55.00	49.50	48.86
604	John Shangrau	308.00	308.00	277.20	273.04
605	James Clincher	42.75	31.75	28.58	28.15
606	Red Horse	110.00	84.00	75.60	74.47
607	Mrs. No Neck	618.75	435.75	392.18	386.30
608	Sarah Gillispie	197.50	133.00	119.70	117.91
609	Ice	40.00	40.00	36.00	35.46

*Hostile. †Did not lose any property. Nothing.

12   CLAIMS OF CERTAIN INDIANS.

Abstract of depredation claims investigated by James A. Cooper, etc.—Continued.

ROSEBUD AGENCY CLAIMS.

No.	Name.	Amount claimed.	Amount allowed.	Less 10 per cent.	Amount recommended, less 1½ per cent.
1	Alex Cromrie	$55.80	$44.55	$40.10	$39.50
2	R. C. Bour	269.05	213.50	192.15	189.27
3	Minnie E. Mead	42.15	37.65	33.89	33.38
4	A. D. Harpold	300.50	221.77	199.60	196.60
5	H. E. Eaton	140.95	108.35	97.52	96.02
6	Henry Young	488.00	399.00	359.10	353.71
7	Lip	40.00	20.00	18.00	17.73
8	Man with Horns	28.00	15.00	13.50	13.30
9	William C. Garrett	632.60	443.99	399.60	393.60
10	Eagle Hawk	70.00	40.00	36.00	35.46
11	Frank L. Lock	133.35	88.55	79.70	78.50
12	Cut	35.00	20.00	18.00	17.73
13	Bull Walk Behind	120.00	60.00	54.00	53.19
14	Plenty Bull	65.00	38.00	34.20	33.69
15	Muggins	40.00	20.00	18.00	17.73
16	Stands for Them	35.00	35.00	31.50	31.03
17	John B. G. Vettal	40.00	40.00	36.00	35.46
18	Red Dog	200.00	105.00	94.50	93.08
19	Coffee	75.00	55.00	49.50	48.75
20	Yellow Wooden Ring	45.00	20.00	18.00	17.73
21	Chas. Smith	95.50	63.15	56.84	56.29
22	Mrs. Ada M. Clark	87.81	77.16	69.45	68.36

CHEYENNE RIVER AGENCY CLAIMS.

No.	Name.	Amount claimed.	Amount allowed.	Less 10 per cent.	Amount recommended, less 1½ per cent.
1	Bridges	$64.30	$47.80	$43.02	$42.37
2	Lazy White Bull	64.00	40.00	36.00	35.46
3	Act the Bear	167.00	121.40	109.16	107.62
4	Eagle Chasing	289.00	157.95	142.16	140.03
5	Touch Cloud	335.00	119.55	107.60	105.99
6	Charger	82.00	81.60	73.44	72.34
7	Little Crow	50.00	50.00	45.00	44.32
8	Pretty Crow	335.00	235.45	211.91	208.74
9	Red Dupui	240.00	120.00	108.00	106.38
10	Bear Eagle	213.00	130.75	117.68	115.92
11	Bear Growling	118.15	41.60	37.44	36.88
12	Straight Head	171.50	119.65	107.69	106.08
13	Red Horse	154.00	117.00	105.30	103.72
14	Yellow Hair Horse	99.30	43.95	39.56	38.97
15	John Black Hawk	97.00	79.85	71.87	70.80
16	Hump	79.00	71.30	64.17	63.21
17	Own the Bob Tail Horse	90.00	75.90	68.31	67.29
18	But of the Horn	269.00	241.65	217.49	214.23
19	High Lodge	156.00	100.85	90.77	89.41
20	Bull Man	117.00	87.60	78.84	77.66
21	Narciss Narcelle	15.00	10.00	9.00	8.87
22	Bear Arm Necklace	201.00	165.25	148.73	146.50
23	Red Rabbit	106.10	85.50	76.95	75.80
24	Takes His Snot	68.00	34.15	30.74	30.23
25	Kills Twice	70.00	40.00	36.00	35.46
26	White Thunder	161.00	114.25	102.83	101.29
27	Brown Thunder	85.00	85.00	76.50	75.35
28	Turtle	185.50	144.75	130.28	128.33
29	Makes Him Long	216.25	121.45	109.31	107.67

STANDING ROCK AGENCY CLAIMS.

No.	Name.	Amount claimed.	Amount allowed.	Less 10 per cent.	Amount recommended, less 1½ per cent.
1	Eagle Man	$616.15	$52.90	$47.61	$46.90
2	Holy Medicine	100.00	40.00	36.00	35.46
3	White Buffalo Man	15.00	15.00	13.50	13.30
4	His One Feather	40.00	40.00	36.00	35.46
5	Louis Premean	1,122.75	1,061.25	955.13	940.80
6	Weasel Bear	24.25	23.25	20.93	20.62
7	Bear Rib	9.25	6.30	5.67	5.59
8	High Eagle	11.50	9.25	8.33	8.21
9	Running Hawk	19.50	14.75	13.28	13.08
10	Looking Elk	4.50	4.50	4.05	4.00
11	White Bird	71.00	36.50	32.85	32.36
12	Red Bear	20.50	18.83	16.20	15.96
13	Rooster	15.75	15.25	13.73	13.53
14	Swift Hawk	2.50	2.50	2.25	2.22
15	Louis Sitting Bull	20.00	15.50	13.95	13.75
16	Adam Hona	8.50	6.75	6.08	5.99
17	Paints Brown	173.80	90.50	81.45	80.23
18	Red Tomahawk	17.75	12.50	11.25	11.08
19	Louis Hat	15.90	12.65	11.39	11.22

CLAIMS OF CERTAIN INDIANS. 13

Abstract of depredation claims investigated by James A. Cooper, etc.—Continued.

TONGUE RIVER AGENCY CLAIMS.

No.	Name.	Amount claimed.	Amount allowed.	Less 10 per cent.	Amount recommended, less 1½ per cent.
1	Little Head	$341.25	$294.50	$265.05	$261.07
2	No Brains	455.00	286.55	257.90	254.03
3	Little Chief	355.50	182.55	164.30	161.84
4	Red Neck	257.00	128.15	115.34	113.61
5	Oil Gum	36.50	29.00	26.10	25.71
6	Old She Bear	383.00	157.70	141.93	139.81
7	Hollow Wood	205.75	163.90	147.51	145.30
8	Little White Man	307.50	149.50	134.55	132.53
9	Beaver Heart	293.00	271.75	244.58	240.91
10	Black Bird	198.50	175.65	158.09	155.72
11	Big Leg	280.70	190.15	171.14	168.57
12	Old Bear	335.50	302.75	272.48	268.39
13	Crawling	267.75	166.60	149.94	147.70
14	Red Fox	126.00	126.00	113.40	111.70
15	Little Hawk	309.60	239.45	215.51	212.28
16	Old Bull	160.75	129.00	116.10	114.36
17	Arapehoe Chief, sr	442.50	388.75	349.88	344.64
18	Grass Hopper	264.50	217.65	195.89	192.96
19	Black Whetstone	262.25	200.35	180.32	177.61
20	Long Teeth	353.50	285.95	257.36	253.50
21	Black Man	961.25	552.50	497.25	489.79
22	Wounded Eye	458.75	277.90	250.11	246.36
23	White Bird	217.00	66.75	60.08	59.18
24	Mrs. Buffalo Rib	82.00	82.00	73.80	72.70
25	His Bad Horse	108.50	97.55	87.80	86.49
26	Medicine Man	113.50	98.55	88.70	87.37
27	The Standing Elk	536.00	273.00	245.70	242.02
28	Sioux	179.25	150.75	135.68	133.65
29	Elk Shoulder	274.75	169.50	152.55	150.26
30	Sharp Nose	77.75	51.90	46.71	46.01
31	Rising Elk	354.00	216.20	194.58	191.66
32	Rock Forehead	48.00	40.00	36.00	35.46
33	Big Foot	181.50	123.00	110.70	109.04
34	Walking Woman	505.25	311.75	280.58	276.37
35	Plenty Camp	268.25	178.45	160.61	158.20
36	Mrs. Kills Back	407.00	214.95	193.46	190.56
37	Loves His Knife	270.00	170.00	153.00	150.70
38	Plenty Crows	140.00	121.00	108.90	107.27
39	Lone Chief	383.50	175.95	158.36	155.99
40	Tangle Hair	523.00	304.20	273.78	269.68
41	Mrs. White Sky	217.00	169.95	152.96	150.67
42	Lame Woman	94.50	60.50	54.45	53.63
43	Eagle Wolf	52.30	27.95	25.16	24.78
44	Mrs. Iron Teeth	192.00	126.00	113.40	111.70
45	Mrs. Twenty Stands	381.00	217.00	195.30	192.37
46	Pawnee	412.50	199.35	179.42	176.73
47	Mrs. Red Breath	135.00	79.50	71.55	70.48
48	Mrs. Crooked Neck	58.00	29.50	26.55	26.15
49	Bear Chum	432.30	248.15	223.34	220.00
50	Black Bea	476.00	176.25	158.63	156.25
51	Wolf Chief	333.00	146.80	132.12	130.14
52	Benjamin Rowland	490.00	175.00	157.50	155.14
53	Women's Leggins	298.25	176.60	158.94	156.56
54	Mrs. Wild Hog	605.50	314.70	283.23	278.98
55	Bessie Standing Elk	166.00	113.50	102.15	100.62
56	Bull Elk	296.00	170.45	153.41	151.11
57	Black Stone	113.45	64.85	58.37	57.49
58	Black Horse	251.25	223.20	200.88	197.87
59	Eugene Standing Elk	1,634.00	375.90	338.31	333.23
60	Round Stone	260.00	150.00	135.00	132.97
61	Spotted Elk	475.50	225.50	202.95	199.91
62	Walks Fanning	245.00	107.65	96.89	95.44
63	Wooden Leg	375.00	168.00	151.20	148.93
64	Mrs. Cut Nose	341.25	151.25	136.13	134.09
65	Mexican Cheyenne	463.00	241.40	217.26	214.00
66	Tall Bull	400.00	205.00	184.50	181.73
67	Arapahoe Chief, jr	401.00	247.50	222.75	219.41
68	Arthur Standing Elk	413.50	210.90	189.81	186.97
69	Lone Elk	331.00	190.50	171.45	168.88
70	Sweet Grass	319.75	171.25	154.13	151.82
71	Burns, Mrs	35.50	21.25	19.13	18.84
72	Bites	223.75	137.85	124.07	122.21
73	Gray Blanket	24.50	11.70	10.53	10.37
74	Bull Thigh	225.00	90.00	81.00	79.78
75	Bear Tusks	358.25	183.90	165.51	163.02
	Grand total	201,455.64	110,976.58	99,880.23	98,383.46

14   CLAIMS OF CERTAIN INDIANS.

I certify on honor that the foregoing "Grand recapitulation of Abstract L," sheets numbered from 1 to 29, inclusive, is correct and true.
Dated at Pine Ridge Agency, S. Dak., February 25, 1892.

JAMES A. COOPER,
Special United States Indian Agent.

WASHINGTON, D. C.
Erasures and interlineations made by me this 30th day of March, 1892.

JAMES A. COOPER,
United States Special Indian Agent.

Appendix H

Chronology of Historical/Legal Events on Sioux Land Claims

Events from 1851 to 1946

1851   The Fort Laramie Treaty of September 17, 1851 (11 Stat. 749), was ratified by the U.S. Senate. Article 5 of the treaty recognized title in the "Sioux or Dahcotah Nation" to approximately 60 million acres of land west of the Missouri River (within the present states of North Dakota, South Dakota, Nebraska, Montana, and Wyoming).

1863   Congress passed an amendment to the Court of Claims' 1855 Enabling Act (10 Stat. 612). The amendment provided that the jurisdiction of the court would not include claims against the United States "growing out of or depending on any treaty stipulation entered into . . . with Indian tribes."

1866   The Sioux bands were engaged at war with the United States in the Powder River country (in the present states of Montana and Wyoming). The United States was attempting to build a road through the 1851 treaty lands, which the Sioux bands considered their best hunting grounds. This road, known as the Bozeman Trail, was intended to protect miners traveling to the Montana goldfields near Bozeman.

1867   By the Act of July 20, 1867 (15 Stat. 17), Congress authorized the president to appoint a peace commission with the power to meet with the Indians then waging war against the United States; to ascertain the causes of their acts of hostility; and to enter into treaties with these Indians which would remove the causes of their complaint, establish security along the railroad line to the Pacific and other thoroughfares of travel to the west, and ensure civilization for the Indians and peace and safety for the whites. The commissioners were also instructed to examine and select a district or districts of country to serve as a permanent reservation for all the Indians residing east of the Rocky Mountains. The peace commissioners (according to the preamble of the 1868 treaty) consisted of Lieutenant-General William T. Sherman, General William S. Harney, General Alfred H. Terry, General C. C. Augur, J. B. Henderson, Nathaniel G. Taylor, John B. Sanborn, and Samuel F. Tappan.

On August 16, 1867, General Augur made a statement to the Indian peace commission. He stated that from the military standpoint the Powder River Road was objectionable. The Indians would fight to the death to retain the Powder River country, and the cost in time, money, and lives to defeat them militarily would far exceed the cost of a peaceful solution (Sioux Tribe v. United States, 42 Ind. Cl. Comm. 214 [1978]).

1868   The Fort Laramie Treaty of April 29, 1868 (15 Stat. 635), was ratified by Congress. The treaty established peace between the Sioux bands and the United States (art. 1); established a 26-million-acre reservation (the Great Sioux Reservation) for the "absolute and undisturbed use and occupation" of the Sioux bands (art. 2); provided that no future cession of the reservation would be valid without the signatures of three-fourths of the adult male population of the Sioux bands (art. 12); provided that the Sioux bands would have hunting rights over their remaining 1851 treaty lands and expanded hunting rights westward to the summits of the Bighorn Mountains and southward to the Republican River so long as the buffalo ranged in such numbers as to justify a chase (art. 11); provided that when agency buildings were constructed by the United States, they would regard the permanent reservation as their permanent home (art. 15); and provided that all remaining 1851 treaty lands would remain "unceded Indian territory" (art. 16).

1874   Lt. Col. George A. Custer led a military expedition into the Black Hills portion of the Great Sioux Reservation. The expedition left from Fort Lincoln (across the Missouri River from present-day Bismarck, North Dakota) and entered the Black Hills from the north. The expedition sent back glowing reports of gold deposits in the Black Hills, which resulted in an influx of miners and settlers into the Black Hills. The Sioux people later referred to Custer's route as "the thieves' road." The expedition's report of gold deposits caused public pressure on the U.S. government to open the Black Hills for mining and settlement.

1875   In a letter dated November 9, 1875, to Brigadier General Alfred H. Terry from General William Tecumseh Sherman, Sherman reported that he had met with President Grant, the secretary of the interior, and the secretary of war, and President Grant had decided that the military should make no further resistance to the occupation of the Black Hills by miners, "it being his belief that such resistance only increased their desire and complicated the troubles." These orders were to be enforced "quietly," and the president's decision was to remain "confidential" (United States v. Sioux Nation of Indians, 448 U.S. 371 [1980]).

President Grant's 1875 order was in direct violation of article 2 of the 1868 treaty which established the Great Sioux Reservation and provided "the United States now solemnly agrees that no persons except those herein designated and authorized so do to, and except such officers, agents, and employees of the Government as may be authorized to enter upon Indian reservations in discharge of duties enjoined by law, shall ever be permitted to pass over, settle upon, or reside in the territory described in this article." In 1875, it was also illegal to make a settlement on any lands "belonging, secured, or granted by treaty with the United States to an Indian tribe." See section 11 of the Act of June 30, 1834 (4 Stat. 730, 25 U.S.C. 180).

With the army's withdrawal from its role as enforcer of the 1868 treaty, the influx of settlers to the Black Hills increased. The secretary of the interior appointed a commission headed by William B. Allison to negotiate an annual rental of the Black Hills for $400,000 or an absolute cession for $6 million. The negotiations broke down (United States v. Sioux Nation of Indians, 448 U.S. 371 [1980]).

1876   In the winter of 1875–76, several bands of Sioux were hunting in the unceded territory north of the North Platte River and east of the summits of the Bighorn Mountains in accordance with articles 11 and 16 of the 1868 treaty. The commissioner of Indian affairs sent instructions to the Indians that they would be declared "hostile" if they did not return to the Great Sioux Reservation by January 31, 1876. Given the severity of the winter, compliance with these instructions was impossible. The secretary of the interior, nevertheless, relinquished his jurisdiction over all "hostile" Sioux, including the Sioux Indians legally exercising their treaty-protected hunting rights in the Powder River Country, to the War Department.

The U.S. Army's campaign against the so-called hostiles in the spring of 1876 resulted in Lt. Col. George A. Custer's attack on an encampment of Sioux Indians (and their Cheyenne-Arapahoe allies) exercising their article 11 and 16 hunting rights on the Little Bighorn River on June 25, 1876. The attack, often referred to as the "Battle of the Little Bighorn" or "Custer's Last Stand," resulted in the defeat of Custer and his Seventh Calvary.

On August 15, 1876, Congress passed an appropriation act (19 Stat. 176) which provided that no further appropriations would be made for the Sioux bands (as required by the 1868 treaty), unless they first relinquished their rights to the hunting grounds outside the Great Sioux Reservation, ceded the Black Hills portion of the reservation, and reached some accommodation with the U.S. government that would enable them to become self-supporting. This appropriation act is now called the "starve or sell" act. A commission, known as the Manypenny Commission, was established to negotiate the sale of the Black Hills pursuant to the act. The commission, however, could only gather signatures from 10 percent of the adult male population of the different Sioux bands instead of the signatures of three-fourths required by article 12 of the 1868 treaty (United States v. Sioux Nation of Indians, 448 U.S. 371 [1980]).

1877 To resolve the "impasse" created by the public's demand for opening the Black Hills for settlement and the Manypenny Commission's failure to obtain the requisite number of signatures necessary to make the 1876 agreement legal, Congress enacted the 1876 agreement into law on February 28, 1877 (19 Stat. 254). The 1877 act had the effect of abrogating article 12 of the 1868 treaty and implementing the terms of the "1876 agreement" on the Sioux bands (United States v. Sioux Nation of Indians, 448 U.S. 371 [1980]).

1920 The Sioux bands, after years of lobbying, finally got Congress to pass a special jurisdictional act which provided them with a forum for adjudication of all claims against the United States "under any treaties, agreements, or laws of Congress, or for the misappropriation of any of the funds or lands of said tribe or band or bands thereof" (Act of June 3, 1920 [41 Stat. 738]).

1923 The Sioux bands hired Washington, D.C., attorney Ralph Case to file their treaty claims under the 1920 special jurisdictional statute. The claims were filed in the Court of Claims as Docket C-531.

1934 Ralph Case amended the original Docket C-531 petition by filing twenty-four separate, amended petitions. The amended petitions were described in a report to the Sioux bands:

Offices of
The Attorneys for the Sioux Nation
1002–1004 National Press Building
Washington, D.C.

Report to the Sioux Nation
June 11th, 1934.

To the Chairmen and Secretaries of the
Tribal Councils and to the Members of
the Sioux Nation

The Attorneys for the Sioux Nation call attention to the date of June 11th, 1934, as thereon we filed in the Court of Claims the separated amended petitions covering all of the band claims included in the original Sioux Petition. Previously and on May 7th, 1934, we filed the separated Tribal Claims. The Tribal Claims are numbered 1 to 11 inclusive, and the Band Claims are numbered 12 to 24 inclusive.

We will shortly send to the President and Secretary of each Tribal Council and as well to the several Superintendents, copies of these 24 separated petitions. It will be impossible for us to supply all of the people of the Sioux

Nation with copies of all of the Petitions. It has required much time and effort to prepare these separated Petitions, but we are convinced that this effort and as well the expense of printing is justified by the advantage we obtain in presenting the issues separately to the Court. We cannot give you here the detail of each one of the separated Amended Petitions, but we do include an outline as comprehensive as possible in this Report.

A. *Tribal Claims*
(Separated Amended Petitions 1 to 11 Inclusive)

Petition No. 1—Education: This Petition deals with the failure of the United States to furnish the school houses, teachers, and supplies to comply with the Treaty of 1868 as extended by the Act of March 2, 1889. We are willing to give credit to the Government for what it expended, but we are asking for payment of money for the failure of the Government to provide the education facilities under the Treaty of 1868.

Petition No. 2—Clothing: This Petition covers the failure of the Government to provide the clothing guaranteed by Article 10 of the Treaty of 1868.

Petition No. 3—Annuities: This Petition covers the failure of the Government to make the appropriation and its failure to disburse. The Government was required to pay the Sioux tribe an annuity of $10.00 per capita for all people roaming and hunting, and $20.00 per capita to all people engaged in farming. We now have proof showing the number of Sioux Indians who were engaged in farming from year to year and we are certain that the Government has failed to make the appropriation to discharge this obligation.

Petition No. 4—Rations: This Petition covers the claim for rations provided by the Treaty of 1868. Under that Treaty, rations were to be provided for four years in specified quantities of food stuff. During the four year period the Government failed to furnish all the food guaranteed by the Treaty and we have made claim for the amount of the shortage.

Petition No. 5—Cows and Oxen: This Petition covers the 1868 Treaty obligation to provide a definite number of cows and oxen for the members of the Sioux Tribe. The Government did purchase and deliver a limited number of animals, but did not fulfill the obligation of the Treaty of 1868, and, therefore we are claiming the shortage as now due.

Petition No. 6—Seeds and Implements: This Petition covers the failure of the Government to provide the seeds and agricultural implements promised to the Sioux people under Article 8 of the Treaty of 1868. This is not a large claim, but the United States disregarded almost entirely its obligation to furnish the seeds and implements required by the Treaty and, therefore, we have made claim for the full amount which should have been expended thereunder.

Petition No. 7—Black Hills: This Petition is the most important of all of the separated Amended Petitions and covers the taking of land by the United

States in 1874 to 1877 inclusive. The land areas finally taken from the Sioux people are of three classes:

Class A. The area taken from the 1868 Treaty Reservation lying between the 43rd and 46th standard parallel to 144th Meridian of the west; on the east the 103rd Meridian and the forks of the Cheyenne River. There are 7,345,157 acres in this area. it is from this area that not less than 400,000,000 dollars in gold has been extracted by white citizens of the United States

Class B. This area includes all of the land outside of the boundaries of the Treaty Reservation of 1868, but inside the boundary agreed to by the Treaty of 1851. The area of this class is nearly 26,000,000 acres, to which the Sioux Tribe had the absolute right of use and occupation.

Class C. The remaining area claimed under this Petition are those lands which by the Treaty of 1851 and the Treaty of 1868 are held and regarded as unceded Indian lands over which the Sioux Tribe had the right to roam and hunt. This area includes 40,500,000 acres of land.

This Claim is based upon the contention that the Sioux Nation has never been compensated for the taking of this vast area of land and we believe that the United States should pay to the Sioux Nation the fair value of the land, together with interest thereon, and against this there may be credited the expenditures made by the United States strictly for the benefit of the people of the Sioux Nation.

Petition No. 8—Lands Added to the 1868 Reservation: This Petition covers the taking of land by the United States from the Sioux Nation, which lands were added to the 1868 Reservation by Executive Order under the terms of the 1868 Treaty. These are the lands east of the Missouri River and west of the 99th Meridian, (exclusive of the Crow Creek Reservation). This area of land was added to the 1868 Treaty Reservation to provide homes for members of the Tribe living on the easterly side of the Missouri River. Without justification and excuse, in the year 1879 the Indians living east of the Missouri River were removed to the westerly side of the river and these lands were thrown open to settlement and sale and homestead entry. Once these lands were added to the 1868 Treaty Reservation as they were by Executive Order, these lands could not be taken away from the Sioux people without just compensation being paid therefor. We have, therefore, asked the Court of Claims to enter judgment in your favor for the value of these lands, which actually belong to the Tribe, but which were taken from them by Executive Order.

Petition No. 9—Wood: This Petition covers the claim for cutting and taking of wood on the 1868 Reservation. We know that the Government cut and used many thousands of cords of wood, either for the uses of the Government or as fuel for steam boats. It is contended that this wood was the private property of the Sioux Nation and we are now asking that the Government pay for the wood which was cut and used, either by the Government or for the benefit of the steamboat lines on the Upper Missouri River.

Petition No. 10—Game: This Petition covers the slaughter of the buffalo and other game animals on the lands of the Sioux Nation owned under the Treaty of 1851 and 1868. The game animals were, as all of us know, the principal food, clothing and housing supply of the Sioux people. The United States guaranteed to the Sioux Nation that the white citizens of the United States should not be permitted to go in and on the Sioux Reservation and take and kill game animals, but, nevertheless, they did so and the buffalo and other animals were slaughtered in numbers running up into the millions. No less than fifteen million animals were slaughtered for their hides only. This wanton destruction of property should be paid for by the United States and we are now asking that the Government properly compensate the Sioux Nation for the destruction of the game animals.

Petition No. 11—Land Cession of 1889: This Petition covers the second most important claim of the Sioux Nation and includes the claim for payment of lands ceded by the Act of of March 2, 1889. We now have the full information covering the exact amount of land open to settlement and entry under this Act of Congress. On March 2, 1889, the Sioux Nation still held title to that portion of Dakota Territory lying west of the boundary of the Crow Creek Indian Reservation and the east bank of the Missouri River; lying north of the 43rd standard parallel, and also including the land north of the Kehapaha and the Niobrara Rivers; lying south of the 46th standard parallel, and likewise including the lands south of the Cannon Ball River; lying east of the 103rd Meridian and the north and south forks of the Cheyenne River.

By the agreement of March 2, 1889, the several separate Reservations were set apart and described. All other lands then owned by the Sioux Nation were ceded to the United States. The United States agreed to put up and did put up three million dollars, which from then on has been known as the Great Sioux Fund. This was to pay in part for the lands. However, the Government never did pay any additional money into the Great Sioux Fund, except for a very small number of dollars. We are now asking that the Government pay to the Sioux Nation what is justly due and owing for the lands ceded to the Government by the Act of March 2, 1889. On March 2, 1889, the Sioux people did not own the lands which were taken previously by the Government on February 28th, 1877 (Black Hills Claim). The Sioux Nation ceded to the Government under the Act of March 2, 1889, only the lands which they, at that time, still owned and controlled, but this area itself which was ceded to the Government included more than ten million acres of land, all of which the Government should have paid for, but which it has never done.

B. *Band Claims*
(Separated Amended Petitions 12–24 Inclusive)

In addition to the foregoing tribal claims, we now have filed Petitions, which are the Separated Band Claims. These band claims are the separate property of the Sioux people on the several Reservations. You will understand that in regard to the band claims the entire Sioux Nation is bringing the suit, but that the proceeds of the band claims belong to the bands and not to the Sioux Nation. From this point on in the Petitions the claims which are asserted by the people of one Reservation belong to those people and the people of another Reservation are not interested except that the entire Nation desires to stand together in the suit. The Sioux Nation therefore is prosecuting the claims of the several bands to recover the money which is due to each band.

Petition No. 12—The Santee Offset: This Petition covers the offset made by the United States in a previous Court of Claims case wherein the Santee people have been charged with all of the money expended under the Treaty of 1868. The '68 Treaty guaranteed to the Santee people certain definite rights and it was the obligation of the United States to make certain disbursements under the Treaty to the Santee people. All of these disbursements up to the time of the decision of the Court of Claims in the Santee case brought under the Act of March 4, 1917, have been charged back against the Santee annuities. This should not have been done and the Santee people are entitled to the amount of money charged against them in the case mentioned which was brought under the Act of March 4, 1917.

Petition No. 13—First Taking of Santee Lands by Executive Order: This Petition covers the taking of lands from the Santee people from the Reservation set apart for the Santees by Executive Order. There is no justification for the taking of these lands without just compensation and, therefore, we have filed this separated action.

Petition No. 14—Second Taking of Santee Lands by Executive Order: This Petition covers the second taking of lands belonging to the Santee people by Executive Order of February 9th, 1885, and this Order took from the Santee people all of the remainder of their lands in Nebraska and the United States should compensate the Santee people for these lands.

Petition No. 15—Sale of Santee Lands in Minnesota, 1861: This Petition covers the sale of 320,000 acres of land in Minnesota at thirty cents an acre. It may be possible to question the price, but we are asking for an accounting from the Government to show us what was done with the $96,000.00 derived from the sale of these lands.

Petition No. 16—Sale of Santee Lands in Minnesota, 1863: This Petition covers the sale of lands in the lower agency in Minnesota under the Act of March 3, 1863.

Petition No. 17—Rosebud—Gregory County Fund: This Petition calls for an accounting for the sale and disposition of lands in Gregory County.

Petition No. 18—Rosebud—Tripp County Fund: This Petition calls for an accounting of the disposition of the moneys derived from the sale of lands in Tripp County.

Petition No. 19—Rosebud—Mellette County Fund: This Petition calls for an accounting of moneys received by the United States for sale of lands in Mellette County.

Petition No. 20—Pine Ridge—Bennett County: This Petition calls for an accounting by the United States covering the moneys received from the sale of lands in Bennett County.

Petition No. 21—Crow Creek Four Percent Fund: This Petition covers the accounting for the fund which was appropriated by the United States to compensate the people of Crow Creek Reservation for the shortage of land imposed upon them by the Act of March 2, 1889.

Petition No. 22—Lower Brule Land Opening: This Petition covers the claim of the Lower Brule people for lands taken from them under the Act of April 21, 1906. Under this Act a portion of the Lower Brule lands was opened to sale and entry, and also under this Act a re-survey of the Reservation was made. This re-survey established the southern boundary some several miles north of the true boundary of the Reservation. The true boundary is the 44th standard parallel, but the actual survey was run three or more miles north of the true boundary of the Reservation. These lands between the survey and the 44th standard parallel were sold or disposed of by the United States, but the title of the Lower Brule people has never been extinguished. Your attorneys are, therefore, asking that the Government pay for these lands and we are asking that payment shall be made of the value of the lands on the date of filing of the original Sioux Petition, May 7th, 1923. We are also asking for an accounting of the disposition of the moneys derived from the sale of lands opened under the Act of April 21, 1906.

Petition No. 23—Cheyenne River Land Opening: This Petition covers an accounting for sale and disposition of lands opened under the Act of 1908, and covering the northerly and westerly portion of the original Cheyenne River Reservation.

Petition No. 24—Standing Rock Land Opening: This Petition covers an accounting for the sale and disposition of lands in the original Standing Rock Reservation opened to sale and entry under the Acts of Congress of 1908 and 1913.

C. *In General*

It should be stated that in filing the Separated Amended Petitions Numbers 1 to 24 inclusive, described briefly above, we have not included any matter or claim not already included in the original Petition filed May 7th, 1923. We are now completing the proof on the Tribal Claims. It is our purpose to urge some of them for trial when the Court of Claims reconvenes in October, 1934. This case throughout its entire progress has been delayed by the slowness of the Government in making and filing its accounting. Even up to the date of writing this Report, the United States has not filed in the Court of Claims the accounting made by the Comptroller General. The Comptroller's report was furnished in April, 1932. The work on this Report was begun January 1, 1925. We have told you many times about this Report and many of your people have seen some of the eight volumes which were prepared by the Comptroller General's office.

We shall now urge that the United States complete whatever proof it has to offer. On our side we are ready to go ahead with the twenty-four cases. We shall make every effort that we can to bring the Tribal Claims to trial in the Fall of this year. All of our time and all of our effort will be given to this end during the coming Summer. . . .

> The Attorneys for the Sioux Nation
> Ralph H. Case, Kingman Brewster
> James S. Y. Ivins, C. C. Calhoun
> Rice Hooe

On June 18, 1934, Congress passed the Indian Reorganization Act (48 Stat. 984). Section 16 of the act allowed one or more tribes or bands residing on the same reservation to consolidate and reorganize as a single "tribe" by adopting constitutions and bylaws.

In 1934, four historic Sioux bands were residing on the Cheyenne River Sioux Reservation in South Dakota, the Minneconjou, Blackfeet, Two Kettle, and No Bows. These four historic Sioux bands consolidated and reorganized under section 16 of the IRA as the "Cheyenne River Sioux Tribe."

In 1934, the historic Oglala band was residing on the Pine Ridge Reservation. The band also consisted of members from other Sioux bands who were incorporated into the tribe (such as Chief Lip's band, whose members were Hunkpapa and Brule Sioux). The historic Oglala band and the members of other Sioux bands residing on the Pine Ridge Reservation consolidated and reorganized under section 16 of the IRA as the "Oglala Sioux Tribe."

1942   The Black Hills Claim (Docket C-531 [7]) was dismissed by the Court of Claims on the basis that the court was not authorized by the 1920 special jurisdictional act to question whether the compensation afforded the Sioux by Congress in 1877 was an adequate price for the Black Hills, and that the Sioux claim in this regard was a moral claim not protected by the Just Compensation Clause of the Fifth Amendment (Sioux Tribe v. United States, 97 Ct. Cl. 613 [1942]).

1943   The U.S. Supreme Court refused to hear the Court of Claims dismissal of the Black Hills claim under the 1920 jurisdictional statute by denying the Sioux bands' petition for a writ of certiorari (Sioux Tribe v. United States, 318 U.S. 789 [1943]).

Events from 1946 to 1960

1946   Congress passed the Indian Claims Commission Act of August 13, 1946 (60 Stat. 1052). Section 2 of the act provided that:

> The Commission shall hear and determine the following claims against the United States on behalf of any Indian tribe, band, or other identifiable group of American Indians residing within the territorial limits of the United States or Alaska: (1) claims in law or equity arising under the Constitution, laws, treaties of the United States, and Executive orders of the President; (2) all other claims in law or equity, including those sounding in tort, with respect to which the claimant would have been entitled to sue in a court of the United States if the United States was subject to suit; (3) claims which would result if the treaties, contracts, and agreements between the United States were revised on the ground of fraud, duress, unconscionable consideration, mutual or unilateral mistake, whether of law or of fact, or any other ground cognizable by a court of equity; (4) claims arising from the taking of the United States, whether as the result of a treaty of cession or otherwise, of lands owned or occupied by the claimant without the payment for such lands of compensation agreed to by the claimant; and (5) claims based on fair and honorable dealings that are not recognized by any existing rule of law or equity. No claim accruing after [August 13, 1946] the date of the approval of this Act shall be considered by the Commission. (60 Stat. 1050, section 2)

Sections 10, 12, 15, and 22 of the act further provided that:

> Any claim within the provisions of this Act may be presented to the Commission by any member of an Indian tribe, band, or other identifiable group of Indians as the representative of all its members; but wherever any tribal organization exists, recognized by the Secretary of the Interior as having authority to represent such tribe, band, or group, such organization shall be accorded the exclusive privilege of representing such Indians, unless fraud, collusion, or laches on the part of such organization be shown to the satisfaction of the Commission. (60 Stat. 1052, section 10)

> The Commission shall receive claims for a period of five years after [August 13, 1946] the date of the approval of this Act and no claim existing before such date but not presented within such period may thereafter be submitted to any court or administrative agency for consideration, nor

will such claim thereafter be entertained by the Congress. (60 Stat. 1052, section 12)

Each such tribe, band, or other identifiable group of Indians may retain to represent its interests in the presentation of claims before the Commission an attorney or attorneys at law, of its own selection, whose practice before the Commission shall be regulated by its adopted procedures. The fees of such attorney or attorneys for all services rendered in prosecuting the claim in question, whether before the Commission or otherwise, shall, unless the amount of such fees is stipulated in the approved contract between the attorney or attorneys and the claimant, be fixed by the Commission at such amount as the Commission, in accordance with standards obtaining for prosecuting similar contingent claims in courts of law, finds to be adequate compensation for services rendered and results obtained, considering the contingent nature of the case, plus reasonable expenses incurred in the prosecution of the claim; but the amount so fixed by the Commission, exclusive of reimbursement for actual expenses, shall not exceed 10 per centum of the amount recovered in any case. . . . (60 Stat. 1052, section 15)

The payment of any claim, after its determination in accordance with this Act, shall be a full discharge of the United States of all claims and demands touching any of the matters involved in the controversy. (60 Stat. 1052, section 22)

1950   Attorney Ralph Case filed the Sioux tribes' original petition in the Indian Claims Commission on August 15, 1950. The case was docketed as "Docket 74."

The following Sioux tribes occupying eight reservations in Montana, North Dakota, South Dakota, and Nebraska were parties to Docket 74:

1. Cheyenne River Sioux Tribe of the Cheyenne River Reservation (South Dakota)
2. Crow Creek Sioux Tribe of the Crow Creek Reservation (South Dakota)
3. Lower Brule Sioux Tribe of the Lower Brule Reservation (South Dakota)
4. Oglala Sioux Tribe of the Pine Ridge Reservation (South Dakota and Nebraska)
5. Rosebud Sioux Tribe of the Rosebud Reservation (South Dakota)
6. Santee Sioux Tribe of Nebraska (Nebraska)
7. Sioux Tribe of the Fort Peck Reservation (Montana)
8. Standing Rock Sioux Tribe of the Standing Rock Reservation (North Dakota and South Dakota)

1954 On April 5, 1954, the Indian Claims Commission dismissed Docket 74 (Sioux Tribe v. United States, 2 Ind. Cl. Comm. 646 [1954]).

1956 On November 7, 1956, the Court of Claims affirmed the Indian Claims Commission's dismissal of Docket 74 (Sioux Tribe of Indians v. United States, 146 F. Supp. 229 [Ct. Cl. 1956]). This resulted in a quandary for elected leaders of the Sioux tribes because their attorney Ralph Case informed them that he intended to appeal the case to the U.S. Supreme Court by filing a petition for a writ of certiorari. Sioux Indian leaders, including Robert Burnette of the Rosebud Sioux Tribe and Helen Peterson of the Oglala Sioux Tribe, questioned Case's litigation strategy when they found out that he failed to make an adequate record before the Indian Claims Commission, and that if the Sioux tribes appealed the case to the Supreme Court, they would lose. The Sioux leaders decided to ask Mr. Case to resign and hire new attorneys to prosecute the case, but the situation was delicate because Mr. Case was extremely popular on the various Sioux reservations and terminating his contract could have caused a backlash among traditional leaders who supported him.

   Helen Peterson was selected to confer with Mr. Case and request his resignation. She was very diplomatic and convinced Case to resign. New attorneys, Arthur Lazarus, Jr., Marvin J. Sonosky, and William Howard Payne, were then sought out and hired to represent the tribes.

1957 On October 4, 1957, before they actually signed their claims attorney contracts, the Lazarus/Sonosky/Payne legal team assisted the eight Sioux tribes in filing a *pro se* motion before the Court of Claims to vacate its 1956 affirmation of the Indian Claims Commission's dismissal of Docket 74 on the basis that Docket 74 had been decided on a distorted and empty record, that Mr. Case agreed with the Government not to press two claims, made concessions which were contrary to fact, and had failed to conduct significant research in the case. See Sioux Tribe v. United States, 500 F.2d 458 (Ct. Cl. 1974).

   On November 5, 1957, the Court of Claims remanded Docket 74 to the Indian Claims Commission for a determination as to: "(1) whether the claimant Indian tribes are entitled on the basis of statements made in support of the above motions to have the proof in this case reopened, and (2) if so, to receive the additional proof sought to be offered and on the basis thereof, together with the record already made, reconsider its prior decision in this matter" (Sioux Tribes v. United States, 182 Ct. Cl. 912 [Ct. Cl. 1957]).

1958 On November 15, 1958, the Court of Claims granted the Sioux tribes' request to reopen Docket 74 and remanded the case to the Indian Claims Commission for a full hearing and to receive additional evidence. See Sioux Tribe v. United States, 182 Ct. Cl. 912 (1968) (Summary of Proceedings).

On November 19, 1958, the Indian Claims Commission reopened Docket 74 and announced it would reconsider its prior judgment on the merits (United States v. Sioux Nation of Indians, 448 U.S. 371 [1980]; also see summary of proceedings in Sioux Tribe v. United States, 182 Ct. Cl. 912 [1968]).

1960   On November 4, 1960, the Indian Claims Commission agreed to allow the Sioux tribes to amend their original Docket 74 petition by substituting two separate petitions to be designated as Docket 74-A and 74-B.

Docket 74-A involved claims for Sioux property outside of western South Dakota that was, according to the United States, voluntarily "ceded" by the Sioux bands under article 2 of the 1868 Fort Laramie Treaty! Docket 74-A consisted of the following claims

1. A recognized title claim for 34 million acres of Sioux lands located west of the Missouri River (outside of western South Dakota) in the states of Montana, Wyoming, North Dakota, and Nebraska; and

2. An aboriginal title claim for 14 million acres of Sioux lands located east of the Missouri River (in the states of North Dakota and South Dakota).

Docket 74-B involved claims for Sioux property confiscated by Congress under the 1877 act in violation of the Just Compensation Clause of the Fifth Amendment. Docket 74-B consisted of the following claims:

1. A claim for 7.3 million acres of the Great Sioux Reservation (the Black Hills) confiscated under article 1 of the 1877 act;

2. A claim for article 11 hunting rights confiscated under article 1 of the 1877 act;

3. A claim for placer (surface) gold removed by trespassing gold miners with U.S. government connivance prior to 1877; and

4. A claim for three rights-of-way confiscated under article 2 of the 1877 act.

DOCKET 74-A (1868 TREATY CLAIMS) FROM 1960 TO 1998

1962   After the Sioux tribes succeeded in reopening Docket 74 in 1960, they attempted three times to amend their petition to allege a wrongful taking under the 1868 treaty. All three amendments were denied by the ICC on May 11, 1960, February 28, 1962, and October 29, 1968 (Sioux Tribe v. United States, 500 F2d 458 [Ct. Cl. 1974]).

1965   The Indian Claims Commission ruled that the 1851 treaty recognized title in the "Sioux or Dahcotah Nation" to approximately 60 million acres of territory situated east of the Missouri River in what is now the states of North Dakota, South Dakota, Nebraska, Wyoming, and Montana (Sioux Tribe v. United States, 15 Ind. Cl. Comm. 577 [1965]).

1969   On December 17, 1969, the Indian Claims Commission allowed the Docket
        74 Sioux tribes to intervene in the suit with the Yankton Sioux (Docket 332-
        C) and include their claims for aboriginal title lands located east of the Mis-
        souri River. It also allowed the Yankton Sioux, for the first time, to assert a
        recognized title claim west and north of the Missouri River on the basis that
        it was a party to the 1851 Fort Laramie Treaty (Sioux Tribe v. United States,
        500 F2d 458 [Ct. Cl. 1974]).

1970   Docket 74-A involved an aboriginal title claim by the Teton and Yanktonai
        divisions to a tract of land largely between the James River and Missouri River
        consisting of approximately 14 million acres (Sioux Nation v. United States,
        23 Ind. Cl. Comm. [1970]). The United States contended that while the Sioux
        exclusively used and occupied much of the 14 million acre aboriginal title
        area, they did not do so either from time immemorial or for a long time prior
        to the United States sovereignty over the area. The ICC rejected this conten-
        tion in 1970, finding that:

> it is clear since the Court of Claims opinion in *Sac and Fox Tribe v. United
> States* . . . that the Sioux need not have exclusively occupied the subject lands
> for a long time prior to United States sovereignty over the area involved.
> The boundaries of the tribe's aboriginal holdings were not frozen as of the
> date of United States sovereignty. . . . It is sufficient that the lands were ex-
> clusively used and occupied for a long time prior to the treaty of cession to
> turn them into domestic territory of the Sioux. . . . That a "long time" ran
> during the period of United States sovereignty over the area involved rath-
> er than during the period of French and Spanish sovereignty is irrelevant
> insofar as the perfecting of Indian title is concerned. (Sioux Nation v. United
> States, 23 Ind. Cl. Comm. 419 [1970]. See also Turtle Mountain Band v.
> United States, 23 Ind. Cl. Comm. 315 [1970] [exclusive use and occupation
> "for a long time" by a tribe is sufficient to give aboriginal title].)

        After finding that the Teton and Yanktonai divisions possessed aboriginal title
        to the 14 million acre area, the ICC determined that "By the Treaty of April
        29, 1868, 15 Stat. 635, which was proclaimed on February 24, 1869, the subject
        lands of the Tetons and Yanktonai were ceded to the United States. . . . The
        valuation date for these lands is February 24, 1869, the date of the proclama-
        tion of the 1868 Treaty" (Sioux Nation v. United States, 23 Ind. Cl. Comm.
        419 [1970]). The boundary of the aboriginal title area is described at 23 Ind.
        Cl. Comm. 424–25.
            The Indian Claims Commission also made the following supplemental
        findings of fact to its August 17, 1969, decision (15 Ind. Cl. Comm. 577) re-
        garding the 34 million acre, 1851 treaty recognized title area involved in Docket
        74-A:

14. The Treaty of Fort Laramie of 1851 (11 Stat. 749) was entered into by the United States and "the chiefs, headmen, and braves of the following Indian nations, residing south of the Missouri River, east of the Rocky Mountains, and north of the lines of Texas and New Mexico, viz: the Sioux or Dahcotahs, Cheyennes, Arrapahoes, Crows, Assiniboines, Gros Ventre, Mandans and Arrickaras." By Article 5 of the treaty the United States recognized title in the "Sioux or Dahcotah Nation" (as that term was used in the treaty) to a designated tract of land (hereinafter "Sioux-Laramie land"). Six Sioux Chiefs signed the treaty; their tribal or band affiliation was not specified. These signers have been identified as five chiefs of the Teton division of Sioux—four of the Brule Band, one of the Two Kettle Band—and one chief of the Yankton division. None of the signers have been identified as being a chief of the Yantonais division of Sioux.

15. The Treaty of Fort Laramie was amended by the Senate and ratified, subject to acceptance of the amendment by the tribal parties. The amendment was accepted separately by the "Sioux of the Platte" and by the "Sioux of the Missouri." Five signatures appear on behalf of the "Sioux of the Missouri." Although the consent does not indicate tribal affiliation, three of the signers have been identified as being Yankton Sioux and two as being Teton Sioux—one of the Miniconjou Band, one of the Sans Arc Band. Ten signatures appear on behalf of the "Sioux of the Platte." No tribal affiliation was specified on the consent, but these signers have been identified as Teton Sioux—five of the Brule Band, and five of the Oglala Band. None of the signers of either of these consents have been identified as Yanktonais.

16. The term "Sioux or Dahcotah Nation" as used in the Treaty of Fort Laramie is ambiguous. In its broadest context, the Sioux Nation is composed of seven divisions: (1) Medawakantons; (2) Sissetons; (3) Wahpakootas; (4) Wahpetons; (5) Yanktons; (6) Yanktonais; and (7) Tetons. The first four of these divisions are collectively referred to as the "Sioux of the Mississippi"; the latter three as the "Sioux of the Missouri." The Sioux of the Mississippi were not part of the "Sioux or Dahcotah Nation" treated with at Fort Laramie.

34. The "Sioux or Dahcotah Nation" with which the United States negotiated at Fort Laramie and in which title was recognized by the Treaty of September 17, 1851, *included the Teton and Yankton divisions of Sioux. Neither the Yanktonai division, nor any of the four Eastern divisions were included in the term "Sioux or Dahcotah Nation"* [emphasis added]. (Sioux Nation v. United States, 24 Ind. Cl. Comm. 147 [1970]).

It should be noted that, in the context of Docket 74, the Court of Claims recognized that there is no *legal entity* called the "Sioux Nation," and that the court "adopted such terminology in the interests of clarity for purposes of a complex case." See Sioux Nation v. United States, 8 Ct. Cl. 80 (1985), [Appendix C at 20 n. 2].

The ICC found that the Yanktonai division of Sioux were not parties to the 1851 treaty because "The Yanktonai, because they resided generally north and east of the Missouri [River] and because they were far removed from either of the roads which the treaty was designated to protect, were not intended to be parties to the treaty" (Sioux Nation v. United States, 24 Ind. Cl. Comm. 147 [1970]).

1974   The Court of Claims ruled that the ICC did not err in excluding the Yanktonai from the 1851 treaty recognized title claim (Sioux Tribe v. United States, 500 F.2d 458 [1974]).

1976   The Indian Claims Commission determined that, as of February 24, 1869, the fair market value of both the recognized title claim (34 million acres) and the aboriginal title claim (14 million acres) in Docket 74-A was $45,685,000.00. This valuation was broken down as follows:

	East of the Missouri	West of the Missouri
Agricultural	$11,135,000	$ 3,790,000
Grazing	$ 9,760,000	$21,000,000
Total	$20,896,000	$24,790,000

See Sioux Tribe v. United States, 38 Ind. Cl. Comm. 485 (1976).

1978   The Indian Claims Commission rendered its final decision on the merits, land valuation, and offsets. The matter came before the ICC on a motion filed by the Sioux tribes for "an order that no offsets, either payments on the claim or gratuities, be deducted" from the award in Docket 74-A (Sioux Nation v. United States, 42 Ind. Cl. Comm. 214 [1978]).

The tribes' position on offsets was that the 1868 treaty "was primarily a treaty of peace rather than a treaty of cession; that the Sioux were unaware that under the treaty the United States was acquiring land; that payments promised by the United States under the treaty were in exchange for peace and other promises made the Sioux; and that therefore, those payments cannot be offset as payments on Plaintiffs' claim for compensation for their lands." The Sioux tribes also asserted that "the nature of the claim and the course of dealings between the parties are such that the Commission should not allow the set off of any gratuitous expenditures by the defendant" (42 Ind. Cl. Comm. 214–15).

The ICC then indicated that "[i]n determining whether certain payments made by the United States are consideration for Indian lands the Commis-

sion must look to see what the parties agreed to" (42 Ind. Cl. Comm. at 216).
In regard to the 1868 treaty, the ICC found that: "In short, the Commission
is unable to determine from the language of the treaty whether the payments
and benefits promised by the United States were in exchange for peace or
other promises, as contended by the plaintiffs, or were in exchange for the
cession of Sioux lands, as urged by the defendant. It is therefore necessary to
examine the history and negotiations leading up to the treaty in an attempt
to ascertain the intent of the parties" (Sioux Nation v. United States, 42 Ind.
Cl. Comm. 214 [1978]).

After examining the history behind the Sioux claim, the ICC found that:

> The Indian Peace Commission presented the proposed treaty to the Sioux
> bands in a series of councils held in the spring of 1868. . . . At these coun-
> cils, after hearing an explanation of the terms of the treaties, the Sioux
> generally voiced these sentiments; . . . 2—*they were unwilling to cede any
> of their lands* [emphasis added]. . . .
>
> [I]t is clear that, based on the representations of the United States ne-
> gotiators, the Indians cannot have regarded the 1868 Treaty as a treaty of
> cession. No-where in the history leading up to the treaty negotiations
> themselves is there any indication that the United States was seeking a land
> cession or that the Sioux were willing to consent to one. On the contrary,
> the evidence is overwhelming that the Sioux would never have signed the
> treaty had they thought they were ceding any land to the United States.
> (Sioux Tribe v. United States, 42 Ind. Cl. Comm. 214 [1978])

The ICC then concluded as follows:

> We conclude as a matter of law that the goods and services promised by
> the United States under the 1868 treaty were not intended by the Sioux
> (or by the government negotiators) to be consideration for any Sioux
> lands. The history of this case makes it clear that this treaty was an attempt
> by the United States to obtain peace on the best terms possible. *Ironical-
> ly, this document, promising harmonious relations, effectuated a vast cession
> of land contrary to the understanding and intent of the Sioux.* Therefore,
> no consideration for the cession of Sioux lands under the 1868 Treaty has
> been promised or paid and the defendant may not offset any part of the
> cost of these goods and services as payments on plaintiffs claim for com-
> pensation [emphasis added]. (Sioux Tribe v. United States, 42 Ind. Cl.
> Comm. 214 [1978])

Note: The findings of the ICC that article 2 of the 1868 treaty effectuated a
"cession" of 48 million acres of Sioux territory as a matter of law even though
the Sioux did not intend to cede any land is outrageous. The findings are also
contrary to the rule of statutory construction that "Indians treaties are to be

interpreted in the sense in which they would naturally be understood by the Indians and any ambiguity is to be resolved in their favor" (Choctaw Nation v. Oklahoma, 397 U.S. 620 [1970]; Winters v. United States, 207 U.S. [1908]; also see Worcester v. Georgia, 32 U.S. 515 [1832]; United States v. Winans, 198 U.S. 371 [1905]; and United States v. Shoshone Tribe of Indians, 304 U.S. 111 [1938]). The findings are also contrary to a previous ruling of the Court of Claims involving the Santee Sioux that the 1868 Fort Laramie Treaty did not effectuate a cession of Sioux territory (Medawakanton and Wahpakoota Bands of Sioux Indians v. United States, 57 Ct. Cl. 357 [1922]).

The Indian Claims Commission also found in 1978 that the Yankton division had a 7 percent interest in the 1851 treaty territory and awarded them compensation for their interest in Docket 332-C. The ICC further found that the Teton division, consisting of the Oglala, Brule, Hunkpapa, Minneconjou, No Bows, Two Kettles, and Blackfeet, owned the remaining 93 percent of the 1851 treaty territory (Sioux Nation v. United States, 42 Ind. Cl. Comm. 214 [1978]; also see Sioux Nation v. United States, 41 Ind. Cl. Comm. 160 [1977], aff'd., 616 F.2d 485 [Ct. Cl. 1980]).

1980   The Court of Claims remanded Docket 74-A to its trial division (United States Claims Court), since the life of the Indian Claims Commission terminated in 1978 and all pending cases in the ICC were transferred to the Court of Claims. The Claims Court determined on remand that the only issue remaining in the case concerned the amount of *offsets* to be allowed against the $43,949,700 land valuation award. The United States made an offer to the tribal claims attorneys (Lazarus/Sonosky/Payne) in 1978 to settle the offset issue in Docket 74-A for $4,200,000. The attorneys accepted the offer with conditions. The conditions were rejected by the United States, but the original offer was left open. The claims attorneys subsequently recommended acceptance of the offer to the Sioux tribes. See Cheyenne River Sioux Tribe v. United States, 806 F.2d 1046 (Fed. Cir. 1986). The Sioux tribes rejected the offer and demanded (among other things) the return of all federal lands in the 48 million acre area.

1983   The United States renewed its offer to settle the offset issue in Docket 74-A. The Sioux tribes refused to consider the offer. The Claims Court then ordered the Sioux Tribes' counsel (Lazarus/Sonosky/Payne) to formally present the settlement offer to the tribes, and further directed the tribes, through their governing bodies, to consider and act upon the offer (Sioux Tribe of Indians v. United States, 3 Cl. Ct. 536 [1983]).

Two Sioux tribes accepted the settlement offer and four Sioux tribes rejected it (Sioux Tribe of Indians v. United States, 8 Cl. Ct. 80 [1985]).

The parties subsequently filed six motions for summary judgment in regards to offsets. Prior to rendering its order to terminate Docket 74-A, the Claims Court ruled on the following three motions:

Summary Judgment Opinion I—Payments on the claims offsets. The court denied the Sioux tribes' request to disapprove these offsets (Sioux Tribe v. United States, Sioux Tribe of Indians v. United States, 6 Cl. Ct. 91 [1984]).

Summary Judgment Opinion II—gratuitous offsets. The court granted the Sioux tribes' request to disapprove these offsets (Sioux Tribe of Indians v. United States, 7 Cl. Ct. 468 [1985]).

Summary Judgment Opinion III—Land Adjustment offsets. The court granted the United States' request to allow these offsets (Sioux Tribe of Indians v. United States, 7 Cl. Ct. 481 [1985]).

The United States claimed approximately $65 million in offsets (Sioux Tribe v. United States, 8 Cl. Ct. 80 [1985]).

1985   On February 22, 1985, the Claims Court, without considering the remaining three motions for summary judgment, entered an order implementing the government's settlement offer of $39,749,000 as its final judgment and terminated Docket 74-A (Sioux Tribe of Indians v. United States, 8 Cl. Ct. 80 [1985]). The court concluded that Docket 74-A had become "an uncontrolled quagmire" and that "[t]he simple fact that four of the reservation tribes are refusing to accept any settlement or award of this Court, which does not include the return of their land, is indicative of the plaintiff's [*sic*] refusal to comprehend, after 35 years of litigation, that this Court can only award money judgments" (ibid.).

On April 23, 1985, the Oglala Sioux Tribe (by and through its attorney Mario Gonzalez) and Cheyenne River Sioux Tribe (by and through its attorney John Peebles) appealed the Claims Court's February 22, 1985, decision terminating Docket 74-A to the U.S. Court of Appeals for the Federal Circuit. The remaining Sioux tribes and the United States filed cross-appeals. The Bureau of Indian Affairs, however, disapproved the Cheyenne River Sioux Tribe's contract with Mr. Peebles on the basis that the Cheyenne River Sioux Tribe already had a contract with counsel for the Sioux Tribe of Indians. Thus, although the appeal was captioned *Cheyenne River Sioux Tribe v. United States,* the Cheyenne River Sioux Tribe did not file a brief or present oral argument in the appeal.

1986   On December 5, 1986, the U.S. Court of Appeals for the Federal Circuit held that the Claims Court improperly imposed upon the parties a settlement offer to which they had not consented, vacated the $39,749,700 award, and remanded the case to the Claims Court "for further proceedings in accordinance with this opinion" (Cheyenne River Sioux Tribe v. United States, 806 F.2d 1046 [Fed. Cir. 1986]). The Federal Circuit made a suggestion to the U.S. attorney and claims attorneys (Lazarus/Sonosky/Payne) on how to bring closure to Docket 74-A:

In vacating the judgment of the Claims Court and remanding for further proceedings, we are not suggesting that a complete trial on all of the offset issues will be required. . . . [T]he parties may be able to stipulate the total dollar amount of various categories of offsets to which the government is entitled. *If the parties can so stipulate, this may be action that counsel for the Sioux Tribe can take as part of the normal conduct of litigation without the necessity for obtaining the approval of their clients* [emphasis added]. (Ibid.)

1987   On March 5, 1987, Claims Court Judge Robert Yock held a conference with claims attorneys Arthur Lazarus, Jr., Marvin J. Sonosky, and William Howard Payne to discuss how to resolve the remaining three summary judgment motions on government offsets.

On March 5, 1987, the Oglala Sioux Tribe (by and through its attorney Mario Gonzalez) filed a Petition for a Writ of Certiorari with the United States Supreme Court to review the final decision of the Federal Circuit. Even though the Oglala Sioux Tribe prevailed in getting the Federal Circuit to vacate the Claims Court's February 22, 1985 decision, the tribe requested the Supreme Court to review the Claims Court's holding that article 2 of the 1868 treaty effectuated a cession of Sioux territory. The U.S. Supreme Court denied the Oglala Sioux Tribe's petition (Oglala Sioux Tribe v. United States, 107 S.Ct. 3184 [1987]).

On July 29, 1987 (after the Supreme Court denied the Oglala Sioux Tribe's Petition for a Writ of Certiorari), the attorneys for the U.S. government and the Sioux tribes (Lazarus/Sonosky/Payne) filed a stipulation of facts "regarding the offsets of the government in this case" and a joint motion "to enter Judgment in accordance with the Stipulation of Facts." The attorneys stipulated to $3,703,892.98 in government offsets, and further stipulated that upon approval of the stipulation by the court, "a final judgment may be entered in the Sum of $40,245,807.02." Both the stipulation and joint motion were signed by Arthur Lazarus, Jr., on behalf of the Sioux tribes (Oglala Sioux Tribe and Rosebud Sioux Tribe v. United States, 862 F2d 275 [Fed. Cir. 1988]).

On July 30, 1987, the Claims Court entered a final judgment that "plaintiff [Sioux Tribe] recover of and from the United States the sum of $43,949,700 less stipulated offsets of $3,703,892.98 for a net amount of $40,245,807.02" (Oglala Sioux Tribe and Rosebud Sioux Tribe v. United States, 862 F2d 275 [Fed. Cir. 1988]).

On September 28, 1987, the Oglala Sioux Tribe and Rosebud Sioux Tribe filed a motion for relief from judgment on the basis that "the attorneys who appeared on behalf of the plaintiffs and agreed to the stipulation and entry of judgment took these actions without notice to or approval of plaintiffs as required by law." The Claims Court denied the motion (Oglala Sioux

Tribe and Rosebud Sioux Tribe v. United States, 862 F2d 275 [Fed. Cir. 1988]).

1988   On November 23, 1988, the U.S. Court of Appeals for the Federal Circuit affirmed the Claims Court's denial of the Oglala Sioux Tribe's and Rosebud Sioux Tribe's motion for relief from judgment (Oglala Sioux Tribe and Rosebud Sioux Tribe v. United States, 862 F2d 275 [Fed. Cir. 1988]). In a dissenting opinion, Judge Newman stated that:

> The entry of judgment is surely not a routine 'evidentiary stipulation' such as is encountered in day-to-day trial management: not only because the stipulation disposes of some 3.7 million dollars in moneys previously adjudged to be due the Sioux Indians; but because counsel for both sides knew that since at least 1979 tribes representing the majority of Sioux Indians had given instructions contrary to the settlement. The record contains two resolutions of the Oglala Sioux Tribal Council informing counsel that it no longer sought money damages, but wanted to pursue legal and legislative strategies to gain return of ancestral lands. These resolutions also directed counsel to have the Oglala Sioux Tribe dismissed from this litigation. . . .
>
> A lawyer can not be authorized by a court to make a settlement and bind the client contrary to the client's wishes. Nor can either the court or the United States ignore the tribes' several attempts to discontinue Mr. Lazarus' representation. The court does not discuss the asserted violation of 25 U.S.C. 81.
>
> In light of this extended history, the Claims Court's acceptance of the Stipulation of Facts and the grant of the Joint Motion To Enter Judgment is incongruous; and its denial of appellants' motion for relief [from judgment] under Rule 60 (b) is in plain error, in light of their undisputed assertion that they were given no prior notice of the settlement. (Ibid.)

1989   On October 10, 1989, Eddie Brown, assistant secretary of the interior for Indian affairs, issued a report entitled "Results of Research Report of Judgment Funds to the Sioux Tribe of Indians in Docket 74 before the United States Claims Court" to the two BIA area offices serving the Docket 74 Sioux tribes.

The "Results of Research Report" for Docket 74-A contained the following language regarding distribution of the $40,245,807.02 award:

> The Act of October 17, 1973, as amended, requires that we submit a Secretarial Plan to Congress within one year from the date of appropriation of the funds. . . . In this case, the Secretarial Plan must be submitted to Congress on or before June 4, 1990. Following a 60-day Congressional review period, the Secretarial Plan will become effective, if a joint resolution of disapproval is not passed by the Congress. The funds will then

become available to the beneficiary entities. *If we do not meet the December 5 deadline and if we do not submit a Secretarial Plan within the specified one year period, as has occurred in the case of Docket 74-B, legislation will be required to provide for the use of the funds* [emphasis added].

Since no plan was adopted by the Sioux bands prior to the June 4, 1990, deadline, the funds cannot be distributed without new legislation authorizing the distribution of funds. In the meantime, the $40,245,807.02 award (minus 10 percent attorney fees) has been deposited in interest bearing accounts by the secretary of the interior.

DOCKET 74-B (BLACK HILLS CLAIM) FROM 1960 TO 1998

1974   The Indian Claims Commission ruled that the 1877 act constituted an unconstitutional taking of the Black Hills and three rights-of-way under the Just Compensation Clause of the Fifth Amendment; that the Congress acted pursuant to its power of eminent domain and was required to pay just compensation to the Docket 74 Sioux. The ICC then awarded the Docket 74 Sioux $17.1 million for the 7.3 million acres of Black Hills land that the United States confiscated, plus 5 percent simple interest from the time of the taking. The ICC also awarded the Docket 74 Sioux compensation for placer (surface) gold removed by trespassing miners prior to 1877, and for the three rights-of-way across the reduced Great Sioux Reservation (Sioux Nation v. United States, 33 Ind. Cl. Comm. 151 [1974]). The total award in Docket 74-B was $105 million.

1975   On appeal, the Court of Claims, without deciding the merits, dismissed the Indian Claims Commission's 1974 final judgment on the basis that the appeal was barred by *res judicata* since the Black Hills claim had been previously decided against the Sioux in 1942. The Docket 74 Sioux argued that the earlier dismissal was for lack of jurisdiction, not a dismissal on the merits of their claims (United States v. Sioux Nation, 207 Ct. Cl. 234, 518 F.2d 1298 [1975]). The Supreme Court subsequently denied a Petition for a Writ of Certiorari filed by the Docket 74 Sioux (Sioux Nation v. United States, 423 U.S. 1016 [1975]).

1978   On March 13, 1978, Congress passed a special jurisdictional statute allowing the Court of Claims to review the Indian Claims Commission's 1974 judgment *de novo* (Act of March 13, 1978 [92 Stat. 153]). The Black Hills Claim (Docket 74-B) was refiled in the Court of Claims under the 1978 jurisdictional statute as Docket 148-78. The parties to Docket 148-78 thereafter stipulated that the Indian Claims Commission's record in Docket 74-B could be used by the Court of Claims to decide the merits of the Black Hills Claim.

1979   The Court of Claims heard the merits of the Black Hills Claim *de novo,* and affirmed the Indian Claims Commission's 1974 judgment (United States v. Sioux Nation of Indians, 220 Ct. Cl. 442, 601 F.2d 1157 [1979]).

1980   On June 30, 1980, the Supreme Court affirmed the 1979 judgment of the Court
        of Claims (United States v. Sioux Nation of Indians, 488 U.S. 371 [1980]). The
        Docket 74 Sioux were awarded $102 million for Black Hills land ($17.1 mil-
        lion in principle and $85 million in simple interest from 1877 to 1980), and
        $3 million for the placer gold and three rights-of-ways. (Note: The Court of
        Claims subsequently awarded the claims attorneys [Lazarus/Sonosky/Payne]
        10 percent of the final $105 million judgment as attorneys' fees.)

        On July 18, 1980, the Oglala Sioux Tribe (by and through its attorney Mario
        Gonzalez) filed an independent class action in U.S. District Court at Rapid
        City, South Dakota, against the United States, several cities and towns, and
        individuals to quiet title to the entire Black Hills taking area and for $11 bil-
        lion in damages for the denial of the absolute and undisturbed use and oc-
        cupation of the Black Hills for 103 years. The Oglala Sioux Tribe argued that
        is was not a party to the 1980 Supreme Court case because it had not autho-
        rized attorney Lazarus to refile the Black Hills case *de novo* under the 1978
        jurisdictional statute; that it had allowed its claims attorney contract with
        Lazarus to expire by its own terms in 1977, and decided to seek land restora-
        tion in the Black Hills, in addition to compensation. The Oglala Sioux Tribe
        also argued that the 1877 act was unconstitutional, not only under the just
        compensation clause of the Fifth Amendment but also under the public
        purpose and due process clauses of the Fifth Amendment.

        On September 11, 1980, the U.S. District Court dismissed the case for lack
        of subject matter jurisdiction (Oglala Sioux Tribe v. United States, Civil No.
        80-5062 [D.S.D. 1980]).

1981   The Court of Claims awarded the Docket 74 claims attorneys (Lazarus/
        Sonosky/Payne) 10 percent of the Black Hills (Docket 74-B) award for attor-
        ney's fees (Sioux Nation v. United States, 650 F.2d 244 [Ct. Cl. 1981]).

        The United States Court of Appeals for the Eighth Circuit, located in St.
        Louis, Missouri, affirmed the district court's dismissal of the Oglala Sioux
        Tribe's quiet title/damages case on the basis that the Indian Claims Commis-
        sion (whose jurisdiction was limited to awards of monetary compensation
        only) was the Oglala Sioux Tribe's "exclusive remedy" for litigating the claim
        (Oglala Sioux Tribe v. United States, 650 F.2d 140 [8th Cir. 1981]).

1982   The U.S. Supreme Court refused to hear the Eighth Circuit's affirmation of
        the U.S. District Court's dismissal of the Oglala Sioux Tribe's quiet title/dam-
        ages case for the Black Hills (Oglala Sioux Tribe v. United States, 455 U.S. 907
        [1982]).

1983   Another case filed by the Oglala Sioux Tribe (by and through its attorney
        Mario Gonzalez) against Homestake Mining Company was also dismissed
        for lack of jurisdiction on the basis that the United States was an indispens-
        able party to the case, and since the United States could not be sued, neither

could Homestake Mining Company (Oglala Sioux Tribe v. Homestake Mining Co., 722 F.2d 1407 [8th Cir. 1983]). Homestake Mining Company operates the largest gold and silver mine in North America located in the Black Hills at Lead, South Dakota.

1985   On July 17, 1985, Senator Bill Bradley of New Jersey introduced "The Sioux Nation Black Hills Act" (S. 1453) in the Ninety-ninth Congress. This bill became known as "the Bradley Bill." A companion bill, H.R. 3651, was introduced in the U.S. House of Representatives by Congressman James Howard of New Jersey, on October 30, 1985.

1986   On July 16, 1986, a hearing was held on S. 1453 before the Senate Select Committee on Indian Affairs in Washington, D.C.

1987   On March 10, 1987, Senator Bradley reintroduced the "Bradley Bill" as S. 705 in the One-hundredth Congress. A companion bill, H.R. 1506, was introduced in the U.S. House of Representatives by Congressman James Howard of New Jersey.

The sponsors and cosponsors of S. 705 and H.R. 1506,
as of June 24, 1988, were all Democrats and included:

United States Senate

Chief Sponsor—Senator Bill Bradley (D-NJ)
Senator Daniel Inouye (D-HA)
Senator Claiborne Pell (D-RI)

United States House of Representatives

Chief Sponsor—Representative James Howard (D-NJ)
Representative Morris Udall (D-AZ)
Representative George Miller (D-CA)
Representative William Lipinski (D-IL)
Representative Walter Fauntroy (D-DC)
Representative Stephen Solarz (D-NY)
Representative Major Owens (D-NY)
Representative John Lewis (D-GA)
Representative Norman Mineta (D-CA)
Representative Robert Garcia (D-NY)
Representative Matthew Martinez (D-CA)
Representative David Bonior (D-MI)
Representative Edolphus Towns (D-NY)
Representative George Brown, Jr. (D-CA)
Representative Claude Pepper (D-FL)

Note: Representative Howard died after H.R. 1506 was introduced in the House of Representatives. No hearings were held on S. 705 or H.R. 1506.

1990   On September 19, 1990, Congressman Matthew Martinez of California introduced the Black Hills Bill (H.R. 5680) developed by the Grey Eagle Society in the One-hundred and first Congress. The bill was an amended version of the Bradley Bill, S. 705. The bill was referred to the Committee on Interior and Insular Affairs. No hearing was held on the bill. Congressman Martinez was also one of the cosponsors of the House version of the Bradley Bill (H.R. 1506) in 1987.

DOCKETS 74-A AND 74-B FROM 1990 TO 1998

1996   On June 6, 1996, Congressman Bill Barrett of Nebraska introduced H.R. 3595 in the U.S. House of Representatives. The bill proposed to pay out the Santee Sioux Tribe of Nebraska's "proportionate share" of Docket 74-A.

   A hearing was held on H.R. 3595 on August 1, 1996, before the Resources Subcommittee on Native American and Insular Affairs. Congressman Barrett and Santee Sioux tribal chairman Arthur "Butch" Denny submitted written testimony in support of the bill. Deborah J. Maddox, director of the Office of Tribal Services, U.S. Department of the Interior, submitted written testimony indicating that the Interior Department had no position on the bill "because it affected eight other tribes."

   Johnson Holy Rock of the Oglala Sioux Tribe submitted written testimony on behalf of the Oglala Sioux Tribe opposing the bill and testified against the bill at the hearing. Others testifying at the hearing against the bill were John Yellow Bird Steele, president of the Oglala Sioux Tribe, Gregg Bourland, chairman of the Cheyenne River Sioux Tribe, and William Kindle, president of the Rosebud Sioux Tribe. The bill died in committee.

1998   Docket 74-A: The larger Sioux tribes continue to reject the cram down of the final $40,245,807.02 judgment in Docket 74-A, demanding instead that the United States return all federal lands to the Sioux tribes in the 48 million acre area.

   Docket 74-B: The anti-Indian forces in South Dakota (such as the Open Hills Association organized by Senator Tom Daschle) still continue to oppose land restoration proposals to settle Docket 74-B.

   On the other hand, as of April 8, 1998, the total award for both the 1868 Treaty Claim (Docket 74-A) and the Black Hills Claim (Docket 74-B, aka Docket 148-78), according to the U.S. Department of the Interior's Division of Trust Fund Services, is as follows:

1. Docket 74-A	$ 67,073,267.88
2. Docket 148-78	$473,161,163.29
Total	$540,234,431.17

See *Indian Country Today,* Apr. 27–May 4, 1998, p. 1.

Although some of the Sioux tribes, like the Fort Peck Sioux Tribe of Montana, continue to request their "proportionate share" of the Docket 74-A award, the larger tribes, the Cheyenne River Sioux Tribe, the Oglala Sioux Tribe, the Rosebud Sioux Tribe, and the Standing Rock Sioux Tribe, continue to remain steadfast in the rejection of both the Docket 74-A and 74-B awards, demanding instead the restoration of federal lands in both claims areas.

The Oglala Sioux Tribe also continues to demand a fair and honorable settlement for Black Hills lands held by *private parties* consistent with Lakota religious beliefs, since the Black Hills are religious property that cannot be sold for any amount of money.

Appendix I

A Resolution Expressing the Federal Government's Deep Regret for the 1890 Wounded Knee Massacre

SENATE CONCURRENT RESOLUTION 153—RELATIVE TO THE 100TH ANNIVERSARY OF THE TRAGEDY AT WOUNDED KNEE CREEK, S.D.

Mr. INOUYE (for himself, Mr. McCain, Mr. Cochran, Mr. Murrowski, Mr. Reid, Mr. Daschle, Mr. Gorton, Mr. DeConcini, Mr. Burdick, Mr. Pressler, Mr. Bradley, and Mr. Hatfield) submitted the following concurrent resolution; which was referred to the Committee on the Judiciary:

S. Con. Res. 153

Whereas, in order to promote racial harmony and cultural understanding, the Governor of the State of South Dakota has declared that 1990 is a Year of Reconciliation between the citizens of South Dakota and the member bands of the Great Sioux Nation:

Whereas the Sioux people who are descendants of the victims and survivors of the Wounded Knee Massacre have been striving to reconcile and, in a culturally appropriate manner, to bring to an end their 100 years of grieving for the tragedy of December 29, 1890;

Whereas historians regard the 1890 Wounded Knee Massacre as the last armed conflict between Indian warriors and the United States Cavalry which brought to a close an era in the history of this country commonly referred to as the Indian wars period characterized by an official government policy of forcibly removing the Indian tribes and bands from the path of westward expansion and settlement through placement on reservations;

Whereas this era of government policy has been replaced by a more enlightened policy of Indian self-determination and respect for human rights characterized by a recognition of the valuable contribution of Indian cultures, traditions, and values to the history and fabric of American society;

Whereas, on September 25, 1990, hearings were conducted in the United States Senate by the Select Committee on Indian Affairs regarding the historical circumstances surrounding the Wounded Knee Massacre and to receive testimony regarding a proposed Wounded Knee Memorial and the need to designate the area an historic site or national monument in order to properly preserve and maintain the terrain; and

Whereas it is proper and timely for the Congress of the United States of America to acknowledge, on the one hundredth anniversary of the Massacre at Wounded Knee Creek, to express its deep regret to the Sioux people and in particular to the descendants of the victims and survivors of this terrible tragedy, and to support the reconciliation efforts of the State of South Dakota and the Wounded Knee Survivors Association: Now, therefore, be it

Resolved by the Senate (the House of Representatives concurring), That—

(1) the Congress, on the occasion of the one hundredth anniversary of the Wounded Knee Massacre of December 29, 1890, hereby acknowledges the historical significance of this event as the last armed conflict of the Indian wars period resulting in the tragic death and injury of approximately 350–375 Indian men, women, and children of Chief Big Foot's band of Minneconjou Sioux and hereby expresses its deep regret on behalf of the United States to the descendants of the victims and the survivors and their respective tribal communities;

(2) the Congress also hereby recognizes and commends the efforts of reconciliation initiated by the State of South Dakota and the Wounded Knee Survivors Association and expresses its support for the establishment of a suitable and appropriate Memorial to those who were so tragically slain at Wounded Knee which could inform the American public of the historic significance of the events at Wounded Knee and accurately portray the heroic and courageous campaign waged by the Sioux people to preserve and protect their lands and their way of life during this period; and

(3) the Congress hereby expresses its commitment to acknowledge and learn from our history, including the Wounded Knee Massacre, in order to provide a proper foundation for building an ever more humane, enlightened, and just society for the future.

Appendix J

A Bill to Establish a Wounded Knee National Tribal Park

A BILL

104th Congress, 12st Session
S. 382
To establish a Wounded Knee National Tribal Park, and for other purposes.

———————

IN THE SENATE OF THE UNITED STATES
February 9 (legislative day, January 30), 1995
Mr. Daschle (for himself, Mr. Pressler, Mr. Campbell, Mr. Simon, Mr. Pell, and Mr. Dorgan) introduced the following bill; which was read twice and referred to the Committee on Indian Affairs.

———————

A Bill
   Be it enacted by the Senate and House of Representatives of the U.S. of America in Congress assembled,

SEC. 1, SHORT TITLE.
   This Act may be cited as the "Wounded Knee National Tribal Park Establishment Act of 1995."

SEC. 2, FINDINGS AND PURPOSES
(a) Findings. The Congress finds that
   (1) in December of 1890, approximately 350 to 375 Sioux men, women, and children under the leadership of Chief Big Foot journeyed from the Cheyenne River Indian Reservation to the Pine Ridge Indian Reservation at the invitation of Chief Red Cloud to help make peace between non-Indians and Indians;

(2) the journey of Chief Big Foot and his band of Minneconjou Sioux occurred during the Ghost Dance Religion period when extreme hostility existed between Sioux Indians and non-Indians residing near the Sioux reservations, and the United States Army assumed control of the Sioux Reservations;

(3) Chief Big Foot and his band were intercepted on the Pine Ridge Indian Reservation at Porcupine Butte by Major Whiteside, surrendered unconditionally under a white flag of truce, and were escorted to Wounded Knee Creek, where Colonel Forsyth assumed command;

(4) on December 29, 1890, an incident occurred in which soldiers under the command of General Forsyth killed and wounded over 300 members of the band of Chief Big Foot, most all of whom were unarmed and entitled to protection of their rights to property, person, and life under Federal law.

(5) the 1890 Wounded Knee Massacre is a historically significant event because the event marks the last military encounter of the Indian wars period of the 19th century;

(6) in S. Con. Res. 153 (101st Cong. 2d Sess.) Congress apologized to the Sioux people for the 1890 Massacre;

(7) (A) paragraph (2) of such concurrent resolution provides that Congress "expresses its support for the establishment of a suitable and appropriate Memorial to those who were so tragically slain at Wounded Knee which could inform the American public of the historic significance of the events at Wounded Knee and accurately portray the heroic and courageous campaign waged by the Sioux people to preserve and protect their lands and their way of life during this period"; and

(B) paragraph (3) of such concurrent resolution provides that Congress "express its commitment to acknowledge and learn from our history, including the Wounded Knee Massacre in order to provide a proper foundation for building an ever more humane, enlightened, and just society for the future";

(8) the Wounded Knee Massacre site, and sites relating to the 1890 Wounded Knee Massacre and Ghost Dance Religion on the Cheyenne River Indian Reservation and Pine Ridge Indian Reservation, are nationally significant cultural and historical sites that must be protected through the designation of the sites as a national tribal park; and

(9) the Wounded Knee Massacre is a nationally significant event that must be memorialized by establishing suitable and appropriate memorials to the Indian victims of the Massacre, located on the Cheyenne River Indian Reservation and Pine Ridge Indian Reservation,

(b) PURPOSES. The purposes of this act are to

(1) establish the Wounded Knee National Tribal Park consisting of

(A) sites relating to the 1890 Wounded Knee Massacre and Ghost Dance Religion located on the Cheyenne River Indian Reservation; and

(B) the 1890 Wounded Knee Massacre Site and sites relating to the Massacre and Ghost Dance Religion located on the Pine Ridge Indian Reservation;

(2) establish suitable and appropriate national monuments within both units of the Wounded Knee National Tribal Park to memorialize the Indian victims of the 1890 Wounded Knee Massacre; and

(3) authorize feasibility studies to

(A) establish the route of Chief Big Foot from the Cheyenne River Indian Reservation to Wounded Knee as a national historic trail; and

(B) establish a visitor information and orientation center on the Cheyenne River Indian Reservation.

SEC. 3 DEFINITIONS.

As used in this Act:

(1) COMMISSION. The term "Commission" means the Wounded Knee National Tribal Park Advisory Commission established under section 8(a).

(2) NORTH UNIT. The term "North Unit" means the area of the Park comprised of the sites referred to in section 2(b) (1) (A).

(3) PARK. The term "Park" means the Wounded Knee National Tribal Park established under section 4.

(4) REAL PROPERTY. For the purposes of this Act, the term "real property" includes lands, and all mineral rights, water rights, easements, permanent structures, and fixtures on such lands.

(5) SECRETARY. The term "Secretary" means the Secretary of the Interior.

(6) SOUTH UNIT. The term "South Unit" means the area of the park comprised of the sites referred to in section 2(b)(1) (B).

SEC. 4. ESTABLISHMENT OF WOUNDED KNEE NATIONAL TRIBAL PARK.

(a) ESTABLISHMENT.

(1) IN GENERAL. The Secretary shall establish a national tribal park to be known as the "Wounded Knee National Tribal Park," as generally described in the third alternative of the report completed by the National Park Service entitled "Draft Study of Alternatives, Environmental assessment, Wounded Knee, South Dakota," and dated January 1993, and as more particularly described in this Act.

(2) AREA INCLUDED IN PARK. The Wounded Knee National Tribal Park shall consist of:

(A) North Unit that may include

(i) such sites relating to the 1890 Wounded Knee Massacre and Ghost Dance Religion, including the campsite of Chief Big Foot at Deep Creek, as the Cheyenne River Sioux Tribe, in consultation with the Director of the National Park Service, considers necessary to include in such unit;

(ii) a cultural center and museum complex;

(iii) projects described in section 9(b)(2); and

(iv) a suitable and appropriate national monument to memorialize Chief Big Foot and his band of Minneconjou Sioux; and

(B) a South Unit that may include

(i) the 1890 Wounded Knee Massacre site, as generally described in the 1990 boundaries studies authorized by the National Park Service, and such other sites relating to the 1890 Wounded Knee Massacre and Ghost Dance Religion as the Oglala Sioux Tribe, in consultation with the Director of the National Park Service, considers necessary to include in such Unit;

(ii) a cultural center and museum complex at or near the Wounded Knee Massacre Site;

(iii) projects described in section 9(b)(2); and

(iv) a suitable and appropriate national monument to memorialize the Sioux Indians involved in the 1890 Wounded Knee Massacre.

(b) COOPERATIVE AGREEMENTS.

(1) IN GENERAL. The Secretary shall enter into a cooperative agreement with the Cheyenne River Sioux Tribe with respect to the North Unit, and the Oglala Sioux Tribe with respect to the South Unit to carry out planning, design, construction, operation, maintenance, and replacement activities, as appropriate, for the units.

(2) REQUIREMENTS FOR COOPERATIVE AGREEMENTS. A cooperative agreement entered into under paragraph (1) shall set forth, in a manner acceptable to the Secretary,

(A)(i) the responsibilities of the parties referred to in paragraph (1) with respect to the North Unit and South Unit; and

(ii) the manner in which contracts to carry out such activities will be administered;

(B) the procedures and requirements for the approval and acceptance of the design of, and construction of the North Unit and South Unit;

(C) such federal management policies described in the publication entitled "Management Policies, U.S. Department of the Interior, National Park Service, 1988" as Secretary considers necessary to qualify both units of the Park for affiliation;

(D) a general management plan for each unit of the Park that shall include plans

(i) to protect and preserve the religious sanctity of the Wounded Knee Massacre site and other religious sites located within each unit;

(ii) to restore the Wounded Knee Massacre site, and other important historic sites located within the units, to the original condition of the sites at the time of the Massacre, including the removal of all buildings and structures that have no historical significance;

(iii) for the enactment of tribal zoning ordinances to protect areas surrounding each unit from commercial development and exploitation;

(iv) for the implementation of a continuing program of public involvement, interpretation, and visitor education concerning the Lakota
Sioux history and culture within each unit;

(v) to protect, interpret, and preserve important archaeological and pa-
leontological sites within each unit;

(vi) for visitor use facilities, and the training and employing of tribal
members within each unit, as provided in subsection (e); and

(vii) to waive or require entrance fees at the Wounded Knee Massacre site;
and

(E) the role and responsibilities of the Advisory Commission established under section 8(a) in relation to both units.

(c) TITLE.

(1) PROPERTY ACQUIRED FOR THE NORTH UNIT. Title to all real property acquired
for the North Unit of the Wounded Knee National Tribal Park shall be held
in trust by the United States for the Cheyenne River Sioux Tribe.

(2) PROPERTY ACQUIRED FOR THE SOUTH UNIT. Title to all real property acquired
in the South Unit of the Wounded Knee National Tribal Park shall be held in
trust by the United States for the Oglala Sioux Tribe.

(d) TECHNICAL ASSISTANCE.

(1) IN GENERAL. The Secretary may provide technical assistance to the Cheyenne
River Sioux Tribe and Oglala Sioux Tribe for carrying out the activities described in subsection (b) (1).

(2) TRAINING. In addition to providing the assistance described in paragraph (1),
the Secretary may train and employ members of the tribes concerning the operation and maintenance of both units, including training in

(A) the provision of public services, management of visitor use facilities, interpretation and visitor education on Sioux history and culture, and ar-
tifact curation at both units; and

(B) the interpretation, management, protection, and preservation of other
historical and natural properties at both units.

(e) APPLICATION OF THE INDIAN SELF-DETERMINATION ACT. Except as otherwise
provided in this Act, the activities described in subsection (b) (1) shall be subject to the Indian Self-Determination Act (25 U.S.C. 450 et seq.).

SEC. 5. ACQUISITION OF LANDS FOR WOUNDED KNEE NATIONAL TRIBAL PARK.

(a) IN GENERAL. The Cheyenne River Sioux Tribe and Oglala Sioux Tribe may acquire
by purchase from a willing seller, by gift or devise, by exchange, or in other manner

(1) surface and subsurface rights to any tract of fee-patented or trust land; or

(2) easements that cover such lands, that those tribes, in consultation with the
Secretary, consider necessary for inclusion in the North Unit or the South Unit
of the Wounded Knee National Tribal Park.

(b) FINANCIAL ASSISTANCE. The Secretary may provide financial assistance to the Cheyenne River Sioux Tribe and the Oglala Sioux Tribe to acquire land and any interest in land or other real property that is necessary for a unit of the Park.

SEC. 6 MANAGEMENT

(a) MANAGEMENT OF NORTH UNIT.

(1) IN GENERAL. The Cheyenne River Sioux Tribe, or a designated agency or authority of that tribe shall operate, maintain, and manage the North Unit pursuant to the terms and conditions contained in a cooperative agreement between the Secretary and the Cheyenne River Sioux Tribe entered into by the Secretary and the tribe pursuant to section 4(b).

(2) EXCLUSION. The Cheyenne River Sioux Tribe shall have no jurisdiction or authority over the South Unit.

(b) MANAGEMENT OF SOUTH UNIT.

(1) IN GENERAL. The Oglala Sioux Tribe, or a designated agency or authority of such tribe, shall operate, maintain, and manage the South Unit pursuant to the terms and conditions contained in a cooperative agreement between the Secretary and the Oglala Sioux Tribe entered into by the Secretary and the tribe pursuant to section 4(b).

(2) EXCLUSION. The Oglala Sioux Tribe shall have no jurisdiction or authority over the North Unit.

SEC. 7 PLANNING AND DESIGN OF NATIONAL MONUMENTS; FEASIBILITY STUDIES.

(a) MONUMENTS.

(1) IN GENERAL. Except as provided in paragraph (2), the national monuments on the North Unit and South Unit authorized by subparagraphs (A) (iv) and (B) (iv) of section 4(a) (2) shall be planned, designed, and constructed by the Secretary, after consultation with an advisory committee that the Secretary shall appoint in consultation with

(A) the Wounded Knee Survivors Association of Cheyenne River Indian Reservation;

(B) the Wounded Knee Survivors Association of the Pine Ridge Indian Reservation, and

(C) direct descendants of the band of Minneconjou Sioux of Chief Big Foot.

(2) AUTHORITY OF THE CHEYENNE RIVER SIOUX TRIBAL COUNCIL AND THE OGLALA SIOUX TRIBAL COUNCIL.

(A) The Cheyenne River Sioux Tribal Council and the Oglala Sioux Tribal Council shall have no authority to plan and design the monuments referred to in paragraph (1).

(B) The Cheyenne River Sioux Tribal Council and the Oglala Sioux Tribal Council shall have the authority to enter into contracts for the construction, operation, maintenance, and replacement of the monuments under the Indian Self-Determination Act (25 U.S.C. 450 f et seq.).

(b) FEASIBILITY STUDIES
  (1) IN GENERAL. The Secretary shall complete feasibility studies to
    (A) establish and mark the route taken by Chief Big Foot and his band from the Cheyenne River Indian Reservation to Wounded Knee as a national historic trail; and
    (B) establish a visitor information and orientation center on the Cheyenne River Indian Reservation.
  (2) REPORT. Not later than 1 year after funds are initially made available to the Secretary for a feasibility study conducted under this subsection, the Secretary shall complete the study and submit a report that contains the findings of the study to Congress.

SEC. 8 WOUNDED KNEE NATIONAL TRIBAL PARK ADVISORY COMMISSION

(a) IN GENERAL. There is established within the Department of the Interior the Wounded Knee National Tribal Park Advisory Commission. The Commission shall advise regularly the Cheyenne River Sioux Tribe and Oglala Sioux Tribe, or any designated agency or authority of either tribe, concerning the management and administration of the North Unit and South Unit.

(b) ROLE AND RESPONSIBILITIES. The role and responsibilities of the Commission shall be defined in the cooperative agreements that the Secretary shall enter into with the Cheyenne River Sioux Tribe and Oglala Sioux Tribe under section 4(b). The Cheyenne River Sioux Tribe and Oglala Sioux Tribe, or any designated agency or authority of either such tribe, shall consult with the Commission not less frequently than 4 times each year.

(c) PERIOD OF OPERATION. The Commission shall exist for such time as either the North Unit or the South Unit is in existence.

(d) MEMBERSHIP. The Secretary shall appoint 17 members of the Commission. In addition, the Director of the National Park Service or a designee of the Director shall serve as an ex-officio member of the Commission. The Secretary shall appoint the members of the Commission after consulting with, and soliciting a recommendation from each of the following:
  (1) The Chairman of the Cheyenne River Sioux Tribe.
  (2) The President of the Oglala Sioux Tribe.
  (3) The Chairman of the Wounded Knee Community Council on the Pine Ridge Indian Reservation.
  (4) The Chairman of the Wounded Knee Subcommunity Council on the Pine Ridge Reservation.
  (5) The Chairman of the White Clay Community Council on the Pine Ridge Indian Reservation.
  (6) The Chairman of District No. 3 on the Cheyenne River Indian Reservation.
  (7) The Chairman of Red Scaffold Community on the Cheyenne River Indian Reservation.

(8) The Chairman of Cherry Creek Community on the Cheyenne River Reservation.

(9) The Chairman of the Bridger Community on the Cheyenne River Reservation.

(10) The Chairman of the Board of Directors of the Oglala Sioux Parks and Recreation Authority.

(11) The President of the Wounded Knee Survivors Association on the Cheyenne River Indian Reservation.

(12) The President of the Wounded Knee Survivors Association on the Pine Ridge Indian Reservation.

(13) The Secretary of the Smithsonian Institution.

(14) (i) The Governor of the State of South Dakota and the historic preservation officer of such state.

(ii) The Governor of the State of Nebraska and the historic preservation officer of such state.

(e) CHAIR. The offices of Chairman and Vice Chairman of the Commission shall be rotated between the Chairman of the Cheyenne River Sioux Tribe (or a designated representative of the Chairman) and the President of the Oglala Sioux Tribe (or a designated representative of the President) on a year-to-year basis. If both the Chairman and the Vice Chairman are absent from any meeting, the members of the Commission who are present at the meeting shall select a member who is present to serve in the place of the chairman for the meeting.

(f) MEETINGS. The Commission shall meet at the call of the Chairman or a majority of its members. In a manner consistent with the public meeting requirements of the Federal Advisory Committee Act (5 U.S.C. App.), the Commission shall from time to time meet with persons concerned with Park issues relating to the North Unit or the South Unit. The Commission shall record all minutes and resolutions of the Commission and make such records available to the public upon request.

(g) ADMINISTRATIVE DIRECTOR.

(1) IN GENERAL. The Secretary, in consultation with the Commissioner, shall employ an administrative Director for the Commission and define the duties of the Administrative Director. The Administrative Director shall be paid at a rate not to exceed the annual rate of basic payable for grade GS 12 of the General Schedule under subchapter IV of chapter 53 of title 5, United States Code, without regard to

(A) the provisions of title 5, United States Code, governing appointments in the competitive service; and

(B) the provisions of chapter 51, and subchapter III of chapter 52 of that title relating to classification and General Schedule pay rates.

(2) OFFICE. The office and staff of the Administrative Director shall be located at such location as the Secretary considers appropriate.

(h) SUPPORT SERVICES. The Administrator of General Services shall provide to the Commission, on a nonreimbursable basis, such administrative support services as the Commission, in consultation with the Secretary may request.

(i) EXPENSES. Members of the Commission who are not otherwise employed by the Federal Government, while away from their homes or regular places of business in the performance of services for the commission, shall be allowed travel and all other related expenses, including per diem in lieu of subsistence, in the same manner as persons employed intermittently in Government service are allowed expenses under section 5703 of title 5, United States Code.

(j) APPLICABILITY OF FEDERAL ADVISORY ACT. Except with respect to any requirement for reissuance of a charter, and except as otherwise provided in this Act, the provisions of the Federal Advisory Committee act (5 U.S.C. App.) shall apply to the Commission established under this Act.

SEC. 9 FUNDRAISER AGREEMENTS WITH NONPROFIT CORPORATIONS.

(a) IN GENERAL. Notwithstanding any other provision of law, the Cheyenne River Sioux Tribe and the Oglala Sioux Tribe, or a designated agency or authority of either tribe, may, with the approval of the Secretary, enter into an agreement with a nonprofit corporation to raise funds from private sources to be used in lieu of, or supplement, any federal funds made available by appropriations pursuant to the authorization under section 11.

(b) NEW PROJECTS. The Cheyenne River Sioux Tribe and the Oglala Sioux Tribe, or a designated agency or authority of either tribe, shall have the power and authority to enter into a separate agreement with a nonprofit corporation to

(1) raise funds from private sources to pay for all obligations, costs, and fees for professional services contracted, incurred, or assumed by the tribe, or a designated agency or authority of the tribe, that are related, directly or indirectly, to the development or establishment of the Park; and

(2) raise funds from private sources to plan, design, construct, operate, maintain, and replace

(A) an international amphitheater dedicated to the Indigenous Peoples of the Americas to be located at or near the Wounded Knee Massacre site which, if constructed, shall become the permanent home of the Francis Jansen sculpture; and

(B) any other project that the Cheyenne River Sioux Tribe or the Oglala Sioux Tribe may, in consultation with the Secretary, choose to include within the North Unit or South Unit.

SEC. 10. DUTIES OF OTHER FEDERAL ENTITIES.

The appropriate official of any Federal entity that conducts or supports activities that directly affect the Park shall consult with the Secretary and the Cheyenne River Sioux Tribe and the Oglala Sioux Tribe with respect to such activities to minimize any adverse effects on the Park.

SEC. 11. AUTHORIZATION OF APPROPRIATIONS.

There are authorized to be appropriated such sums as may be necessary to carry out this Act.

SEC. 12. RULE OF STATUTORY CONSTRUCTION.

Nothing contained in this Act is intended to abrogate, modify, or impair any rights or claims of the Cheyenne River Sioux Tribe or Oglala Sioux Tribe, that are based on any treaty, Executive order, agreement, Act of Congress, or other legal basis.

Notes

PREFACE

1. Johnson v. McIntosh, 21 U.S. (8 Wheat.) 543 (1823).

2. The rule in the *Johnson v. McIntosh* case, that grants of fee title made by a European government to individuals under the Doctrine of Discovery "have been understood by all, to convey title to the grantees, subject only to the Indian right of occupancy," was recognized by the Supreme Court as applicable to land grants made by Spanish governors in Chouteau v. Molony, 57 U.S. (16 How.) 203 (1853). The rule was also applied to the United States as the "successor" to Great Britain in Holden v. Joy, 84 U.S. 211 (1872) and as successor to Mexico (in the Mexican cession area) in United States ex rel. Haulpai Indians v. Santa Fe Pacific Railroad Co., 314 U.S. 339 (1941). The fee title to the Indian lands granted by these governments has been called a "naked fee," since the grantee cannot disturb the occupancy of the Indian tribes until the underlying aboriginal title to the land is extinguished. See, e.g., Beecher v. Wetherby, 95 U.S. (Otto) 517 (1877) ("The grantee . . . would take only the naked fee, and could not disturb the occupancy of the Indians").

The manner of extinguishment of aboriginal title has also evolved over time. Although the Supreme Court ruled in the 1823 *Johnson v. McIntosh* case that extinguishment of aboriginal title could occur "either by purchase or by conquest," later Court decisions have held that extinguishment could occur "whether it be done by treaty, by the sword, by purchase, by the exercise of complete dominion adverse to the right of occupancy, or otherwise," but "[t]he intent must be clear, however, 'an extinguishment cannot be lightly implied'" (United States v. Dann, 706 F.2d 919 (9th Cir. 1983). In Tee-Hit-Ton Indians v. United States (348 U.S. 272 [1955]), the Supreme Court also ruled that extinguishment of aboriginal title by the United States does not create a legal obligation to pay just compensation!

European governments and their successors can also *grant fee title to an Indian tribe* for lands already held by the tribe under aboriginal title. These grants are called "recognized Indian title." In Sac and Fox Tribe of Indians v. United States (315 F.2d

896 [Ct. C.. 1963]), the U.S. Court of Claims ruled that for Indian title to be recognized, "Congress, acting through a treaty or statute, . . . must grant legal rights of permanent occupancy within a sufficiently defined territory. . . . There must be an intention to accord or recognize a legal interest in the land."

3. Cherokee Nation v. Georgia, 30 U.S. (5 Pet.) 1 (1831).

4. In 1883, the Supreme Court decided Ex Parte Crow Dog (109 U.S. 556 [1883]), which held that the Dakota Territorial Court lacked jurisdiction to try a Sioux Indian for the crime of murder and that serious disputes in Indian country such as murder must be resolved by tribal custom (as they had been for thousands of years). Indian agents and other U.S. citizens, however, felt the punishment for Indians for such crimes should be based on retribution (according to non-Indian standards) rather than restitution (according to tribal custom) and convinced Congress to pass legislation which listed seven major crimes committed by Indians that would be punishable under federal law. This legislation, called the Seven Major Crimes Act (23 Stat. 385), was passed in 1885 and was the first major encroachment on tribal sovereignty by the U.S. government. The act has since been expanded to include other crimes, and presently reads as follows:

> Any Indian who commits against the person or property of another Indian or other person any of the following offenses, namely, murder, manslaughter, kidnapping, maiming, a felony under chapter 109A, incest, assault with intent to commit murder, assault with a dangerous weapon, assault resulting in serious bodily injury (as defined in section 1365 of this title), an assault against an individual who has not attained the age of 16 years, arson, burglary, robbery, and a felony under section 661 of this title within the Indian country, shall be subject to the same law and penalties as all other persons committing any of the above offenses, within the exclusive jurisdiction of the United States. (18 U.S.C. 1153[a])

5. In 1953, during a period known as the "termination era," Congress passed Public Law 280, which purported to relinquish civil and criminal jurisdiction over reservation Indians from the federal government to state governments. See 25 U.S.C. 1321–26; 18 U.S.C. 1162. P.L. 280 was amended by the 1968 Indian Civil Rights Act and now requires the *consent* of the Indian people in a referendum election called by the secretary of the interior before civil and criminal jurisdiction can be assumed by a state government:

> State jurisdiction acquired pursuant to this subchapter with respect to criminal offenses or civil causes of action, or with respect to both, shall be applicable in Indian country only where the enrolled Indians within the affected area of such Indian country accept such jurisdiction by a majority vote of the adult Indians voting at a special election held for that purpose. The Secretary of the Interior shall call such special election under such rules and regulations as he may prescribe, when requested to do so by the tribal council or other governing body, or by 20 per centum of such enrolled adults. (Act of April 11, 1968, 82 Stat. 80)

Also see Kennerly v. District Court of Montana, 400 U.S. 423 (1971) (Blackfeet Tribal Council had no authority to relinquish civil jurisdiction to State of Montana without the majority vote of the enrolled members of the tribe voting in an election called by the secretary of the interior under 25 U.S.C. 1326).

6. Worcester v. Georgia, 31 U.S. (6 Pet.) 515 (1832).

7. Williams v. Lee, 358 U.S. 217 (1959). See also White Mountain Apache Tribe v. Bracker, 65 L.Ed.2d 665 (1980).

8. Most federal cases are decided under the "governing act of Congress" (federal preemption) standard. A clearly correct application of the infringement test is Eastern Band of Cherokee Indians v. North Carolina Wildlife Resources Commission (588 F.2d 75 [4th Cir. 1978], cert. dismissed 446 U.S. 960 [1980], in which the Fourth Circuit Court of Appeals held that the infringement test prevented a state from licensing and regulating non-Indians who fished in reservation streams stocked entirely by an Indian tribe and the federal government.

9. Nathan R. Margold, *Powers of Indian Tribes,* 55 I.D. 14 (October 25, 1934). Also see Iron Crow v. Ogallala Sioux Tribe, 129 F. Supp. 15 (D.S.D. 1955), where the district court found that "[f]rom time immemorial the members of the Ogallala Sioux Tribe have exercised powers of local self-government, regulating domestic problems and conducting foreign affairs, including in later years the negotiation of treaties and agreements with the United States." When the *Iron Crow* case was appealed, the court of appeals further found "that Indian tribes, such as the . . . Oglala Sioux Tribe . . . still possess their inherent sovereignty excepting only where it has been specifically taken from them either by treaty or by Congressional Act." See Iron Crow v. Oglala Sioux Tribe, 231 F.2d 89 (8th Cir. 1956). In another case, Barta v. Oglala Sioux Tribe, 259 F.2d 553 (8th Cir. 1958), the court of appeals further recognized that "Indian tribes retain attributes of sovereignty over both their members and their territory."

Many Indian tribes adopted western-style governments under section 16 of the Indian Reorganization Act of 1934 (25 U.S.C. 476) and section 3 of the Oklahoma Welfare Act (25 U.S.C. 503). Section 16 of the IRA provided that in addition to inherent sovereign powers already recognized to be vested in an Indian tribe, tribes organized under the IRA could exercise certain other powers delegated to them by the United States.

10. See, e.g., Lone Wolf v. Hitchcok, 187 U.S. 553 (1903), qualified in Delaware Tribal Council v. Weeks, 430 U.S. 73 (1977) and United States v. Sioux Nation of Indians, 448 U.S. 371 (1980). *Merriam Webster's Collegiate Dictionary* defines "plenary" as "complete in every respect," "absolute," "unqualified" or "full."

11. Trust responsibility, as it evolved in the federal courts, appears to be based on international customs relating to conquest, as incorporated into federal common law or federal statutory law. It can also be based on the mutual agreement of parties to Indian treaties and agreements. The use of the trust responsibility of the United States to extinguish title to Indian lands was discussed in United States v. Sioux Nation of Indians (448 U.S. 371 [1980]) as follows:

In reaching its conclusion that the 1877 Act affected a taking of the Black Hills for which just compensation was due the Sioux under the Fifth Amendment, the Court of Claims relied upon the 'good faith effort' test developed in its earlier decision in *Three Tribes of the Fort Berthold Reservation v. United States,* 182 Ct. Cl. 543, 390 F.2d 686 (1968). The Fort Berthold test had been designed to reconcile two lines of cases decided by this Court that seemingly were in conflict. The first line, exemplified by *Lone Wolf v. Hitchcock,* 187 U.S. 553, 23 S.Ct. 216, 47 L.Ed. 229 (1903), recognizes "that Congress possesse[s] a paramount power over the property of the Indians, by reason of its exercise of guardianship over their interests, and that such authority might be implied, even though opposed to the strict letter of a treaty with the Indians." Id., at 565, 23 S.Ct., at 221. The second line, exemplified by the more recent decision in *Shoshoni Tribe v. United States,* 299 U.S. 476, 57 S.Ct. 244, 81 L.Ed. 360 (1937), concedes Congress' paramount power over Indian property, but holds, nonetheless, that "[t]he power does not extend so far as to enable the Government 'to give the tribal lands to others, or to appropriate them to its own purpose, without rendering, or assuming an obligation to render, just compensation.'" Id. at 497, 57 S.Ct. 252 (quoting *United States v. Creek Nation,* 295 U.S. 103, 110, 55 S.Ct. 681, 684, 79 L.Ed. 1331 [1935]). . . .

The *Fort Berthold* test distinguishes between cases in which one or the other principle is applicable:

"It is obvious that Congress cannot simultaneously (1) act as trustee for the benefit of the Indians, exercising its plenary powers over the Indians and their property, as it thinks is in their best interests, and (2) exercise its sovereign power of eminent domain, taking the Indians' property within the meaning of the Fifth Amendment to the Constitution. In any given situation in which Congress has acted with regard to Indian people, it must have acted either in one capacity or the other. Congress can own two hats, but it cannot wear them both at the same time.

"Some guideline must be established so that a court can identify in which capacity Congress is acting. The following guidelines would best give recognition to the basic distinction between the two types of congressional action. Where Congress makes a good faith effort to give the Indians the full value of the land and thus merely transmute the property from land to money, there is no taking. This is a mere substitution of assets or change of form and is a traditional function of a trustee." 182 Ct. Cl., at 553, 390 F.2d, at 691

In the case of the Black Hills, the Court found that Congress did not make a good faith effort to give the Sioux Indians the full value of the land and therefore its action in confiscating the Black Hills violated the Just Compensation clause of the Fifth Amendment.

The "good faith effort" test has also been used to justify the diminishment of reservation boundaries (theft of additional lands) under the so-called surplus land acts. If

Congress was wearing its own hat when it passed a surplus land act, reservation boundaries were held to be diminished; if Congress was wearing its trustee hat when it passed
a surplus land act, reservation boundaries were held not to be diminished. See generally Rosebud Sioux Tribe v. Kneip, 430 U.S. 584 (1977), and cases cited therein.

The Sioux Indian tribes regard any taking of their treaty lands by the United States
to be outright thievery, regardless of which hat the United States chooses to use, when
their lands are taken without the signatures of three-fourths of the adult male population required to effectuate a valid cession under article 12 of the 1868 Fort Laramie
Treaty. (See appendix A for the text of article 12 of the 1868 treaty.)

12. See appendix H for the chronology of Sioux land claims.

INTRODUCTION

1. Maya Angelou, *On the Pulse of Morning;* Angelou read this poem at the inauguration of President Bill Clinton, Jan. 20, 1993 (emphasis added).

2. On the importance of mutual respect and cooperation between indigenous
peoples and the former colonial powers, see Rigoberta Menchú's Nobel lecture, delivered in Oslo on December 10, 1992.

3. Robert Quiver, Mario Gonzalez's great-great-grandfather had two Indian
names: "Quiver" and "Nantan Hinapan" (Comes Out Charging). In 1979, Mario's
great-uncle Enos Poor Bear, Sr., gave him the name "Nantan Hinapan" in a sacred
name-giving ceremony at Wanblee, South Dakota. A traditional dinner and give-away
was held and a horse with money tied to its mane and tail was given by Mario to
Grover Horned Antelope, a Lakota religious leader.

4. See Treaty of April 29, 1868, 15 Stat. 635.

5. The legislation developed for the Grey Eagle Society was introduced in Congress by Congressman Mathew Martinez in 1990 as H.R. 5680.

6. See Black Hills Act of February 28, 1877.

7. Edward Lazarus, *Black Hills, White Justice: The Sioux Nation versus the United
States, 1775 to the Present.* Cook-Lynn's review of this book appears in the *Wicazo Sa
Review.*

8. Vine Deloria, Jr., "Reflections," p. 34.

9. In *Rethinking Indian Law,* Steven Tullberg and Robert Coulter note:

The first part of the taking clause of the Fifth Amendment, which provides that the
government may not take private property except for a legitimate public purpose
by use of its eminent domain powers, was not applied by the Supreme Court to rule
the initial seizure of the Black Hills as an unconstitutional act. The constitutional
argument is now being made for the first time by a Sioux Indian lawyer [Mario
Gonzalez] representing the Oglala Sioux Tribe in a new lawsuit which rejects the
offered money damages and which seeks return of the Black Hills instead.

Inexplicably . . . and certainly without the approval of the Sioux people . . . the
white lawyer [Arthur Lazarus] representing the Sioux Nation in the Supreme
Court argument of the *Sioux Nation v. U.S.* case conceded that the United States

government had the lawful power to abrogate the Fort Laramie Treaty and to take the Black Hills from the Sioux people, even though the purpose of the taking was to give that Indian land and its gold to non-Indians (such a taking would obviously not meet the "public purpose" test of the Fifth Amendment). All the Constitution required, the white lawyer argued, is that the Indian people be given compensation, with interest, whenever Indian land is taken by the federal government:

> QUESTION BY THE COURT: Under a treaty a reservation is set up for an Indian Tribe and at sometime later, the Government, the Congress just says, "Well, we think that reservation is too big. We are going to cut it in half and open the rest up." So it just cuts it in half and redraws the reservation.
> Now, is that a breach of the treaty or is it a taking or both?
> ATTORNEY FOR THE SIOUX NATION: It is a breach of the treaty and the United States has the power to breach the treaty.
> QUESTION BY THE COURT: That is *Lone Wolf.*
> ATTORNEY FOR THE SIOUX NATION: That is *Lone Wolf.*
> QUESTION BY THE COURT: Right.
> ATTORNEY FOR THE SIOUX NATION: *Lone Wolf* tells us that Congress . . . if Congress determines that the reservation should be cut in half, Congress can come in and do it; it can do it without the consent of the Indians and it can do it in violation of a treaty. It is also a taking and when Congress does it, it has to pay for it.

Going even further, the attorney for the Sioux Nation [Lazarus] conceded that the United States government and not his Sioux clients, was the actual owner of all Sioux lands and all other Indian lands as well:

> QUESTION BY THE COURT: The question such as in the *Decoteau* case and others as to whether or not the reservation has been terminated is a question of congressional intent, but here this was not an Indian reservation, this was . . . this belonged to the Sioux Nation, didn't it?
> ATTORNEY FOR THE SIOUX NATION: Well, this . . . all reservations, the beneficial ownership and all the incidents of ownership are in the Indian Tribe. The bare legal title is in the United States.
> QUESTION BY THE COURT: And that was true here too?
> ATTORNEY FOR THE SIOUX NATION: Yes.
> QUESTION BY THE COURT: It was.
> QUESTION BY THE COURT: But this was more than aboriginal title. Even if originally it had been aboriginal title it was recognized by treaty and it constituted a reservation.
> ATTORNEY FOR THE SIOUX NATION: That is correct. It was recognized twice over.
> QUESTION BY THE COURT: It was Federal land?
> ATTORNEY FOR THE SIOUX NATION: It was a federal Indian reservation, recognized title that . . .

QUESTION BY THE COURT: That title was in the Sioux Nation and not the Federal, Government.

ATTORNEY FOR THE SIOUX NATION: Well, all of the incidents of ownership if you want to say who has all the incidents of ownership, it is the Sioux Nation. Where does the bare legal title rest, it is in the United States as it is with respect to all Indian lands. That is what establishes the trust.

But when the United States takes it . . . and *Shoshone* makes this quite clear . . . when the United States takes it, the Indians have a 100 percent interest for purposes of determining just compensation.

You value it at full value.

Rather than arguing that the Sioux actually held title to the land and rather than arguing that the Sioux land rights should be constitutionally protected from confiscation by the federal government just as all other property is, the lawyer for the Sioux focussed on the objective of money damages. (Ten percent of the damages awarded to the Sioux have gone to the lawyers as attorney's fees . . . over ten million dollars.) (National Lawyers Guild, Committee on Native American Struggles, *Rethinking Indian Law,* p. 53.) [Ed. note: Is it any wonder that there is fear and suspicion on the part of tribal members, Indian officials, and reservation residents as they enter into an agreement concerning the Wounded Knee memorial site on the Pine Ridge and Cheyenne River homelands?]

It was left up to Gonzalez to redirect the argument, to begin a new rationale, and he has worked toward that understanding ever since in the face of the astounding racism to be found in mainstream legal thought.

10. See appendix I.

11. Rattling Hawk is the great-great-grandmother of Mario Gonzalez. Rattling Hawk's mother's name was Jealous of Her rather than Jealous At. Rattling Hawk married Robert Quiver (a.k.a. Nantan Hinapan), a Lower Brule Sioux, and the couple had four children, including Harry Quiver, the father of Mario's maternal grandmother Anna Quiver Wilcox (Winyan Wankan).

12. See Paul High Horse's account in *Pute Tiyospaye (Lip's Camp): The History and Culture of a Sioux Indian Village.*

13. Don Doll, *Vision Quest,* p. 93. This collection of photos and brief interviews is intended to give a true picture of contemporary, modern tribal leadership in roles ranging from politics to art.

INTRODUCTION TO DIARIES AND CHRONICLES

1. Johnson v. McIntosh, 21 U.S. (8 Wheat.) 543 (1903); Tee-Hit-Ton Indians v. United States, 348 U.S. 272 (1955).

2. Cherokee Nation v. Georgia, 30 U.S. (5 Pet.) 1 (1831).

3. See, e.g., Talton v. Mayes, 163 U.S. 376 (1895) (Fifth Amendment not applicable to Indian Nations); Barta v. Oglala Sioux Tribe, 259 F.2d 553 (8th Cir. 1958) (Fourteenth

Amendment inapplicable to Indian Nation); Native American Church v. Navajo Tribal Council, 272 F.2d 131 (10th Cir. 1959) (First Amendment inapplicable to Indian Nation).

4. Recognition goes to Sidney Keith for the rendering of the essential Ghost Horse story. It appears in the 1991 Wounded Knee monument hearing transcripts ("Proposed Wounded Knee Park and Memorial," Hearing before the Select Committee on Indian Affairs, U.S. Senate, 102d Cong., 1st sess. [April 30, 1991]). Keith's translation work and the story itself is essential to *The Politics of Hallowed Ground* for it is the source of modern understanding and storytelling. Though diary keeping and the writing of chronicles may be on the rise among the indigenous peoples of the world, they are still the rarity. What is not so rare is the recognition that the Lakotaness of the art and storytelling which have developed within the native circle of history making is still the source for everything.

PART 1: THE DILEMMA OF ETHICAL SYSTEMS AND LEGAL IDEAS

1. See Act of February 28, 1877 (19 Stat. 254).

2. 1868 Fort Laramie Treaty, art. 1 (15 Stat. 635), in Charles J. Kappler, *Indian Affairs: Laws and Treaties*, vol. 2.

3. See Act of February 28, 1877, 19 Stat. 254.

4. See Act of February 22, 1889, 25 Stat. 888.

5. Many historians have varying theories about the cause of the Wounded Knee Massacre, most of which we consider to be examples of colonial orthodoxy. Unfortunately, these historical accounts have now become virtually unchallengeable doctrine. For example, see Raymond J. DeMallie, "The Lakota Ghost Dance: An Ethnohistorical Account," in which he reviews the James Mooney theory of religion as cause; Robert M. Utley, *Frontier Regulars* (esp. p. 408) and *The Last Days of the Sioux Nation* (esp. p. 126), reviewing much of the same interpretation; and James O. Gump, *The Dust Rose like Smoke* (esp. p. 115), suggesting Indian aggression as the cause and claiming ultimately that Wounded Knee symbolizes "the denouement in Sioux efforts to resurrect the open frontier." He too intimates that the Ghost Dancers were the cause of the event. For a contemporary tribal viewpoint, see Gonzalez's introduction to the appendixes.

6. In 1863, Congress passed an amendment to the Court of Claims' 1855 Enabling Act (10 Stat. 612), which expressly excluded Indian tribes from the Court of Claims by providing that jurisdiction of the court "shall not extend to or include any claim against the Government not pending in said court on December 1, 1862, growing out of or depending on any treaty stipulation entered into with foreign nations or with Indian tribes" (Act of March 3, 1863, 12 Stat. 765, sec. 9).

7. Act of June 3, 1920 (41 Stat. 738).

8. See Sioux Tribe v. United States, 97 Ct. Cl. 613 (1942), *cert. denied,* 318 U.S. 789 (1943).

9. See sec. 22 of the Indian Claims Commission Act of August 13, 1946, which provided that:

(a) When the report of the Commission determining any claimant to be entitled to recover has been filed with Congress, such report shall have the effect of a final judgment of the Court of Claims, and there is hereby authorized to be appropriated such sums as are necessary to pay the final determination of the Commission.

The payment of any claim, after its determination in accordance with this Act [25 USCS sec. 70 and notes-70n, 700–70v-1], shall be a full discharge of the United States of all claims and demands touching any of the matters involved in the controversy.

(b) A final determination against a claimant made and reported in accordance with this Act [25 USCS sec. 70 and notes-70n, 700–70v-1] shall forever bar any further claim or demand against the United States arising out of the matter involved in the controversy. (60 Stat. 1049, sec. 22; 25 U.S.C. 70u)

It is not an accident that the Indian Claims Commission Act was passed by the U.S. Congress in 1946; rather it was an act of contrition, a forced U.S. congressional response to world events. Between 1945 and 1946 the United States and its allies were trying Nazis war criminals at Nuremburg, Germany, on the theory that the Nazis were men who *implemented policies which led to death, disease, and starvation.* They could hardly do that without looking critically at U.S. Indian policy, which resulted in the illegal taking of lands, the deaths of thousands of Indians, and massive starvation and disease during the previous decades. As a conquest-oriented people, however, they never meant to return the land they stole. For more information, see Indian Claims Commission, *Final Report.*

10. Secs. 8–12 of the 1889 act (25 Stat. 888) also provided for allotments on the Sioux reservations in western South Dakota. Sec. 9 contained a proviso that the sections on allotment would not be binding until the majority of adults on any of the individual reservations created by the act agreed to allotment. At Pine Ridge, the majority of the adults resisted allotment from 1889 to 1904, when the secretary ignored their opposition and directed the reservation to be allotted. Thus, the Pine Ridge Reservation was allotted in direct violation of sec. 9 by the secretary of the interior. See Indian Law Resource Center, "A Brief History of Allotment on the Pine Ridge Reservation" (n.p., n.d.).

11. Much information on Red Cloud emerges from the oral storytelling tradition of the Lakotas. More on Red Cloud's politics, however, may be read in a doctoral thesis, "Chiefs, Headmen and Warriors: Oglala Politics, 1851–1889," submitted to the faculty at Purdue University in 1987 by Catherine Margaret Price, which has since been published as *The Oglala People, 1841–1879.* Good sources for background reading are James C. Olson, *Red Cloud and the Sioux Problem,* and George Hyde, *Red Cloud's Folk* and *Sioux Chronicle.*

12. See Price, "Chiefs, Headmen and Warriors."

13. Ex Parte Crow Dog, 109 U.S. 556 (1883). For discussion of this case, see Sidney L. Harring's *Crow Dog's Case: American Indian Sovereignty, Tribal Law, and United States Law in the Nineteenth Century.*

14. The initial courts established to regulate law and order on the Sioux reservations were called Courts of Indian Offenses. They were governed by a Code of Indian Offenses. Both the courts and the code were created by regulations issued by the secretary of the interior.

In a 1935 solicitor's opinion, Solicitor Nathan R. Margold, in upholding the legality of Courts of Indian Offenses, discussed their history as follows:

> In 1883 Commissioner Price under the approval and direction of the Secretary, issued regulations calling for the establishment on each reservation of a "court of Indian offenses" to be composed of three Indians selected by the agent (with the approval of the Commissioner) because of their prestige in the tribe and understanding of Indian ways. The court was to have jurisdiction of offenses defined in the departmental regulations, of civil suits between the Indians on the reservation, of liquor traffic by Indians and of all questions presented to it for consideration by the agent. The punishment might be the withholding of rations, a fine or hard labor, imprisonment, or the making of compensation to the injured party. The decisions of the court were to be subject to the approval of the agent with appeal to the Indian Office. The Indian offenses listed in the regulations were, briefly, participation in the "sun-dance" and other similar dances, polygamy, the practice of medicine men, theft or destruction of property, the purchase of girls for cohabitation purposes, and "misdemeanors committed by Indians belonging to the reservation." These regulations were included as Section 486 in the *Regulations of the Indian Office 1884* and were reissued in the same form in the *Regulations of the Indian Office 1894* (Section 580) *and 1904* (Section 584). To date the set-up of the court has not been changed, though from the first it became apparent that the court would not be able to be established on all reservations because of various local conditions; it was established on the majority. (See *Opinions of the Solicitor of the Department of the Interior Relating to Indian Affairs, 1917–1974*, vol. 1, p. 533.)

The Courts of Indian Offenses and Code of Indian Offenses existed on the Sioux reservations until they were replaced by tribal courts and codes established under constitutions and bylaws adopted by the tribes pursuant to the 1934 Indian Reorganization Act (25 U.S.C. 461 et seq.). These Courts of Indian Offenses, or "C.F.R. Courts," as they are commonly called, still exist on some Indian reservations. See 25 C.F.R., part 11 (1996 Rev.). C.F.R. Courts are now classified as tribal courts under the 1968 Indian Civil Rights Act (25 U.S.C. 1301 [3]).

15. Copies of this bill can be obtained from any federal depository library, from the Rapid City Public Library, or from the Sinte Gleska University archives.

16. The front page of the February 10, 1988, edition of the *Lakota Times* carried an article entitled "Erroneous Rapid City Journal Article Creates Confusion on Reservations." The following excerpts are taken from that article:

> An article in the Feb. 6 *Rapid City Journal* on the appointment of California millionaire Philip J. Stevens as a war chief of the Sioux was apparently erroneous.

The press release prompted a meeting of the Grey Eagle Society on Feb. 7 at Dupree on the Cheyenne River Reservation. . . . Pine Ridge Grey Eagle President Royal Bull Bear, who attended the meeting, said the appointment of Stevens as a war chief did not come from the Grey Eagles. "It is just a family honoring him," Bull Bear said. "According to our traditions, he has to go through certain things to become a war chief." . . .

The ceremony honoring Stevens began on the Rosebud Reservation. Homer Whirlwind Soldier's *tiospaye* planned to honor Stevens and asked support from the other reservations. "Each clan chose their own leaders," said Ed Charging Elk, long-time Rosebud resident. "It is handed down from father to son." Charging Elk said that even if the [Stevens] proposal [to regain the Black Hills] is defeated, Stevens can still be a war chief of Whirlwind Soldier's *tiospaye.*

Another article that appeared on the front page of the March 23, 1988, edition of the *Lakota Times* entitled "Grey Eagle Society Clarifies Position," stated that "Royal Bull Bear, president of the Pine Ridge Grey Eagle Society, has clarified the position of the Society in regard to the Special Chief's Honoring Ceremony to be held at Mission on the Rosebud Reservation on March 26. . . . 'Although the Pine Ridge Grey Eagles support Stevens, they cannot officially endorse the Special Chief's Honoring Ceremony,' he said."

17. See "Editorial Perspective: The Man Who Would Be Chief," *Lakota Times,* Mar. 25, 1988, p. 1.

18. *Lakota Times,* Jan. 12, 1994.

19. See Mario Gonzalez, "The Black Hills: The Sacred Land of the Lakota and Tsististas."

20. An example of Indians being shot by settlers after the turn of the century is the ambush of Sioux Indians from the Pine Ridge Reservation in Wyoming in 1903. Two parties of Indians were given passes by Agent J. R. Brennan to gather berries, roots, and herbs off the reservation and were ambushed by a sheriff's posse at Lightning Creek, located thirty-five miles north of Lusk, Wyoming, on October 31, 1903. The Indians comprised two different parties from the reservation that met accidentally and united. One of the parties was headed by an Indian man named William Brown, who left the reservation under a pass dated September 30, 1903, with fifteen men, women, and children. The other party was headed by Charles Smith, an educated mix-blood (said to be a graduate of Carlisle Indian School), who left the reservation under a pass dated October 20, 1903, with thirteen men, women, and children. The united party included fifteen wagons and several ponies.

The number of Indians killed and wounded is described in a November 17, 1903, letter to the commissioner of Indian affairs from Agent Brennan:

Total number of Indians killed, so far as I am able to learn, was 4—one old man, Black Kettle, aged 58 years; one boy, Philip White Elk, aged 11 years; Charles Smith, aged 37 years, and Gray Bear, aged 48 years. Two wounded—Smith's wife, shot in shoulder from behind, and an old man named Last Bear, 70 years of age, was shot in the back, the ball coming out in front, almost opposite where it went in. Will probably recover. The 11-year-old boy killed was shot in the head. The whole top of his head was blown off, indicating that the party who did the shooting was pretty close to the boy.

Outside of a party of 9 old Indians, men and women, that the sheriff arrested five or six days previous to the fight and were being held at Newcastle, and whom I had released on my first trip there, there was not to exceed 35 persons, men and women, young and old, in the party that had the trouble with the sheriff, and in fact were the only Indians in that section of the country. These people were composed of two parties, one known as the Smith party and the other as the Brown party. These two parties were mostly old people, were given permits to visit outside of the reservation in the Black Hills and vicinity for the purpose of gathering berries, roots, and herbs. They were not given a permit to hunt. The two parties met accidentally some few days before the trouble and arranged to go together.

Two members of the posse were killed, Sheriff William Miller and Deputy Falkenberg of Newcastle, Wyoming (where the posse was organized).

After the incident, on November 3, 1903, the survivors, including nine Indian men and their families, who were returning to the reservation, were arrested by another sheriff's posse near Edgemont, South Dakota, and were taken to Douglas, Wyoming, and tried for murder. They were acquitted by a judge and released from jail.

Correspondence and newspaper reports regarding the Lightning Creek incident can be found in a U.S. Senate Report entitled "Encounter between Sioux Indians of the Pine Ridge Agency, S.Dak., and a Sheriff's Posse of Wyoming" (see Senate Report No. 128, 58th Cong., 2d sess. [January 27, 1904]).

21. Alfred Runte's *National Parks: The American Experience,* is an excellent treatment of bureaucratic motivations.

22. Herbert Hoover, "Centennial West's Celebration of the Northern Tier States' Heritage." This 1989 booklet is available from the Montana State Historical Society in Helena or the South Dakota State Historical Society in Pierre. It was printed with funding by the National Endowment for the Humanities. Hoover does not make much of the illegal Custer expedition's "muscling" its way into the Black Hills in 1874 as illegally violating the 1868 treaty. President Ulysses S. Grant's order to withdraw troops to allow the invasion of the Black Hills by U.S. citizens to go forward has been part of the discussion in the courts and should have been included in Hoover's assessment; his failure to include these facts and interpretations can only be called historical bias.

23. 650 F.2d 140 (8th Cir. 1981).

24. See the Act of March 3, 1871 (16 Stat. 544), which provided that "[n]o Indian Nation or tribe within the territory of the United States shall be acknowledged or recognized as an independent nation, tribe, or power with whom the United States may contract with treaty, *but no obligation of any treaty lawfully made with any Indi-*

an nation or tribe prior to March 3, 1871, shall be hereby invalidated or impaired." (Emphasis added.)

25. Marbury v. Madison, 1 Cranch 137, 2 L.Ed. 60 (1803).

26. Cohens v. Virginia, 6 Wheat. 264 (1821).

27. Transcript of oral arguments in Oglala Sioux Tribe v. United States, 650 F.2d 140 (8th Cir. 1981).

28. Act of August 10, 1988 (102 Stat. 903).

29. Christina Hoff Sommers's position in *Who Stole Feminism?* is that "advocacy research" entered into by feminist ideologues is as dangerous and as stultifying as the male domination theoretical models have been throughout history (p. 60).

30. "Daschle's Campaign," *Rapid City Journal,* Mar. 5, 1994.

31. Act of June 8, 1906 (34 Stat. 225).

32. Vine Deloria, Jr., refers to the 1891 act on depredations (26 Stat. 851) in "Congress in Its Wisdom." Depredations acts were intended to compensate non-Indian victims but they have been used, on occasion, to compensate Indians. The so-called 1891 Sioux Depredation Act was actually part of the 1891 Appropriation Act, which read: "Payment to friendly Indians, etc., for property destroyed: The sum of one hundred thousand dollars, or so much thereof as may be necessary, is hereby appropriated out of any money in the Treasury not otherwise appropriated, to be immediately available, for the prompt payment to the friendly Sioux and legal residents on the Sioux Reservation, for property destroyed or appropriated by the roving bands of disaffected Indians during the recent Sioux trouble, to be expended under the direction and control of the Secretary of Interior, and upon satisfactory proof made to him in each case of the loss sustained" (26 Stat. 1002). See appendix G.

33. This is supposed to be the 1968 Pine Ridge Aerial Gunnery Range Act (Act of August 8, 1968 [82 Stat. 663]).

34. "Wounded Knee Memorial and Historic Site—Little Big Horn National Monument Battlefield," Hearing before the Select Committee on Indian Affairs, U.S. Senate, 101st Cong., 2d sess. (September 25, 1990). What was being revealed at these hearings was that since 1492 tribal peoples had been subjected to a colonial mythology that robbed them of their right to be themselves and enter into the dialogues of America as equal partners in humanity. Ted Jojola (of Isleta Pueblo), longtime director of Native American Studies at the University of New Mexico, has commented upon the struggle of the indigenes to reclaim their lands, artifacts, and identities in an article published in the *American Indian Quarterly,* "Recently, native lawyers and lobbyists have attempted to gain federal legislation to further strengthen and protect indigenous cultural integrity and property. Most of the resulting laws address the protection of objects, artifacts, and burial sites, and the reparation of bones macabrely stashed by the ton in museums and anthropology labs around the country. Attempts to protect indigenous cultural definition and identity have been made as well. Currently, the United Nations is in the process of developing principles on the rights of indigenous peoples, which will include cultural rights. The impact of

such federal legislation as the Native American Graves Protection and Repatriation Act, the American Indian Freedom of Religion Act, the Act to Promote Development of Indian Arts and Crafts, and the Native American Languages Acts have been significant. Combined they serve to lay the foundation for the development of a patent on culture and historical interpretation." This kind of research and legislation is not unrelated to the effort of the Minneconjou and Oglala to develop their memorial. The next several Diary and Chronicle entries include references to Alan Parker, an old friend of Gonzalez. Both Parker and Gonzalez participated in the Indian Law Program at the University of New Mexico School of Law. Funding for the program was initiated by Sioux intellectual Jim Wilson, who was head of the OEO Indian Desk in Washington, D.C., for many years. Mario's summer class of 1969 also included Tom Fredericks, Richard Trudell, Ray Emery, Enoch LaPointe, John Oguin, Rod Lewis, George Goodwin, Floyd Westerman, John Sinclair, Phil LaCourse, Gary Kimble, John Chavez, Ralph Keen, and many others. The significance of Wilson's influence in the field of legal training for Indians cannot be overemphasized, since he initiated programs in which Indian participants became a core of professionals destined to do the vital work for the tribal nations. Fredericks was for many years with the Native American Rights Fund (NARF); Richard Trudell and Parker began the American Indian Lawyer Training Program (AILTP) in Oakland, California; Rod Lewis became the first male Indian lawyer to argue before the U.S. Supreme Court; John Sinclair is chief judge of the Wind River Reservation; Kimble is the current director of the Administration for Native Americans; and the list of accomplishments goes on and on.

35. For an account of Chief Lip's Band, see the introduction (pp. 8–9).

36. See *Congressional Record* S. 15289 (Oct. 15, 1990). For the text of S.C.R. 153, see appendix I.

37. In light of critical and sometimes angry discourse concerning Indian/non-Indian relations in the state of South Dakota, the motivations inherent in Governor George Mickelson's speech at the 1990 hearing are far from clear. However, it can be suggested that this boundary drawing of particular problems such as health care and education and economic development was necessary, since the governor had previously made several declarations during this period that the Black Hills land theft issue could *not* be part of the dialogue since it was a federal matter, not a state matter. Some have suggested that this behavior on the governor's part was masterful since what he did was to put tribal leadership *under* him, delineating the terms on which the tribes could deal with his government. Instead of dealing with the Sioux leadership on a government-to-government basis, he dealt with them as tribal enclaves within his jurisdiction and attempted to co-opt their sovereignty in favor of state power. This has always been at the heart of jurisdictional matters since tribal governments established their sovereign relationship with the federal government before states like South Dakota even existed. State power in the West, say Indian scholars, does not take precedence over the tribal-federal relationship because treaties were signed prior to statehood and only the federal government can treat with Indian

tribes. For the most part, Mickelson's strategy was successful since Indian leaders of that time seemed to be so brainwashed with colonialism that many of them didn't see or comment upon the significant symbolism of the governor's paternalistic actions. This became a very divisive issue in Indian communities and indicated to many that the so-called reconciliation was just another strategy to thwart Indian intentions.

38. Gramsci is usually regarded as being in the Marxist tradition. His work, summarized in *Selections from the Prison Notebooks,* edited and translated by Quinten Hoare and G. N. Smith, argues that the so-called elites who control society (culture, media, religion, and education) set in place strategies to get "consent" for their rule. See also *Politics and Society* by James C. Scott. One of the reasons for the failure of Gramsci's analysis to be used very productively in the Indian/non-Indian discussions in the United States is that he was one of the founders of Italy's Communist Party and his very useful ideas were therefore demeaned by many U.S. intellectuals during the cold war. More recently, in *Weapons of the Weak: Everyday Forms of Peasant Resistance,* James C. Scott sheds some light on class structure issues, though he tends to set everything only in economic terms rather than in treaty sovereign/nationalistic terms.

PART 2: WORD SEARCHERS AND BIG FOOT RIDERS

1. Reports on environmental assessment for the Wounded Knee Study of Alternatives, begun in 1991 and finished in March, 1992, may be obtained through the National Park Service of the U.S. Department of Interior, Rocky Mountain Regional Office, 12795 W. Alameda Parkway, P.O. Box 23287, Denver, CO, 80225-0287. Wyss Associates, Inc., can be reached at 522 7th Street, #214, Rapid City, SD 57701; the South Dakota Historical Preservation Center can be reached at 3 E. Main, Vermillion, SD 57069-0917.

2. Peter Matthiessen, *In the Spirit of Crazy Horse,* pp. 130–32, 250. This book received much public acclaim and made a reputation for the author as an advocate of Indian rights. Actually, prior to this success, Matthiessen had written on Indian themes. As early as 1965, he published *At Play in the Fields of the Lord,* a story about a displaced Cheyenne Indian character, a vision quest, and the destruction of Indian environment by Euroamericans. That novel became a successful movie.

3. Sally Roesch Wagner's testimony in "Wounded Knee Memorial and Historic Site—Little Big Horn National Monument Battlefield, Hearing (September 25, 1990)," pp. 86–89.

4. The Act of June 18, 1934 (48 Stat. 984).

5. Annie Tallent, *The Black Hills; or The Last Hunting Ground of the Dakotahs.*

6. *Rapid City Journal,* July 12, 1997.

7. Robert Utley, *The Lance and the Shield: The Life and Times of Sitting Bull.* Utley has changed his historical stance toward the Sioux very little since an early effort at historiography appeared in 1963 from Yale University Press, entitled *The Last Days of the Sioux Nation.* In this work he speaks of the "reduction" of the Great Sioux

Reservation (not the theft of lands), and the last page of the book carries a photo of the Wounded Knee site, which he called a battle site, not a massacre site, and about which he says: "in the foreground is the ravine 'pocket' from which the Sioux inflicted heavy casualties on the troops before artillery drove them out." *Last Days* is a badly flawed history seen now in the light of recent works, which Utley tends to call revisionism. Its chapters, with such titles as "Tightening the Ring" and "The Final Reckoning," reveal a turn-of-the-century bias characteristic of much of the work which emerged from Frederick Jackson Turner's famous 1893 frontier thesis, which sees Indians as a barrier to progress.

8. See Treaty of September 17, 1851 (11 Stat. 749); Treaty of April 29, 1868 (15 Stat. 635).

9. On July 10, 1980, the Oglala Sioux Tribe passed Oglala Sioux Tribal Executive Committee Resolution No. 80-31XB, which provided:

THEREFORE, BE IT RESOLVED that Mario Gonzalez take whatever legal action is necessary in the Black Hills case to protect the interest of the Oglala Sioux Tribe in the Black Hills litigation and to file any additional proceedings necessary in United States District Court to protect the interests of the Oglala Sioux Tribe, and BE IT FURTHER RESOLVED, that the Executive Committee endorses this proposed action subject to approval by the Tribal Council.

On July 16, 1980, the Oglala Sioux Tribal Coucil passed Resolution No. 80-62 confirming the Tribal Executive Committee's action (Resolution No. 80-31XB). Based on this authorization, Mario Gonzalez initiated a civil action in the U.S. District Court at Rapid City, South Dakota, on July 18, 1980, entitled Oglala Sioux Tribe of the Pine Ridge Indian Reservation v. the United States of America et al. (Civil Case No. 80-5062) to quiet title to 7.3 million acres of Black Hills territory confiscated unlawfully and unconstitutionally by the United States in 1877, and for $11 billion in damages for committing trespass and waste on the land, and for denying the tribe access to and use of the land from 1877 to 1980.

Just prior to filing the case, Mario was informed by Robert Fast Horse (who later changed his name to Robert Grey Eagle), a close friend of Russel Means, that the American Indian Movement's solution to the payment of the Indian Claims Commission's money judgment for the Black Hills was to publish the names of every Sioux Indian who accepted a per capita payment so future generations would know who the sellouts were. The American Indian Movement had absolutely no influence on the Oglala Sioux Tribe's decision to file Civil Case No. 80-5062.

10. Further readings on the Washington State issues including Oliphant v. Suquamish Indian Tribe, 435 U.S. 191 (1978) can be found in *Indian Tribes: A Continuing Quest for Survival,* a 1981 report by the U.S. Commission on Civil Rights. Members of the commission were Arthur S. Flemming, Mary F. Berry, Stephen Horn, Blandena Cardenas Ramirez, Jill Ruckelshaus, and Murray Saltzman. Louis Nuñez was staff director. See also "The States versus Indian Off-Reservation Fishing: A U.S. Supreme

Court Error" by Ralph W. Johnson, which chronicles the continuing aftermath of the Oliphant decision in Indian legal issues throughout the country. Further analysis can be found in *Justice in Indian Country*. Janklow's role in helping to finance *Oliphant* is detailed in Russel L. Barsh and James Youngblood Henderson, "The Betrayal: *Oliphant v. Suquamish Indian Tribe* and the Hunting of the Snark": "South Dakota Attorney General (now Governor) William Janklow, for example, has been cited as stating that 'South Dakota officials prepared the briefs and other legal material [in *Oliphant*] which cost the state about $20,000.' *Indian Jurisdiction Case Prepared by South Dakotans*, Rapid City Journal, Mar. 9, 1978, at 2, col. 1. Janklow further stated that *Oliphant* 'was a test case from the state of Washington but it was basically funded by the state of South Dakota. . . . It was really our lawsuit.' *Id*. Janklow added, finally, that 11 other states participated in the Oliphant case. *Id*."

11. The *Sioux Falls Argus Leader*, the *Rapid City Journal*, *Indian Country Today*, and the *Aberdeen American News* are the major newspapers in the state of South Dakota and provide a good source for understanding the attitudes of white South Dakotans.

12. The photos of the authors used elsewhere in the text, as well as the photo of the Big Foot Riders in this section, come from the collection of a Jesuit Catholic priest, Don Doll, who has taught at Creighton University in Omaha, Nebraska, and is the author of *Vision Quest: Men, Women and Sacred Sites of the Sioux Nation*. He previously published *Crying for a Vision: A Rosebud Sioux Trilogy: 1886–1976*.

13. See Zuni-Cíbola Act of 1988, 102 Stat. 2847.

14. U.S.C. 25 sec. 450 et seq.

PART 3: WOCOWOYAKE (TRUE STORIES)

1. "Proposed Wounded Knee Park and Memorial," Hearing (April 30, 1991).

2. For example, see Scott, *Politics and Society*.

3. "Proposed Wounded Knee Park and Memorial," Hearing (April 30, 1991), p. 83.

4. Ibid., p. 26.

5. "Congress passed the Indian Depredations Act on March 3, 1891 to resolve this issue [of settlers' complaints against tribes]. People with claims against the Indians still filed with the Secretary of the Interior for a decision, but appeals could be taken by the tribe or government to the Court of Claims" (Vine Deloria, Jr., "Congress in Its Wisdom," p. 112; see 26 Stat. 851).

Though there is some controversy on this point, the "Sioux Depredations Act" of 1891 was passed just months after the Wounded Knee Massacre so that ranchers, farmers, and "friendly" Indians could recoup losses of war even though no condition of "war" existed that time and the 1868 peace treaty had been signed. Those Indians called "hostile" and what was left of Chief Big Foot's Minneconjou people were excluded from such reparations (see 26 Stat. 1002). These facts make up a significant part of the ongoing disagreement concerning historical interpretations of events and policies issues. In the mid-sixties Indians began to question many of the rules and procedures of the process of reparation.

6. "Proposed Wounded Knee Park and Memorial," Hearing (April 30, 1991).

7. The original Black Hills bill introduced by Senator Bill Bradley of New Jersey was S. 1453, which was reintroduced by Bradley in 1987, in the 100th Congress, as S. 705. An amended version of the Bradley Bill was introduced by Congressman Matthew Martinez of California in 1990 as H.R. 5680.

8. Act of August 13, 1946, sec. 22 (60 Stat. 1055).

9. Many sources for American Indian Movement activities are available. Two significant references used here are "Occupation of Wounded Knee," Hearings before the Subcommittee on Indian Affairs of the Committee on Interior and Insular Affairs, U.S. Senate, 93d Cong. (June 16, 1973, at Pine Ridge, S.Dak., and June 17, 1973, at Kyle, S.Dak.), and Rolland Dewing, *Wounded Knee: The Meaning and Significance of the Second Incident.* While the introduction is said to be replete with inaccuracies and biases, Dewing's book is the source for much of our information as it is a work which tells a story about cultural opposition to Western domination. The book has never been taken up by a major publisher but was rereleased in 1995 as *Wounded Knee II,* shortened from 416 pages to 213 pages and printed by Great Plains Network and Pine Hill Press. The notes at the end of the original book are invaluable to researchers, grouped under the following chapter headings: America's Most Neglected Minority, Red Power, The New Indian Wars, Return to Wounded Knee, An Impasse, Reaching an Accord, Over the Brink, A Caldron of Violence, and Conclusion. The trading post story is covered extensively in this text. In the early 1900s, Congress passed the so-called surplus land acts which allowed non-Indians to take Indian lands on reservations as homesteads. The justification was to place non-Indian farmers in the midst of Indian allottees to teach them how to farm. It was really nothing more than a clever way to steal more Indian lands for European immigrants. Bennett County on the Pine Ridge Indian Reservation was open for non-Indian settlement under a 1910 surplus land act (36 Stat. 440).

Next came forced fee patents in 1917, under which the federal government sent competency commissions to Indian reservations. If an allottee was deemed "competent" enough to manage his own affairs he was issued a "forced fee patent" to his allotment notwithstanding the fact that the allottee never made an application for the patent and the 25-year trust period established under the 1889 act had not expired. Once the allottee got his "fee patent," the allotment became subject to county property taxes and tax foreclosure, another form of theft. Much treaty-protected land was also lost to unscrupulous non-Indians who cheated Indians out of their lands since restrictions on alienation were removed upon issuance of the fee patents. (See Macgregor, *Warriors without Weapons.*)

In 1948, the supervised sale act was passed (62 Stat. 236). Many Indians have since that time sold their allotted lands or inherited allotments to non-Indians through BIA supervised sales. The result of this has been a "checkerboarding" of non-Indian-owned, county taxable lands within the boundaries of the reservations. Recently, these non-Indian landholders and their heirs have started campaigning for "rights" on Indian reservations. Several works, most notably Fergus Bordewich's *Killing the White Man's Indian*, call for a solution to this "equal rights" problem. Bordewich says that permanent residents of reservations who are not enrolled members (i.e., non-Indian persons) do not have "representation" on the reservations where they reside and that the denial of their rights should cause the people of the United States to write an amendment to the Constitution clearly stating that Indian tribes are "subjects" of the United States and therefore "subject" to all of its laws. This writer does not much like the idea of "sovereignty" for Indian Nations within the United States, and suggests that the sovereign rights of Indians to claim their own citizenship as tribal members and their homelands as treaty-protected is a risk to the cultural definition of America, another facet of the Balkanization of the United States. What all of this means, one supposes, is that the adversaries to Indian life and limb, the land thieves, the "controllers," and the "colonizers" are still in place.

10. Mario's father's family came to the United States from the city of Loreto, located in the state of Zacatecas, Mexico. His paternal great-grandparents are Faustino Gonzalez and Andrea Bernal Gonzalez.

The Gonzalez family came to Loreto from Aguascalientes. The Bernals were already a prominent family there. Andrea's nephew Juan Bernal (a son of her brother Eluterio) served as a magistrate of Loreto in the 1940s.

Faustino's family migrated to the United States from the Hacienda de San Marcos in the early part of this century, first to Piedras Negras, Coahuila, Mexico, where family members worked in the coal mines. Then to Texas, where the family did migrant work as far north as the Brazos River. Andrea died in 1914 at Munford, Texas. Faustino moved back to Piedras Negras, where he died in the early 1920s.

Mario's grandfather Urbano Gonzalez was one of Faustino and Andrea's ten children. He married Guadalupe Delgado of Las Norias (a farming community near Loreto). Mario's father, Gabriel Gonzalez, was born in 1918 at Rio Escondidos, a town located south of Piedras Negras.

Urbano and his family worked in the asphalt mines at Cline, Texas, during the 1920s. They moved to San Antonio, Texas, in 1932 (when the asphalt mines closed) and resided there the remainder of their lives.

In 1942 Gabriel enlisted in the U.S. Army Air Corps at San Antonio and was stationed at Alliance, Nebraska, when he met Mario's mother, Geneva Wilcox Gonzalez (Winyan Waste), a half-blood Oglala Sioux from the village of Wanblee on the Pine Ridge Indian Reservation. In 1946, after his father was discharged from the U.S. Army Air Corps, Mario's parents moved to South Dakota, where they have resided up to the present time.

In January, 1946, Mario made a trip to Loreto with his parents and grandmother Guadalupe, who had made a pledge to take each of her sons to the Cathedral of San Juan de los Lagos (San Juan by the Lakes) for prayers if they returned home safely from World War II. Mario's parents described their experiences on the trip, and the history of the area his grandparents came from, in a 1992 conversation (taken from a December 20, 1992, diary entry):

Gabriel: We left San Antonio and traveled by bus to Eagle Pass, Texas, then crossed the Rio Grande at Eagle Pass to Piedras Negras, where we spent the night with my uncle Jesús and his family. The next day, we caught a train for Loreto. We traveled through several cities, including Monclova, Saltillo, Torreón, and Zacatecas, before we reached Loreto. The mountains between Saltillo and Zacatecas were beautiful. At times the train was near the top of the mountains and we could look down and see far below. Sometimes the train traveled slow, maybe 30 miles per hour, through the mountains. We once looked out of a window and saw another train. It turned out to be the same train we were riding on, making a circular turn.

Geneva: It took three days to reach Loreto from San Antonio. Your grandfather Urbano Gonzalez's brother, Refugio 'Cuco' Gonzalez, met us at the train station in Loreto. His sons, Gonzalo and Gabriel, who were young boys, were selling oranges at the train station when we arrived. We stayed at their home during our stay. The day after we arrived, Juan Bernal came to see us. He was living in a community called Asientos, and walked all the way to Loreto just to see us. He was an old man at this time, with a long bushy mustache and short beard. He was wearing a white shirt, white pants, sandals, a serape, and a straw hat.

Gabriel: Cuco's wife's name was Concepción Medina Gonzalez. She was a member of the Chichimeca Indian Tribe from the Tierra Blanca (White Earth) Indian Reservation located near San Marcos.

   We had a lot of fun the day we went to the Hacienda de San Marcos. The Hacienda de San Marcos is also referred to as the "Casa Grande." We walked the whole distance, about 10 to 15 miles from Loreto, but it didn't seem that far. We took turns riding in a cart pulled by a burro. The trip to the cathedral was also memorable. Cuco took us in his car to Aguascalientes, and from there we rode by bus. The bus was old and the ride was very rough. We bounced around as we traveled down the road. The bus driver stopped along the way to pick up two Indians, a boy and a girl. They conversed in an Indian language, although the boy knew Spanish. When the bus driver asked them for their fare in Spanish, the boy told him that they didn't have any money. The bus driver told them that he would give them a ride if they would dance Indian, so they both danced.

Geneva: When we arrived at the cathedral, Gabriel and his mother walked up several flights of stairs to the altar on their knees. His mother carried a candle.

Gabriel: There were many candle shops located all around the cathedral, and candles everywhere. And another thing I remember about the trip is an Indian man I saw standing at the entrance of a bar in Loreto, begging for a beer (in

Spanish). I told him "come on, I'll buy you a drink." When we entered the bar, the bartender told me that I could be arrested because it was illegal to buy alcoholic beverages for an Indian. He said that the Mexican government forbids the sale of alcoholic beverages to Indians because they get crazy when they get drunk. A few months later I visited South Dakota for the first time and was very surprised to learn that it was also a violation of federal law to buy alcoholic beverages for Indians in the United States.

Geneva: On our return trip, we came through San Luis Potosí and almost got stranded there. City health officials imposed a quarantine on the city because of a scarlet fever epidemic.

Gabriel: My father was born at Aguascalientes. When he was thirteen years old, he worked on the dam, called "La Presa" ("the Dam"), which was U-shaped. His job was to carry grout-cement in a sack, which had a strap or cap that fit on his forehead to help him carry it on his back. The dam and the Hacienda de San Marcos were built by a rich Spaniard named Gennaro García. He was a millionaire who traveled back and forth to Europe. He built the dam for irrigation. The hacienda was built with imported materials, marble and other materials. García hired my uncle Pablo Gonzalez as one of the keepers of the hacienda. During the revolution, García took off and later died in France. I believe the Mexican government confiscated his property.

My father told me that during the revolution, there was a battle at the Hacienda de San Marcos. There were bodies lying all over, some for about a week. When it wasn't too hot, people would drag the bodies into trenches and bury them. Also during the revolution, Anita Lara's brother was gone for a long time. No one knew what happened to him until he came back as a captain in the Mexican army. Anita Lara was the wife of my uncle Francisco "Pancho" Gonzalez.

My mother's father was Basilio Delgado, who had a ranch in a farming area called "Las Norias" ("the wells") near Loreto. My mother told me that the Mexican government confiscated the ranch during a period called the "Agrarian Reform."

The surname Gonzalez means the "son of" Gonzalo.

(Note: Indians were not allowed to purchase liquor in the United States until the Eisenhower administration.)

11. Phil Hogen is an enrolled member of the Oglala Sioux Tribe and a former classmate of Gonzalez at Kadoka, South Dakota.

12. "Message of Lincoln to the Senate," Dec. 11, 1862, reprinted in *The Collected Works of Abraham Lincoln,* ed. Roy P. Basler, vol. 5, pp. 550–51.

13. "It is a striking fact that no life was forfeited and no sentence of fine and imprisonment carried out in any judicial proceeding for treason arising out of the 're-

bellion' [Civil War]," according to James G. Randall in *Constitutional Problems under Lincoln*, p. 91.

14. See David H. Burton, *Theodore Roosevelt*, p. 43, quoting Theodore Roosevelt, *Hunting Trips of a Ranchman*, in *Works*, vol. 1, p. 19.

15. The Oglala Sioux Rural Water Supply System was established by sec. 3 of P.L. 100-516, 102 Stat. 2566.

16. David Seals, "The Lakota Nation: Another Breakaway Republic."

17. Seals, who goes by the name Davydd ap Saille, is a producer for Thunder Nations Productions. A petition for a court-ordered injunction was filed in June, 1995, by the Oglala Lakota Cultural Committee and its chairman, Philip Under Baggage, to prevent the making of a movie on Crazy Horse by one Seals production company (*Indian Country Today*, June 23, 1995).

18. Carl Boggs, *Gramsci's Marxism*, pp. 39–40.

19. Gonzalez could not accompany the Lakota delegation to Europe to meet with Austrian, German, and Swedish governmental officials because his wife was admitted to a hospital for surgery when the delegation was ready to leave. He kept in contact with the delegation by telephone each day, and issued press releases to inform reservation people of the meetings that were taking place. The meetings were historically significant because for the first time in the twentieth century the head of an Indian Reorganization Act government met with heads of state (i.e., the chancellor of Austria, the prime minister of Sweden, and the head of the German Green Party) to discuss foreign affairs, the sponsorship of the Oglala Sioux Tribe in the World Court so it could obtain an advisory opinion on whether the United States confiscation of the Black Hills in 1877 violated international law. The *Bennett County Booster II* at Martin, SD, printed the press releases but the *Lakota Times* refused to report on the meetings because its owner/editor, Tim Giago, Jr., as a tribal member was personally against President American Horse and the Oglala delegation using tribal funds to make the trip. Other members of the delegation included Mike Her Many Horses, Fred "Budger" Brewer, and Birgil Kills Straight.

20. Petra Kelly to the German parliament (1984). The International Indian Treaty Council (IITC) was originally established as an organization of indigenous peoples from North, Central, and South America and the Pacific working for recognition of their sovereignty and protection of their human rights, cultures, and sacred lands. The IITC was founded in 1974 at a gathering called by the American Indian Movement on the Standing Rock Reservation, attended by more than 5,000 representatives of ninety-eight indigenous nations. In 1977 the IITC was recognized as a nongovernmental organization (NGO) with consultative status to the United Nations Economic and Social Council. The IITC submits testimony and documentation to these and other U.N. forums as well as to international bodies such as the International Union for the Conservation of Nature (IUCN) and the World Archeological Congress, in order to systematically address concerns vital to indigenous peoples.

21. The following individuals were awarded a Medal of Honor for the 1890 Wounded Knee Massacre, according to *The Medal of Honor of the United States Army:* William G. Austin, John E. Clancy, Mosheim Feaster, Ernest A. Garlington, John C. Gresham, Mathew H. Hamilton, Joshua B. Hartzog, Harry L. Hawthorne, Marvin C. Hillock, George Hobday, George Loyd, Albert W. McMillan, Thomas Sullivan, Frederick E. Toy, Jacob Trautman, James Ward, Paul H. Weinert, and Hermann Ziegner.

22. In a July 29, 1993, hearing on (among other topics) the Wounded Knee National Memorial, Senator Ben Nighthorse Campbell (the only Native American senator to be serving in the U.S. Congress) had this to say about the Medals of Honor:

I am a Korean Vet, and like many American Indians are, very proud of the military. American Indians have served with distinction in virtually every war in memory, including World War I, World War II, and Korea, and Vietnam; and, in fact, in Kuwait. There were 12,500 Indians fighting under the American flag in Kuwait.

Two of the first six, in fact, in Kuwait—two of the first six Americans that were killed, were American Indians. And one was a Sioux, a Lakota; his name was Came From the Stars, as I remember. He was, by the way, they were killed by Americans. They were killed in friendly fire, the 2 that were killed in Kuwait, unfortunately.

But there is no question that American Indians have had kind of an interesting phenomenon take place, ending up 100 years later, fighting and protecting a flag that was, that represents freedoms that they were often denied in the history of this country.

But nevertheless there were over a dozen medals of honor given at Wounded Knee. They were not Congressional Medals of Honor, they were medals of honor given before Congress initiated them, they were Army medals of honor. But to this day I cannot believe anybody would be given a medal of honor for killing babies. But that is basically what they were for. And if they had been Congressional Medals of Honor, I would try and attach an amendment to this bill, very frankly, to revoke those Medals of Honor. But they were not in our jurisdiction; they were Army medals of honor, so there is not much we can do about that. (U.S. Congress, Senate, *Hearing before the Subcommittee on Public Lands, National Parks and Forests of the Committee on Energy and Natural Resources,* 103rd Cong., 1st sess. [1993].)

Campbell then went on the record as supporting the legislation for a monument.

It has never been the Lakota/Dakota view that Congress is separate from the Army, that the feds are separate from the state, that the people are separate from the government, that the courts are separate from something else, and so on and so on. This statement by Campbell, though it was taken in with politeness, was interpreted by some as just another excuse. Though a bit far afield from the specific issues here, there is an interesting new book on Indian veterans called *Strong Hearts, Wounded Souls: Native American Veterans of the Vietnam War,* by Tom Holm.

23. The National Parks and Conservation Association was established in 1919 and is the only national, nonprofit, membership organization that focuses on defending, promoting, and improving the national park system in the United States while educating the public about the parks.

24. Ed Lemmon, *Boss Cowman: The Recollections of Ed Lemmon (1857–1946)*, p. 151.

25. Flood's written testimony presented at "Wounded Knee Memorial and Historic Site—Little Big Horn National Monument Battlefield," Hearing (September 25, 1990).

26. Act of November 16, 1990 (104 Stat. 3048, 25 U.S.C. 3001 et seq.).

27. Types of land ownership: To break up tribal power, the Allotment Act of 1887 (Dawes Severalty Act) was passed by the U.S. Congress without the consent of Indian Nations to allot tracts of tribal land to individual Indians. Within twenty years 138,000,000 acres of treaty-protected land was diminished by two-thirds. Some say this was an effort to assimilate Indians into non-Indian society. Others say it was a matter of simple greed. Today about half of the allotted lands are in multiple "heirship" status often expressed in fractional interests with a common denominator of 1,000,000 and has resulted in landless Indians gripped in poverty. The U.S. government as "trustee" of Indian tribes has confiscated thousands upon thousands of acres of Indian land over the last century, often citing "the public good" as the rationale. Many other categories of land possession exist on Indian reservations throughout the United States, for example "sub-marginal lands" are those reservation lands purchased by the federal government during the drought period of the 1930s but never restored to tribal ownership (when oil was discovered on submarginal lands on the Fort Peck Reservation in Montana). These lands were finally returned to tribal ownership in 1975. See Act of October 17, 1975 (89 Stat. 577, 25 U.S.C. 459 et seq.). Administration of land activities on Indian reservations is in the hands of the Bureau of Indian Affairs, which responds to every whim of a greedy economically driven Congress. Many economists and historians have said that without land reform native Americans will continue to be poor and exploited. The Sioux Tribes, too, in refusing to compromise on the "buy-out" scheme in the Black Hills, know that land restoration and a fair and honorable settlement for the denial of the absolute and undisturbed use and occupation of the Black Hills for the past 121 years is the answer to their survival.

28. Neil Larson and Pete Larson, two white men who grew up on or near the Rosebud Sioux Reservation in South Dakota, removed a complete Tyrannosaurus rex dinosaur fossil from the Cheyenne River Sioux Reservation and allegedly paid $5,000 to an Indian rancher, Maurice Williams, from whose land the bones were taken. The dinosaur relic was recently auctioned by Sotheby's in New York City for more than $8 million and will be the property of the Museum of Natural History in Chicago. Denying that they were mercenary fossil hunters or thieves of Indian property, the brothers placed the fossilized skeleton in a building called the Black Hills Institute

of Geological Research at Hill City, South Dakota, and began charging entrance fees to the tourists in the Hills. Federal criminal charges were eventually brought against the men. The federal government took possession of the huge fossil in 1991 and placed it in a repository at the South Dakota School of Mines and Technology. A local non-Indian jury found the fossil hunters not guilty of many of the charges against them, and the local non-Indian press declared them "innocent." The Cheyenne River Sioux Tribe, according to Williams, attempted to "steal" the fossil by arguing that Williams failed to buy a $100 tribal business permit and therefore forfeited his rights to it. The non-Indian brothers, of course, contend it is they who must be protected from the federal government's seizure of the fossil remains. This is another case which exemplifies the fact that Indians are almost powerless to stop vandalism, commerce, and theft and that the legal system is biased against them. Though there has been little public discussion of this kind of questionable activity, the protection of Indian property on Indian reservations, namely, relics and bones, from mercenaries is probably more necessary now than at any time in history.

29. True Clown, Sr., stated at the September 21, 1991, WKSA meeting that his great-grandmother was Iron Cedar Woman, a sister to Chief Crazy Horse. Some historians believe that Iron Cedar Woman appears to be related to Chief Crazy Horse not by blood but by marriage. This is based on the fact that an Oglala named Kicking Bird has been identified as a cousin of Crazy Horse and that Kicking Bird's parents Black Fox and Iron Cedar Woman were not related to those of Crazy Horse, so the kinship association to Crazy Horse must have been established through marriage. See David H. Miller, *Ghost Dance,* p. 11; and Major Israel McCreight, *Firewater and Forked Tongues,* p. xxi.

30. Big Woman married a man named One Horse. The couple's two daughters married a half-blood Sioux named George Standing Bear (whose English surname, according to Oglala historian Wallace Amiotte, was "Arcoren"). Standing Bear had several children from these wives including Luther (from the first wife) and Henry, Willard, Ellis, Emily, and Victoria (from the second wife). Emily married Peter Dillon and Victoria married Harry Conroy.

31. Chief Crazy Horse also had a half-brother named Little Hawk, whose mother was one of the two sisters of Chief Spotted Tail that Worm had married after Rattle Blanket Woman left him.

32. For many years, Sioux Indians asserted claims for loss of horses, arms, and other equipment of a military nature taken from them by U.S. military authorities subsequent to 1876. A suit filed in the Court of Claims on June 7, 1923 (C-531), by attorney Ralph Case asserted claims for individuals, but the court determined that the special jurisdictional act the case was filed under did not give the court jurisdiction to determine claims of a purely individual character.

In a December 3, 1940, memorandum to the secretary of the interior explaining the pony claims, Interior Department Solicitor Nathan R. Margold gave a synopsis of the history and character of the Sioux pony claims:

For your information I am setting forth a synopsis of the history and character of the Sioux pony claims. For many years the Sioux have asserted claims for personal property, particularly horses and arms taken from them by military authority on various occasions in the latter part of the nineteenth century and particularly in 1876. Three acts of Congress were passed appropriating fixed sums to pay pony claims at designated agencies. The act of March 2, 1889 (25 Stat. 888,899), authorized payment up to $28,200 to such individual Indians of the Red Cloud and Red Leaf Bands of Sioux as were deprived by the United States of their ponies in 1876, at the rate of $40 for each pony. The act of January 18, 1891 (26 Stat. 720), authorized payment up to $200,000 to such individual Indians of the Standing Rock and Cheyenne River Reservations as were deprived of ponies in 1876, at the same rate per pony. The act of June 21, 1906 (34 Stat. 325,374), authorized payment of $6,320 to 15 Sioux Indians of the Pine Ridge Agency for the loss of property for reasons of military expediency while they were in amity with the United States. The Act of May 3, 1928, was the first act to authorize a general investigation of such claims, leaving the amount of compensation to be determined by the Secretary of the Interior and reported to Congress for latter Appropriation.

In his memorandum, Mr. Margold also discussed the construction and application of the term "hostility" in the 1928 act, which provided:

That the Secretary of the Interior be, and he is hereby, authorized and directed to investigate, hear, and determine the claims of the individual Indians whose names are enrolled on the approved rolls of the following Indian agencies: Rosebud, Pine Ridge, Lower Brule, Crow Creek, Cheyenne River, Yankton, Sisseton, and Flandreaux in the State of South Dakota; Fort Peck, in the State of Montana; Fort Totton, in the State of North Dakota; Standing Rock, in the States of North and South Dakota; and Santee, in the State of Nebraska: Provided, That the Secretary of the Interior is authorized to make all rules and regulations necessary to carry out the provisions of this Act: Provided further, That the claims which shall be investigated under this Act shall be individual claims for allotments of land and for loss of personal property or improvements where the claimants or those through whom the claims originated were not members of any band of Indians engaged in hostilities against the United States at the time the losses occurred. If any such claims shall be considered meritorious, the Secretary of the Interior shall adjust same where there is existing law to authorize their adjustment, and such other meritorious claims he shall report to Congress with appropriate recommendations.

Between 15,000 and 20,000 claims of all types were filed by individual Sioux Indians under the act and investigated by the secretary of the interior. Four claims were allowed of the 511 filed by the Indians at Pine Ridge Agency. Four claims were allowed of the 520 claims filed at Cheyenne River Agency. At Rosebud Agency, in place of the 289 claims for ponies taken by the U.S. military from 1874 to 1884, there were substituted two lists of claims prepared by Lt. Lee covering ponies and cattle stolen by U.S. citizens from 1875 to 1878. The claims on Lt. Lee's list amount to $10,555, all of which were allowed. The total claims from all agencies amounted to $19,357.

On February 16, 1933, Congress passed an act (47 Stat. 818) to authorize an appropriation to carry out the provisions of the Act of May 3, 1928:

> That there is hereby authorized to be appropriated out of any money in the Treasury of the United States of America not otherwise appropriated, $19,357 to pay certain individual enrolled Indians under the Pine Ridge, Standing Rock, Cheyenne River, and Rosebud Agencies, in full settlement of such claims against the Government, the amounts which they have been awarded by the Secretary of the Interior under the Act of Congress of May 3, 1928 (45 Stat. 484): Provided, That the Secretary of the Interior is authorized and directed to determine what attorney or attorneys have rendered services of value in behalf of said Indians and to pay such attorney or attorneys on such findings when appropriation is available the reasonable value of such services, not to exceed 10 per centum of the recovery on any individual claim, which payment shall be in full settlement for all services rendered by such attorney or attorneys to said claimants.

On March 2, 1932, the secretary of the interior approved the recommendations of the commissioner of Indian Affairs for the approval of four of the 511 claims filed at Pine Ridge Agency. One of the four claims was a claim filed on behalf of Flying Horse for one horse killed during the Wounded Knee Massacre: "No. 3, P.R. 1298,—Flying Horse, for one horse killed by the military at the battle of Wounded Knee. It appears that the father of Claimant was engaged in rounding up some of his stock during this battle and was not in any way connected with Chief Big Foot or his band with whom this battle was fought. The father of claimant was mistaken for a hostile, fired upon by the troops and he and his horse were killed. The claimed value of the horse is $40.00, and this claim is listed under Class 2 (c)."

At Rosebud Agency, the 289 filed were categorized as follows:

Class 2 (a)	189 Claims,	$80,520.00
Class 2 (c)	49 Claims,	26,442.25
Class 2 (f)	2 Claims,	560.00
Unclassified	32 Claims,	16,662.75
Withdrawn, or no	17 Claims,	5,496.12
hearing held for	289 Claims,	129,681.12
sufficient cause,		

Class 2 (a) claims were for loss of ponies taken by U.S. military authorities from 1874 to 1884. Included under Class 2 (a) claims was R. 30 for one horse owned by Chief Crazy Horse's father, Wagula (who was also known by the name of Crazy Horse), that was stolen by U.S. military authorities at Spotted Tail Agency in 1877.

Practically every claim submitted under the 1928 act at Rosebud Agency was found to be without merit because the claimants were deemed to be "hostile" at the time the loss occurred or were determined to have already been paid. An exception were those claims investigated, certified, and recommended for payment fifty years earlier (in 1878) by Lt. J. M. Lee, Ninth Infantry, acting agent in charge of Spotted Tail Agency, Dakota Territory, under Article 1 of the 1868 treaty and section 2158 of the Revised Statutes of the United States. Congress never authorized payment for any of the claims recommended for payment by Lt. Lee; consequently, many of these claims were refiled under the 1928 act. Lt. Lee's lists of claims were printed in House Ex. Doc. 125, 49th Cong., 1st sess., as Schedule B (pp. 280–83), nos. 678–784 and 785–808. Lt. Lee's lists included the claim for the pony owned by Chief Crazy Horse's father:

SCHEDULE 5.—A list of claims for losses sustained by Sioux Indians at the Spotted Tail Agency, Dakota, on account of depredations by white citizens of the United States at the time set opposite the Indians' name, respectively, and reported upon by J. M. Lee, Lieutenant, Ninth United States Infantry, acting Indian Agent.
[Subscribed and sworn to before J. M. Lee, March, 1878]

No.	When	Ponies Stolen	Value	Name of Claimant	Where and by whom stolen
791	Apr. 1866	1	15.00	Crazy Horse	Old agency, Neb. by whites

In 1877, Spotted Tail Agency was located on Beaver Creek, north of present-day Hay Springs, Nebraska. Waglula was living at Spotted Tail Agency with his two wives, both sisters of Chief Spotted Tail, when his son Chief Crazy Horse was killed at Fort Robinson, Nebraska, in September, 1877. Chief Crazy Horse was brought to Beaver Creek and placed on a death scaffold constructed on a tree. Later, his parents moved his body several times before taking it to its final resting place east of Wanblee, South Dakota. Waglula and his two wives spent the remainder of their lives among the Indians at Spotted Tail Agency (which later became the Rosebud Indian Reservation) to be near their son's body.

After Congress appropriated money to pay the horse claims, it became necessary for the secretary of the interior to determine the heirs of deceased claimants. A controversy arose over the estate of Crazy Horse for the amount awarded by the U.S. government for one pony claim. It was not known whether the pony claim belonged to Chief Crazy Horse's father Waglula (aka Crazy Horse) who married two of Chief Spotted Tail's sisters and died on the Rosebud Reservation, or the man who married Chief Crazy Horse's half-blood wife (after he was killed at Fort Robinson in 1877) and assumed his name so he could use his ration card. The following are statements and correspondence that occurred between federal officials at Rosebud Agency and Pine Ridge Agency in an effort to determine which Crazy Horse the pony claim belonged to:

25811

PERSONAL PROPERTY OR IMPROVEMENTS

CLAIM NUMBER   *Rosebud* Agency

R. 30, Class 2 (a)   *$80.00* Amount

TO THE SECRETARY OF THE INTERIOR:

Comes now *Making Coffee,* Heir of *Crazy Horse* Deceased, as determined by Probate finding of Interior Department, under date of *(left blank),* and makes claim, under oath, under the [date] of May 3, 1928, Public No. 347, 70th Congress, as follows:

Claimant says that *he is* enrolled on the approved rolls of the *Rosebud* Agency. That the loss for which this claim is made is the loss of *2 horses* belonging to said deceased *Crazy Horse.* That the amount claimed is *$80.00.* That at the time the loss occurred, to-wit: *(left blank)* day of *1877,* Decedent's band of Indians was not engaged in hostilities against the United States.

That neither the Decedent, nor the claimant has ever received payment in full or in part, for said losses, except as follows: *(left blank).*

That the details of this claim are as follows: *Band to which deceased claimant was a member was engaged in hostilities against the U.S.; as was claimant. The horses were turned out in the evening and in the morning they were missing; that claimant does not know who took the horses, but believes it to have been white men.*

WHEREFORE, Claimant prays the Secretary of the Interior to adjust this claim under existing law, or report this claim to Congress, with recommendation that it be paid.

Signed Rudolph E. Miles   *(Thumb print of Making Coffee)*
                                                                          Claimant

Signed Foster Jannis
Witnesses

Subscribed and sworn to before me this *23rd* day of *March,* 1931.

                                                            Signed Rudolph E. Miles
Official Representative   Official Title

STATE OF SOUTH DAKOTA)
) ss
COUNTY OF *Todd*   )

We *Kills The Enemy Cold and Stephen Brave Bird* are enrolled members of the *Sioux tribe* of *Rosebud Indians* being duly sworn, do depose and say that we have had read and interpreted to us the foregoing sworn statements of *Making Coffee* and know of our own knowledge that the facts therein set forth are true and correct.

Witnesses to mark

Rudolph E. Miles   *(Thumb print of Kills The Enemy Cold)*
                                                   Signature of Affiant

Foster Jannis   *(Thumb print of Stephen Brave Bird)*
                                                   Signature of Affiant

Subscribed and sworn to before me on this *23rd* day of *March*, 1931.

Signed Rudolph E. Miles
Assistant Clerk

I certify that I interpreted the aforesaid deposition to *Kills The Enemy Cold and Stephen Brave Bird* who clearly understand the same.

Signed Foster Jannis
Interpreter

Date *March 23, 1931*

Claim No. *R. 30* Class 2 *(a)*
Claim of *Crazy Horse*
Presented by *Making Coffee*
Interpreter *Foster Jannis*
Oath Administered

Q. Are you enrolled on the approved rolls of the Rosebud Agency?
A. Yes.
Q. To what band do you belong?
A. Crazy Horse.
Q. Was Crazy Horse a member of the same band?
A. Yes.
Q. Was this band engaged in hostilities against the U.S. at the time the loss occurred?
A. Yes.
Q. Was Crazy Horse engaged in hostilities against the U.S. at the time the loss occurred?
A. Yes.
Q. What is the loss you are claiming?
A. 2 horses at $40.00 each.
Q. When did the loss occur?
A. 1877.
Q. Where did this loss occur?
A. Niobrara River in Nebraska.
Q. How did Crazy Horse lose the horses?

A. They were put out in the evening and were missing in the morning.

Q. Who told you of this loss?

A. He went out looking for the horses and they were missing.

Q. Did Crazy Horse see the horses taken?

A. No.

Q. Did he know who took the horses?

A. He never saw who took them, but he knows the white men took them.

Q. How long ago did Crazy Horse die?

A. 1888.

Q. How old are you?

A. 73.

Q. Did Kills The Enemy Cold and Stephen Brave Bird see the horses taken?

A. They didn't see who took them, but they heard that they were taken.

Q. Has this claim ever been presented to the government before for payment?

A. No.

Q. Did Crazy Horse, or have you ever received any payment either in money or supplies or any consideration whatsoever from the U.S. from any official of the government for this loss?

A. No.

Witnesses:

Signed Foster Jannis   (*Thumb print of Making Coffee*)

Rosebud Indian Agency

Rosebud, South Dakota

June 14, 1934

Mr. James H. McGregor, Supt.

Pine Ridge Agency

Pine Ridge, South Dakota

Dear Mr. McGregor:

Included in the sum transferred to your agency for claims allowed for lost ponies was the amount of $13.50 for claim of Crazy Horse for one pony. One of our Indians by the name of Coffee No. 2 feels that he should receive a part of this sum as he insists that he is an heir. Please advise if it has been paid to the heirs and if so the names of the heirs. Coffee No. 2 makes frequent inquiries about [SIC] and we will appreciate the above information in order that we may advise him.

   Yours very truly,

                              W. O. Roberts
                              Superintendent

88

In reply Please Refer to:
268

UNITED STATES
DEPARTMENT OF THE INTERIOR
OFFICE OF INDIAN AFFAIRS
Field Service

Pine Ridge Agency,
Pine Ridge, So. Dak.
June 21, 1934.

Mr. W. O. Roberts, Superintendent,
Rosebud, South Dakota.

Dear Mr. Roberts:

This will acknowledge receipt of your letter of June 14, 1934, regarding Coffee No. 2 and his probable interest in the pony claim of Crazy Horse.

This money has not been distributed for the reason that we have been unable to ascertain which Crazy Horse it was that lost these horses but we have been informed by quite a number of Pine Ridge Indians that the Crazy Horse from whom the pony was taken was our allottee #3955, and if this is the case Coffee No. 2 would not be one of the heirs.

The Crazy Horse that we think has this claim lived on the Eagle Nest District and his allotment was near the mouth of Pass Creek in Washabaugh county. I will appreciate it very much if you will question Coffee No. 2 and see if that Crazy Horse [is] the proper man. Another way you can identify him to Coffee No. 2 is that he was married to a half breed woman who was the daughter of old Todd Randall.

I will appreciated anything you can do to help us to identify this Indian for we are anxious to get this money distributed to the heirs.

Very truly yours,
Signed   James H. McGregor,
Superintendent

MM:MAM

Rosebud Indian Agency
Rosebud, South Dakota
July 2, 1934

Mr. James H. McGregor, Supt.
Pine Ridge Agency,
Pine Ridge, South Dakota.

Dear Mr. McGregor:

Referring to your letter of June 21, there is enclosed statement of Coffee No. 2 in regard to the pony claim allowed Crazy Horse. Coffee No. 2 is very deaf and it is difficult to get testimony from him. We trust the enclosed statement will be of assistance in settling this case.

Yours very truly,
W. O. Roberts
Superintendent

88
encl.

Statement of Coffee No. 2 in regard to pony claim allowed Crazy Horse.

There were three Crazy Horses. Out of those only one Crazy Horse was allotted and he was allotted on the Pine Ridge Reservation and died at Wanblee on the Pine Ridge Reservation not very long ago. The second Crazy Horse was the famous Crazy Horse killed by soldiers at Fort Robinson, Nebraska. The third Crazy Horse is the old man who put in a claim for 1 lost pony and which was allowed by the government. This claimant had one daughter and one son. The daughter's name was Looks At Her and she was my mother. I am the only child. The son's name was Crazy Horse and he was the famous Crazy Horse who was killed by soldiers at Fort Robinson, Nebraska.

The allotted Crazy Horse who died at Wanblee recently was known as Crazy Horse because his mixed blood wife was formerly the wife of the famous Crazy Horse who was killed by soldiers.

WITNESSES:
Lottie Georgenson   (*Thumb print of Coffee No. 2*)
Jacob LaPointe
Subscribed and sworn to before me this 26th day of June, 1934.

Signed Charles Brooks
Chas. Brooks, Senior Clerk

Your No. 268

Rosebud Indian Agency
Rosebud, South Dakota,
July 7, 1934

Mr. James H. McGregor, Supt.
Pine Ridge Agency
Pine Ridge, South Dakota.

Dear Mr. McGregor:

Referring further to your letter of June 21, there is enclosed herewith testimony of Brave Bird and Afraid of Eagle in connection with the claim allowed Crazy Horse for a lost pony.

Yours very truly,
Chas. Brooks,
Clerk in Charge

88
encl.

ESTATE OF CRAZY HORSE

Q. State your names, ages, residences, and tribe.

A. Brave Bird, age 76, residence Rosebud, Rosebud Sioux Indian; Afraid of Eagle, age 76, post office address Parmelee, S.D., Rosebud Sioux.

Q. A claim for one lost pony has been allowed Crazy Horse. Did you know this Crazy Horse?

A. Yes.

Q. When did he die?

A. Four years after this agency was established. (Agency established in 1879).

Q. How many times was he married?

A. Twice.

Q. Who was his first wife?

A. We don't know the names of either wife but they were sisters he was married to.

Q. Did he have any children by the first wife?

A. They had two daughters. One died when she was small and the second is the mother of this man, Coffee #2. The first daughter died before her parent.

Q. When did the second daughter die?

A. The summer before this agency was established.

Q. How many times was she married?

A. Just once.

Q. What other children did she have besides Coffee, #2?

A. She had three children, and Coffee #2 is one of them. The other two died long ago before this agency was established, before their parents, single and with no issue.

Q. When did her husband, that is the father of Coffee #2, die?

A. He died long before this agency was established. He died before his wife.

Q. When did the second wife of Crazy Horse die?

A. She died three years after her husband died.

Q. What children did she and Crazy Horse have?

A. They had three girls and one boy.

Q. Are they living or when did they die?

A. They are all dead now. All the girls died single, and with no issue before their father and mother. He has married twice. His first wife died before her husband. They had one son died before 1876, single and with no issue. His second wife died not very long ago at Wanblee on the Pine Ridge Reservation. I don't know her name. They had no children.

Q. Did she have a husband when she died?

A. After this famous Crazy Horse died she married another man by the name of Crazy Horse. Soon after she died her second husband, Crazy Horse, died. They had no children.

Q. Is there anything further you want to say?

A. No. That is all.

WITNESSES:

Lottie Jeorgenson	*(Thumb print of Brave Bird)*
Jacob LaPointe	*(Thumb print of Afraid of Eagle)*

In addition to the foregoing correspondence and statements, the following diary entry regarding Crazy Horse from Mario's diary is also worth mentioning:

Diary: September 1, 1995

I had breakfast with Ray Martinez of Kyle, South Dakota, this morning and talked to him about family relationships on the Pine Ridge Reservation. . . . Ray said that his grandfather's name was Manuel Martinez, and that his real surname was Mesteth (original spelling was probably Maestas). . . . He said that he is related to the Mesteth family that currently resides on the reservation. Children of his grandfather Manuel are:

Joseph (Ray's father)
Philip (a full brother to Joseph)
Jim (a half brother to Joseph)
Dick (a half brother to Joseph)

Joseph Martinez married Julia Harvey. . . . Julia's father was George Harvey and his wife was Maggie Cicler Harvey. Maggie's mother was Parts Her Hair, a relative of Chief Crazy Horse. Thus, Ray is related to Crazy Horse through his grandfather Harvey. (Note: this reminds me of a conversation I had with Jack Runnels. Jack told me that his grandfather John Conroy [a.k.a. American Man in pre-reservation days] personally knew Crazy Horse and had a photograph of a man that he said resembled Chief Crazy Horse. Jack said he saw the photograph, and the man in the photograph resembled George Harvey. The George Harvey that Jack referred to was his first cousin who was probably named after Ray Martinez's grandfather, his aunt Mary Conroy Harvey's son. Mary Conroy Harvey was also the sister of my father-in-law Gerry Conroy.)

Ray said that one of his grandmothers lived with a man named Elridge, but had no children from him; his grandmother's children all went by the name of Elridge instead of Martinez, however, because of the prejudice that exists against Spanish-surnamed people on the reservation.

Ray said that Frank Kicking Bear's mother was related to Chief Crazy Horse; her name was Iron Cedar Woman and she was a sister to Crazy Horse's mother. (Note: I recall Ellen In The Woods of Dupree, South Dakota, mentioning Iron Cedar Woman when we discussed True Clown, Sr., being related to Chief Crazy Horse through his real mother, Rattle Blanket Woman. True claims to be a direct descendant of Chief Crazy Horse.) I asked Ray where he got the information on Iron Cedar Woman and he said his brother Walter Martinez has a book that talked about her.

Ray said that he was told that the reason Chief Crazy Horse's parents moved his body so much is because they were afraid the soldiers were going to cut off his head and take it back east as a trophy. I told him that soldiers were cutting off heads of Indian warriors in the 1870s so scientists could study the size of Indian skulls to determine if Indians were inferior to non-Indians intellectually; that the Smithsonian Institution has the skulls of many warriors taken from battles with the U.S. Army for this reason.

I also told Ray about a conversation I had with Robert Dillon before he died. Robert Dillon, who was the son of Emily Standing Bear Dillon and nephew of Henry Standing Bear, said that Chief Crazy Horse's body was moved several times, first from Beaver Creek in Nebraska to Manderson, South Dakota, then to Eagle Nest Butte north of Wanblee, and to its final resting place east of Wanblee, South Dakota. He said it would take his father and mother one day to travel from Dillon's ranch north of Wanblee to the burial site in a wagon.

Ray also said that he was told Frank Kicking Bear married one of Sitting Bull's nieces and didn't get along with Sitting Bull. He said that one old Indian told him that Sitting Bull didn't have any children of his own; that all his children, including Crow Foot, were adopted children. He said that old Indians didn't lie and told what they believed to be true; that some of those old Indians could really stare you down; they had piercing eyes.

33. While for many, the discourse of the legislative effort seemed to move the tribes and the United States government into a modern relationship in which the "trust" responsibilities would be examined and transformed, others disagreed, largely, it was thought, for the publicity it would bring to their organization and leadership and

for the right to sit at the discussion table. Gerald Ice, Walter Little Moon, and Ben George Little Moon, members of the Oglala Sioux Tribe, as late as March, 1998, continue their opposition even though the proposed Wounded Knee bill has not been introduced in the last two sessions of Congress. Ice and his non-Indian wife at the time, Pamela Ice, formed a group called Wapaha Canku Luta, Inc., gave a Wounded Knee, South Dakota, address, as well as an address in San Diego. The following statement is what they put out on the Internet and faxed to numerous newspapers: "Another Attempt by the U.S. Government to Reclaim Wounded Knee, South Dakota." Stirring the controversy, they said the following: "We would like to bring to your attention yet another attempt by the United States Government to subversively steal treaty lands from the Native Americans. What makes this attempt even more shocking is that the lands being taken are the sacred grounds of Wounded Knee. On Saturday the Wounded Knee Landowners Association and the WCL, Inc., will hold a demonstration. We will start here and then go to Washington D.C., to fight in court and Congress if necessary. Speakers at the March demonstration will be Leonard Crow Dog, Gerald Ice, Francis He Crow, Manson Garreaux, Melvin Garreaux, Sr., Jasper Spotted Elk, Walter Little Moon, Gene Poor Bear, Neva Standing Bear and Bernard Ice. There have been two bloody incidents at Wounded Knee . . . a massacre of Indians by the [cavalry] in the 1890's and a bloody standoff between the Lakotas (Sioux), and FBI Agents, U.S. Marshalls, tribal police and all branches of the U.S. Armed Forces (except the Navy) in the 1970's. By arranging this peaceful demonstration we are trying to avoid a third incident. We urge you to consider covering the demonstrations and reasons for it in your program. We believe that both of us will benefit: we will receive the national publicity our cause so desperately needs and you will get in on the ground floor of a story that may reach historic proportions, enhance your journalistic integrity, and in all probability, deliver great ratings to your network." Contact numbers were given for Pamela Ice, Tom Clifford, and Walter Little Moon. This idea, while inaccurate and counterproductive, may be believed by an uninformed public. When considering autonomy for American Indian Nations within the American framework, it is often a challenge to get the right information and act upon it.

The question of who speaks for Indians is a real dilemma in America. The politicians in Washington, when they speak to anyone at all, will only speak with tribal chairmen, duly elected officials. The media will speak to anyone with long hair and a headband. Gullible tourists and new-agers will believe anything that is told to them by anyone who "looks Indian." And, now, anyone can put anything on the Internet. While most recognize that there are Jewish intellectuals who ask the difficult and sometimes unanswerable questions of the people, while there is now recognized a black intellectualism which has become part of the nation's discourse, the idea that there is a native intellectual base for inquiring minds is thought by most people to be absurd. There are only the "militants," that is, AIM, or the "shamans," or those of the "primitive mind set," reformed alcoholics, and the "wonderful old people," or the white "experts" who have "lived with the natives," many of them claiming to have had "spiritual" experiences, and been given Indian names. American Indian intellectualism seems to most Americans a bizarre phrase falling quaintly on unaccustomed ears. But, the truth is, there are native, tribally based lawyers, writers, professors, college presidents, politicians, program developers, social scientists, nurses and physicians, linguists, farmers and ranchers, grassroots people of consequence like the now-deceased Royal Bull Bear as heads of long-standing tribal organizations who will and must ask what it means to be an Indian in tribal America. They are seeking the appropriate answers to difficult questions and trying not to distort the story. The ultimate price of resistance for American Indians in past centuries has been to give up their very lives. Assassination. Massacre. Assimilation. It is the hope of all those who have made this story and those who have read it that working together, we can find alternatives to that reality.

PART 4: THE IMAGINED SENSE AND THE COMMUNITY
AS TRIBAL NATION

1. Severt Young Bear and R. D. Theisz, *Standing in the Light.*
2. Marla N. Powers, *Oglala Women,* p. 205.
3. It is difficult for enlightened Americans to fathom the racial hatred that must have been a characteristic of those Indian/White war periods. Some of the Indian hating, however, which is at the root of today's South Dakota's race relations, has been recorded. Just a quick look at old newspaper files reveals much about the period when Hunkpapa Chieftain Sitting Bull fought for the right to be an Indian in America. Five months after the assassination of Sitting Bull and the subsequent slaughter of the unarmed women and children of Big Foot's band by U.S. soldiers, the invective concerning his heroic leadership of the Sioux Nation was unrelenting. This editorial appeared in a major regional newspaper and is reprinted here as an example of the hundreds of such public expressions of the era. It should not be dismissed as "the climate of the times" or a "minority view" or journalistic hyperbole. Instead, it should be read and studied as the not insignificant opinion of the masses of Europeans who made up the immigrant population in the region of the northern plains whose descendants still occupy the land. The legacy of this philosophy is alive and well even at the close of a very remarkable twentieth century.

"The Last of Sitting Bull"
St. Louis Republic, St. Louis, Missouri
Wednesday, Dec. 17, 1890

The death of Sitting Bull removes one of the obstacles to civilization. He was a greasy savage, who rarely bathed and was liable at any time to become infected with vermin. During the whole of his life he entertained the remarkable delusion that he was a free-born American with some rights in the country of his ancestors. Under this delusion, when civilized immigrants pushed over the Black Hills country in search of gold he considered them trespassers on the lands of his people and tried to keep them out. He was engaged in this absurd and wicked attempt when General Custer surprised his camp in the interests of civilization. Unfortunately for civilization General Custer was mistaken in the number of the savages who had assembled to fight for the land, which they foolishly believed was their birthright, and "a massacre" ensued. That is, it was one of those rare occasions when savagery for the moment had the best of it in a pitched battle with civilization. It was, of course, only for the moment, and Sitting Bull and his followers, who might have been easily and legally hanged as murderers, were granted a temporary respite.

This graciousness of the Great Father they have constantly abused by obstructing civilization in every possible way, especially in the worst way possible by trying to keep their land in a state of barbarism, and by insisting on their own understanding of treaties, regardless of necessary changes in translation into a highly civilized language, and of necessary amendments made in Congress. They have gone on holding ghost dances, complaining about the rations issued to them under treaties, objecting to the way their money was handled by the government, and it is charged on excellent civilized authority, actually stealing from civilized people who have settled on their lands.

Under such circumstances there could have been only one ending for Sitting Bull, and now that it has come he has no complaint to make. There is every reason to believe, therefore, that it was perfectly satisfactory to him. He himself had recognized it as inevitable and had fully made up his mind to it, preferring it to death in what in his barbaric way he called the "stone houses of the Great Father," meaning thereby the penitentiaries in which the Great Father, with the aid of Hon. Powell Clayton, Hon. Poker J. McClure and others of his Sanhedrin, attempts on occasion to incarcerate those who disagree with him in such a way as to inconvenience him.

So when Sitting Bull was surprised and overpowered by the agents of the Great Father, he set his greasy, stolid face into the expression it always took when he was most overcome by the delusion that he was born a native American from native American ancestry. Disarmed and defenceless he sat in the saddle in which he had been put as a preliminary to taking him to prison, and without a change of countenance urged his handful of greasy followers to die free. This idiotic proceeding he kept up until he was shot out of the saddle.

So died Sitting Bull. So was removed one of the last obstacles in the path of progress. He will now make excellent manure for the crops, which will grow over him when his reservation is civilized.

The work of redeeming these excellent lands from barbarism has now reached a point where it can be at once carried to completion. The filth and vermin-infested Sioux and other savages who have pretended a desire to live even under starvation rations and broken treaties will be persuaded by Sitting Bull's example, and a little skillful management of the same kind which converted him from a brutal savage into a good Indian, to stand up where they can be shot out of the way of advancing progress.

Mr. Harrison should continue to act with the same promptness and firmness he has shown in Sitting Bull's case. While one of these barbarians lives to claim an acre of unentered land in the United States he will remain as an obstacle to progress. A firm persistence by the President in the admirably progressive policy he has illustrated in Sitting Bull's case will make good Indians of all the rest of them, bucks, squaws and pappooses. And the future historian will say of them, no doubt, that they died justly, because they owned lands and would not use fine-toothed combs."

4. As Vine Deloria, Jr., notes in "Congress in Its Wisdom": "Many traditional Indians then argued that they had dual citizenship, both tribal and American, but the Iroquois, believing that the imposition of American citizenship would injure their tribal affiliation, promptly sent the President notice of their rejection of American Citizenship" (p. 117). On Indian citizenship, see also Felix S. Cohen's *Handbook of Federal Indian Law*, pp. 153–57.

When the U.S. Constitution was adopted in 1789, Black people and Indian people were defined in the Constitution. Black people were defined as property. See Dred Scott v. Sandford, 19 How. 393 (1857). Indians were defined as "Indians not taxed." The status of Black people was changed after the Civil War; they became people and not property by virtue of the Thirteenth Amendment, and federal and state citizens by virtue of the Fourteenth Amendment. An argument can be made that the status of Indians has never changed since there is no *constitutional amendment* making them U.S. citizens or citizens of the states wherein they reside.

"Indians not taxed" is a constitutional category excluding Indian tribes from political representation in the House of Representatives. See U.S. Const., art. 1, sec. 2, cl. 3. This provision had been interpreted to mean that Indian tribes are not part of the political community of the United States or the states or territories from which their reservations were exempted. See S. Rep. no. 268, Effect of the Fourteenth Amendment upon Indian Tribes, 41st Cong., 2d sess. (1870). Thus, they are citizens of their own Indian nations with no representation in Congress. Because Indians were not part of federalism, the Supreme Court and lower federal courts have held that the Bill of Rights in the U.S. Constitution is not applicable to reservation Indians vis-à-vis their own tribal governments. See Native American Church v. Navajo Tribal Council, 272 F.2d 131 (10th Cir. 1959) (First Amendment does not apply to Indian tribes); Talton v. Mayes, 163 U.S. 376 (1895) (Fifth Amendment not applicable to Indian tribes); Barta v. Oglala Sioux Tribe, 259 F.2d 553 (8th Cir. 1958) (Fourteenth Amendment does not apply to Indian tribes). Congress felt it had to remedy this situation by enacting the 1968 Indian Civil Rights Act, which extended the protections of the Bill of Rights to reservation Indians. See 25 U.S.C. 1301 et seq.

Early Supreme Court cases held that voluntary relinquishment of tribal membership alone could not confer U.S. citizenship or state citizenship (under the Fourteenth

Amendment) on Indians; that Congress had to pass legislation naturalizing them before they could become citizens. See Elk v. Wilkins, 112 U.S. 94 (1884). Moreover, prior to the 1924 Citizenship Act, U.S. citizenship and membership in an Indian tribe were viewed as incompatible. The 1924 act changed this situation by providing "[t]hat all non-citizen Indians born within the territorial limits of the United States be, and they are hereby, declared to be citizens of the United States: *Provided: That the granting of such citizenship shall not in any manner impair or otherwise affect the right of any Indian to tribal or other property*" (emphasis added). See 43 Stat. 253, 8 U.S.C. 1401.

During World War I, many reservation Indians were drafted into the U.S. military illegally since they were non-citizens. The U.S. government "rewarded" these soldiers by passing the World War I Veterans' Citizenship Act of November 6, 1919 (41 Stat. 350), thereby covering up the illegality of the draft. Federal citizenship was later extended to all Indians under the 1924 Indian Citizenship Act (41 Stat. 350). Over time, Indians won the right to seek elective office and vote in federal and state elections. See, e.g., Harrison v. Laveen, 67 Ariz. 308, 271 P. 411 (1928) (granting Indians the right to vote in state elections).

It can be argued that the 1924 Citizenship Act is *unconstitutional* since Congress cannot change the U.S. Constitution by an act of Congress. Only a constitutional amendment can change the status of Indians in the Constitution.

Moreover, the imposition of federal income taxes on reservation Indians without affording them direct representation in the House of Representatives constitutes "taxation without representation."

5. Renée Sansom Flood's November 20, 1991, letter is printed in this book with the permission of the author.

6. Bureau of Ethnology, *Annual Report* 14, part 2 (1892–93).

7. See Thisba Hutson Morgan, "Reminiscences of My Days in the Land of the Ogallala Sioux," pp. 54–56.

8. Renée Sansom Flood's book, *Lost Bird of Wounded Knee: Spirit of the Lakota,* was very well received and has won for the author a nomination for a Pulitzer Prize. Flood made donations which were received by Sam Eaglestaff on behalf of the WKSAs and other Indian organizations.

9. See Act of August 26, 1954 (68 Stat. 868, 25 U.S.C. 677 et seq.). The purpose of the Ute Termination Act was "to provide for the partition and distribution of the assets of the Ute Indian Tribe of the Uintah and Ouray Reservation in Utah between the mixed-blood and full-blood members thereof; for the termination of Federal supervision over the trust, and restricted property, of mixed-blood members of said tribe; and for the development of programs for the full-blood members thereof, to assist them in preparing for termination of Federal supervision over their property." 25 U.S.C. 677.

10. The Wounded Knee Survivors' Associations' proposed legislation was first introduced on August 12, 1992, as S. 3213. It was sponsored by Senators Daschle, Pressler, Kerry, Burns, and Pell. This version was based on the 1988 Zuni-Cíbola Act

(102 Stat. 2847) in which tribal lands (including the 40-acre tract in which the mass grave is located) at Wounded Knee would be "leased" to the National Park Service for a national park. The 40-acre Gildersleeve tract located south of the mass grave would have been acquired in the name of the Oglala Sioux Tribe and leased back to the National Park Service along with other tribally owned lands.

S. 3213 was reintroduced in the Senate as S. 278 on February 2, 1993, and in the House of Representatives as H.R. 2435 on June 16, 1993. The Senate version was sponsored by Senators Daschle, Pressler, Campbell, and Simon. This version was also based on the 1988 Zuni-Cíbola Act model.

The new "national tribal park" version of the WKSAs' proposed legislation, based on the third alternative of the National Park Service study of alternatives, was introduced in the Senate as S. 382 and in the House of Representatives as H.R. 877 on February 9, 1995. It was sponsored by Senators Daschle, Pressler, Campbell, Simon, Pell, and Dorgan. The House version was sponsored by Congressmen Johnson, Williams, Underwood, Richardson, Faleomavaega, and Miller.

11. See the Act of October 24, 1988 (102 Stat. 2566).

12. Mario Gonzalez continues to write and lecture. In 1995 he was selected as the Poundmaker Lecturer at the Indian Law Centre of Canada, University of Saskatchewan, Saskatoon, a position named after Chief Poundmaker who negotiated a key treaty between the Cree and the Canadian government. *Cultural Survival Quarterly* published an important essay by him entitled "The Black Hills: The Sacred Land of the Lakota and Tsistsistas."

13. 21 U.S. (8 Wheat.) 543 (1823).

Sources

Angelou, Maya. *On the Pulse of Morning*. New York: Random House, 1993.

Barsh, Russel Lawrence, and James Youngblood Henderson. "The Betrayal: *Oliphant v. Suquamish Indian Tribe* and the Hunting of the Snark." *Minnesota Law Review* 63 (Apr., 1979).

Boggs, Carl. *Gramsci's Marxism*. London: Pluto Press, 1976.

Bordewich, Fergus M. *Killing the White Man's Indian: Reinventing Native Americans at the End of the Twentieth Century*. New York: Doubleday, 1996.

Brown, Dee. *Bury My Heart at Wounded Knee: An Indian History of the American West*. New York: Holt, Rinehart and Winston. 1970.

Bureau of Ethnology. *Annual Report* 14, part 2 (1892–93).

Burton, David H. *Theodore Roosevelt*. New York: Twayne Publishers, 1972.

Cadwalader, Sandra L., and Vine Deloria, Jr., eds. *The Aggressions of Civilization*. Philadelphia: Temple University Press. 1984.

Cohen, Felix. *Handbook of Federal Indian Law*. Washington, D.C.: GPO, 1942.

Cook-Lynn, Elizabeth. *From the River's Edge*. New York: Arcade, 1991.

———. Review of *Black Hills, White Justice* by Edward Lazarus. *Wicazo Sa Review* 8 (Spring, 1992).

Deloria, Vine, Jr. "Congress in Its Wisdom: The Course of Indian Legislation." In *The Aggressions of Civilization*. Edited by Sandra L. Cadwalader and Vine Deloria, Jr. Philadelphia: Temple University Press. 1984.

———. *God Is Red*. Denver: North American Press, Fulcrum Publishing. 1992.

———. "Reflections." *Wicazo Sa Review* 4 (Spring, 1988): 33–38.

———. *We Talk, You Listen: New Tribes, New Turf*. New York: Macmillan, 1970.

DeMallie, Raymond J. "The Lakota Ghost Dance: An Ethnohistorical Account." *Pacific Historical Review* 51 (Nov., 1982): 385–504

Dewing, Rolland. *Wounded Knee: The Meaning and Significance of the Second Incident*. New York: Irvington Publishers, 1984. 2d ed. 1995.

————. *Wounded Knee II.* Chadron, Neb.: Great Plains Network, 1995.

Doll, Don, and Jim Alinder, eds. *Crying for a Vision: A Rosebud Sioux Trilogy: 1886–1976.* Dobbs Ferry, N.Y.: Morgan & Morgan, 1976.

————. *Vision Quest: Men, Women, and Sacred Sites of the Sioux Nation.* New York: Crown Publishers, Inc., 1994

Flood, Renée Sansom. *Lost Bird of Wounded Knee: Spirit of the Lakota.* New York: Scribner's, 1995.

Gonzalez, Mario. "The Black Hills, The Sacred Land of the Lakota and Tsistsistas." *Cultural Survival Quarterly* (Winter, 1996): 63–69.

Gramsci, Antonio. *Further Selections from the Prison Notebooks.* Edited and translated by Derek Boothman. Minneapolis: University of Minnesota Press, 1995.

————. *Gramsci's Marxism.* Reprint. London: Pluto Press, 1976.

————. *Selections from the Prison Notebooks.* Edited and translated by Quinten Hoare and G. N. Smith. London: Lawrence and Wishart, 1971.

Gump, James O. *The Dust Rose like Smoke.* Lincoln: University of Nebraska Press. 1994.

Harring, Sidney L. *Crow Dog's Case: American Indian Sovereignty, Tribal Law in the Nineteenth Century.* Cambridge: Cambridge University Press, 1994.

Holm, Tom. *Strong Hearts, Wounded Souls: Native American Veterans of the Vietnam War.* Austin: University of Texas Press, 1996.

Hoover, Herbert. "Centennial West's Celebration of the Northern Tier States Heritage." Booklet. Helena: State Historial Society of Montana; and Pierre: State Historical Society of South Dakota, 1989.

Hyde, George. *Red Cloud's Folk: A History of the Oglala Sioux Indians.* 1937. Reprint. Norman: University of Oklahoma Press, 1984.

————. *A Sioux Chronicle.* 1956. Reprint. Norman: University of Oklahoma Press, 1993.

Jackson, Helen Hunt. *A Century of Dishonor: The Early Crusade for Indian Reform.* Edited by Andrew F. Rolle. New York: Harper & Row, 1965.

Jensen, Richard E. "Big Foot's Followers at Wounded Knee." *Nebraska History* 71 (Winter, 1990): 194–212.

Johnson, Ralph W. "The States versus Indian Off-Reservation Fishing: A Supreme Court Error." *Washington State Law Review* 47, no. 2 (1972).

Jojola, Ted. "On Revision and Revisionism: American Indian Representations in New Mexico." *American Indian Quarterly* 20 (Winter, 1996): 41–47.

Justice in Indian Country. American Indian Lawyer Training Program, Oakland, Ca.

Kappler, Charles J. *Indian Affairs: Laws and Treaties.* 5 vols. Washington, D.C.: Government Printing Office, 1904.

Lawson, Michael. *Dammed Indians.* Norman: University of Oklahoma Press, 1982.

Lazarus, Edward. *Black Hills, White Justice.* New York: HarperCollins, 1992.

Lemmon, Ed. *Boss Cowman: The Recollections of Ed Lemmon, 1857–1946.* Edited by Nellie Irene Snyder Yost. Lincoln: University of Nebraska Press, 1974.

Lincoln, Abraham. *The Collected Works of Abraham Lincoln.* Edited by Roy P. Basler. 8 vols. New Brunswick, N.J.: Rutgers University Press, 1953–55.

Macgregor, Gordon. *Warriors without Weapons: A Study of the Society and Personality Development of the Pine Ridge Sioux.* 1946. Reprint. Chicago: University of Chicago Press, 1975.

Matthiessen, Peter. *In The Spirit of Crazy Horse.* New York: Viking Press, 1980.

McCreight, Major Israel. *Firewater and Forked Tongues: A Sioux Chief Interprets U.S. History.* Pasadena, Calif.: Trail's End Pub., 1947.

The Medal of Honor of the United States Army. Washington, D.C.: Government Printing Office, 1948.

Miller, David H. *Ghost Dance.* New York: Duell, Sloane and Pearce, 1959.

Morgan, Thisba Hutson. "Reminiscences of My Days in the Land of the Ogllala Sioux." *South Dakota Historical Collections* 29 (1958): 21–62.

National Lawyers Guild, Committee on Native American Struggles. *Rethinking Indian Law.* New York: The Committee, 1982.

Olson, James C. *Red Cloud and the Sioux Problem.* Lincoln: University of Nebraska Press, 1965.

"Periscope." *Newsweek,* Dec. 31, 1990.

Powers, Marla. *Oglala Women: Myth, Ritual, and Reality.* Chicago: University of Chicago Press, 1986.

Price, Catherine Margaret. "Chiefs, Headmen and Warriors: Oglala Politics, 1851–1889." Ph.D. dissertation, Purdue University, 1987.

———. *The Oglala People, 1841–1879: A Political History.* Lincoln: University of Nebraska Press, 1996.

Pute Tiospaye (Lip's Camp): The History and Culture of a Sioux Indian Village. Written and compiled by students and faculty of Crazy Horse School in Wanblee, South Dakota, on the Pine Ridge Reservation. Albuquerque: Sloves-Bunnell, 1978.

Randall, James G. *Constitutional Problems under Lincoln.* Rev. ed. Urbana: University of Illinois Press, 1964.

Roosevelt, Theodore. *The Works of Theodore Roosevelt.* Edited by Hermann Hagedorn. 24 vols. New York: Charles Scribner's Sons, 1923–26.

Runte, Alfred. *National Parks: The American Experience.* 2d. ed. Lincoln: University of Nebraska Press, 1987.

The Sacred: Ways of Knowledge, Sources of Life. Edited by Peggy V. Beck, Anna Lee Walters, and Nia Francesco. Redesigned ed. Tsaile, Ariz.: Navajo Community College Press, 1992.

Scott, James C. *Politics and Society.* New York: Praeger, 1977.

———. *Weapons of the Weak: Everyday Forms of Peasant Resistance.* New Haven: Yale University Press, 1985.

Seals, David. "The Lakota Nation: Another Breakaway Republic." *Lies of Our Times* 2, no. 11 (Nov., 1991).

————. *Sweet Medicine.* The Library of the American Indian. New York: Orion Press, 1993.

Smith, Donald B. *From the Land of Shadows.* Saskatoon, Saskatchewan: Western Producer Prairie Books, 1990.

Sommers, Christina Hoff. *Who Stole Feminism? How Women Have Betrayed Women.* New York: Simon and Schuster, 1994.

Tallent, Annie. *The Black Hills; or The Last Hunting Ground of the Dakotahs.* St. Louis: Nixon-Jones Printing Co., 1899. Reprint. Sioux Falls, S.Dak.: Brevet Press, 1974.

U.S. Commission on Civil Rights. *Indian Tribes: A Continuing Quest for Survival.* Washington, D.C.: Government Printing Office, 1981.

U.S. Congress. Senate. Select Committee on Indian Affairs. "Wounded Knee Memorial and Historic Site—Little Big Horn National Monument Battlefield." *Hearing to Establish Wounded Knee Memorial and Historic Site and Proposal to Establish Monument Commemorating Indian Participants of Little Big Horn and to Redesignate Name of Monument from Custer Battlefield to Little Big Horn National Monument Battlefield.* 101st Cong., 2d sess. 1990.

————. Select Committee on Indian Affairs. "Proposed Wounded Knee Park and Memorial." *Hearing to Establish a National Park and Memorial at Wounded Knee.* 102d Cong., 1st sess. 1991.

————. Subcommittee on Indian Affairs of the Committee on Interior and Insular Affairs, "Occupation of Wounded Knee." *Hearings on June 16, 1973, at Pine Ridge, S.Dak., and June 17, 1973, at Kyle, S.Dak.* 93d Cong. 1973.

U.S. Department of the Interior. Office of the Solicitor. *Opinions of the Solicitor of the Department of the Interior Relating to Indian Affairs, 1917–1974.* 2 vols. Washington, D.C.: Dept. of the Interior, 1979.

U.S. Indian Claims Commission. *Final Report: August 13, 1946–September 30, 1978.* Washington, D.C.: The Commission, 1978.

Utley, Robert M. *Frontier Regulars: The U.S. Army and the Indian, 1866–1891.* New York: Macmillan, 1973. Reprint. Lincoln: University of Nebraska Press, 1984.

————. *The Lance and the Shield: The Life and Times of Sitting Bull.* New York: Henry Holt and Company, 1993.

————. *The Last Days of the Sioux Nation.* New Haven: Yale University Press, 1963.

Young Bear, Severt, and R. D. Theisz. *Standing in the Light: A Lakota Way of Seeing.* Lincoln: University of Nebraska Press, 1994.

Index

Dillon, Emily Standing Bear, 189
Dillon, Robert, 189
dinosaur fossils, 187, 393–94
Docket 74, 342–44
Docket 74-A, 344–53, 356–57
Docket 74-B, 344, 353–57
Doctrine of Discovery, xi–xii, xiii, xiv, 167, 229
Dred Scott v. Sandford, 244
Ducheneaux, Wayne, 46, 56, 141
Duke, David, 73–74, 74–75
Duncan, Luke, 87, 147

Eagle Deer, Jancita, 99–100
Eaglestaff, Kathy, 188, 201, 216, 217, 223
Eaglestaff, Kay, 219
Eaglestaff, Sam, 3, 7, 32, 33, 46, 50, 55, 64, 87, 93, 97–98, 101, 152, 157, 172, 178, 179, 180, 185–86, 188, 197–98, 199, 200, 201–2, 204–5, 206, 212, 215, 217, 218, 219, 220; apology issue, 75; congressional support, 39; eulogy for, 223; Harjo-Ducheneaux debacle, 56–57; health concerns, 114; letter to Inouye, 216
Ecoffey, Anita, 190, 225
Ecoffey, Bob, 225
Edmunds Commission, 260–63; failure, 263–67
electoral system, 75
Emery, Ray, 383
Emery, Steve, 141
eminent domain, 43
English, Jack, 90
equitable relief, 43, 44
Erdman, Tim, 60, 61
Erdoes, Richard, 144
ethics and political life, 159–60
ethnic cleansing, 40, 177
Executive Order of January 24, 1882, 241
Executive Order of January 25, 1904, 242–43
Ex Parte Crow Dog (1883), 31–32, 371
extermination policy, 88
extradition procedures, 65

Fast Horse, Robert (Robert Grey Eagle), 385
federal lands, 185
feminist scholars, 49–50
Fiddler, Terry, 118, 136, 141, 211

Fifth Amendment (U.S. Constitution), 41, 42, 45, 46, 374; just compensation clause, 243; text, 241
Fire Thunder, Chris, 125
First Amendment (U.S. Constitution), 45
Firstenberg, Suzanne, 58, 60
flagpole incident, 85
Flood, Renée Sansom, 150, 151, 175–77, 215, 217, 219–20; Moreno suit, 206; opposition to Plenty USA, 208; Pulitzer nomination, 410
Fools Crow, Frank, 155
Fort Berthold test, 373
Fort Laramie, 30
Fort Laramie Treaty (1851), 237, 331
Fort Laramie Treaty (1868), 4; consent issue, 269–83; description, 332; major provisions, 258; miners violating, 41; misunderstandings, 258–59; Red Cloud's role, 31; selected text, 237–39; summarized, 250; as treaty of cession, 348; tribes' position, 347; violations, 41, 65, 332–33
Fort Robinson, 142–43
Four Directions Council, 159
Fourteenth Amendment (U.S. Constitution), 244–45
Fredericks, Tom, 383
Friday Scares, Victoria, 33
fund-raising, 59, 198, 199–200; commercialization of site, 222; Gary Rhine, 206–9

Gall, 31
Garreau, Manson, 184, 211, 406
Garreau, Melvin, Sr., 33, 55, 117, 125, 143, 151–52, 172, 178, 179, 184–85, 198, 218, 219, 406
Garrett, Jim, 48, 81–82
genealogy, 188–89; Mario Gonzalez's ancestors, 376
German Green Party, 164
German parliament, 164–64
Ghost Dance religion, 26, 175, 252, 377
Ghost Horse, Alice: description of Wounded Knee massacre, 15–21; significance, 231
Giago, Tim, 36; year of reconciliation, 68, 70
Gildersleeve family, 135, 138, 187
Glazer, Rabbi, 50
Goffin Collection, 197
Gold Rush (Black Hills), 250, 332

MARIO GONZALEZ is the attorney general of the Kickapoo Tribe in Kansas. He is an enrolled member of the Oglala Sioux Tribe, Pine Ridge, South Dakota, and gained a national reputation in Indian law when he worked for the Oglala Sioux Tribe on the Black Hills Claim. He is the first recipient of the Distinguished Aboriginal Lawyer Achievement Award, given by the University of Saskatchewan in 1995. He is the author of two Black Hills bills, the 1987 Bradley Bill (S. 705) and the 1990 Martinez Bill (H.R. 5680). His Lakota name is Nantan Hinapan.

◆

ELIZABETH COOK-LYNN is professor emerita of English and Native American Studies at Eastern Washington University, Cheney. She is an enrolled member of the Crow Creek Sioux Tribe, Fort Thompson, South Dakota, and is a novelist, poet, and founder of a scholarly journal, the *Wicazo Sa Review*, published semiannually by the University of Minnesota Press. She lives with her husband, C. J. Lynn, in the Black Hills of South Dakota, and also during some periods in a log house on the west end of the Spokane Reservation near the Columbia River. Her book, *Why I Can't Read Wallace Stegner* (University of Wisconsin Press, 1996), won the Gustav Meyer Award for Human Rights. Her Dakota family name is Renville/ Bowed Head.

◆

Beyond working in the professional fields of law, literature, and teaching, Cook-Lynn and Gonzalez have continued in the tradition of their ancestors to assist in the modern struggle of Native American tribes toward sovereignty and the nation-within-a-nation status described in the treaty-making process of indigenous history.

This book is set in
10.5/13 Minion text
designed by Robert Slimbach
with Eden Light display.
Book design by Dennis Roberts.
Composed by Jim Proefrock
at the University of Illinois Press.
Manufactured by Cushing-Malloy, Inc.

♦